Bernard O'Hara

MAYO

MAYO

Aspects of its Heritage

Edited by Bernard O'Hara

First published in 1982 by
The Archaeological, Historical and Folklore Society,
Regional Technical College,
Galway,
Ireland.

British Library Cataloguing in Publication Data
Mayo.
1. Mayo (County) — History
I. O'Hara, Bernard
941.7'3   DA990. M3
ISBN 0-9508233 0-9
ISBN 0-9508233 1-7

Printed by Corrib Printers Ltd., Galway, Ireland.

To Edward Fox

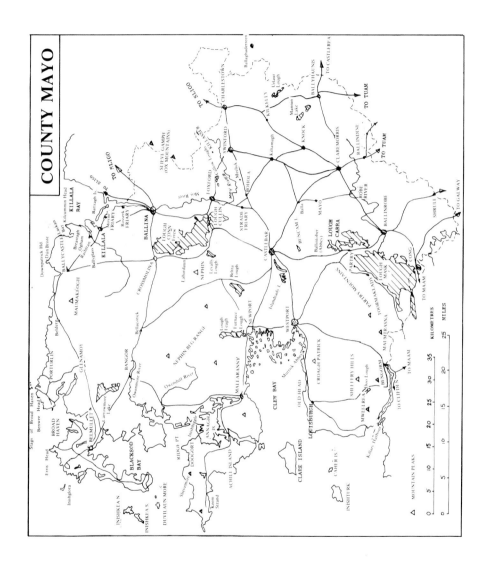

COUNTY MAYO

CONTENTS

LIST OF ILLUSTRATIONS

PREFACE

This book is an attempt to give the reader an appreciation of some aspects of the heritage of County Mayo. It is highly selective, both in subject matter and depth of treatment. The topics covered include: the origin of the county, its baronies, parishes and population statistics; history; archaeology; placenames; Ulster migration to Mayo; The Year of the French; Mayo Elections 1801-1982; the 1857 Mayo Election; folksongs; geology; mountains; wildlife; industries; The Reek; Knock Shrine; a miscellany of historical information, and biographical notes on some famous Mayo people. In respect of the latter, only one living person has been included, Fr. Patrick Peyton — "The Rosary Priest"; John Moore and John Dillon have been included because of their association with Mayo.

The chief sources used are recorded at the end of each article; a full list of sources and some other publications relevant to Mayo are included in the bibliography.

The Ordnance Survey spelling of a placename is followed, except in the list of Mayo Industries, where the registered address of each industry is used. Consequently, you will see Ballintober, Kiltamagh, Lahardaun, Toormakeady, Mallaranny and Strade used instead of the conventional, Ballintubber, Kiltimagh, Lahardane, Tourmakeady, Mulranny and Straide. In the case of Swinford, both the Ordnance Survey version Swineford and Swinford are used; it would appear that the inclusion of the *e* was a mistake.

The Archaeological/Historical and Folklore Society of Galway Regional Technical College (Publisher) was founded in 1977 by Edward Fox, to whom this book is dedicated.

The officers of the Society in June 1982 were:

President	Peadar O'Dowd
Vice President	Maura Hynes
Auditor	Louise Johnston
Chairperson	Catherine Kennedy
Hon. Secretary	Tina Walshe
Hon. Treasurer	Helen O'Connell
Assistant Treasurer	Mary Shaughnessy

Thirteen people co-operated with me in this project, all of whom gave of their time and talent gratuitously. Any profit will be divided equally between the following:
The Archaeological/Historical/Folklore Society, Galway R.T.C., The Killasser Museum Project, Co. Mayo, and The Michael Davitt Centre, Strade, Co. Mayo.

A special thanks is due to the staff of Corrib Printers Ltd., Galway.

I would like to record my thanks to Mary Cunningham and Kevin Dooley, Galway R.T.C., Tomás P. Ó Néill, University College, Galway, Rev. Martin Jennings, Swinford, and especially to Nollaig Ó Muraíle for his help and advice in addition to his own articles.

Finally, a special word of thanks to my wife, Mary, for all her help and understanding. Rath Dé ort.

Bernard O'Hara.
28-08-1982

COUNTY MAYO

by Bernard O'Hara

"Anois teacht an Earraigh beidh an lá dul chun síneadh,
Is tar éis na Féil' Bríde ardóidh mé mo sheol,
Ó chuir mé i mo cheann é ní stopfaidh mé choíche,
Go seasfaidh mé thíos i lár Chontae Mhaigh Eo."

Antoine Ó Raifterí

County Mayo is a maritime county in the West of Ireland, bounded on the north and west by the Atlantic Ocean, on the east by the Counties of Sligo and Roscommon, and on the south by County Galway. It extends from 53^0 28' to 54^0 21' north latitude and from 8^0 25' to 10^0 5' west longitude. Mayo is the third largest county in Ireland, with an area of 5,398 sq. km. (2,084 sq. miles). The Irish for Mayo is Maigh Eo, which means "the plain of the yews".

County Mayo was formally established on the initiative of Sir Henry Sidney (1529-1586), who was Queen Elizabeth I's Lord Deputy in Ireland from 1565 to 1571, and from 1575 to 1578. Mayo was designated a administrative unit about 1570. County Mayo got its name from the diocese of Mayo, which evolved from the monastery established at Mayo Abbey, near Balla, by St. Colmán of Lindisfarne (c. A.D. 605 - 676). The monastery was an important centre of learning, and attracted many students from the continent. Mayo became a diocese in the twelfth century, a reflection of the esteem in which the monastery was held. Mayo diocese comprised the following parishes: Kilcolman, Kilvine, Crossboyne, Tagheen, Balla and Manulla, Roslee, Robeen, Touaghty, Burriscarra, Drum, Ballyhean, Ballintober, Ballyovey, part of Ballinrobe north of the Robe, Aglish, Islandeady, Turlough, Kildacommoge, Breaghwy, Aghagower, Oughaval, Kilgeever, Kilmeena, Kilmaclasser, Burrishoole and Achill. The diocese had a chequered history and was amalgamated with Tuam in the seventeenth century.

BARONIES

Ancient Gaelic Ireland was divided into small tribal areas, known as tuatha. Some of the post-Norman baronies corresponded to these earlier divisions. Nine baronies formed County Mayo in the sixteenth century, i.e. Burrishoole, Carra, Clanmorris, Costello, Erris, Gallen, Kilmaine, Murrisk and Tirawley.

Table 1 shows the names of the civil parishes in each Mayo barony until 1898, and Table 2 the population of each in 1841 and 1861. The establishment of county councils in 1898 was followed by some changes in the Mayo boundary. A portion of the barony of Costello was transferred to County Roscommon, i.e. the parishes of Castlemore and Kilcolman and part of Kilbeagh. A portion of the barony of Tireragh in Sligo was transferred to Mayo, i.e. parts of the parishes of Castleconor and Kilmoremoy. A section of the barony of Ross in Galway was also transferred to Mayo, i.e. parts of the parishes of Ross, Ballinchalla and Ballinrobe. Baronies ceased to be administrative units in 1898.

TABLE 1 MAYO BARONIES (1570 — 1898)

Burrishoole	Carra	Clanmorris	Costello
Achill Aghagower (Pt.) Ballintober (Pt.) Burrishoole Islandeady (Pt.) Kilmaclasser Kilmeena	Aglish Ballintober (Pt.) Ballyhean Islandeady (Pt.) Ballyovey Breaghwy Burriscarra Drum Kildacommoge (Pt.) Manulla Rosslee Touaghty Turlough	Balla Crossboyne Kilcolman Kilvine Knock (Pt.) Mayo (Pt.) Tagheen	Aghamore Annagh Bekan (1) Castlemore (Pt.) Kilbeagh (2) Kilcolman (Pt.) Kilmovee (3) Kilturra (Pt.) Knock
Erris Kilcommon Kilmore			NOTES (1) The remainder was in the barony of Frenchpark, Co. Roscommon. (2) The remainder was in the barony of Frenchpark and in the barony of Coolavin, Co. Sligo. (3) The remainder was in the barony of Corran, Co. Sligo.
Gallen	**Kilmaine**	**Murrisk**	**Tirawley**
Attymass Bohola Kilconduff Kildacommoge (Pt.) Kilgarvan Killasser Killedan Meelick Templemore Toomore	(1) Ballinachalla (Pt.) (2) Ballinrobe (Pt.) (3) Cong (Pt.) Kilcommon Kilmainebeg Kilmainemore Kilmolara Mayo (Pt.) Moorgagagh Robeen Shrule	Aghagower (Pt.) Inishbofin Kilgeever Oughaval	Addergoole Ardagh Ballynahaglish Ballysakeery Crossmolina Doonfeeny Kilbelfad Kilbride Kilcummin Kilfian Killala (1) Kilmoremoy (Pt.) Lackan Moygawnagh Rathreagh Templemurry
Pt. = Part of	(1, 2, 3) The remainder was in the barony of Ross, Co. Galway.		(1) The remainder was in the barony of Tireragh Co.Sligo.

2

TABLE 2 POPULATION OF MAYO BARONIES IN 1841 AND 1861

Baronies	Area A. R. P.			Population 1841	Population 1861	Houses 1841	Houses 1861
Burrishoole	145,172	0	0	39,853	21,520	7,506	4,100
Carra	134,206	3	13	52,238	28,647	9,511	5,380
Clanmorris	69,252	1	1	27,437	18,222	4,897	3,334
Costello	143,874	2	36	48,389	46,237	8,869	8,321
Erris	230,452	2	3	26,428	19,397	4,655	3,631
Gallen	119,153	3	15	46,566	37,695	8,439	7,168
Kilmaine	95,284	1	15	42,342	24,934	7,651	4,703
Murrisk	137,061	3	34	34,402	19,332	6,258	3,306
Tirawley	246,822	3	39	71,232	38,787	12,756	7,142
Merchant Seamen					25		
	1,321281	1	36	388,887	254,796	70,542	47,025

PARISHES

The parish concept in Ireland is thought to have had its origin in the fifth or sixth century, and may have been based on a tribal or monastic area. The ecclesiastical parishes were formally constituted during the twelfth century, after the Synod of Rath Breasail in 1111 and the Synod of Kells in 1152. They appear to have been based on the pre-existing parish units and boundaries were determined by the politico-ecclesiastical and demographic considerations obtaining at that time. The boundaries were fixed by surveys in the seventeenth century. The civil parishes were used by the Established Church (Church of Ireland), but after Catholic Emancipation in 1829, the civil and Catholic parish units diverged in most areas. The Catholic Church authorities ignored the civil boundaries, and marked out new parish units more in keeping with the demographic and ecclesiastical requirements of the time. The Church of Ireland retained the civil parish unit, but amalgamated parishes for ecclesiastical administration. The word parish today can refer to three different units, the civil parish, the Catholic Church parish, and the Church of Ireland parish.

CIVIL PARISHES

There are now seventy two civil parishes in County Mayo. They are: Achill, Addergoole, Aghagower, Aghamore, Aglish, Annagh, Ardagh, Attymass, Balla, Ballinchalla, Ballinrobe, Ballintober, Ballyhean, Ballynahaglish, Ballyovey, Ballysakeery, Bekan, Bohola, Breaghwy, Burriscarra, Burrishoole, Castleconor (Pt.), Cong (Pt.), Crossboyne, Crossmolina, Doonfeeny, Drum, Islandeady, Kilbeagh (Pt.), Kilbelfad, Kilbride, Kilcolman, Kilcommon (Pt. Erris Barony), Kilcommon (Kilmaine Barony), Kilconduff, Kilcummin, Kildacommoge, Kilfian, Kilgarvan, Kilgeever, Killala, Killasser, Killedan, Kilmaclasser, Kilmainebeg, Kilmainemore, Kilmeena, Kilmolara, Kilmore, Kilmoremoy, Kilmovee, Kilturra (Pt.), Kilvine, Knock, Lackan, Manulla, Mayo, Meelick, Moorgagagh, Moygawnagh, Oughaval, Rathreagh, Robeen, Ross (Pt.),

3

Rosslee, Shrule, Tagheen, Templemore, Templemurry, Toomore, Touaghty and Turlough.

CATHOLIC PARISHES

There are four Catholic dioceses in Mayo, Achonry, Galway-Kilmacduagh-Kilfenora, Killala and Tuam, all in the Archdiocese of Tuam. There are fifty six Catholic parishes in County Mayo. Table 3 shows the Catholic parishes of Mayo under each diocese. (Historical names given in brackets).

TABLE 3 CATHOLIC PARISHES OF MAYO 1982

Tuam	Achonry	Killala	Galway, Kilmac-duagh and Kilfenora
Patron St. Jarlath (6th June)	Patron St. Nathy (9th August) St. Attracta (12th August)	Patron St. Muredach (12th August)	Patron Our Lady Assumed into Heaven 15th August

Achill
Castlebar (Aglish,
  Ballyheane and
  Breaghwy)
Ballyhaunis (Annagh)
Aughagower
Aghamore
Westport (Aughaval)
Balla and Manulla
Ballinrobe
Partry
Bekan
Carrownacon
Newport
Clare Island
Cong
Crossboyne
Islandeady
Keelogues
Claremorris (Kilcol-
  man)
Roundfort (Kilcommon)
Louisburgh (Kilgeever)
Kilmaine
Kilmeena
Ballindine (Kilvine)
Knock
Mayo Abbey
Parke
Robeen
Leenaun (Kilbride)
(Pt. of)
	Attymass
	Bohola
	Carracastle
	Kilconduff & Meelick
	Kilbeagh
	Kilgarvan
	Killasser
	Killedan
	Kilmovee
	Templemore
	Toomore
		Ballina (Kilmoremoy)
		Backs
		Ardagh
		Ballycastle (Kilbride
		  & Doonfeeny)
		Ballycroy
		Ballysokeary
		Belmullet
		Crossmolina
		Kilcommon - Erris
		Kilfian
		Killala
		Kilmore - Erris
		Kiltane
		Lackan
		Lahardaun
		  (Addergoole)
		Moygawnagh
			Shrule

MAYO CHURCH OF IRELAND PARISHES 1982

County Mayo is part of the United Diocese of Tuam, Killala and Achonry for Church of Ireland administration. There are three parishes of the

4

diocese of Tuam in Mayo, i.e. Aughaval (Westport), Castlebar, and part of Tuam/Cong. There are two Mayo parishes in the diocese of Killala and Achonry, i.e. Kilmoremoy (Ballina) and Killala/Crossmolina.

Co. Mayo Diocesan Boundaries

(These are the Roman Catholic diocesan boundaries; the Church of Ireland boundaries differ little, except that there is no diocese of Galway. The Catholic diocese of Galway was only established in 1831. The boundaries of the medieval diocese of Mayo are also indicated here.)

THE MAYO CREST

The Mayo Crest consists of nine yew trees, a Patriarchal Cross and three Passion Crosses, with a ship and waves. The word Maigh Eo means "the plain of the yews", and the nine yew trees express that fact, with one for each barony of the county. The Patriarchal Cross (a cross with two bars) symbolises the Catholic Archdiocese of Tuam, and the three Passion Crosses represent the other three Catholic dioceses in Mayo, i.e. Achonry, Killala, and Galway-Kilmacduagh-Kilfenora. Mayo is a maritime county, and that fact is represented by the ship and waves. The colour scheme of the crest incorporates the Mayo G.A.A. colours, green and red.

POPULATION

The population of Mayo declined from 388,887 in 1841 to 109,525 in 1971, a decrease of 71.83%. The population decline from 1841 to 1851 was

5

114,388, or 29.41%. Since the Great Famine (1845-1849) County Mayo has been synonymous with emigration. Charlestown-born journalist John Healy shocked the conscience of many in 1968 with the publication of *"The Death of an Irish Town"*, in which he vividly described the effects of emigration in and around his native town. It was a story equally applicable to every town and parish in Mayo. The 1979 Census recorded an increase in the population of County Mayo for the first time since the Great Famine. It showed an increase of 4,494 on the 1971 figure. The 1981 Census recorded an increase of 529 on the 1979 figure. Table 4 shows the population of Mayo from 1821 to 1981, and table 5 the average annual rates of births, deaths, and net emigration per 1,000 of the population, of County Mayo from 1926 to 1981.

Table 6 shows the population of each civil parish in County Mayo as recorded in the Census of 1841, 1851, 1861, 1871, 1881, 1891 and 1979.

TABLE 4 POPULATION OF COUNTY MAYO 1821 — 1981

Year	Males	Females	Total	Percentage Change
1821	146,137	146,975	293,112	—
1831	179,595	186,733	366,328	+ 24.98
1841	194,198	194,689	388,887	+ 6.16
1851	133,264	141,235	274,499	- 29.41
1861	125,636	129,160	254,796	- 7.18
1871	120,877	125,153	246,030	- 3.44
1881	119,421	125,791	245,212	- 0.33
1891	107,498	111,536	219,034	- 10.68
1901	97,564	101,602	199,166	- 9.07
1911	96,345	95,832	192,177	- 3.51
1926	86,778	85,912	172,690	- 10.14
1936	83,213	78,136	161,349	- 6.57
1946	75.073	73.047	148,120	- 8.20
1951	73,345	68,522	141,867	- 4.22
1956	68,879	64,173	133,052	- 6.21
1961	63,844	59,486	123,330	- 7.31
1966	59,829	55,718	115,547	- 6.31
1971	56,402	53,123	109,525	- 5.21
1979	58,489	55,530	114,019	+ 4.1
1981	58,898	55,650	114,548	+ 0.46

TABLE 5 AVERAGE ANNUAL RATES OF BIRTHS, DEATHS AND NET MIGRATION PER 1,000 IN MAYO 1926—1981

Intercensal Period	Births	Deaths	Natural Increase	Net Migration
1926-'36	18.5	12.8	5.6	- 6.8
1936-'46	19.3	14.3	5.1	- 8.5
1946-'56	19.4	13.1	6.3	- 19.1
1956-'61	18.2	13.1	5.1	- 20.3
1961-'66	16.9	12.9	4.0	- 17.1
1966-'71	16.8	13.5	3.3	- 14.0
1971-'79	17.8	13.0	4.8	+ 0.2
1979-'81	19.0	13.0	6.0	- 3.7 (e)

TABLE 6 POPULATION OF THE CIVIL PARISHES OF COUNTY MAYO

Parish	1841	1851	1861	1871	1881	1891	1911	1979
Achill	6,392	4,950	5,776	6,263	6,732	6,235	6,919	3,994
Addergoole	7,379	5,085	4,644	4,707	4,672	4,145	3,496	1,586
Aghagower	12,235	6,511	5,068	4,471	4,314	4,009	3,595	2,078
Aghamore	7,675	6,097	6,782	7,145	7,128	6,580	5,699	2,105
Aglish	10,464	9,135	5,995	6,075	6,295	5,763	5,675	8,754
Annagh	7,904	6,105	6,139	6,175	6,251	5,549	4,916	2,175
Ardagh	2,621	1,497	1,283	1,155	1,080	950	778	485
Attymass	3,435	2,431	2,816	2,741	2,733	2,558	2,077	832
Balla	1,934	1,272	1,165	1,159	1,131	1,049	896	689
Ballinchalla (Pt. pre 1898) (See Note 1)	1,722	1,420	1,329	1,331	1,286	1,060	1,420	637
Ballinrobe (Pt. pre 1898) (Note 2)	10,115	9,326	6,157	5,806	5,534	4,586	4,651	2,918
Ballintober	7,219	3,438	3,101	3,143	3,142	2,903	2,457	1,282
Ballyhean	4,032	1,987	1,913	1,734	1,689	1,500	1,253	1,018
Ballynahaglish	5,397	3,397	3,572	3,625	3,546	3,108	2,678	2,247
Ballyovey	4,505	3,073	2,837	2,807	2,817	2,688	2,351	1,247
Ballysakeery	6,034	2,951	2,323	2,163	2,104	1,914	1,520	947
Bekan	5,589	4,724	5,005	4,797	4,969	4,502	3,834	2,126
Bohola	4,301	2,907	3,183	3,279	3,419	2,880	2,580	781
Breaghwy	2,452	1,136	1,079	1,002	987	851	692	706
Burriscarra	1,681	913	892	848	805	661	516	362
Burrishoole	11,942	7,528	6,318	6,100	5,872	5,000	4,226	2,081
Castleconor (Pt.) (Note 9)							243	150
Castlemore (Pt.) (Note 3)	2,944	2,831	2,625	2,527	2,360	2,260		
Cong (Pt.) (Notes 4 and 10)	5,359	3,839	3,343	2,773	2,547	2,252	1,658	1,048
Crossboyne	6,702	4,963	4,206	3,947	3,937	3,347	2,570	1,890
Crossmolina	12,221	7,236	6,547	5,739	5,738	4,976	4,065	3,469
Doonfeeny	4,819	2,720	2,582	2,302	2,228	1,965	1,747	833
Drum	4,127	2,732	2,565	2,449	2,338	1,944	1,635	833
Inishbofin (Note 8)	1,612	1,047	1,236	1,262				
Islandeady	8,463	4,699	4,209	4,058	4,178	3,731	3,402	1,539
Kilbeagh (Pt. post 1898) (Note 11)	9,963	9,733	10,733	11,145	11,148	10,266	8,586	3,013
Kilbelfad	3,681	2,296	2,313	2,273	2,229	1,951	1,640	989
Kilbride	1,963	1,144	968	839	866	851	745	247
Kilcolman (Clanmorris barony)	9,451	7,421	7,091	6,879	7,289	6,404	5,772	3,522
Kilcolman (Costello barony) (Note 5)	4,365	4,151	4,496	4,365	4,285	3,615		
Kilcommon (Erris barony)	17,000	12,253	12,945	12,401	13,286	12,393	12,266	7,498
Kilcommon (Kilmaine barony)	7,456	5,255	4,529	3,898	3,774	3,242	2,505	1,584
Kilconduff	7,072	6,909	7,271	7,653	8,172	7,097	6,466	2,954
Kilcummin	2,791	1,552	1,491	1,479	1,465	1,419	1,236	436
Kildacommoge	3,923	2,234	2,320	2,649	2,663	2,261	2,014	848
Kilfian	6,064	3,348	2,791	2,233	2,241	2,053	1,750	858
Kilgarvan	4,158	3,194	3,171	3,314	3,483	3,433	2,860	1,227
Kilgeever	12,573	6,892	6,442	5,830	5,918	5,538	4,602	2,107
Killala	3,253	2,919	1,729	1,392	1,329	1,051	872	1,028
Killasser	6,962	4,852	5,682	5,404	5,547	4,839	4,213	1,403
Killedan	6,410	5,158	5,639	5,802	5,886	5,421	4,887	2,448
Kilmaclasser	3,548	1,614	1,274	1,261	1,312	1,192	1,131	603

Parish	1841	1851	1861	1871	1881	1891	1911	1979
Kilmainebeg	1,491	895	733	684	701	585	475	395
Kilmainemore	4,877	3,293	2,696	2,480	2,281	1,879	1,655	1,417
Kilmeena	7,876	5,108	3,542	2,894	2,742	2,525	1,907	1,062
Kilmolara	1,296	864	849	941	957	809	636	312
Kilmore	9,428	7,379	6,452	5,552	5,327	4,111	4,059	2,831
Kilmoremoy (Pt. Pre 1898 Note 6)	7,028	6,393	5,382	4,952	4,911	4,215	7,022	9,387
Kilmovee	5,844	5,882	6,515	6,807	6,701	6,389	5,521	1,692
Kilturra (Pt.) (Notes 7 & 12)	1,350	1,023	1,187	1,236	1,269	1,160	888	275
Kilvine	2,236	1,697	1,595	1,637	1,735	1,542	1,402	658
Knock	3,374	3,174	3,271	3,242	3,241	2,981	2,550	1,143
Lackan	2,943	1,176	1,102	948	878	888	698	355
Manulla	2,336	1,387	1,492	1,506	1,442	1,233	1,002	540
Mayo	4,179	2,379	2,243	2,141	2,084	1,915	1,617	986
Meelick	3,915	2,692	3,045	3,278	3,245	2,611	2,483	835
Moorgagagh	627	294	275	229	217	175	155	171
Moygawnagh	2,107	1,181	963	894	950	833	679	363
Oughavel	13,441	13,282	8,802	7,906	7,944	7,216	6,259	5,064
Rathreagh	1,664	790	642	526	510	453	388	290
Robeen	3,544	2,522	2,196	2,021	1,793	1,529	1,161	607
Ross (Pt. Note 13)	—	—	—	—	—	—	563	166
Rosslee	1,283	694	612	592	579	450	334	339
Shrule	5,087	3,004	2,394	2,169	2,101	1,830	1,402	1,155
Tagheen	3,084	2,051	1,839	1,745	1,719	1,483	1,075	486
Templemore	4,251	2,387	2,560	2,532	2,411	2,154	1,938	798
Templemurry	1,291	514	455	357	398	395	316	195
Toomore	3,744	2,498	2,899	2,646	2,484	2,234	2,082	1,163
Touaghty	1,297	884	843	749	708	559	448	293
Turlough	7,430	4,516	4,612	4,966	5,159	4,888	4,368	1,464
Total for County	388,887	274,499	254,796	246,030	245,212	219,034	192,177	114,019

Sir Henry Sidney, who formally established Co. Mayo c. 1570
(National Portrait Gallery, London)

8

SOURCES

i. Central Statistics Office, Census of Population.
ii. Michael Ross, E.S.R.I.
iii. Nollaig Ó Muraíle, The Placenames Office, Ordnance Survey, Dublin.

NOTES ON THE CIVIL PARISHES

Part = Part of
The figure in brackets in the following notes was the population of the entire parish in 1861.

PRE 1898

1. The remainder of the parish of Ballinchalla was in the barony of Ross, Co. Galway. It was transferred to Mayo in 1898. (1,839)
2. The remainder of the parish of Ballinrobe was in the barony of Ross, Co. Galway. It was transferred to Mayo in 1898. (7,164).
3. The remainder of the parish of Castlemore was in the barony of Frenchpark, Co. Roscommon (3,178). All the parish was transferred to Roscommon in 1898.
4. The remainder of the parish of Cong was in the barony of Ross, Co. Galway (5,753).
5. The remainder of the parish of Kilcolman was in the barony of Frenchpark, Co. Roscommon and in the barony of Coolavin, Co. Sligo. The Mayo section of the parish was transferred to Roscommon in 1898. (6,576).
6. The remainder of the parish of Kilmoremoy was in the barony of Tireragh, Co. Sligo. It was transferred to Mayo in 1898. (9,311).
7. The remainder of the parish of Kilturra was in the barony of Corran, Co. Sligo. (2,035).
8. Inishbofin was recorded as a separate parish until 1871.

POST 1898

Parts of the parishes of Castleconor and Ross were transferred to Mayo in 1898.
9. The remainder of the parish of Castleconor is in Co. Sligo.

10. The remainder of the parish of Cong is in Co. Galway.

11. The remainder of the parish of Kilbeagh is in Co. Roscommon.

12. Part of the parish of Kilturra is in Co. Sligo.

13. Part of the parish of Ross is in Co. Galway.

AN OUTLINE HISTORY
OF COUNTY MAYO

by Nollaig Ó Muraíle

To speak of the 'history of County Mayo' before the latter part of the 16th century is in a sense anachronistic, for the county, as such, did not exist before Queen Elizabeth's Lord Deputy in Ireland, Sir Henry Sidney, and his subordinates undertook the shiring of Connacht about the year 1570. In the following pages, however, an attempt is made to recount, as concisely as possible, the principal events which have gone to shape the history of the area now designated, 'County Mayo'. It may need to be emphasised that some of the developments referred to were not confined to Mayo, but were part of the story of a much wider area, while others were of quite local significance, being confined perhaps to a small area within the county. An effort is also made to at least mention individuals, whose actions, whether good or bad, left their mark on the subsequent history of the county.

Having drawn attention to some of the inherent limitations of a study such as this, we begin by looking briefly at the earliest evidence for the presence of man in this corner of Ireland, long before the dawn of recorded history.

PREHISTORY

Archaeological investigations have shown that Neolithic man was settled along the north Mayo coast as far back as 4,500 years ago. As the blanket bog which has covered much of the county in recent millenia has been stripped away, dramatic evidence has come to light — particularly in the Belderg-Glenulra area — of the types of dwelling, field-systems, and methods of cultivation used by these late Stone-Age farmers. These early 'Mayomen' have left a very tangible reminder of their presence by the kind of tombs in which they buried their dead. Tombs of a type known as Court Tombs — and numbering over 300 — are to be found mainly in north Connacht and south Ulster. Of these, the largest concentration — about a fifth of the total — is located in Co. Mayo, especially in the area west and north-west of Killala.

As we move on to the early Bronze Age, we have evidence (from some examples of a type of tomb known as a Wedge Tomb) of settlers in the Belderg area who may have exploited a seam of copper laid bare by coastal erosion. Excavations in the Glenree valley, east of Ballina, on the lower slopes of the Ox mountains, have uncovered the remains of a Bronze Age farmstead dating back almost 3,000 years. Numerous huge cairns, and a fine group of stone circles, such as that at Nymphsfield, near Cong in south Mayo, testify to the fact that this fertile limestone area was heavily populated in early Bronze Age times. (Native antiquarians in the late medieval period selected the Nymphsfield area as the site of a mythical 'second battle of Mag Tuired', supposedly between the Tuatha Dé Danann and the Fomoire; the equally mythical 'first battle of Mag Tuired', between the Tuatha Dé Danann and the Fir Bolg, was located in the townland of Moytirra, near Lough Arrow in south-east Co. Sligo).

THE DAWN OF HISTORY

Despite what the archaeologists can tell us of the various groups of prehistoric settlers, we are separated from them by an unbridgeable gulf. For example, we can never know by what name they called themselves, nor indeed what kind of language they spoke. Accordingly, we bid them farewell and leap across several centuries to the beginning of recorded history in Ireland, about the fifth century of the Christian era.

From echoes in the tales which comprise what is known as 'the Ulster Cycle' — the most important of which is *Táin Bó Cuailnge* — and in related materials, we get some idea, however vague and uncertain, of the names and location of population-groups and tribal kingdoms (called *tuatha*) in north Connacht in the period immediately preceding, and perhaps immediately following, the introduction of Christianity to Ireland. The earlier name of Erris, Irrus Domnann, contains the name of a people — Domnainn or Fir Domnann — who would appear to have been related to a British people, the *Dumnonii,* who were settled over a large part of England and southern Scotland in Roman times and have given their name to Devon in the south of England. An important branch of the Domnainn were the Gamanraid, one of whose heroes was called Fer Diad mac Damáin; his tragic death at the hands of his boyhood companion, Cú Chulainn, is one of the best-known and most moving episodes in the Táin. Other ancient peoples of whom remnants existed in early historical times — and in some instances down to the Norman period and beyond — were the Calraige in north Mayo, the Partraige in the south (their name survives in present-day Partry), the Conmaicne Críche north of Lough Mask and the Conmaicne Cúile Talad in the barony of Kilmaine, the Ciarraige in east Mayo, particularly around Lough Mannin (called Loch na nÁirned), and the Gailenga who have given their name to the barony of Gallen.

In the early Christian period we find much of Connacht under the sway of a dynasty called the Uí Fiachrach, claiming descent from one Fiachra Foltsnathach, an elder brother of Niall Noígiallach ('Niall of the Nine Hostages'), an early-5th-century king of Tara. Much of present-day Co. Mayo was at this time — if later traditions may be believed — the patrimony, or at least the 'sphere of influence', of a branch of the Uí Fiachrach called the Uí Fiachrach Muaide ('of the river Moy'), whose chieftains in the later middle ages bore the surname Ua Dubda (O'Dowd).

11

The political history of Connacht up to the 11th century is obscure and frequently confusing, but the main development to be noted is the supersession, from the late 8th century onwards, of the Uí Fiachrach by the rival dynasty of Uí Briúin, who claimed descent from Brión, another brother of Fiachra Foltsnathach. An important segment of the Uí Briúin in later centuries was called Síl Muiredaig, from which sprang the royal house of O'Conor, one of whom, Tairdelbach Mór Ua Conchobair (or Turlogh More O'Conor), became virtual monarch of Ireland in the early 12th century.

THE EARLY CHRISTIAN CENTURIES

The circumstances surrounding the introduction and spread of Christianity in 5th-century Ireland is the subject of much controversy among historians of early Ireland. Suffice it to say here that the cult of the British missionary bishop, Patrick, appears to have been established in Mayo at an early date. Whether the saint ever visited north Connacht — as later accounts claim — is quite impossible to say, but the belief that he did is due, in no small measure, to the exertions of a 7th-century 'Mayoman', the bishop Tírechán from Tír Amolngid (Tirawley), whose memoir of Patrick survives in the early-9th-century *Book of Armagh*. Writing around 670, Tírechán was one of the two main progenitors of what was to become 'the Saint Patrick Legend'. His work, which is essentially propaganda on behalf of the church of Armagh, may be of little value in relation to the life and works of the historical Patrick, but it is of the utmost interest as a reflection of the political topography of late-7th-century Ireland.

Of the numerous Patrician sites in Mayo mentioned by Tírechán and later authors, or merely attested in folk-tradition, the best-known were Cruach Pátraic (formerly Cruachán Aigle, 'mount of the eagle'), the great conical mountain on the south shore of Clew Bay, Aghagower (Achad Fobuir), nine miles to the east, and, north of Lough Carra, Baile Topair Pátraic (Ballintober — well-known nowadays for its medieval abbey, which has continued in unbroken use, through all vicissitudes, since its foundation by Cathal Crobderg O'Conor in 1216). Mention may also be made of Foghill near Killala, which has been identified by some writers — prompted by Tírechán — with the Silva Vocluti, 'the wood of Fochluth (or Fochlad) beside the western sea', mentioned by Patrick himself in his *Confessio.*

It is not possible, in the space available, to make more than a passing reference to some of the better-known early monastic sites in Mayo. (I give the names of reputed founders, but much of the story of these early sites is heavily encrusted with legend and therefore unreliable.) Among the sites which are most worthy of note are: Cong, founded by the 6th-century St. Fechín of Fore; Balla, founded in the 7th century by Crónán, alias Mo-Chúa; Meelick, attributed to a St. Broccaidh; Errew on Lough Cong, founded by St. Tigernach; Inishmaine on Lough Mask, founded by a 7th-century St. Cormac on the site of the dún of a 6th-century king named

Eogan Bél. Mention must also be made of the now uninhabited islands off the north-west coast of Mayo, such as Iniskea North, Duvillaun More, and Inishglora, which show traces of early anchoritic settlements similar to those found on other coastal islands such as Sceilg Mhichíl in Kerry and Inismurray in Sligo. A dubiously historical bishop named Cellach is linked with Killala in a 'life' which is a late literary romance; in fact, little can be said with certainty about the early history of the site.

'MAYO OF THE SAXONS'

One of the most interesting monastic sites in Co. Mayo was that from which the county derives its name — Maigh Eo. Colmán of Lindisfarne, having been defeated by the 'Romanist' party at the synod of Whitby (in Northumbria, in the north-east of England) in 663, withdrew with his followers, via Iona, to Inishbofin off the west coast of Galway. As a result of disagreement between the Irish and the English monks in the little community, the latter moved to the 'plain of yews', about sixteen kilometres south-east of the present town of Castlebar. The monastery they established there, known as Mag nÉo na Sachsan ('of the Saxons'), became renowned as a centre of learning, and continued to attract monks of English birth for a century and more after its foundation.

It is an indication of Mayo's importance in the middle ages that, when, in 1152, the synod of Kells introduced a system of diocesan organisation to the Irish church, one of the dioceses established west of the Shannon was that of Mayo. Admittedly, Rome sought to end its separate existence early in the 13th century, but we find it reappearing with its own bishops in the 15th and 16th centuries. In the aftermath of the Reformation, the Established Church united the see to Tuam — as the Roman authorities had wished to do as far back as 1202. The last Catholic bishop of Mayo was Adam Magauran, who was appointed in 1585; the diocese was finally absorbed by Tuam, by papal decree, some time after 1631.

The monastery at Mayo became a collegiate church sometime early in the 13th century, and about 1370 it became an abbey (St. Michael's) of Augustinian Canons. It survived until the dissolution of the monasteries after the Reformation; its possessions were finally disposed of, to an Englishman, in 1594. It will be clear from the foregoing that 'Mayo', as the name of the abbey and, more importantly, of the diocese, was very much in circulation around 1570, when it came to naming the new county established by Sir Henry Sidney.

THE COMING OF THE NORMANS

Having looked briefly at the early centuries of Christianity in the area now called 'County Mayo', it is necessary to return to a consideration of political developments in the area over the same period. In the centuries which saw the rise to power of various segments of the Uí Bhriúin dynasty, particularly Síl Muiredaig — culminating in the reigns, in the 12th century, of Tairdelbach Mór Ua Conchobair and his son Ruaidrí as among the first virtually undisputed kings of Ireland — Mayo was something of a backwater. It formed a hinterland to the main O'Conor territory, which lay chiefly along the Tuam-Roscommon axis. The young Ruaidrí O'Conor had just won the almost universal acceptance as national monarch which had so often just eluded his father when the deposed king of Leinster, Diarmait Mac Murchada, sought to recover his kingdom with the aid of a band of sturdy and adventurous Norman knights from Wales.

The repercussions of the Norman landings in 1160-70 were not felt directly in Connacht for more than half a century. The hapless Ruaidrí O'Conor, having been deposed, died in the monastery of Cong in 1198, and it was only after the death of his younger brother and successor, Cathal Crobderg ('Cathal More of the Wine-red Hand'), in 1224 that a Norman named Richard de Burgo, nephew of Hubert, the royal justiciar, got himself a grant of the 'Land of Connacht', consisting of the whole province except for part of Co. Roscommon which was left to the O'Conors.

The actual conquest of Connacht was not achieved until 1235, when all the great names of feudal Ireland followed de Burgo and his ally, Maurice Fitz Gerald, in a lightning campaign to overthrow the new king, Felim O'Conor. Connacht was quickly carved up among the invaders, with de Burgo taking all the rich land in Co. Galway and a large area in Co. Mayo. FitzGerald received most of Co. Sligo, as well as parts of Mayo and Galway. From de Burgo's principal allies in the venture sprang the great Norman families of Mayo — Prendergasts, Stauntons, d'Exeters, and de Angulos. From the rank and file of his army were planted the Barretts, Lynnots, Walshes, and Merricks — known as 'the Welshmen of Tirawley' — while, in the south — in the area still known as Dúiche Sheoigheach — were planted the Joyces.

'MORE IRISH THAN THE IRISH'

Although the advent of the Normans meant the eclipse of many Gaelic lords and chieftains — most notably of all the O'Conors — it was arguably not a disaster for Gaelic civilisation in general, for the eminently adaptable invaders — who, after all, were comparatively few in number, and had retained an almost wholly Gaelic tenantry — had, within the space of century, shed their veneer of French speech, adopted peculiarly Gaelic customs, and begun to intermarry with the native Irish, becoming, as the old phrase has it, *hiberniores ipsis Hibernis* ('more Irish than the Irish themselves'). The transformation was illustrated dramatically a century after their invasion of Connacht, when William de Burgo, known as 'the Brown Earl' (the de Burgos having become earls of Ulster as well as lords of Connacht), was assassinated at Carrigfergus, leaving no male heirs but one daughter, who later married Lionel, Duke of Clarence, second son of King Edward III. (This last point was to prove significant three centuries later, in 1635). The Brown Earl's grandfather's first cousin, William Liath (who had defeated the great Irish army under Felim O'Conor at Athenry during the Bruce campaign in 1316), had two sons, Ulick and Edmund Albanach. Taking their stand on the Gaelic law of succession, these now laid claim to the lordship of Connacht. Ulick seized the family lands in Co. Galway and founded the line which some generations later became known as the Clanrickard Burkes, and whose chieftains adopted the Gaelic patronymic Mac Uilliam Uachtarach ('Upper Mac William'). Émonn Albanach's descendants became the great, and rival, family of Mac Uilliam Íochtarach (or Íochtair), the Burkes of Mayo, whose lordship was roughly identical in area to the present county Mayo.

These two great families, lording it over most of Connacht, with — in English eyes — no legal title but with little outside interference, for over two centuries, epitomised the revival in Irish (meaning both Gaelic and Hiberno-Norman) fortunes which took place in the 14th and 15th centuries. The process of Gaelicisation is nowhere better exemplified than in the adoption by various Norman families, and branches of families, of new surnames based on Gaelic-style patronymics. Many of the de Angulos in east Mayo became, at a very early stage, Mac Goisdelbh (later Mac Coisdealbha — Costello), and a branch of the family later adopted the name Mac Baildrín (Waldron). The descendants of Jordan d'Exeter in Gallen became Mac Siúrtáin (Jordan), while an offshoot took the name Mac Stiofáin. Some of the Prendergasts in Clanmorris became Mac Muiris (Morris or Fitzmaurice), while an important branch of the Stauntons in Carra took the name Mac an Mhílidh (MacEvilly), with lesser branches called Mac Uilcín (Quilkin, Culkeen or Culkin) and Mac Páidín. The Barretts in Tirawley also had a branch called Mac Páidín, while other branches were called Mac Aindriú, Mac an Fhailghigh (Nally), Mac Toimín, and Mac Baitín. The Burkes, however, as might be expected of the predominant Hiberno-Norman family in the county, outshone all the other families with their variety of patronymics. Some of the more important of these were: Mac Giobúin (Gibbons) in Burrishoole, Mac Seoinín (Jennings) in Kilmaine, Mac Philbín, Mac Daibhéid (Davitt), Mac Uáitéir (Mac Walter), Mac Maoilir (Mac Miler), Mac Tiobóid, Mac Séathrúin, and many others.

The very rapid Gaelicisation of the Normans in Mayo did not, however, mean that those Gaelic families who had lost their lands to the invaders came any nearer to regaining possession. The O'Garas and O'Haras who were expelled out of Gallen and north Costello, the O'Dowds from Tirawley, and various branches of the O'Conors, mainly from Carra, simply ceased to the considered 'Mayo' families, and were forced to carve out new, reduced, territories in the neighbouring counties of Sligo and Roscommon. Only the O'Malleys were conspicuously successful in holding on to their wild and largely barren patrimony around Clew Bay, the defence of which was facilitated by their prowess as seafarers and pirates.

THE NEW ABBEYS AND FRIARIES

A noteworthy feature of the period with which we have been dealing was the building of abbeys or friaries for the new mendicant orders — Augustinians, Carmelites, Dominicans and Franciscans — principally by the Hiberno-Norman families. A number of early monastic sites — such as Cong, Inishmaine, Ballintober, Errew, and Mayo — had been chosen as locations for abbeys of the Augustinian Canons Regular, built under the patronage of Gaelic families (particularly the O'Conors) in the 12th and 13th centuries.

The first friary founded under Norman auspices in Mayo was that of Strade, established for the Franciscans by Jordan de Exeter, probably between 1240 and 1250. It was very soon (in 1252) transferred to the Dominicans. Another Dominican house, also thought to have been founded by a de Exeter, was Rathfran, dating from 1274. The Prendergasts founded Ballinasmalla, near Claremorris, for the Carmelites around 1288. Another Carmelite foundation, dating from 1298, was Burriscarra, which was built by the Stauntons. Abandoned after about eighty years by the Carmelites, it was later occupied by the Augustinian friars. The Augustinians were given a house in Ballinrobe around 1313, by one of the de Burgo's. No other notable foundation is recorded for over a century, until about 1430, when the Mac Costellos established the Dominicans in Urlaur and the Augustinians in Ballyhaunis. A decade later Rosserk Friary was founded for the Franciscan Third Order by one Joye (or Joyce). Nearby Moyne Friary was built for the Franciscan friars by Mac Uilliam Íochtarach (de Burgo) around 1455, while, a couple of years later, the only Gaelic foundation of the period, Murrisk, in the shadow of Croagh Patrick, was established for the Augustinians by Tadhg Ó Máille, the local chieftain. The latest foundation of any significance was the Dominican Friary of Burrishoole, built around 1469 by Mac Uilliam Íochtarach, Richard de Burgo of Turlough.

Almost all the foundations mentioned above were suppressed in the wake of the Reformation in the 16th century. One or two have been rebuilt and restored to use, but in most cases, only the ruins survive, pleasing, if poignant, late Gothic relics of what must have been among the most striking buildings in the countryside of pre-Tudor Ireland.

THE LORDSHIP OF MACWILLIAM EIGHTER

The 15th century was marked by frequent quarrels between the Mayo Burkes (as the people of Mac Uilliam Íochtair may be called for convenience) and the Clanrickard Burkes of what is now Co. Galway, as well as by much internecine fighting among the minor Norman lords of Mayo. From mid-century onwards, the O'Donnells, the great Gaelic lords of Tír Chonaill (in present-day Co. Donegal), interfered frequently in the affairs of north Connacht, as they sought to extend their sway southwards. They met with opposition from the Burkes, who were also quite often embroiled in the affairs of their eastern neighbours, the O'Conors of Roscommon and Sligo. Another Gaelic family, the O'Kellys of east Galway and south Roscommon were usually to be found in alliance with the Burkes of Mayo.

The turn of the century saw the Lord Deputy, Garrett Mór Fitzgerald, the great Earl of Kildare, ruling as virtual king of Ireland. In August 1504 he demonstrated his power by inflicting a crushing defeat on his son-in-law, Ulick Burke, Earl of Clanrickard, in a battle at Cnoc Tuagh (Knockdoe) near Galway. Among those who joined the great alliance against Clanrickard and his Munster allies were his cousins and rivals, the Mayo Burkes.

A mere thirty years after Cnoc Tuagh the great House of Kildare succumbed to the growing might of the Tudor monarchy, and by mid-century English power was making itself felt in Connacht, where the rivalry between the Mayo and Clanrickard Burkes had flared up again into war. By the late 1560s the Lord Deputy, Sir Henry Sidney, had procured the submission of both de Burgo lords, and was making provision for the future government of the province in the interests of the Crown. In July 1569 Sir Edward Fitton was appointed President, or Governor, of Connacht. One of the first tasks facing him and his council was to lay down the boundaries of the new counties of Connacht and Thomond. Almost immediately he was faced with what was to become a commonplace over the next thirty years — a rebellion by the Mayo Burkes. Fitton, with various allies, including Clanrickard, met them in battle at Shrule in June 1570. The outcome of the battle was somewhat indecisive, but Mac Uilliam Íochtair submitted and made peace shortly afterwards. 1572 saw another short-lived revolt, this time in alliance with two sons of Clanrickard. When Clanrickard's sons rebelled again in 1576, however, the Mayo Burkes remained loyal, holding Castlebar for the Queen.

It was in this last campaign, in 1576, that the remarkable 'sea-queen' from the shores of Clew Bay, Gráinne Ní Mháille (variously anglicised Granie ny Maille, Grace O'Malley, Granuaile, etc.) first makes her appearance in history, offering the services of her galleys and two hundred fighting men to Lord Deputy Sidney. But within two years Gráinne's second husband, Risteard an Iarainn — a Burke, and claimant to the MacWilliamship — was in revolt; his rebellion simmered on until 1582, when the new Lord Deputy, Sir Nicholas Malbie, recognised him as MacWilliam, and later knighted him.

THE 'COMPOSSICION OF CONOUGHT' AND AFTER

By 1585, both Risteard an Iarainn and Malbie were dead, and the new Lord Deputy, Sir John Perrott, determined to settle the land-tenure question in Connacht and Clare by bringing the Gaelic chiefs and Hiberno-Norman lords under the Crown, giving them legal titles to their estates under English law, and setting out the terms under which their tenants could hold land from them. The office and title of chieftain were abolished, and the system of primogeniture in the male line — to which the Normans, unlike their Gaelic neighbours, had long adhered — was made the norm for succession to property. This far-reaching measure — known as the 'Composition of Connacht' — brought an unprecedented degree of stability to the system of land-holding in the province, and seemed likely to remove a prime cause of the turbulence and strife which had for so long afflicted the area. The composition signified an important increase in the authority and influence of the Crown west of the Shannon, but the allowance it made for a continuation of Gaelic law and custom was sufficient to ensure that it caused comparatively little resentment among most of the population. It would appear to have been widely welcomed, both by the lords who had agreed to it, and whom it confirmed in their holdings, and by the mass of the common people who had had to bear the brunt of the incessant quarrels and petty wars occasioned by aristocratic squabbling over rights to land.

If Perrott, however, had expected the Composition to immediately pacify the province, and particularly the Mayo Burkes, he was sadly mistaken. One important effect of the agreement had been to abolish the MacWilliamship, and much of the turmoil of the next decade and a half derived from the refusal of various claimants to the title to accept its abolition; instead they attempted to enforce their rights, in the traditional Gaelic manner, on those who had always been their subordinates. A rebellion in 1585 by various branches of the Burkes was suppressed by the formidable new Governor, Sir Richard Bingham, with a harshness of which the county was to witness many examples in the coming years. A month after the rebellion ended, a force of nearly two thousand Scots *galloglaigh* (mercenaries) entered Connacht to assist the Burkes, but they were attacked near Ardnaree on the Moy (beside Ballina) by Bingham and routed with great slaughter.

The summer of 1588 saw the galleons of the Spanish Armada wrecked along the west coast of Ireland. The hapless Spaniards received little assistance in Mayo, being slaughtered by the O'Malleys and robbed and imprisoned by some of the Burkes. However, one Justin MacDonnell of Erris was hanged by Bingham for having attempted to help a Spanish force which had ensconced itself in a castle near Ballycroy.

The long-running feud between Bingham and the Burkes continued over the next seven years. The latter had thrown off all pretence of loyalty to the Crown, inaugurating one of their number — known as 'the Blind Abbot' — MacWilliam in the Irish fashion, and going into open rebellion. Bingham's efforts to suppress the outbreak were severely hampered by the mutual hostility between himself and the Lord Deputy, Fitzwilliam, which resulted in his replacement in 1595 by the ill-fated Sir Conyers Clifford.

18

RED HUGH O'DONNELL AND THE REBELLION IN CONNACHT

The Connacht rebellion took a more serious turn when Sligo fell to Red Hugh O'Donnell in June 1595. In December of that year O'Donnell presided over a great gathering of the Gaelic and Norman lords of Mayo — MacJordan, MacCostello, MacMorris, O'Malley, O'Dowd, and various Burkes — at the Gaelic-style inauguration-site of the Burkes near Kilmaine, to see the re-establishment of the MacWilliam title which the English had thought to abolish a decade before. There were at least eight contenders for the title, and O'Donnell made a serious error of judgment in choosing as MacWilliam one of those with least title to be so named — one Theobald, son of Walter Kittagh (Ciotach). The appointment offended almost every branch of the Burkes, and aroused the enmity in particular of another Theobald Burke, a son of Gráinne Ní Mháille known as Tióbóid na Long (or, as the State Papers usually render it, Tibbot ne Long). As a result, Theobald, son of Walter Kittagh, could attempt to function as The MacWilliam only when he had O'Donnell in the vicinity to support him.

While most of the Mayo Burkes, because of O'Donnell's misjudgment, were willing to submit to the Queen, most of the other lords in the county, both Norman and Gaelic, rallied to O'Donnell. The new governor, Sir Conyers Clifford, had some success in re-establishing English control in Connacht during 1597, by the end of which year only The MacWilliam and the O'Malleys were still in rebellion, but all his work was undone by the great Irish victory of Hugh O'Neill and his allies at the Yellow Ford on 14 August 1598. A year and a day later, another attempt by Clifford to re-impose government control in the west came to grief when his army was routed, and he himself killed, by the forces of O'Donnell and his allies, O'Rourke and MacDermott, in the Curlew mountains north of Boyle, Co. Roscommon.

In December 1599 O'Donnell came to Mayo and made peace between his puppet 'MacWilliam' and Tibbot na Long, who had refused to be swayed from his vital support for the English. As a result of this agreement Mayo was left in reasonable peace until 1601. Meanwhile, Sir Henry Dowcra's new and effective tactics were threatening O'Donnell's home-territory in Donegal, while Connacht, which he still dominated, was generally left alone by the English. The year 1601 saw the quarrel between The MacWilliam and Tibbot na Long flare up again, but the year ended with the former accompanying his patron and protector to Kinsale. After the disaster which befell the Gaelic cause on Christmas Eve 1601, Theobald, son of Walter Kittagh — The MacWilliam — went with Red Hugh to Spain, and the proud title which he bore disappeared forever.

STRAFFORD AND MAYO

As Irish resistance petered out after Kinsale, Sir Oliver Lambert had little difficulty in finally establishing government control in Connacht. Unlike Ulster, which was soon to be subjected to the most thorough 'plantation' in

Irish history, Connacht was left comparatively undisturbed as regards land-ownership. The settlement agreed under the composition of Connacht was generally adhered to. When Thomas Wentworth, Lord Lieutenant of Ireland and later Earl of Strafford, was preparing a plantation of Connacht in 1635, he had the province surveyed, and in the resulting document (the so-called 'Strafford Inquisition') the amount of land in Protestant hands in Mayo is given as only a little over 10%, divided among a dozen individuals. The remaining 88% or so was in the hands of about a thousand Catholic landowners.

The most important Protestant landholder, with a large estate in Erris and Achill, was the royalist Earl of Ormond, while a grand-nephew of Sir Richard Bingham had a large holding around Castlebar. Among the new arrivals in the county the most notable were the families of three Elizabethan officials, John Browne of the Neale, ancestor of the Marquis of Sligo and of Lord Kilmaine, John Moore, who settled at Brees (or Brize) Castle, near Claremorris, and Theobald Dillon, who had dispossessed the MacCostellos from their barony in east Mayo after they had, rather naively, placed themselves under his protection. Dillon, who became the first Viscount Dillon, was soon one of the two chief noblemen in the county, the other being Viscount Mayo — the first of that title (created in 1627) was none other than Tibbot na Long, Gráinne Ní Mháille's son, who died in 1629. Other arrivals in Mayo in the early 17th century included Ulstermen who settled in the north and west of the county; among the most notable of these were two sons of Niall Garbh O'Donnell who obtained land around Westport.

Given the success of the Ulster plantation, it was to be expected that greedy eyes would soon be cast in the direction of Connacht, still largely in Catholic hands. A scheme for planting Mayo, Sligo and Roscommon failed to find much favour, but the scheme proposed by Lord Deputy Wentworth, to which reference has already been made, came much nearer implementation. A jury of local landowners, meeting in Ballinrobe on 31 July 1635, was bullied into finding the king's title to Co. Mayo, on the basis that the king was heir to the estate of the 14th-century 'Brown Earl of Ulster', whose title had been usurped by Ulick and Edmund Albanach de Burgo. Wentworth's ingenious plan for raising additional revenue for his royal master by planting Connacht eventually came to nothing; its author had made too many enemies for himself, and the prince in whom he had put his trust, Charles I, was unable to save him from the scaffold in 1641.

THE CROMWELLIAN SETTLEMENT

The Irish uprising which commenced in 1641 ended a decade later with a stern Cromwellian regime in absolute control of the country and grimly determined to reward its friends and punish its enemies. The most significant feature of the 'Cromwellian Settlement', as it is known, was the plan to repay Commonwealth soldiers and adventurers for their services with grants of land in ten Irish counties. The landowners displaced as a consequence of implementing this scheme were, if found to be innocent of participation in 'the late rebellion', to be given lands, in proportion to their original estates, in four counties west of the Shannon — Mayo (except the barony of Tirawley), Galway, Roscommon, and Clare. The 'transplantation to Connacht' also involved transplantation *within* Connacht, as existing landowners west of the Shannon, displaced to make way for the new arrivals, had to be found estates elsewhere in the province.

In the case of Mayo, Tirawley was reserved for Cromwellian soldiers, and, of the remaining eight baronies, three — Carra, Clanmorris and Kilmaine — were intended for transplanters from counties Antrim and Down, and four — Murrisk, Burrishoole, Erris, and Costello — were for transplanters from other Ulster counties. The assignment of Gallen entailed some initial confusion, but eventually some forty transplanters from twenty counties were given land there. Things, however, did not turn out quite as planned. The total number of transplanters to Mayo was about 200; there were about 70 more who were transplanted from one part of Mayo to another. Of the 200, more than a third came from elsewhere in Connacht (mainly from Galway), another third came from Leinster (more than twenty from Wexford alone), a fifth from Munster (sixteen from Tipperary), and only a dozen from the whole of Ulster. Two important estates — those of Lord Mayo, who had been executed in 1652 after being found guilty on some very flimsy charges, and of Lord Dillon — had been confiscated because of their owners' involvement in the Confederate Wars, while the city of Gloucester received a grant of land near Ballinrobe because of its support for the parliamentary cause. A few years later, after the Restoration, this last piece of land passed to General Monck, created Duke of Albemarle as a reward for helping Charles II regain his throne.

The Restoration led to great confusion with regard to landholding in Mayo. Many who had been dispossessed, or had had their estates greatly reduced, now hoped to recover their lands, and some, such as Lords Dillon and Mayo (the latter the son of the executed Third Viscount), were successful, but many more were unable to dislodge the new proprietors. Many of the cases dragged on through various courts for nearly a quarter of a century, while some of the dispossessed, denied redress through lawful means, had recourse to methods outside the law. One of these was Dudley Costello (Dubhaltach Mac Coisdealbha) who, having fought for Charles II, had hopes of recovering the family lands in east Mayo which had earlier been lost to the Dillons. Being disappointed in this, Costello turned Tory, and waged a private war against the Dillons until they eventually cornered and killed him in Coolcarney (in north Gallen) in 1667.

The net result of the events in the half century after Wentworth's abortive preparations for plantation was that the 88% or so of Mayo land in Catholic hands in the time of Charles I had been reduced to less than half that figure (43%) by the close of the reign of his son, Charles II. The

Williamite (or Jacobite) War of 1689-91 led to a further, albeit slight, change in the balance — down to 39%; this resulted from the confiscation of the lands of those who had gone to France and so were not protected by the terms of the treaty of Limerick. The percentage of land in Catholic hands declined drastically in the following century, not — for the most part — through any change of ownership, but because, under the pressure of the penal code against Catholics, the majority of Catholic landowners conformed to the Established Church rather than risk the loss of their estates.

THE EIGHTEENTH CENTURY

Except for the momentous occurrences at the very close of the century, the history of Mayo in the 18th century is quite lacking in events of any historical moment. In many respects, the county's story in that century is of a piece with that of Ireland as a whole in the same period. For the great mass of the people it was a time of general and unrelieved misery. Although information on the specific conditions obtaining in Mayo is not easy to come by, it is probable that the county suffered severely from the terrible famine of 1739-40, and from the deadly outbreak of typhus which followed it. There were several epidemics of both typhus and smallpox in the course of the century, and eye-diseases, tuberculosis, and various other types of bronchial complaint were widespread. The lot of the people in some areas was eased by the comparatively humane and progressive policies of certain landlords, but, in general, the landowning class was not distinguished by its concern for the welfare of the tenantry. Like his co-religionists in other counties, a Mayo Catholic in the 18th century had virtually no hope of advancement — while he remained in his native land. Should he choose exile, however, the prospects could be rather brighter — as they were for William Brown, who left Foxford at the age of nine in 1786 and thirty years later was an admiral in the fledgling Argentine navy, having defeated the Spaniards in two engagements.

Culturally, 18th-century Mayo was a particularly obscure corner of the 'hidden Ireland', producing no poet of the calibre of Munster's Aodhagán Ó Rathaille or Eoghan Rua Ó Súilleabháin to give expression to the feelings of a vanquished and leaderless people. The blind harper, Turlough O'Carolan (d. 1738) visited the county in the early years of the century, and received hospitality in the big houses of the Burkes, the Dillons, and some of the later arrivals to the county, in return for which he composed several beautiful airs, and some far less memorable verses. There were a number of minor poets around in the earlier part of the century, one of the most colourful being Tomás Ó Caiside, whose varied career included a while as an Augustinian friar in Ballyhaunis and an adventure-filled period of service in various continental armies. Some of his songs — particularly the beautiful 'Caisideach Bán' — have remained popular down to the present day. Two other poets, of a slightly later period, whose works have retained considerable popularity in the west were Riocard Bairéad (d. 1819) from the Mullet, whose songs included 'Eoghan Cóir', 'Preab san Ól' and 'Tarraingt na Móna', and blind Anthony Raftery (d. 1835) from Killedan, near Kiltamagh, who spent most of his life in south and east Galway, and whose numerous compositions included the ever-popular 'Máire Ní Eidhin' 'Aithrí Reaftaraí' and, of course, 'Cill Liadáin'.

The gradual growth among the Anglo-Irish ascendancy in the 18th century of a kind of colonial nationalism — leading, in the last quarter of the century, to the founding of the Volunteer movement, and to efforts by Henry Grattan and his colleagues to reform the corrupt and unrepresentive Dublin parliament and, later still, to the more radical reform movement, the United Irishmen — had comparatively little impact on counties like Mayo, which seemed remote, inaccessible, and backward to middle-class Dublin reformers. There were some stirrings in the west in the 1790s, with reports of agrarian disturbances in Tirawley, and an influx into Mayo of Catholic refugees from Ulster following the sectarian clashes in north Armagh in 1795 which led to the formation of the Orange Society. Nevertheless, when the United Irishmen were forced by government repression to move from working openly for reform to secretly plotting revolution, and when Leinster and east Ulster blazed into rebellion in June of 1798, no one expected Mayo to play a memorable role in the bloody drama about to commence. The man who dragged Mayo onto the stage of Irish history in 1798 was a French general from Lorraine, a former dealer in goat and rabbit skins named Joseph Amable Humbert.

'THE YEAR OF THE FRENCH'

Ten weeks after the United Irishmen had been crushed at Ballynahinch, Co. Down, and two months after the fall of the rebel camp at Vinegar Hill, near Enniscorthy in Co. Wexford, Humbert landed at Kilcummin strand, on Killala bay, with about 1,100 officers and men of the army of the French Republic. Four days later, on Sunday, 26 August, having taken Ballina, Humbert led about 700 of his men, and about the same number of untrained Irish recruits, in an amazing all-night march down the almost trackless west shore of Lough Conn, arriving next morning in front of the startled British garrison of Castlebar. The force opposing Humbert numbered about 1,700, under the command of General Lake, and consisted mainly of Irish militia. After a short, sharp engagement, the militia broke and fled, and were quickly joined by the remainder of the garrison in a headlong flight which, for some of them, did not end till they reached the safety of Tuam, Co. Galway. The episode, still remembered as 'the races of Castlebar', was an ignominious defeat for the government forces and a corresponding morale-booster for the small force opposing them, but it was in no way decisive.

Humbert realised that without additional aid from France his expedition was doomed to failure. He remained in Castlebar for eight days awaiting further orders from his superiors, and while he waited he established a 'Republic of Connacht', with a young Catholic gentleman, John Moore from Moore Hall on the shores of Lough Carra, as its president. When neither orders nor help were forthcoming, Humbert marched his little army towards Sligo, winning a skirmish at Collooney. Then, hearing reports of a rising in the midlands, he swung south-eastwards through Leitrim into Longford where, on September 8 the force of 850 French troops and about a thousand Irish allies faced a force over five times as strong under Lord Cornwallis and General Lake.

The token battle at Ballinamuck ended with Humbert's surrender after barely half an hour. The French soldiers were treated honourably, but for the Irish the surrender meant slaughter. There was more slaughter a fortnight later when Killala finally fell to General Trench's forces. The little garrison (including its commander, Ferdy O'Donnell) was massacred. The government forces were turned loose on the countryside. The insurgents, or anyone suspected of having been involved in the rising, were hunted down and butchered without mercy. In all, it is estimated that some four to six hundred were killed in the battle for Killala and in the course of the 'mopping-up operations' which continued for some weeks, while others died on the scaffold in towns like Castlebar and Claremorris, where the high sheriff for Co. Mayo, the Honourable Denis Browne, M.P., brother of Lord Altamont, wreaked a terrible vengeance — thus earning for himself the nickname which has survived in folk-memory to the present day, 'Donnchadh an Rópa' (Denis of the Rope). The awful aftermath of those few stirring weeks, in what was long remembered, with a mixture of pride and horror, as *Bliain na bhFrancach* ('The year of the French') ensured that it was many a long year before the people of Mayo felt free to celebrate in song the exploits of 'The men of the West' and to remind their countrymen that *'When Éire lay broken at Wexford she looked for revenge to the West'*.

MAYO BEFORE THE FAMINE

The early decades of the 19th century saw a new outbreak of agrarian agitation with the rise of the 'Ribbon Societies' in Connacht. These sought to protect tenants against eviction by landlords who wished to clear their lands for grazing — to avail of the high prices for cattle prevailing in the years immediately after the Napoleonic Wars. Ribbonism had a strong sectarian tinge, being influenced by inflammatory pamphlets which were widely circulated at the time and which predicted the imminent overthrow of 'the Reformation'. (The most notable of these, particularly in the years leading up to Catholic Emancipation — 1829 — was a work popularly known as 'Pastorini's Prophecies', by a bishop and theologian named Charles Walmesley, which was first published in 1771.)

Sectarian tensions were further increased in this period by the activities of evangelical protestant missionaries seeking to 'redeem the Irish poor from the errors of Popery'. One of the best-known missions of this kind was that founded at Dugort, in Achill, in 1831 by a Meathman, the Rev. Edward Nangle. The activities of the missionaries and bible societies were strongly disapproved of by many, perhaps most, of the clergy of the Established Church, but they received important encouragement from two successive Protestant bishops of Tuam, Power le Poer Trench (d. 1839) and Thomas Plunkett, as well as from Bishop Daly of Cashel. Their staunchest opponent was the Mayo-born Catholic archbishop of Tuam, John MacHale, a supporter of Daniel O'Connell, a promoter of the Irish language, and a sturdy polemicist, who died at the age of ninety in 1881.

These too were the years of the campaign for Catholic Emancipation and, later, for the abolition of the tithes which a predominantly Catholic population was forced to pay for the upkeep of the clergy of the Established Church. Taken together with the missionary campaign, these were ideal conditions for the inflaming of sectarian passions. The activities of the evangelical missionaries, in particular, gave rise to the charge of 'souperism' — the use of food as an instrument for proselytism. Although the evidence in support of the charge was rather thin, the important thing was that it was widely believed and resulted in bitterness which took several generations to assuage. The use of food as a weapon against a people's beliefs was looked on with particular horror in later years in view of the catastrophe which overtook the Irish people, and particularly those in the west of the country, in the great famine of the 1840s.

'THE BAD TIMES'

There had been previous disasters in the Ireland of the early 19th century. The potato, the staple food of the ordinary Irish people at the time, had failed in 1817, 1819, 1821, and 1831-2, and this last failure had been followed by a terrible cholera epidemic, but all these disasters were dwarfed by the scale of the 1840s' catastrophe which began to be felt in Mayo by the Winter of 1846. In a county whose population in 1841 is thought to have been close to half a million (25% higher than the official census figures), there was a total lack of the amenities needed to cope with a disaster of the magnitude which now loomed. All through 1847 helpless officials reported harrowing scenes of distress throughout the county, but their superiors in Dublin and London were unable, and to a great extent unwilling, to do anything which might interfere with the free play of market forces.

Early in 'black forty-seven' an even greater killer than starvation appeared — so-called 'famine-fever'. Mayo landlords, with a few honourable exceptions (notably Colonel Vaughan Jackson near Ballina, and George Henry Moore of Moore Hall), acquitted themselves badly throughout this catastrophic period, meting out merciless treatment to helpless tenants unable to pay their rents. By 1848 Mayo was a scene of total disorder, with any attempts at distributing food (such as maize, called 'Indian meal' or 'yellow meal') and organising relief work in complete disarray. When the potato crop failed again in Mayo in 1848, the result was a wholesale and desperate effort to get away from what had become a land of death and despair. People took to the roads in their thousands to make their way to a port, where they hoped to get passage to England or get on board a possibly unseaworthy ship (one of the so-called 'coffin-ships') for the hazardous voyage to America. As a final blow to a hapless land, Asiatic cholera struck Ireland in 1849, and soon spread to Mayo, where there were no means of dealing with the epidemic.

How many died in Mayo in those terrible years from 1846 to 1849 no one will ever know. One Mayoman, James Daly, who later had a hand in starting what became known as 'the Land War', wrote that '200,000 people died of hunger in Mayo, after living on nettles and asses' flesh'. This was no doubt an exaggeration, but it is true that Mayo lost approximately that number of people — both by death and emigration — between 1841 and 1851. (On Clare Island, Gráinne Ní Mháille's old stronghold, there were 576 deaths from starvation during the Famine-years — out of a total population of 1,700.) Apart from the thousands who joined the exodus to England and America, Mayo probably lost a quarter, and maybe a third, of her people from hunger and the side effects of hunger, such as famine-fever, in what was in later years referred to, euphemistically, as 'an drochshaol' (the bad times).

Rather ironically perhaps, the great reduction in Mayo's population, and especially the virtual annihilation of the formerly numerous class of landless cottiers who had been hardest hit by the Great Famine, enabled those who remained to considerably improve their standard of living in the following decades. The new National Schools — despite the opposition of those, such as Archbishop MacHale, who regarded them, with some justification, as agents of anglicisation — succeeded in reducing the rate of illiteracy by almost half in the forty years between 1841 and 1881. The result was a population with rising expectations, and with growing confidence in their own strength and in their ability to bring about a change in conditions, and so, when bad harvests in 1877 and '78 and a disastrous one in 1879 brought the threat of another serious famine, particularly in the west, the people were far better prepared to protect themselves than they had been thirty years before.

THE LAND WAR

A signal of the new militancy in Mayo came in 1874 with the election to Parliament of the young pro-Fenian John O'Connor Power, in the face of opposition from — strangely enough — Archbishop MacHale. It was one of the new M.P.'s lieutenants, James Daly, editor of the *Connaught Telegraph,* who was largely responsible for organising a historic meeting at the tiny village of Irishtown, near Ballindine, on Sunday, 20 April 1879. The meeting, at which the attendance was variously estimated at between four and fifteen thousand, arose out of a threat to evict a number of tenants for arrears of rent from the estate of a local absentee landlord. The meeting led not only to the cancellation of the proposed evictions but to a general reduction of rents. Of far greater consequence, however, were the wider political effects of the meeting, whose reverberations were to be felt throughout the whole of Ireland over the next quarter of a century.

On 1 June 1879, the Fenian leader, John Devoy, a Fenian prisoner on ticket-of-leave, Michael Davitt (born in Strade and reared in Lancashire), and the county Wicklow landlord, and M.P. for Meath, Charles Stewart Parnell, met in Dublin, and apparently agreed on 'the new departure', whereby the Fenians and the constitutional nationalists agreed to combine in a struggle to reform — or perhaps revolutionise — the Irish land-system. One week later Parnell urged a meeting of tenants in Westport 'to hold a firm grip on your homesteads and lands'. His call came as potato blight was spreading once more through the west, and the number of evictions for non-payment of rent was rising steadily. On 16 August, under Davitt's leadership, the National Land League of Mayo was founded in Castlebar, and two months later the campaign moved well beyond the borders of Mayo with the inauguration in Dublin of the Irish National Land League, with Parnell as its President.

The story of the 'Land War' over the next two decades is part of Irish history rather than of the Mayo story specifically. Mayo, however, played a prominent, and sometimes violent, role in the struggle. Almost half of what were termed 'agrarian outrages' (maiming of cattle, destruction of property, wounding and even killing of land agents, landlords, and those who were considered 'land grabbers') in the early 1880s occurred in Mayo, Kerry and west Galway. At the same time, Mayo attracted international attention, and in the process gave a new word to the English language, by initiating a rather novel form of non-violent protest. This involved a campaign of ostracisation against Lord Erne's Mayo agent, a Norfolk man named Captain Charles Cunningham Boycott, whose efforts to secure the harvest from the estate on the eastern shore of Lough Mask necessitated the importation of some fifty Orangemen, mostly from Cavan, and a force of about a thousand soldiers and police to protect them. The campaign against the 'Boycott Relief Expedition' was orchestrated by Father John O'Malley, parish priest of Kilmolara (resident in the Neale), and it was he who suggested the term 'boycotting' as being easier for his parishioners to pronounce than 'ostracisation'. The unfortunate Boycott realised by late November 1880 that all his efforts had been in vain (the harvest had cost over £10,000 — 'a shilling for every turnip dug' said Parnell), and so, taking his family with him, he returned to England until the agitation had subsided.

The episode at Lough Mask House was indeed a bloodless victory over landlordism, but bloody deeds were common in the west. The violence was fuelled by the fact that two-thirds of Mayo tenants were not eligible for rent-reductions under the 1881 Land Act. When an Arrears Act came into

27

force the following year there was a dramatic, and speedy, reduction in the number of violent incidents.

By 1882 the fight for the land was virtually won, although various land acts, culminating in that brought in by Chief Secretary, Wyndham in 1903 increased the pace and the scope of the transfer of ownership from landlord to tenant. It was perhaps appropriate that the agrarian revolution begun by Mayomen such as Daly and Davitt, should have been rounded off, as it were, by another Mayoman, Sir Antony MacDonnell — later Baron MacDonnell of Swinford — who, as permanent Under Secretary for Ireland, played an important role in preparing the Land Purchase Act of 1903 which within a decade or two had made Irish landlordism a thing of the past.

LOCAL GOVERNMENT REFORM AND NATIONAL RENAISSANCE

A major reform of the system of local government, involving a significant extension of democracy at local level, and reflecting too the eclipse of landlordism, occurred in 1898, when the Local Government (Ireland) Act replaced the old Grand Juries — which had consisted of the principal landowners in each county — with a system of County Councils. The new councils were elected by adult male suffrage (not quite 'one man, one vote' yet — that came later), and possessed quite considerable powers.

Under the Local Government Act there was a certain readjustment of county boundaries, and Mayo was affected more than most in this respect. For reasons which are not altogether clear, an area of some 7,700 hectares in the barony of Costello — including Ballaghaderreen, one of the principal towns of east Mayo — was detached from Mayo and given to Co. Roscommon, while 4,000 hectares of the Sligo barony of Tireragh — to the south-east of Ballina — were transferred to Mayo, and, in the south, about 9,700 hectares of the barony of Ross — almost a quarter of its total area — were gained at the expense of Co. Galway.

The new century witnessed a great national revival, both in the cultural and, later, in the political field, and Mayo did not go untouched by the new movement. Travelling teachers of the newly-founded Conradh na Gaeilge (the Gaelic League) sought to reimplant respect for, and knowledge of, the language so recently abandoned — as a badge of poverty and backwardness — by the people of the west. *Feiseanna* sprang up in many centres, and parts of the county which were still Irish-speaking experienced an influx of enthusiasts anxious to learn the language from native speakers. One particularly popular area was Tuar Mhic Éadaigh, with its Coláiste Samhraidh (summer college) overlooking Lough Mask. (Among the attendance there in the summer of 1909 were two young teachers from Dublin, Éamon de Valera and Sinéad Flanagan.) Established almost a decade before the Gaelic League, the Gaelic Athletic Association spread rapidly too, and soon there were clubs in many parishes. (The man who in 1884 suggested the foundation of the G.A.A. to Michael Cusack was a fine athlete and prominent member of the Irish Republican Brotherhood from Balla, Patrick W. Nally; he died in Mountjoy Jail in 1891, as he neared the end of a sentence of ten years for his part in the so-called 'Crossmolina Conspiracy').

Another facet of those years was exhibited in the riots which greeted the staging of a play entitled *General John Regan* in Westport in 1913. The play was based on a novel by the Belfast-born author, George A. Birmingham, (the pseudonym of the Rev. John O. Hannay who had been rector of Westport since 1892). The play gave offence because it appeared to lampoon a Catholic priest; this was taken as a slur on Irish Catholics in general, and a people which had come through a century of such suffering, crowned by such dramatic achievements, a people just beginning to regain its self-respect and confidence after such degradation and despair, was in no mood to be tolerant or to display much of a sense of humour in the face of what it considered sneers or insults. (The Rev. Hannay, it is worth recalling, had been a leading figure in the Gaelic League until about 1906, when his attacks on what he considered the abuse of clerical power generated a heated controversy which led to his eventual disillusionment with the League.)

The 'Ulster Crisis' (also called the 'Home Rule Crisis') of 1912-14 saw the emergence of two forces of Volunteers in the country. One of the chief organisers, and first Inspector-General, of the Irish Volunteers after their foundation in November 1913 was Colonel Maurice Moore of the Connaught Rangers, a brother of the noted novelist, George Moore, and a member of the Catholic landowning family from Moore Hall to which the young 'President of the Republic of Connaught' in 1798 had belonged. When the Volunteers split into followers of the Irish Parliamentary Party leader, John Redmond, and the more Republican followers of MacNeill and Pearse after the outbreak of the Great War in August 1914, Moore, as a friend and supporter of Redmond, sided with the faction known as the 'National Volunteers'. (Two decades later he helped initiate the campaign to withhold payment to Britain of the 'Land Annuities' — the money lent by the British Government under land acts such as Wyndham's to buy out the landlords.)

THE STRUGGLE FOR INDEPENDENCE

The rising of Easter Week 1916, in which the predominant role was played by the Volunteer faction which had followed Pearse in 1914, was largely confined to Dublin, but one of the fourteen men executed in Kilmainham Jail in the aftermath of the rising was a Mayoman, Major John MacBride from Westport. Although his role in the rising was a relatively minor one, he had fought the British before, having led a small Irish Brigade in the Boer War in South Africa, and some considered this a factor in the British decision to have him shot. (MacBride was married for a time to the beautiful Maud Gonne — the love of the poet W. B. Yeats's life — and their son, Seán, was later to become an internationally respected jurist, noted spokesman for the cause of Irish Republicanism, founder of the Clann na Poblachta party, Minister for External Affairs in the first interparty government — 1948-51 — and winner of the Nobel and Lenin Peace Prizes.)

In the historic general election of December 1918 — in which Sinn Féin's landslide victory seemed to give retrospective endorsement to the 'Men of Easter Week' — the leaders of the respective parties, de Valera for Sinn Féin and John Dillon for the Irish Parliamentary Party, faced each other in the east Mayo constituency. Although the Parliamentary Party vote was a good deal higher there than in neighbouring constituencies (it was, after all, Dillon's home-constituency), de Valera obtained nearly two-thirds of the vote. (East Mayo also won the reputation of being the worst constituency in the country for intimidation during the election campaign!)

The attempt by the new Dáil Éireann to establish alternative institutions of government to those operated by the Crown evoked a ready response in Mayo. The first public session in Ireland of the new Republican law courts (the so-called 'Sinn Fein Courts') was held in Ballinrobe on 17 May 1919. Collection of money for the Dáil Éireann Loan proceeded apace, as did recruitment to the Irish Volunteers and Cumann na mBan. The organisation and training of the Volunteers (by now more commonly referred to as 'the I.R.A.') was interspersed with incidents which pointed inexorably to the violence to come: raids for arms, burning of deserted R.I.C. barracks, reprisal raids by Crown forces, the arrest of suspects, banning or harrassment of public meeetings, all leading eventually, and, it would appear, inevitably, to armed attacks and loss of life on both sides. An early casualty was J.C. Milling, a resident magistrate, shot dead at his home in Westport on 29 March 1919. In July 1920 a police sergeant was killed in Ballina, and this was followed by reprisals by the newly-arrived Black and Tans. There were incidents of indiscipline by troops in Balla in November, and in January 1921 a tailor with deformed feet named Michael Tolan, who was rather marginally involved with the I.R.A., was arrested in Ballina by Black and Tans, and, after being badly ill-treated, was killed and his body buried in a bog near Foxford, where it was found several months later. An even more innocent victim of the Black and Tans was Michael Coen of Ballyhaunis, who was killed outside the town in May 1921. The Ballyhaunis area too saw the death at their hands on 1 April 1921 of the Commandant of the I.R.A.'s East Mayo Brigade, Seán Corcoran from Kiltamagh, who was killed at Crossard while making preparations for an ambush.

By spring of 1921 the Mayo I.R.A. had formed a number of flying columns, of which two in particular — those under Michael Kilroy in west Mayo, and Tom Maguire in south Mayo — were becoming increasingly daring in their attacks on Crown forces. The killing in March of a police sergeant, and later of two constables, by Kilroy's men, led to reprisals by

Black and Tans in Westport. Two Volunteers died in an abortive ambush at Islandeady on 1 May. Two days later, an ambush by Maguire and thirty of his men near Toormakeady was only partially successful, and the flying column was forced to withdraw to the mountains, where they held off a force of several hundred soldiers until, under cover of darkness, they were able to slip through the cordon which was seeking to encircle them. Maguire was wounded in the engagement and his adjutant, Michael O'Brien, was killed. British casualties, as in a number of other similar engagements, were not revealed. Just over a fortnight later, on 19 May, another unsuccessful ambush at Kilmeena left five Volunteers dead and three wounded. It was only the courageous, and single-handed, rearguard action fought by Michael Kilroy which prevented the column being wiped out. As the survivors attempted to evade encirclement another Volunteer was killed, as was an R.I.C. Head Constable. On 2 June, however, the tables were turned when, at Carrowkennedy, Kilroy's men attacked several lorries of R.I.C., killing six policemen and wounding four, two of them fatally. The remaining seventeen police surrendered with all their arms and equipment.

TRUCE, TREATY AND CIVIL WAR

Six weeks after the Carrowkennedy ambush came the Truce, followed four months later, on 6 December, by the Anglo-Irish Treaty. The subsequent split in Republican ranks, culminating in the outbreak of the tragic civil war on 28 June 1922, left a majority of Mayo Volunteers on the Anti-Treaty side; in this they followed the lead of the respective commanding officers of the Second, Third and Fourth Western Divisions of the I.R.A. to which they were attached — Tom Maguire, Liam Pilkington and Michael Kilroy. The Anti-Treaty side had a good deal of popular support in Mayo, Sligo - Mayo East being the only contested constituency in the general election of June 1922 to show an Anti-Treaty majority, but this was gradually alienated by the economic disruption caused — sometimes intentionally — by the activities of the Anti-Treaty forces. Such actions led to much hardship in areas like Foxford, where the famous woollen mills, employing over 300 people, were forced to close. As a result, the arrival of Pro-Treaty troops in the county, shortly after the outbreak of civil war, was greeted with a certain amount of relief, even by those who were unhappy with the terms of the Treaty.

The military campaign in Mayo was of fairly short duration, and the fighting was not particularly fierce. The bitterness which characterised the later stages of the civil war had not yet made its appearance, and each side seemed reluctant to inflict heavy casualties on its opponents. The strategy of the Pro-Treatyites was both simple and effective. A column of troops from Roscommon advanced on Claremorris, where they waited until more troops were landed by sea at Westport. Then both forces moved on Castlebar which was occupied without incident on 25 July 1922. Three days later Ballina was taken after the Anti-Treaty forces had left the town.

31

Other towns, including Killala, Ballycastle, Belmullet and Foxford, were quickly captured. In mid-August a party of Pro-Treaty soldiers, under Colonel Tony Lawlor, was ambushed at Ballinamore near Kiltamagh. Early in September there was an unsuccessful counter-attack on Castlebar, and on the 12th Michael Kilroy's men retook Ballina, but evacuated it again soon afterwards. This was followed shortly by a fierce but indecisive battle at Glenamoy between Kilroy with about 160 men and a smaller force of Pro-Treaty soldiers. October saw a night-attack on Ballina, and there was also an unsuccessful assault on Ballyhaunis. On 24 November, Newport fell to Lawlor's forces after a battle in which five government soldiers died, but which resulted in the capture of Michael Kilroy and seventy of his men. This effectively ended the war in Mayo, just as the conflict elsewhere was about to enter a new and much more savage phase of summary executions, assassinations, and squalid killings of defenceless people on both sides of the tragic divide. Mayo was fortunate to escape this last terrible part of the 'war of brothers' which left wounds that took decades to heal.

MAYO SINCE 1922

The story of Mayo over the past sixty years is little different from that of the rest of rural Ireland, and particularly the west, in the same period — except that here, perhaps, the degree of economic stagnation and social decay was greater and the seemingly incurable haemorrhage of emigration more acute than elsewhere. (The estimated population of close on half a million in 1841 had by 1901 declined to under 200,000, and this figure had been almost halved again — to 110,000 — by 1971; in the 1940s alone, Mayo lost almost 40,000 of its people, the highest rate of emigration from any county in Ireland, apart from Dublin, in those years.) In line with the disastrous loss of population from virtually all parts of the county, the few remaining Gaeltacht areas — in Erris and Achill and, in the south, around Toormakeady — continued to contract at an alarming rate, and, despite (or, perhaps, because of?) some belated attempts at industrial development in those areas, the decline over recent decades has been precipitate.

In the sphere of national politics, it could be argued that Mayo has made a more than proportionate contribution in the decades since independence. Two political party leaders were born and reared in Mayo, and one, Taoiseach Charles J. Haughey, was born in Castlebar but reared in Dublin. Thomas J. O'Connell from Bekan, T.D. for south Mayo, one-time general secretary of the Irish National Teachers' Organisation and founder-member of the Educational Building Society, succeeded Thomas Johnston as leader of the Labour Party in 1927; he pursued a policy of general support for the Fianna Fáil party in the period leading up to its electoral victory of 1932, in which year he was in turn succeeded as party leader by William Norton. Joseph Blowick from near Balla led the small-farmers' party, Clann na Talmhan, in the first interparty government (1948-51), in which he served as Minister for Lands and Fisheries. (Joseph

Blowick's brother, Fr. John, was co-founder of the Columban Fathers — the famous 'Maynooth Mission to China' — whose first headquarters, after their foundation in 1916, was at Dalgan Park near Shrule.) Two members of Éamon de Valera's early cabinets were Mayomen: Thomas Derrig, from Westport, served as Minister for Education throughout the 1930s and '40s, and as Minister for Lands in the early 1950s, while P. J. Ruttledge, from Ballina, held various portfolios in the 1930s and '40s. Four other Mayomen, Micheál Ó Móráin, Seán Flanagan, Denis Gallagher, and Pádraig Flynn, served in later Fianna Fáil governments. A Claremorris man, Conor A. Maguire — later Chief Justice — served as Attorney General from 1932 to 1936. Three Cumann na nGael/Fine Gael deputies from Mayo served in government: J. Fitzgerald Kenny was Minister for Justice in W. T. Cosgrave's administration from 1927 to '32, Patrick Lindsay was Minister for the Gaeltacht in the second interparty government in 1956-57, and Patrick O'Toole was Minister for the Gaeltacht from June 1981 until March 1982. (Mention should also be made of two Mayomen who contributed to the political life of the land where so many from Mayo have found a home — William and Paul O'Dwyer from Bohola, who attained prominence as Democratic Party politicians in New York.)

As we approach the time of writing this brief sketch of Mayo history it becomes increasingly difficult to maintain the necessary historical perspective. What appears of over-riding importance from the standpoint of the 1980s may seem of much less significance to an observer a hundred years hence. Nevertheless, it is more than likely that historians of the future will take particular note of the economic transformation which began to overtake Mayo in the 1970s, and which has brought in its wake social changes whose consequences can as yet only be guessed at. One positive, indeed historic, development, which one hopes will be permanent, is what appears to be the staunching — at last — of the terrible flow of emigration, which over the years has left many a Mayo hearth desolate and deprived the county of sorely-needed talent. One may be permitted the hope that the sad refrain 'they too are exiled from the County Mayo' will be heard no more, that those who leave their native county in years to come will do so from choice, rather than as the result of hard economic necessity!

Giant modern industrial plants (like the great Asahi chemical fibres complex at Killala), substantial E.E.C. grants for agricultural and industrial development, and a quite dramatic rise in the general level of prosperity in the county (reflected most strikingly, perhaps, in house-building, but also in other facets of popular lifestyle) — all these are taken as signs of new and brighter days for Mayo. A less material sign, calling people back to more traditional values, was the visit of Pope John Paul II to Knock in the autumn of 1979, an event which focussed world attention on Co. Mayo — a Mayo very different from the poverty-stricken, famine-haunted, agitation-wracked county of August 1879, where the strange

33

reports from the little village of Knock would one day lead the Roman Pontiff to visit what he described, on that misty but memorable Sunday in September, as 'the goal of my Irish journey', the great Marian shrine of Cnoc Mhuire.

Interest in the county was further increased by the success enjoyed on both sides of the Atlantic, by Thomas Flanagan's great historical novel *The Year of the French,* which vividly tells the story of Mayo in 1798, and whose impact is likely to be greatly augmented by the film-adaptation of the book for television audiences. The building of a major airport in east Mayo may be seen as reflecting the confidence that many overseas visitors will be attracted to this north-western corner of Ireland, and that many of Mayo's exiled sons and daughters will be persuaded to pay more frequent visits to the county of their birth. So we may hope that this western outpost, to which man first made a perilous voyage more than four thousand years ago, the lordship of the Lower MacWilliam Burke to which Gráinne Ní Mháille's galleys brought exotic wares from Spain and Portugal and plunder from ships on the stormy Atlantic, will soon see visitors from many lands travel in comfort, by the most modern means of air transport, to see and enjoy the unrivalled, and still largely unspoilt, scenery of this historic 'county of the plain of yews' — Contae Mhaigh Eo.

SOURCES

A wide variety of sources was consulted in the preparation of this 'Outline'. This note will only deal with the more important of these. Other books and articles which were availed of to a lesser extent are included in the general bibliography at the end of the book.

For the pre-historic section, three articles, 'The megalithic tombs of Ireland' by Seán Ó Nualláin, 'Neolithic fields: the Irish evidence' by Séamus Caulfield, and 'A bronze age farmstead at Glenree, Co. Mayo' by Michael Herity, were particularly useful. I also benefitted from the advice and helpful suggestions of my colleague, Dr. Seán Ó Nualláin.

For the political history of the pre-Norman period the three pioneering works of Francis John Byrne, Gearóid Mac Niocaill and Donnchadh Ó Corráin — respectively entitled *Irish kings and high-kings, Ireland before the Vikings* and *Ireland before the Normans* — were of immense assistance.

On the thorny 'Patrician question' there is of course a voluminous literature in existance; deserving of special mention, however, is Professor D. A. Binchy's magisterial essay on 'Patrick and his biographers: ancient and modern'. For the history of the earlier monastic sites and of the medieval abbeys and friaries I am very indebted to two sources in particular, Killanin and Duignan's *Shell guide to Ireland* and Gwynn and Hadcock's *Medieval religious houses: Ireland.*

For the political history of the post-Norman period I consulted G. H. Orpen's great work *Ireland under the Normans, 1169-1333,* as well as the two fine works by Edmund Curtis and A. J. Otway-Ruthven, both entitled *A history of medieval Ireland.* (In the case of Curtis, I used the second, extensively revised edition of 1938.) Another work of Curtis's which was consulted with profit, particularly in relation to parts of the 16th century, was his *History of Ireland.* A work which is indispensable for the history of Mayo in the late medieval period — although at times not very readable, mainly due to the author's tendency to reproduce source material in rather undigested form — is H. T. Knox's *History of the county of Mayo.* I also made use of a number of articles by Knox on the Norman conquest of Connacht and on the history of the Burkes.

We are fortunate in having modern scholarly editions of a number of valuable documents relating to important developments in the Mayo story between the late 16th and later 17th centuries; these include A. M. Freeman, *Compossicion Booke of Conought,* William

34

O'Sullivan, *Strafford inquisition of Co. Mayo,* and Robert C. Simington, *Book of survey and distribution: Co. Mayo* and *Transplantation to Connacht, 1654-58.* A very valuable article which analyses some of the sources just mentioned is J. G. Simms: 'Mayo landowners of the seventeenth century'. Also invaluable for the 16th and 17th centuries were several chapters of *A new history of Ireland,* vol. iii: *Early modern Ireland, 1534-1691.*

Edith Mary Johnston's *Ireland in the eighteenth century* was drawn on for her account of the conditions enjoyed (or, rather, suffered!) by the great mass of the population in that century. The account of the 'Year of the French' is greatly indebted to Thomas Pakenham, *The year of liberty* and to Richard Hayes, *The last invasion of Ireland.*

For the period from 1800 almost to the present day two recently-published general works of reference proved of great assistance: D. J. Hickey and J. E. Doherty, *A dictionary of Irish history since 1800* and Henry Boylan, *A dictionary of Irish biography.* Gearóid Ó Tuathaigh's very useful *Ireland before the famine, 1798-1848* was consulted for the early 19th century, while Cecil Woodham-Smith's now classic *The great hunger* was the main source for the section on the terrible catastrophe of the 1840s.

Among the sources which proved useful for the second half of the 19th century, and particularly for the period of the 'Land War', were F.S.L. Lyons's great work *Ireland since the famine* and his *Charles Stewart Parnell,* Tom Corfe, *The Phoenix Park murders,* and Joseph Lee's stimulating and challenging work, *The modernisation of Irish society, 1848-1918.*

I only obtained a copy of T. W. Moody's masterly *Davitt and Irish revolution, 1846-82* as this article was going to print, but I was able to draw on certain other published works on Davitt and the Land League by this great scholar, as well as on a series of lectures on the same subject which he delivered in Mayo in 1979.

The main sources for events in Mayo in the period between the rising of 1916 and the civil war were a series of articles on 'Mayo in the fight for freedom' by Anthony Lavelle which was published in the *Western People* in the mid-1960s, and Dorothy Macardle's *The Irish republic.* The account of Mayo's rather brief involvement in the civil war is based on the works of Calton Younger and Eoin Nesson, respectively entitled *Ireland's civil war* and *The civil war in Ireland, 1922-1923.*

I should perhaps mention that I would have liked to devote rather more space than I have done to certain periods and episodes in the Mayo story (particularly the 16th century and the Great Famine), but such disproportionate treatment of certain sections at the expense of others would have detracted from the aim of providing a fairly balanced overall coverage. If this has resulted in a too summary, even simplistic, treatment of certain developments, I beg the reader's indulgence — but may we dare to hope that this *opéritif* will tempt him/her to sample some of the meatier works mentioned above?

THE ARCHAEOLOGY OF MAYO

by Peadar O'Dowd

Archaeology is the interpretation of our past from the study of man-made objects (artifacts) left behind by our ancestors. In the Irish context, County Mayo can be said to provide artifacts to delight the archaeologist and intrigue the layman.

Our story unfolds with the arrival of the first people in Ireland about 8,000 B.C. during the Middle Stone Age (Mesolithic). They probably came across the narrow neck of water separating Ireland from Scotland. They were Stone Age hunters, who hunted wild game using stone artifacts such as axes and flint-headed spears. They also fished our rivers and, when in season, gathered shell-fish and hazel-nuts. These hunting and food-gathering people moved around in small groups and built no permanent structures, such as stone huts or tombs. Consequently only limited archaeological traces of Mesolithic man have been found, the nearest to County Mayo being at Lough Gara in County Sligo. More substantial evidence has come to light in recent discoveries by Dr. Peter Woodman at Mount Sandel in County Antrim and by Michael Ryan at Boora Bog in County Offaly.

NEOLITHIC SETTLERS

About 3,500 B.C. a new and exciting type of newcomer landed on our shores — Neolithic (New Stone Age) Man — our first farmers, who in time merged with the native hunters. These new settlers brought knowledge of crop cultivation and animal husbandry to Ireland. They cleared large areas of forests using polished stone axeheads, and planted wheat and barley. The evidence these new settlers left on our countryside, such as their megalithic (large stone) tombs, tell us that County Mayo was one of the first places they occupied in Ireland. There are about 330 known Court Tombs in the whole of the country, and County Mayo can boast of having over 60, the highest number of such tombs in any county.

When we look at the actual make-up of a Court Tomb, we see that County Mayo has also what can be classed as a distinctive Mayo type. A Court Tomb was a monument erected to house the bones (usually cremated) of the dead and consisted of a long straight-sided cairn or mound of stones, wider at the front than at the back. Usually there was a semi-circular open space, called a court, at the front facing east, surrounded by tall erect standing-stones acting as a retaining facade. Ceremonies were held in the court before the remains were brought into the gallery (long narrow chamber) and placed in one of its compartments. Large stones lined the sides of the gallery and the roof was also made of large slabs.

The distinct Mayo type, of which eight out of nine known examples are found in the vicinity of Killala Bay, have two small side-chambers or, in archaeological terms, transepted galleries. These have been classed as the "finished" design compared with those elsewhere in the country. Out of the 60 or so known Mayo Court Tombs, (according to the 1964 survey carried out by de Valéra and Ó Nualláin) a large cluster of 29 are in the Bunatrahir Bay region, near Ballycastle. It could, as has been suggested, possibly indicate the primary landing place of these new arrivals. Another school of thought suggests that the original newcomers settled in the east and gradually moved to the west, and so had perfected their tomb-building techniques by the time they reached Mayo. Unfortunately, after 5,000 years, very little remains of any of the tomb structures to help us settle the question without further excavation. In most cases only the largest boulders or stone slabs survive, and some may have fallen from their former positions. It may be difficult to see some such tombs due to overgrowth. The mounds covering the burial chambers have in most cases been denuded, due to the smaller stones being used to build nearby walls or roads. Considering the condition of the surviving tombs, there are probably more such sites to be discovered in Mayo. Diagram 1 illustrates the fate of one such Court Tomb at Cartronmacmanus in the parish of Killasser.

The following is a list of Court Tombs in County Mayo, as published by de Valéra and Ó Nualláin, in Vol. II of *Survey of the Megalithic Tombs of Ireland;* (Sites are grouped together to relate to present centres of population):

Ballina	Ballyholan, Carrowleagh, Ardagh, Creggaun, Ballybeg, Mullaghawny, Drumrevagh, Ballymacredmond, Carrownaglogh;
Ballycastle	Behy, Belderg More, Glenulra (2), Sralagagh, Ballyglass (2), Rathoonagh (2), Lecarrowtemple (2), Aghoo, Aghaleague, Barnhill Upper, Ballybeg, Creevagh More (2), Ballybeg, Rooghan, Cloonboy, Carbad More, Cashel;
Ballycroy	Drumgollagh.
Belmullet	Dooncarton, Rosdoagh, Shanaghy, Muingerroon South (2), Tristia;
Claremorris	Shinganagh, Ballynastangford Lower.
Cong	Killimore, Knocknageeha;
Crossmolina	Tawnywaddyduff (2), Shanvodinnaun, Eskeragh, Carowkilleen, Ballyduffy;

Foxford/Swinford	Coolcronaun, Cartronmacmanus, Collagagh, Pollnagawna, Ballinillaun;
Keel	Keel East (2), Bal of Dookinelly;
Louisburgh	Aillemore, Formoyle;
Newport	Rosbeg, Cloondaff.

Diagram 1 (a) Conjectural Drawing of Court Tomb at Cartronmacmanus in the parish of Killasser.

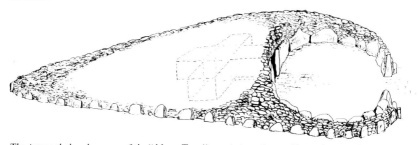

The internal chambers are of the "Mayo Type" consisting of a cruciform shape and are denoted by broken lines.

(b) What remains today - part of the court facade still stands but only a few stones of the gallary and side-chamber are still evident.

NEOLITHIC PRE-BOG FIELD SYSTEMS

Due to the rapid growth of blanket bog around 1,000 B.C., the field systems, habitation sites, and tombs of these early farmers were in many areas of Mayo buried under a protective covering of peat. This is especially true of the north-western region of Mayo where Dr. Séamus Caulfield of

U.C.D. is making an intensive study of the Behy-Glenulra and Belderg areas, a few kilometres west of Ballycastle. Over 30 pre-bog field systems have been discovered as the bog is being cut away by local farmers. The area is one of the largest "digs" of any archaeological site in Europe. A Court Tomb found under the bog at Behy was excavated by Dr. de Valéra. Dr. Caulfield is now conducting a survey of the associated extensive farming settlement in the area. Long parallel stone walls, divided by shorter ones, have been discovered under the vast uncut bog area extending for kilometres along the coast at Behy-Glenulra. The whole area must have been a well-organised farming community some 5,000 years ago.

NEOLITHIC TILLAGE PLOTS

Further west, even more interesting archaeological discoveries were made at Belderg Valley, where Dr. Caulfield discovered evidence of Neolithic tillage plots. The discovery here of actual plough-marks, similar to those of other prehistoric sites elsewhere in Europe, was the first discovery of its kind in Ireland. He also discovered evidence of a series of ridges and a circular earth-and-stone structure under the peat. This could have been a pre-historic granary, as a number of saddle querns for grinding corn were discovered there. It is a truly remarkable archaeological site, now fenced off, laid out and sign-posted. It is a very important open-air "museum" and well worth a visit.

Dr. Michael Herity of U.C.D. discovered other ridge and furrow cultivation marks under bog at Glenree, north east of Ballina.

PORTAL DOLMENS

Another type of megalithic tomb also made its appearance on the Mayo landscape during Neolithic times. It is known by various names, such as Portal Dolmen, Cromlech, and Diarmuid and Grainne's Bed. It was a singled-chambered tomb, mostly freestanding, but sometimes associated with a long mound or cairn. Nowadays the mound is normally denuded and the construction of the chamber itself is usually evident. A huge capstone rests on two large jambstones forming a portal or entrance into the chamber itself. This capstone is usually balanced on a backstone. Side-stones fill in the gaps to form a large stone box, which was the actual burial chamber. Burials usually took the form of cremation, and were communal, i.e. more than one person buried in each tomb.

Diagram 2 shows what a Portal Dolmen looked like when first built and what is usually left after nearly 5,000 years.

Over 160 Portal Dolmens have been identified in Ireland, with most in the east of the country. The following six have been identified in County Mayo in the Survey carried out by de Valéra and Ó Nualláin: two in Ballyknock, near Ballycastle; one in Claggan, near Ballycroy; one at Gortbrack North and another at Knocknalower, near Belmullet; and one at Doogort West, near Keel, on Achill Island.

(b) What might remain today.

PASSAGE TOMBS

The next type of megalithic tomb to be built was the Passage Tomb. It was constructed under a circular mound, which was in many cases huge. Newgrange and Knowth, in the Boyne Valley in County Meath, are the best-known examples of this type of tomb in the country. Inside the mound, a passage or tunnel was constructed to the central chamber. Sometimes side-chambers were constructed, and some of these contained stone basins in which the cremated remains were placed. Many of the stones in the main chambers, passages, and kerbs, which surrounded these tombs, were decorated with carved designs. These designs consisted of spirals, zig-zags, triangles, circles, lozenges, etc., incised into the stone and are very much like what is found in similar-type tombs in Brittany. This could possibly suggest a link between the two countries.

Passage Tombs were usually constructed in large cemeteries, occupying the various hilltops in the district. The nearest of these to County Mayo are Carrowkeel and Carrowmore, both in County Sligo. The latter is the largest in the country, containing approximately a hundred tombs.

Mayo has some monuments which could yet be classified as Passage Tombs, such as, Eochy's Cairn, near Ballinrobe, and the Cairn at Ballymacgibbon, just north of the road between Cross and Cong. Only excavation will reveal the true identity of these monuments, which, for all

Diagram 3 (a) Passage Tomb mound showing entrance.

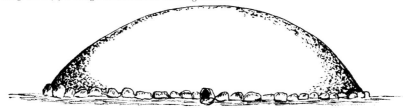

(b) Cross-section showing long passage ending in a cruciform chamber.

practical purposes, are intact. Another site which possibly could have contained a tomb of this sort is to be found in the townland of Carrowreagh on the west side of the Ox Mountains. All that remains of the monument is a large circle of stones, which could have been kerb-stones around a Passage Tomb.

WEDGE TOMBS

The last type of megalithic tomb to be built was the Wedge Tomb. These were in use from the late Neolithic to the Early Bronze Age c. 2000 — 1,500 B.C. Out of about 400 such tombs known in the country, 19 have been located by the de Valéra/ Ó Nualláin Survey of County Mayo. Wedge Tombs were constructed under a round or oval-shaped mound. The surviving stones give us the wedge shape and the tomb its name. Again, we are talking about a large stone chamber, but this time the front is wider and higher, and the whole unit gets lower and narrower as one goes to the back. There are some variations to be found in their construction, and many have a small back chamber and/or a small portico, or porch, at the entrance facing west.

These tombs were also used for communal burials for both the normal-type burial and cremation. It is believed that such tombs were introduced to Ireland by immigrants from north-western France. While the new immigrants, who introduced this type of tomb, may have been our first metal-workers, farming, especially cattle rearing, was their chief occupation. Other tombs are to be found near deposits of copper, especially in the peninsulas of Cork and Kerry, and near the Silvermines in County Tipperary. A large concentration is to be found in County Clare, especially in the Burren, where over 90 such tombs have been identified.

41

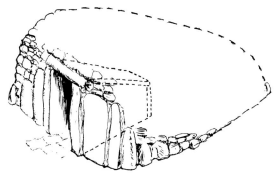

Diagram 4 Conjectural Drawing of Wedge Tomb of the "County Clare" type with single-stone sides and roof. The standard tomb would have sides and roof consisting of three or more rows of stones.

Recent discoveries suggest that the present-day bare limestone fields probably had a good covering of soil when these Wedge Tomb peoples occupied the area. Smaller concentrations extend up through Counties Galway and Mayo and right through to Ulster and Leinster.

The Mayo Wedge Tombs listed in the 1964 Survey seem to occur in two groups. Five are in the west and include one at Lettera, two at Castlehill near Ballycroy; one at Srahwee near Louisburgh and one in the Belderg valley. The remainder are located at Breastagh, Rathfranpark and Townplots West, near Killala; Feamore, Lisduff and Knockadoon, near Irishtown; Harefield, near Claremorris; Greenwood, near Ballyhaunis; Carrowgarve South, near Crossmolina; Carrowleagh and Carrowcrom, near Ballina; Doonty, Callow, Cuillaun and Knockshanbally, near Strade.

Shortly after 2,000 B.C. the era of megalithic tomb-building was coming to an end in Ireland. It is worth noting, at this point, that more tomb-sites undoubtedly have yet to be discovered in Mayo and are awaiting their discoverers. No buried treasure is to be found in them as they were practically all built, except for some wedge tombs, before the use of metal came to this country. The usual finds are pieces of pottery, stone implements, beads, etc., all of which are of value only to the archaeologist in his/her work.

BRONZE AGE

The use of metal began in Ireland with the arrival of the Bronze Age, which lasted, from about 2,000 B.C. to about 400 B.C. or after. New settlers began to arrive with metallurgic skills and started to make implements, first out of copper, then from bronze, and also various types of ornaments from native Irish gold. They also brought in a new burial rite, namely single burial, i.e. one corpse per grave, which supplemented the Wedge Tomb rite initially but in time superseded it. No large stones marked their graves overground, except in a few instances, and so the locations of the vast majority of their burials are unknown.

CIST BURIALS

Cist burials were single burials with the corpse placed underground in a crouched position (body bent with knees to chin) in a small stone box called a Cist. With such burials a pottery vessel, known archaeologically as a Food Vessel, (although never containing remains of food — they were probably for drink of some sort), is often found; rarely anything else. These graves are sometimes discovered by farmers ploughing or during sandpit quarrying. Diagram No. 5 b gives an indication of what a cist-grave may look like when the cover-stone has been removed.

Diagram 5 (a) Side view of Cist Grave. Sometimes found by deep ploughing.

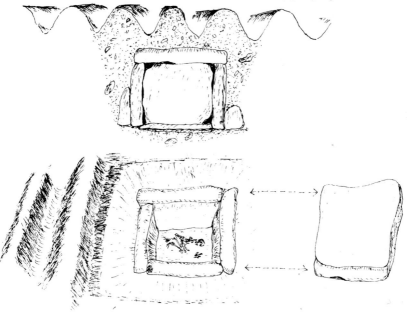

(b) Top view of Cist Grave with top stone removed. Grave contains skeleton in crouched position.

The next type of burial was Pit-Burials. In this type of burial the cremated ashes were placed in a plain pit in the ground, often under a pottery vessel known as a Cinerary Urn to archaeologists. This type of burial began to appear about 1,500 B.C. Like the cist-graves, pit-burials are usually difficult to locate. This is because the grave-markers, which were usually of wood, have long since disappeared. These graves are only discovered by chance, due to ploughing or to quarrying in sandpits. Sometimes they are found in mounds, often with cist-burials; mounds with such multiple burials are known as Cemetery Cairns.

Some have been discovered in Mayo and Dr. John Waddell of U.C.G. in his article in the *Journal of the Galway Archaeological and Historical*

43

Society (1970) lists the following townlands in which they were discovered: Aghalahard; Ballinchalla; Carrickanas; Carrowlisdooaun near Ballinrobe, where a flat bronze axe was found; Carrownacon, west of Ballycastle; Turnincorragh, between Westport and Castlebar, where Professor Etienne Rynne of U.C.G. discovered a Food Vessel in a multiple-cist mound; Corrower, near Ballina, a cemetery mound where three of the nine graves were cists and five Bowl Food Vessels were found; Cuillare; Gortmellia; Kilbroney; Kinard; Letterkeen in the Nephin Beg mountain range, which again was a multiple-cist mound and contained a Vase-type Food Vessel; Moytura/Nymphsfield, near Cong, which also contained a Vase-type Food Vessel; Rathduff; Srahrevagh; Stonepark; Stuckeen and Thornhill.

STONE CIRCLES AND STANDING-STONES

Stone Circles are other evidence of the Bronze Age. These circles were used for ritual purposes and usually consisted of free-standing stones placed erect in the ground to form a circle. Sometimes there was a single stone standing outside, associated with, but not part of the circle, as at Dooncarton, on the coast, just west of Belderg.

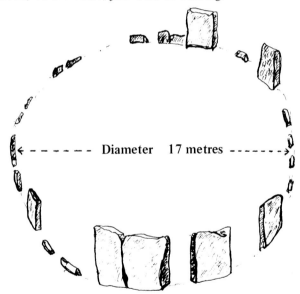

Diameter   17 metres

Diagram 6 Stone Circle at Nymphsfield, Cong.

One may also come across long oblong stones standing erect in the ground, sometimes reaching to a height of six metres. These could have been used to mark a cist-burial, or for orientation or ritual purposes. If standing alone they are classified by the term "Standing-Stone", while a number in a straight line is classed as a "Stone Alignment".

Diagram 7 Standing Stone called 'The Long Stone Of The Neale'.

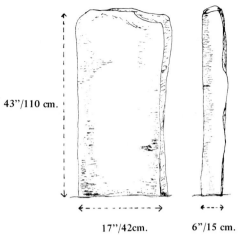

43"/110 cm.

17"/42cm.   6"/15 cm.

These monuments are another manifestation of the Bronze Age and are sometimes found where metal ores were mined. The native ore used was copper, and the craftsmen of that time mixed it with imported tin from southern Britain to make the more usable bronze. Such activity occurred in the peninsulas of Counties Cork and Kerry, where many Standing-Stones, Stone Alignments and Stone Circles are to be found.

County Mayo seems to have such an area in the region of Cong, along the north shore of Lough Corrib, where copper ore was found in the surrounding hills. A fine Stone Circle stands nearby at Nymphsfield, on the right of the road from Cong to The Neale. (See diagram No. 6). The "Long Stone of The Neale" stands at a road junction between Cong and the Neale. Other Stone Circles are situated at Rosdoagh, near Belmullet, at Rathfran, near Killala; at Knockfarnaght on the west shore of Lough Conn, and a fine, if small one, at Dooncarton, near Belderg, which has an outlying Standing Stone associated with it.

Other possible evidence for Bronze Age workings and habitation is found in the Belderg valley where, overlying the previously mentioned Neolithic artifacts, Dr. Caulfield has discovered evidence of Bronze Age activity. He has obtained a radiocarbon date of 1500 B.C. from a block of burnt wood found in a circular structure there, which definitely places these later workings in the Bronze Age. There is a Wedge Tomb nearby and a rich vein of copper in the adjacent cliffs.

BRONZE AND GOLD OBJECTS

The most important objects associated with the Bronze Age are the actual objects made from copper, bronze and gold. Thousands of objects were made from these metals, such as axes, halberds, (blades mounted at right angles to a wooden handle), daggers, spears, razors, brooches, other dress

45

adornments, clothes-fasteners, buckets and cauldrons, horse bridles and musical horns of weird shapes and sizes. Many such artifacts were discovered in County Mayo and can be seen in the National Museum.

Two of the four categories of halberd were discovered in Mayo. Type 1, the earliest type dating from 1,600 B.C. and made from copper, was found at Carn, Co. Mayo. This great find is unique in that the wooden haft was discovered practically intact, after all those years. Type 3 is represented by the one found at Breaghwy and is the only type made from bronze. Archaeologists are still not sure what use was made of halberds. Possibly they were used only for ceremonial purposes.

As a defence against these new-type weapons defensive equipment was also made. Wooden or leather shields (bronze was too soft) were made for protection, and out of five discovered to date two were found in Mayo, one in Cloonlara, near Swinford, and the other in Churchfield, near Knock. Other County Mayo items on exhibition in the National Museum include a copper axehead from Castletown; bronze spear ferrule from Knockaunakill; bronze horse-equipment from Ballinacostello; leaf-shaped bronze swords from Ballina and Ballintober; bronze dagger from Agheragh and a bronze spear-socket from Ballynagarha.

GOLD ORNAMENTS

The Irish Bronze Age craftsmen regularly used gold and their work was traded throughout Europe. Ireland was rich in gold during that time. Bronze ornaments made in other countries were copied in gold in Ireland. One of the earliest types of ornament was the "Sun Disc", a round disc made of thin sheet-gold. They usually had geometric decorations, including a cross-shaped design in the centre, and usually occurred in pairs. One of the six pairs found in Ireland came from the Ballina area, and like all such bronze or gold discoveries was a chance find.

In the Early Bronze Age also another gold ornament called a Lunula was made. This was a crescent-shaped decoration hung around the neck. Of the 60 or so lunulae found in Ireland at least four have come from the Mayo region. Later in the Middle Bronze Age, about 1200 B.C., neck, arm and ankle ornaments, were made from twisted bar-gold called Bar Torcs, and out of 31 found in Ireland two came from Mayo. One was found near Swinford in 1868, by men digging peat, and is now in the British Museum. None of the 10 gold neck collars called Gorgets made in the Late Bronze Age, about 700 B.C., were discovered in Mayo, but a beautiful gold Sunflower Pin of that period was found in Ballinrobe. Mayo is represented by gold artifacts from the Early, Middle and Late Bronze Ages, a time when Ireland led Europe in gold craftsmanship.

IRON AGE

From about 1,000 B.C a great change occurred in Ireland, with a general decline in agricultural activity, due possibly to the climate getting wetter, and massive bog growth ensued. Tribal unrest in Ireland was augmented by the influx of Celtic-speaking peoples from Europe, who brought with them iron technology, and so from about 400 B.C. weapons and many everyday utensils were manufactured in Ireland from iron.

HABITATION SITES

Many actual occupation sites of the Iron Age and later periods survive in Ireland. They were ringforts, which in time totalled 30,000 — 40,000, augmented by about 400 promontory forts and about 50 hill forts. A ringfort consisted of an area of ground surrounded by a protective bank of earth or stones. Promontory and hill fort builders used the natural physical assets of the site to build a defensive wall, or walls, to which the whole tribe might retire when attacked. In many cases, such sites were also used for ritual purposes. An example of a promontory fort, in County Mayo, is found at Doonamo, near Belmullet. This fort was defended by a stone wall over 61 metres long across the narrow neck entrance. Outside, rows of broken stones, as at Dún Aengus in the Aran Islands, called chevaux-de-frise, were used to impede would-be attackers. The Dangan promontory fort at Achillbeg is another example; it could only have been approached from an easily defended side.

RINGFORTS

The ringfort was the main occupation site of the Iron Age people. It was also referred to as a Ráth, Lios, Dún, Cathair or Cashel and such titles form the names of many townlands in Ireland today. Ringforts were the dwelling places of Irish farmers from the end of the Bronze Age (c. 400 B.C.) up to the 16th century. Hundreds are to be found in Mayo, especially in the eastern section of the county. Large concentrations occur around Ballina, south-east to Swinford and Castlebar, over to Claremorris, Knock and Ballyhaunis, south, via Ballinrobe to Shrule and Kilmaine and across to Cong. From over 50 excavations of ringforts in Ireland, it can be said that the typical fort consisted of a circular enclosure, varying from 15 to 61 metres in diameter, surrounded by one or more ditches with the removed earth built into a corresponding bank. A gap was left for an entrance gate. Originally the bank may have contained a wooden fence or palisade to act as a further defensive feature, but evidence for this is negligible. In rocky areas, as in the Burren in County Clare, a stone bank formed the perimeter of the ancient farmstead. Thus the ringforts were the forerunners of the modern farmyards. The farm animals were brought inside the enclosure at night. They were then safe from cattle raiding, which was a favourite past-time of the Celtic people, as evidenced by the saga of the Táin Bó Cuailgne. The enclosure also contained the main dwelling-house, made from wicker, wood or mud, or combinations of these items, while the roof was usually thatched. In rocky areas the dwellings were made of stone, the walls of which may still survive in some areas.

47

SOUTERRAINS

Another feature to be often found inside a ringfort is an artificial cave called a Souterrain. This stone cave and chamber was used for food storage and probably as a refuge at other times. They were constructed from stone slabs laid horizontally on stone walls built under the ground, and often extended for many metres, sometimes in a zig-zag fashion. In many cases souterrains are all that remain when the ringforts have been destroyed, and are often discovered during ploughing, or when they naturally cave in. A typical example is to be found at Cill Duin, on the road between Cross village and The Neale. Countless souterrains exist in Mayo and a fine example of one in a ringfort can be seen in the townland of Carrowmore, in the parish of Killasser. This one runs practically the length of the fort, in a zig-zag manner, culminating in a beautiful circular chamber, 3.6 metres in diameter, complete with a corbelled (each stone overlaps the other) roof, about 1.5 metres high.

CRANNÓGS

Another type of Iron Age dwelling was the Crannóg, an artificial island in a lake, on which the usual ringfort type dwelling was constructed. The word Crannóg is derived from the Irish word 'Crann' for tree and denotes that wood was used in its construction. Built primarily for defence, crannógs were occupied right down to Elizabethan times. Today, all that may remain is just a small overgrown mound on the lakeshore or a hump in a marshy bog. A crannóg can be seen in Callow Lake, in Killasser parish between Swinford and Foxford.

The Fulacht Fiadh is another monument of that period. These were the ancient cooking places where heated stones were placed in a trough of water to cook the hunters' meat. These stones were then discarded and in time formed a horse-shoe shaped mound. Many of these are now being discovered, and can be identified if any of the stones from the mound crumble at your touch.

Diagram 8 Fulacht Fiadh – what the ancient cooking place may look like today - a low horse-shoe shaped mound covered usually by grass or other vegation.

THE EARLY CHRISTIAN PERIOD

The next type of archaeological monument relates to the advent of Christianity to Ireland, in the 5th century. Roman Christianity, based on the diocesan system, was introduced first, but was completely alien to the Irish rural tribal system of that time. The Roman armies of the previous centuries never got to Ireland to build cities, or to set up networks of communications, as in Britain and Europe. Consequently, it was not surprising that early Christianity in Ireland evolved into a Celtic monastic system. This consisted of monks gradually gathering followers around them and creating small monastic enclosures in sparsely-populated areas around the country. One of the main features in these enclosures was the church building, which gradually evolved into the small stone structure of the pre-Viking centuries. Some of these enclosures became the more formal type of monasteries of slightly later times, housing hundreds of monks and scholars in many small clay or wattle structures. The early Irish monks adopted the traditional Irish ringfort system and built a circular earthen or stone-enclosure bank, with their little church, monks' cells and other buildings inside. Hundreds of these monastic sites were constructed, but many have now disappeared — the only trace remaining being an element such as "Kill" in the name of the townland. Others continued for long periods, with one church replacing another down the years, and in more recent times some of the enclosures have been used as burial-grounds for unbaptised children.

EARLY MONASTIC SITE LAYOUT

The chief structure inside the monastic enclosure was the church. Originally built from wood, then of stone, the early church was very small, with high gables, a doorway facing west, with a large stone lintel over it. Excavations show other structures, such as the cells of the monks, called clocháns if made of stone as on Skellig Michael off Kerry. Stone monuments were also erected within the monastic enclosures. Some, it seems, were vertical stone slabs, erected between the 5th and 7th centuries, as memorials to the dead. Later, monastic graves were marked by recumbent slabs, often bearing the name of the dead person and a figure of a cross. Another type was the cross slab, similar to modern tombstones, and often with elaborate ornamental detail and inscriptions. From the 8th century the familiar High Cross became relatively common, possibly originating from wooden prototypes, and finally evolving into the beautiful examples to be seen at Monasterboice, Clonmacnoise and Kilfenora.

Mayo has many early monastic sites. Duvillaun More, a small island, south of the Mullet peninsula, has a good example of a monastic site. It includes a circular stone enclosure, which incorporates a small stone church or oratory, stone cells (clocháns), and a cross-pillar with a representation of the Crucifixion, all dating to the 7th century. On the nearby island of Inishkea North a monastic site has another small church.

49

Inishkea South has a large standing slab with incised crosses, one of the earliest examples in the country. Other early sites were at Balla, where St. Mochua founded a church in the 7th century; Aghagower, near Westport, founded by St. Senach in the 5th century; Cong, founded by St. Feichin in 627, Killala, 5th century; Turlough, near Castlebar, 5th century; Doonfeeny near Ballycastle, with a 5.5 metre pillar with incised crosses; Kilmore Erris, near Belmullet, with a stone enclosure and cross slab; Moyne, near Cross, with a huge stone enclosure; Mayo itself near Balla, founded in the 6th century by St. Colman and many more, too numerous to mention here.

Up to the 8th century beautiful religious objects, incorporating the best of Celtic designs involving intricate spirals and other fascinating motifs, were produced with the highest degree of workmanship possible. During that time the Book of Durrow c. 640 A.D., Tara Brooch c. 720 A.D., Ardagh Chalice c. 730 A.D. and the Book of Kells c. 800 A.D. were all completed.

All this came to an end with the arrival of the Vikings (or, to be more precise, the Norsemen) in Ireland in A.D. 795 and to Co. Mayo around the start of the 9th century. They initially came to plunder, and monasteries around our coasts and near rivers became prime targets. Partly as a result, new structures were erected in the monastic enclosures, the Round Towers.

ROUND TOWERS

Round Towers are tall circular stone towers. They were used as watch-towers/bell-towers/and places of refuge in times of attack. About 100 may have been built, but only 65 survive today. Some rise to 31 metres in height and taper to a conical stone cap. The external door was usually constructed several metres above ground level for defensive purposes and a removable ladder used for entry, the latter was pulled up after the monks had entered the structure.

Possibly the best known of the five remaining in Mayo is Killala's fine tower, which rises to 25.6 metres. The others are at Aghagower, (16m.), Meelick, near Swinford (20m.), Turlough, near Castlebar, which is smaller and wider than the normal with a very squat shape (22.9m.) and Balla (10m.).

NEW RELIGIOUS ORDERS

The advent of the 12th century saw big changes in church-building in this country, due to various church synods replacing the old monastic system with a continental diocesan and parochial system. More building of churches, involving a Hiberno-Romanesque architecture, took place, with emphasis on rounded doorways and windows. This was later replaced by the Gothic style, introduced by the new religious orders, which came to Ireland about this time. The first to come were the Benedictines, but they made little impression. They, in time, were followed by the Cistercians, with their strict orderly way of life. They were followed by the Augustinians, Dominicans, and Franciscans, and their buildings dot the Irish countryside today. Most of their abbeys and friaries are now in ruins due to the sacking of the monasteries during the Reformation. The buildings were constructed in accordance with a well designed plan. This plan usually consisted of various buildings built around an open square or cloister, with the church itself forming the northern section. On the east stood the sacristy and meeting-room and at the south end the kitchen and refectory, or eating-room. On the other side the dormitories were situated.

These monasteries were built all around the country and, in this regard, Mayo can be said to have had more than its fair share. The Augustinians came to Cong in the 12th century, to Inishmaine, near Ballinrobe, in the 13th century, to Errew on Lough Conn in 1413, and to Murrisk, near Westport, in 1457. The Cistercians came to Clare Island in 1220 and the Dominicans to Rathfran, near Killala, in 1274. Some of the best builders, the Franciscans, came to Strade in the 13th century and built great friaries at Moyne in 1460 and at nearby Rosserk, near Killala.

BALLINTOBER ABBEY

Probably the best known abbey in Mayo, if not in Ireland, is at Ballintober, founded in 1216 by King Cathal Crobderg O'Conor. Mass has been offered there, without a break, since its inception. Thanks to the trojan work of the late Fr. Egan, P.P., the church section has been re-roofed, and its many artifacts are now on view including a fine example of a medieval tomb i.e. of "Toby" de Burgo in the church sacristy. Unfortunately, parts of the figures on the sides of it were defaced, probably by Cromwellian troops, when they partially destroyed the abbey in 1653. Ballintober Abbey is well worth a visit, because it is a monument from the past still in use, surely an archaeological paradox.

THE CROSS OF CONG

The mention of King Cathal Crobderg O'Conor leads us to look at what is perhaps Mayo's most famous archaeological treasure — the Cross of Cong. It was another O'Conor, King Turlough, who, c. 1123 commissioned this lovely processional cross. Intended initially for Tuam, it was eventually placed in the loving care of the monks of Cong. They used it on special church occasions only and held it in the deepest veneration, because it contained a relic of the True Cross. Even after the suppression of the abbey in the 16th century, the cross was held by the abbot, who resided locally. The last abbot died in 1829. In 1893 the cross was presented to the Royal Irish Academy and is now in the National Museum. The relic itself is mounted on a big oaken cross, 76.2 centimetres high with arms reaching to a distance of 48.25 centimetres. The tiny fragment of the True Cross is placed at the intersection, under a large crystal, which was used for magnification purposes. The whole surface of the cross is covered with bronze sheets, containing a network of ornaments consisting mainly of beautiful gilt-bronze animal-interlacings, with red and yellow enamels adding even more colour. This cross is acknowledged as one of the finest specimens of 12th century Irish monastic craftsmanship in existence. The name of the maker of the cross, Maoilíosa Ó Echán, is inscribed on it and he surely deserves our thanks and prayers.

The Cross of Cong.
(National Museum of Ireland)

52

TOWER HOUSES

Soon other more sinister medieval monuments began to dot the Mayo landscape — the castles of the invading Normans. The Normans under the leadership of the De Burgos gradually gained control, especially in the east of the county. They began to build castles and those dating from 1440 onwards were called Tower Houses. About 140 castles were built in Mayo and most were of the Tower-House type. In time these newcomers assimilated with the Irish and "grew more Irish than the Irish themselves". This did not stop the native Irish from copying them and building Tower Houses for themselves. Obviously, these structures were more homely and easier to defend than the ringfort.

Possibly the most famous owner of one was Grace O'Malley, Mayo's famous lady sea captain. The best known of her castles was situated on Clare Island, where it still stands today, ever defiant, as was its owner. She was also associated with those at Carrigahowley and Carrickkildavnet, both on the north of Clew Bay. Mention can only be made of one or two others, but those at Ballylahan (near Foxford), Shrule and Moyne on the Black River, are interesting examples. Most of the others are gone or are in a bad state of ruin, due to neglect and lack of interest. They represent important archaeological monuments of the troubled times from the 14th to the 17th centuries, not alone in Mayo, but also throughout the whole country.

The typical tower house was 4-5 storeys high, with one-third of the space normally devoted to servants/soldiers' quarters. The large section was usually divided as follows: the ground floor consisted of a cellar or store, servants' kitchen on first floor, with the lord's living room and bedroom on the second and third floors, and the fourth floor the dining-room where visitors were entertained. The early Irish castles had no chimney, but instead a fire was lit on this floor in a brazier. Later more sophisticated fixtures were added, such as fine chimney-pieces, garderobes (toilets), window-shutters, etc. The earlier castle had no large window below 10 metres (due to considerations of defence) and all windows below that were of the slit variety. The upper section contained an attic, under a slated roof, and a guard-walk on the parapets, usually the domain of the defenders of the castle. Most castles had outside buildings and a surrounding wall.

Tower Houses were occupied during the many upheavals resulting from the wars between the Irish and their English adversaries. Plantations and confiscations led eventually to the landlord (in the Big House) and tenant (in the thatched cottage) system, of the 19th century. By that time the native Irish had left their wicker and mud dwellings and may have found their thatched cabins something of an improvement.

In the first half of the 19th century, the population of Ireland reached nearly eight million. The vast majority lived in rural areas, occupying countless small cottages and holdings, scattered throughout the countryside. The majority were tenants of the local landlords, and for most, life was very hard, with a great dependence on the potato. When the potato failed in 1846-49 thousands died, and within a matter of years the population dropped to about four million. Many survivors were forced to emigrate. Mayo was one of the hardest hit counties in this regard and the pitiful archaeological artifacts of that period are often, too often, evident. Nearly every townland has the remains of at least one Famine cottage to remind us of that dreadful time, and even in some areas whole villages now stand in ruins with the names of the occupants long forgotten. Here and there one may come across rows and rows of gently rolling grassy hillocks. These were the well-worked ridges of the pre-Famine farmers. Other grim remains remind us of that dreadful time. These are the ruins of the Soup Kitchens and especially the notorious Workhouses which became the final resting places of many a Mayo person.

LAND WAR

In the second half of the 19th century a land war broke out between the tenants and the landlords with Mayo showing the rest of the country the way. Many families were evicted and their cottages destroyed. The landlords eventually sold out their estates. Both the ruin of the humble cottage and the stark shell of the "Big House" are mute archaeological testimonials to that period in our history.

They are part and parcel of the Mayo landscape. In their midst, at Strade, stands a Celtic Cross Memorial, marking the grave of local man Michael Davitt. This 20th century version of the early Christian cross is a suitable memorial to Mayo's most famous son, an archaeological monument that spans a thousand years!

SOURCES

1. The List of Megalithic tombs is reproduced from Volume 2 of *"Survey of the Megalithic Tombs of Ireland"* by Ruaidhrí de Valéra and Seán Ó Nualláin, with permission of the Government.(Stationery Office 1964.)

2. The information on the BEHY-GLENULRA and BELDERG sites was taken from a Paper on "Two Neolithic Farms in County Mayo" given by Dr. Séamus Caulfield of U.C.D. to the Archaeological, Historical & Folklore Society of Galway Regional Technical College on 28 November 1978.

3. The other sources used are included in the bibliography.

NOTE: I am grateful to Professor Etienne Rynne and Thomas A. Fanning of the Department of Archaeology, U.C.G. for reading the first draft of this article and making helpful suggestions.

MAYO PLACENAMES

by *Nollaig Ó Muraíle*

The names of all the baronies and parishes and of most of the towns and villages in Co. Mayo are, in linguistic terms, Irish (or Gaelic), although the forms in general use among English-speakers represent attempts to write Irish-language names according to the conventions of an anglicised orthography. Some of these attempts, many of which date back several centuries, have been reasonably successful, inasmuch as they have not grievously distorted the original Irish forms; others have been markedly less successful.

In the following notes, in which the names of the baronies, the parishes, and the towns/villages are dealt with in turn, the aim is to try and recover those original Irish forms, to document some of the more significant, and interesting, occurrences of each name down through the centuries, to recommend a suitable present-day Irish form and, finally, to suggest what is frequently, of necessity, a rather tentative translation or interpretation of each name.

County Mayo, from the time of its formation in the latter part of the 16th century until the very end of the 19th century, comprised nine baronies — although an additional one, Ross, was considered part of Mayo in the uncertain early years, up to about 1585. Under the Local Government Act of 1898 part of Costello barony was transferred to Co. Roscommon, while portions of two baronies, Ross in Co. Galway and Tireragh in Co. Sligo, were transferred to Co. Mayo. The county at present comprises 72 parishes, having lost two (Castlemore and Kilcolman — plus part of Kilbeagh — in Costello) and gained two (Castleconor — plus a part of Kilmoremoy — in Tireragh, and Ross — plus part of Ballinchalla and part of Ballinrobe — in Ross) in 1898. All the 72 parishes in present-day Mayo, and also the two which were lost in 1898, are dealt with in section II below. (The parishes in question here are the *civil parishes,* which in most cases date back to medieval times at least. They sometimes differ fairly considerably, both in names and in boundaries, from the Roman Catholic parishes, many of which date from the period after Catholic Emancipation, 1829. The civil parishes, albeit in large amalgamations, are generally preserved by the Church of Ireland.) On the lowest tier of the old administrative pyramid are the townlands; there are about 3,200 of these in Mayo, far too large a number to be dealt with, even in the most summary fashion, in the space available here.

Almost half the parish-names in the following list, as well as all the barony-names and the town and village-names, have already had Irish forms officially recommended by the Placenames Office of the Ordnance Survey. Those names (such as town and village names) which are the names of post offices have had statutory recognition granted to their Irish forms under the Placenames Act of 1973, and it is envisaged that similar recognition will be afforded in due course to all other name-forms emanating from the Placenames Office. These forms, it should be emphasised, are the result of detailed scholarly research, using a wide range of sources in a variety of languages, including Old, Middle and Modern Irish, Latin, Norman-French and English. Nevertheless, it will be clear from the following notes that the form recommended, due to the unsatisfactory nature of the evidence *in the case of certain names,* will sometimes be little more than an educated guess, and that anything from 15 to 25% of the forms recommended should be taken as probable rather than altogether certain, while a small number of forms must be deemed quite uncertain.

NOTE ON SOURCES

Tírechán: The writings of the late-7th-cent. bishop Tírechán (from Tirawley) on the life of St. Patrick; known as the *Breviarium* and the *Additamenta,* they are preserved in the early-9th-cent. manuscript known as the 'Book of Armagh'.

Tripartite Life: The 'Vita Tripartita' of St. Patrick which scholars over the past half century or so have generally held to have been written (in Old Irish) about the year 900; a more recent study, however, would assign the work (at least in its present form) to the 11th century — the Middle Irish period.

Pont. Hib.: *Pontificia Hibernica, a collection of medieval papal chancery documents concerning Ireland, 640–1261,* ed. Maurice P. Sheehy, in two vols., 1962 and 1965.

AConn: *Annála Connacht, The Annals of Connacht (A.D. 1224–1544),* ed. A. Martin Freeman, 1944.

Tax. 1302: Ecclesiastical Taxation of dioceses of Tuam, Achonry and Killala, c. 1302; ed. by H. S. Sweetman in *Calendar of Documents, Ireland,* vol. v, 1886.

Annates: 'Obligationes pro annatis provinciae Tuamensis', published in *Archivium Hibernicum,* vol. xxvi, 1963. (The 'Annates' are a calendar of first fruits' fees levied on papal appointments in the ecclesiastical province of Tuam between 1413 and 1548.)

Cal. of Papal Letters: *Calendar of Papal Registers, Papal Letters.* vol. xii, A.D. 1458-1471, ed. J. A. Twemlow, 1933.

Ormond Deeds: *Calendar of Ormond Deeds* (vol. v, 1547—1584 A.D.) ed. Edmund Curtis, (1941).

Visit. 1565: 'Visitations of the Dioceses of Clonfert, Tuam and Kilmacduagh, c. 1565-7', ed. K. W. Nicholls in *Analecta Hibernica,* vol. xxvi, 1970.

Division of Connaught: Division of Connaught into Counties and Baronies, with notes of chief counties and special castles — taken from State Papers, Ireland, from the reign of Elizabeth, vol. xxx, no. 81, dated 27, Aug. 1570. Portion relating to Mayo — Mac William Eighter, chief' published in Knox's *History of Co. Mayo,* p. 346.

Browne's Map: Map of Co. Mayo (except baronies of Clanmorris, Costello and Gallen) drawn by John Browne of the Neale for Sir Richard Bingham in the Summer of 1584; published (along with Browne's letter to Sir Francis Walsingham, Secretary of State in England, dated 'Athlone, the 10th June, 1585') in the *Journal of the Galway Archaeological and Historical Society,* vol. v, no. 3, 1908.

CBC: *The Compossicion Booke of Conought,* (1585), ed. A. M. Freeman, 1936.

Straff: *The Strafford Inquisition of County Mayo* (1635), ed. William O'Sullivan, 1958.

BSD: *Books of Survey and Distribution, 1636–1703, vol. ii, County of Mayo,* ed. Robert C. Simington, 1956.

Hib. Del.: *Hiberniae Delineatio* (also known as 'Petty's Atlas'), based on Sir William Petty's great 'Down Survey' of the 1650s; the plates of the 'Atlas' were engraved c. 1663, but the work did not actually appear until 1685.

Bald: William Bald, *A Map of the Maritime County of Mayo,* in 25 sheets; surveyed between 1809 and 1817 and published in 1830.

Namebook: Ordnance Survey Parish Namebooks, still preserved in the Ordnance Survey, Phoenix Park, Dublin; the Mayo Namebooks date from 1838.

I. BARONIES

(Areas, in sq. kilometres, in brackets).

1) BURRISHOOLE (594), *Buiríos Umhaill.*
See also the parish-name in Sect. II, no. 21. As barony-name, *Burriswyle* in Division of Connaught, 1570; *Borries Owyll, the Burries alias Ballyneborieshe* in Ormond Deeds, 1576; *Owles of Boroshoule* and *Boroshole* in Browne's Map, 1584; *Borrishowle* in CBC, 1585. The second element in the name is *Umhall,* the name of an ancient territory around Clew Bay; it appears as *finum Humail* in Tírechán, late 7th cent.; *Umall* and *fir Umaill* in the Tripartite Life of Patrick, c. 900. A note on Browne's Map, 1584, states: 'Moriske or Owles O Mayle, Boroshole, Irres: the three are commonly called the Owles'. In the Ormond Deeds, 1576, there is also mention of 'the three Ulles, viz., Ull I Waly, Ull Chlynphillibyne and Ullieghtrigh' (=Umhall Uí Mháille, Umhall Chloinn' Philbín, Umhall

57

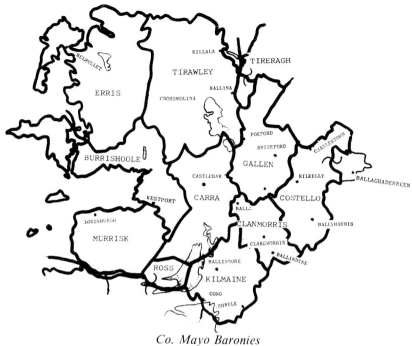

Co. Mayo Baronies

Included here is the portion of Costello transferred to Co. Roscommon in 1898.

Iochtarach). In the late-16th-cent. Book of Howth there is a reference to *O Mayle of Pomo,* the latter name being the dative of the Latin *pomum,* 'an apple'; this word is used in a number of 16th cent. sources to designate *Umhall* because of the latter's similarity to the Irish word *ubhall* (nowadays spelt *úll*), 'an apple'!

2) CARRA (594), *Ceara.*

Barony-name: *Burresker* in Division of Connaught, 1570; *Trohechiad Kárry alias Mc Evile's country* in Ormond Deeds, 1576 (*trohechiad = tricha cét,* literally 'thirty hundred', an early Irish territorial division); *Carra* on Browne's Map, 1584; *Borishkara alias Kerra* in CBC, 1585. *Ceara* (earlier *Cera*) is a very ancient name; *Ceru* (dative) appears in Tírechan, late 7th cent. and in two 12th-cent. MSS, one of them the Book of Leinster; *Mag Cerae* ('the plain of Cera') occurs in the Tripartite Life of Patrick, c. 900. The legendary account of Irish prehistory found in the medieval Lebor Gabála Érenn ('book of the taking of Ireland') purported to drive the latter name from one Cera, daughter-in-law of Nemed who supposedly led one of the pre-Goidelic invasions. As to the meaning of *Cera,* there are two nouns found in Early Irish texts, both of which appear to take this form. Both are poorly attested; one may mean 'tribute', the other is said to mean 'blood' and, used adjectivally, 'red'. The *Fir Chera* ('men of Cera') were one of the two main branches of Uí Fiachrach in Tuaiscirt, tracing their

58

ancestry back to *Macc-Ercae,* son of Fiachra Foltsnathach, brother of Niall Noígiallach ('N. of the Nine Hostages') and ancestor of the Uí Fiachrach. Tírechán, immediately after mentioning *Ceri* (=*Cera*), refers to *regiones Maicc Ercae,* while the Tripartite Life has *Maige Maicc Ercae.*

3)   CLANMORRIS (279), *Clann Mhuiris.*
Barony-name: *Crosbohin* in Division of Connaught, 1570 (see Sect. II, no. 25, below); *Clanmoris* on Browne's Map, 1584; *Crossbohin alias Clanmorrish* in CBC, 1585. The name *Clann Mhuiris* appears to derive from one *Muiris Sucach mac Gerailt* Prendergast whose *floruit* might be placed in the late-13th and early-14th cents. (The epithet *Sucach* has been interpreted as *súgach,* 'merry', but it might also refer to the river Suck, in which case the word, as it appears in the annals, would require no emendation. The patronymic *mac Gerailt* gave rise to the surname variously anglicised *MacGarrett* — found in the name *Castlemacgarrett* near Claremorris — and *Fitzgerald,* this latter not to be confused with the famous Fitzgeralds of Kildare.) *Clann Muris tSucaig* is mentioned in AConn at the year 1335. The family was better known throughout the late medieval period as *Clann Muiris na mBrí* from their stronghold at *Brees* (also anglicised *Brize*) between Claremorris and Balla. The family bore the surname *Mac Muiris* which was anglicised *Mac Morris* and, more commonly at a later period, *Fitzmaurice.*

4)   COSTELLO (506; formerly 584), *Coistealaigh.*
Barony-name: *Bellahaunes* in Division of Connaught, 1570; *Mac Costula otherwise Castell-more* on Browne's Map, 1584; *Clancostillo* in CBC, 1585, and *the barony of Bellahawnesse commonly called Mac Costillo his country* in a report by Lord Deputy Sir John Perott's commissioners, 1587. The Mayo family whose surname is now anglicised 'Costello' trace their ancestry back to one William de Angulo who first appears in one of the Ormond Deeds dated about 1176. This William was son of Jocelyn (spelt *Gocelin* in the deed just cited) and was called in Irish *Mac Goisdelb;* this patronymic was soon adopted as a surname by his descendants who were carving out a territory for themselves in east Mayo. As Knox remarks, 'they were the first colonists of their high rank who adopted Gaelic names'.

5)   ERRIS (942), *Iorras.*
Barony-name: *Envermore* in Division of Connaught, 1570; *Trohechiad* (= *tricha cét,* see no. 2, above) *Irres* in Ormond Deeds, 1576; *Irres* on Browne's Map, 1584; *Irrus or the Owles of Irres* in Browne's letter to Walsingham, 1585; *Irrish alias Invirmore* in CBC, 1585. The name appears, as *Irrus Domnann* ('*Iorras* of the people called the *Domhnainn'*), or some corresponding form, in a great many Irish sources — for instance, in the famous early-12th-cent. MS known as *Lebor na hUidre* ('the book of the dun cow') the forms *Irruiss* (genitive) and *Urros Domnand* occur, the former in the oldest version of the greatest of the early Irish heroic tales, the *Táin Bó Cúailnge. Orrus* appears in an Inquisition dated 1335. The word *iorras* has been variously interpreted as meaning 'a borderland', 'a headland or promontory', 'a peninsula'.

6)   GALLEN (483), *Gaileanga.*
Barony-name: *Bellalaghen* (*=Baile Átha Leathain*) in Division of Connaught, 1570; *the lordship or county called Gallyn* in Ormond Deeds, 1576; *Galen* and *Gallen* on Browne's Map, 1584; *Beallalahin alias Gallen* in CBC, 1585. The *Gailenga* were a very ancient population-group who were closely associated with the people called the *Luigni* who have left their name on the neighbouring Co. Sligo barony of *Leyny.* (The two groups were also settled together in what is now Co. Meath where they have given name to the baronies of *Lune* and *Morgallion* — the latter from *Machaire Gaileang.*) The name appears frequently in the annals: AConn, 1412, for example, has *a nGailengaib* referring to the territory *(crích Gaileng* sub anno 1512*)* and *Gailengaig* referring to the inhabitants of Gallen. That the name had not been quite forgotten by the early 19th cent. is indicated by Anthony Raftery's reference to *Gaillionn* (as it appears in a manuscript dated 1835) in the opening stanza of his famous song in praise of Killedan.

7)   KILMAINE (429), *Cill Mheáin.*
See also the parish-name in Sect. II, no. 48. Barony-name: *Kilvane* in Division of Connaught, 1570; *Kilmayne* on Browne's Map, *Kilmaine* and *Kilmane* in CBC, 1585. Most of this barony and of the neighbouring barony of Ross was anciently the territory of the Conmaicne Cúile Tolad.

8)   MURRISK (554), *Muraisc.*
Barony-name: Morysky in Division of Connaught, 1570; *Moriske or Owles O Mayle* on Browne's Map, 1584; *Murriske in the Owles* in CBC, 1585. Murrisk (the Irish word means 'sea-swamp, or low-lying coast-land') occurs as *Muiriscc Aigli* (dative) in Tírechán, late 7th cent., and in the Tripartite Life of Patrick, c. 900. (The second element in that version of the name is that which also found in the name *Cruachán Aigli* — earlier, in Tírechán, *Mons Egli* — the older name for *Cruach Phádraig/Croagh Patrick.)* The name *Leithearwmursge* (recté *Leithcarwmursge* = *Leithcheathrú Mhuirisce,* 'the half-quarter of Muirisc'?) occurs in a document dated 1456 which is recorded in the Calendar of Papal Registers and refers to the Augustinian abbey establised at Murrisk about that time. The abbey is mentioned, as *Mainisteir Buirsge,* in an annalistic fragment in Irish dealing with the years 1467 and 1468. (The fragment was apparently written for Sir George Carew — using a variety of sources — early in the 17th cent. and has only recently (1981) been edited.) The form *Buirsge* prompts the thought that the name *the Burries alias Ballneborieshe* in Ormond Deeds, 1576 — which has been cited above as referring to Burrishoole — might conceivably refer instead to Murrisk. The interchange of initial 'm' and 'b' is not uncommon in Irish; indeed there are a number of examples in Irish (even in Mayo) placenames, e.g. *Bunnyconnellan* from *Muine Chonalláin.* (The recommended Irish form *Muraisc* is simply a late variant of *Muiresc* or *Muirisc.)*

9)   ROSS (97), *Ros.*
See also the parish-name in Sect. II, no. 67. Barony-name: *Rosse* in

Division of Connaught, 1570, Browne's Map, 1584, and CBC, 1585. Ross appears on Browne's Map, 1584, as part of Co. Mayo, but this was disputed by Co. Galway and it was dealt with as part of the latter county in the Composition of Connacht, 1585. About a third of the barony was transferred back to Mayo under the Local Government Act of 1898.

10) TIRAWLEY (1,316), *Tír Amhlaidh.*
Barony-name: *Moyne* in Division of Connaught, 1570; *Tyrauly* on Browne's Map, 1584; *Moyne alias Tireawly* in CBC, 1585. The name is, however, attested far earlier than the 16th cent., for example *Tir Amalgaid* in AConn, 1225, *Tyrau(n)lyf* in an Inquisition dated 1335; *Tyramalayd* in Annates, 1441. It derives from *Amalgaid* (earlier *Amolngid*), son of Fiachra Foltsnathach (see under no. 2 above); indeed Dubhaltach Mac Fhirbhisigh, c. 1650, refers to the territory as *Tír Amhalgaidh meic Fiachrach.* Tírechán, late 7th cent., mentions the sons of Amolngid, one of whom (a direct ancestor of Tírechán's) is referred to as 'Endeus filius Amolngid . . filii Fechrach filii Echach'. The Tripartite Life of Patrick, c. 900, also refers to 'xii filii Amalgada maicc Fíachrach maicc Echoch'.

11) TIRERAGH (39), *Tír Fhiachrach.*
This barony was never part of Mayo until a small portion was transferred from Co. Sligo under the Local Government Act of 1898. The present-day anglicised form appears in CBC, 1585. The 17th-cent. genealogist, scribe and antiquarian, Dubhaltach Mac Fhirbhisigh of *Leacán* (Lecan or Lackan), whose family had for centuries previously been the leading learned family of Tireragh, invariably referred to the place as *Tír Fhiachrach Muaidhe* ('Tireragh of the Moy'). While, at first sight, one would expect the name to derive from the early 5th-cent. Fiachra Foltsnathach (see under nos. 2 and 10 above), eponymous ancestor of the *Uí Fiachrach,* there is a passage in the Book of Lecan, c. 1400 (and repeated by Dubhaltach Mac Fhirbhisigh), which alleges that *Tír Fhiachrach* derives instead from that Fiachra's grandson, *Fiachra Ealgach,* son of Dath Í, or Nath Í. The main difficulty with this, however, is that it seems quite certain that no such person as 'Fiachra Ealgach' ever existed! The name is the result of the conflation of two quite distinct individuals, Nath Í's son Fiachna (*not* Fiachra!) and the latter's son Ealgach. We can take it, therefore, that *Tír Fhiachrach* after all derives from the ancestor of the Uí Fhiachrach generally, whose sons *(filii Fiechrach)* are mentioned by Tírechán. The Tripartite Life of Patrick, c. 900, refers to *crích Oa Fiacrach la muir* ('the territory of the Uí Fhiachrach by the sea'). *Tír Fiachrach* occurs quite frequently in the annals, e.g. AConn, 1249, 1266 and 1471.

II CIVIL PARISHES
(Numbers denote area in sq. kilometres)
1) ACHILL (B Burrishoole, 208), *Acaill* (meaning uncertain).

The name appears as *Ecaill, Eccuill, Accuill* in various Irish sources, including AConn, 1235, and as *Akill, Akle, The Aukilles,* etc. in late-16th-century English sources. The name occurs elsewhere throughout Ireland, most notably as the ancient name of the Hill of Skreen in Co. Meath. It has been suggested that the name may mean 'look-out point, prospect'; the idea sometimes advanced that it may be related to the Latin word *aquila,* 'an eagle', seems groundless.

2) ADDERGOOLE (B Tirawley, 148), *Eadarghabhal* (possibly 'a place in a river-fork', i.e. between two prongs of a river).

The name appears as *Adergoole* in BSD (17th cent.), but it occurs as early as 1199 in a document in Pont. Hib. as *Dargauillachon;* this may be emended to read *(E)dargauil Lach (a Chon)* = *Edargabail* of Lough Conn.

3) AGHAGOWER (B Burrishoole, 52; B Murrisk, 171), *Achadh Ghobhair* ('field of (the) goat'?)

Ached Fobuir (meaning 'field of (the) spring', i.e. spring well) in writings of Bishop Tírechán (late-7th-cent.); a similar form occurs in the early 10-11th-cent. Tripartite Life of Patrick. *Achad Gobra* ('field of (the) horse, or mare') in Martyrology of Tallaght (c. 800), which is preserved in the late-12th-cent. Book of Leinster. *Achad Gobair* in Book of Lecan (c. 1400), and, in a work derived from the last-mentioned source (Dubhaltach Mac Fhirbhisigh's great Book of Genealogies, c. 1650), *Achadh Gabhair.* *Achedever* in Tax, 1302; *Achadabair* in Pont. Hib., 1216; *Achaabair* in Annates, 1443; *Acagouayr* in Visit., 1565; *Aghagowre* in CBC, 1585, and Straff., 1635.

4) AGHAMORE (B Costello, 92), *Achadh Mór* ('big field').

In Annates, 1430, as *Achamor de Kiarraiduchtaraidloch nanaireada* (= *Achad Mór* de *Ciarraige Uachtarach Locha na nÁirnead,* the latter being an ancient territory around Mannin Lake — formerly *Loch na nÁirneadh*). *Athamor* in Annates, 1492. *Aghavore* in Inquisition, 1625, and *Ahamore* in BSD.

5) AGLISH (B Carra, 59.5), *An Eaglais* ('the church').

Eglishcoyne in BSD, representing *Eaglais Chuáin;* this latter was probably an abbreviation of **Eaglais Chlainne Cuáin,* from the territorial name (originally a tribal or sept name) *Clann Chuáin,* which was itself used as the name of the parish in the 15th and 16th cents. — *Clancuan, Clencoayn* and *Clanchubayn* in Annates, 1432, 1440 and 1477 respectively, and *Cla(n)cuyn* in Visit., 1565.

6) ANNAGH (B Costello, 83), *Eanach* ('a marsh').

Enagh in Tax., 1302; the present-day anglicised form occurs in BSD. The name probably derives from the townland of *Annagh* which now lies in the parish of Aghamore.

7) ARDAGH (B Tirawley, 22), *Ardach* (earlier *Ardachadh,* 'high field').

Arrdachad usuanig (= *Ardachad Úa Súanaig,* 'the high field of the *Uí Shuanaigh*') in Pont. Hib., 1199. Abbreviated form *Arddach* in Tax., 1302.

Ardachad in Book of Lecan, c. 1400. *Ardagh* in Straff., 1635, and BSD.

8) ATTYMASS (B Gallen, 45), *Áth Tí an Mheasaigh* ('the ford of the house of *An Measach*').

Ath Tigi in Mesaig in AConn, 1225; *Authigymnessik* in Tax., 1302; *Aittigymeassa* in Annates, 1426; *Attymass(e)* in BSD. *An Measach* would appear to represent a surname, but what the correct original form of that surname might be is far from clear.

9) BALLA (B Clanmorris, 22), *Balla* ('a bath').

A borrowing from the Latin *balneum* 'a bath', the form *Balni* (genitive) appears in Annals of Ulster, *sub annis* 603, 779, *Ballni* in Martyrology of Tallaght (c. 800), *Balnai* in Cáin Adomnáin (8th cent.). *Balla* was established by the time of the Tax. of 1302; it also appears in Annates, 1429, 1492, and Visit., 1565. It need hardly be said that the name has no connection with the Modern Irish word *balla* 'a wall' which is a late borrowing from English. The form *Ball Álainn* which has sometimes been suggested as the Irish name for Balla derives from a fanciful etymology found in the Life of St. Mochua of Balla in the late 15th-cent. Book of Lismore; it concerns a miraculous well which Mochua is said to have brought with him from Bangor to Ros nDairbrech in Co. Mayo; it is referred to as *topur balláluinn* 'a lovely-limbed well', and this description is said to have given rise to the name *Balla*. Another, equally fanciful, explanation links the name to the Latin word *bulla* 'a bubble'.

10) BALLINCHALLA (B Kilmaine, 34; B Ross, 26), *Baile an Chalaidh* ('the town of the ferry').

Baly Ycollidy in Pont. Hib., 1223; *Ba(l)ynkalay* and *Ballencally* in Visit., 1565; *Ballycally* in BSD. *Caladh* may mean a ferry or ferry-station and also a riverside meadow; the former meaning is probably the one intended here.

11) BALLINROBE (B Kilmaine, 71; B Ross, 27), *Baile an Róba* ('the town of the river Robe').

Referred to in early sources as the parish of *Rodba*, as in Tax., 1302; distinction is made in Annates, 1430 and 1441, between *Roba in Conmacgneculi* (= *Conmaicne Cúile*) and *Roba in Kera*. *Ballemroba* in Annates, 1485; *Ballinrobe* in CBC, 1585; *Ballenrobe alias Templemore Parish* in BSD. (The word *rodba* appears, as an adjective — possibly meaning 'pointed, sharp, aggressive' — in a small number of Early Irish texts.)

12) BALLINTOBER (B Burrishoole, 2; B Carra, 91), *Baile an Tobair* ('the town of the well').

Baile in Topair in 12th-cent. Martyrology of Ua Gormáin; *Topur Patraicc* in AConn, 1224, and *Baili Topair Patricc* in AConn, 1248; *Baili Thobair Padraic* in Book of Lecan, c. 1400; *Fons Sancti Patricii* in Annates, 1430; *monasterium Villefontis Sancti Patricii* in Annates, 1441;

Ballintobber and Ballintober in CBC, 1585. (Ballintober in Co. Roscommon was anciently known as *Baile Tobair Bhríde*).

13) BALLYHEAN (B Carra, 31), *Béal Átha hÉin* ('the ford-mouth of the bird').

Balachaen in Annates, 1510; *Belahen* in Visit., 1565; *Ballyheane* in Straff., 1635; *Ballahine* in BSD. The Irish form is not altogether certain. The form given in the Namebook, 1838 — *Beul atha h-éun* = *Béal Átha hÉan* . . 'of (the) birds' — might be more satisfactory.

14) BALLYNAHAGLISH (B Tirawley, 52), *Baile na hEaglaise* ('the town of the church').

Ballynaheglis, Ballineheglas, etc., in BSD. This parish and that of *Kilbelfad* together form the Catholic parish of *Backs,* which itself is a name of respectable antiquity — *An Bac* in the Annals of Loch Cé, 1225, and *in Da Bac* in the Book of Lecan, c. 1400. (*Bac,* earlier *bacc,* may mean 'an angle, a bend, a corner').

15) BALLYOVEY (B Carra, 111), *Baile Óbha* ('the town of *Óbha',* earlier *Odhbha*).

Baleove in Visit., 1565, and *Balleovy* in CBC, 1585. The second element is a territorial name which occurs in the Life of St. Mochua of Balla in the late 15th-cent. Book of Lismore, as *Odhba.* It appears, in slightly corrupt form, as the parish name in the Annates, *Ome,* 1430, *Homy,* 1471, and *One vel Oue,* 1502. The word *odba* may mean 'a mound'. Ballyovey corresponds to the Catholic parish of *Partry,* Irish *Partraí,* earlier *Partraige,* the name of an early population-group.

16) BALLYSAKEERY (B Tirawley, 52), *Baile Easa Caoire* ('the town of the waterfall of *Caoire',* or *Caoille?*).

Balieascaerig in Annates, 1428; *Baile eassa carri* in Annates, 1535; *Ballassekery* in CBC, 1585; *Baile esa caoirigh* in Senchus Búrcach, c. 1578. But *Ballyassakeely* in a Fiant dated 1593; *Ballyasakilly* and *Ballysakeely* in Straff., 1635; both *Ballessekire* and *Ballyshikilly* in BSD. The forms with 'l' instead of 'r' correspond to *Baile Easa-Caoille* in Dubhaltach Mac Fhirbhisigh's Book of Genealogies, c. 1650. The name *Eas Caoille* also occurs in a poem by Tadhg Dall Ó hUiginn composed in or around 1581. Although forms with 'l(l)' are not attested before the later 16th cent., these may in fact represent the original form. It may be noted that an ancient territory called *Cailli Conaill* (mod. *Caoille* C.) lay some distance to the north of Ballysakeery — between Rathfran and Kilcummin, according to the late-14th-cent. Sligo MS, the Book of Lecan. *Caílle* appears to have denoted an ancient division of land; it may have originally meant simply a narrow strip of land.

17) BEKAN (B Costello, 62), *Béacán,* (meaning unknown).

Beakan in a Fiant dated 1586; *Bekane* in Straff., 1635. The recommended

Irish form was recorded in the Namebook as the form in use among local Irish-speakers around 1838. John O'Donovan was unable to explain the name, but, as he was wont to do when confronted with a word he did not understand, suggested it might represent a personal name; he therefore put forward, very tentatively, the interpretation 'St. Becan's Parish'.

18) BOHOLA (B Gallen, 35), *Both Chomhla* ('hut of shelter'?).

Bothcomla in Tax., 1302, and rather similar forms in Annates, 1429 and 1430; *Boycollo* in CBC, 1585; *Bohollo* and *Bocholla* in Straff., 1635. The word *comla* in Early Irish meant 'a door' (as opposed to *dorus,* 'a doorway'), 'a shutter, a covering' and, by extension, 'protection, shelter'.

19) BREAGHWY (B Carra, 21), *Bréachmhaigh* ('wolf-plain').

Breaghfoy in an Inquisition dated 1607; the present-day anglicised form appears in Straff., 1635, and in the BSD. *Breachmuigh* (dative) in a list of extinct bishoprics compiled by Dubhaltach Mac Fhirbhisigh in 1666.

20) BURRISCARRA (B Carra, 23), *Buiríos Ceara* ('the burgage, or borough-town, of *Ceara*').

Villanova alias Burgiskera in Annates, 1428; *Burgeskera* in Visit., 1565; *Borishkara* in CBC, 1585. (The earlier form of *buiríos* was *buirgés*.)

21) BURRISHOOLE (B Burrishoole, 224), *Buiríos Umhaill* ('the burgage of *Umhall*').

Burgis Wmayl in Annates, 1492; *Burges Wyll* in Visit., 1565; *Burressowle* and *Borrishowle* in CBC, 1585; *Borrizoule* and *Borrishoule* in Straff., 1635. *Mainister Bhuirgheisi Umhaill* in the will of Cú Choigchríche Ó Cléirigh, 1664.

22) CASTLECONOR (B Tireragh, 6; + Co. Sligo), *Caisleán Conchúir* ('the castle of *Conchúr*').

Castroconhor in Tax., 1302; *Caislén Conchobhair* in Allans of Loch Cé, 1316 and 1580; *Caisleanconchubar* in Annates, 1426; *Caslean Conchubayr alias Castro Cornelii* in same source, 1438, and many other examples of similar forms in Annates from 1439 to 1517. But the entry in AConn corresponding to that in Annals of Loch Cé, 1316, has *Caislén meic Conchobair,* and a similar form appears in the Annals of the Four Masters, sub annis 1371 and 1438, and in the Book of Lecan, c. 1400; in his mid-17th-cent. recension of the Lecan text Dubhaltach Mac Fhirbhisigh has *Caisleun (no Dún) mc. Conchabhair,* and both he and the Book of Lecan elsewhere mention *Dun mc. Concobair* (or *Dún Mc.-Conchabair*). Whether *Dún Mhic Conchúir* represents an earlier form of *Caisleán Mhic Conchúir,* and whether *Caisleán Mhic Conchúir* and *Caisleán Conchúir* both refer to Castleconor are matters for debate. What is rather more certain, however, is that the form recorded in the Namebook as the name of the parish among Irish-speakers around 1838 is *p(aráiste) Chaislean Crochuir,* which corresponds to the form first attested in the early 14th century.

* 23)   CASTLEMORE (B Costello, [* now in Co. Roscommon] 10½), *An Caisleán Mór* ('the great castle').

de Castro Magno in Tax., 1302; *Caislen Slebi Luga* in AConn, 1270; *Caislen Mor Mc. Goisdelb* and *an Caislen Mor* in AConn, 1336 and 1527 respectively; *Castell-more* in Browne's Map, 1584, and *Castlemore* in Straff., 1635, and BSD.

24)   CONG (B Kilmaine, 60; + Co. Galway), *Conga* ('a narrow neck of land').

Cunga in the Book of Leinster (late 12th cent.) and in Tax., 1302; *Cunga Feichín* in AConn, 1224, 1225, etc.; *Concha* in Annates, 1511; *Conga, Conge* in Visit., 1565; *Congae, Coing,* etc., in CBC, 1585. The word appears to be related to the word *cuing* 'a yoke' which is used in a geographical context to denote 'an isthmus'. This latter usage is exemplified by the townlands of *Cuing Beg* and *Cuing More* on the isthmus between Lough Conn and Lough Cullin (just east of Pontoon). It has also been suggested that *conga* might denote a short, narrow stream joining two (generally large) stretches of water. This meaning might appear to suit *Ballycong (Béal Átha Conga),* in the parish of Attymass, whose name may derive from the short stream connecting Carrowkeribly Lough with the smaller Ballycong Lough. In the case of Cong it is difficult to decide whether the name was suggested by the 'yoke' of land connecting the land to the east and to the west of the great lakes or by the 'yoke' of water (in the form of a small river) joining the two great expanses of water.

25)   CROSSBOYNE (B Clanmorris, 66), *Crois Bhaoithín* ('*Baoithín's* cross').

Crosbithin in Tax., 1302; *Crosboyny* in Visit., 1565; *Cros(s)bohin* in CBC, 1585; *Crosseboyhinne* in Straff., 1635.

26)   CROSSMOLINA (B Tirawley, 272), *Crois Mhaoilíona* ('*Maoil(fh)íona's* Cross ').

Crosmolyne in Tax., 1302; *Crossmianlina* and *Croiswailina* in Annates, 1441 and 1535 respectively; *Cros Mhaoilína* in AConn, 1526. Mac Fhirbhisigh in his Book of Genealogies (c. 1650) interprets the latter portion of the name as a surname — *Cros-Ui-Mhaoilfhíona* — and indeed there is record, in the Book of Lecan (c. 1400), of the surname *hUa Mailina* (which Dubhaltach Mac Fhirbhisigh renders *O Maoilfhiona*) as one of the ruling families in the Crossmolina area. There is more than sufficient evidence, however, to show that it is the forename and not the surname which is to be found in the Irish name of Crossmolina.

27)   DOONFEENY (B Tirawley, 127), *Dún Fhíne* ('*Fíne's* fort').

Dun Fine in the Book of Leinster (later 12th cent.) and in the late-14th-cent. Sligo MSS, the Books of Ballymote and Lecan; Dubhaltach Mac Fhirbhisigh, c. 1650, writes *Dún Fíne* and *Dún Fhíne,* while the Early Modern Irish text, Betha Chellaigh, has *i nDún Fhidne. Dooniny, Dooneny* and *Doonefiny* in BSD.

28)   DRUM (B Carra, 31), *An Droim* ('the ridge').

de Drum in Tax., 1302, but *Dromenenaghane* in Straff., 1635, and *Dromonenohan* in BSD, while H.T. Knox cites other similar examples, such as *Drummonechain*, 1462, and *Dromenichain*, 1591. The prevalence in this area of the surname *Heneghan (Ó hÉanacháin, Ó hÉineacháin*, earlier *Ó hÉighneacháin, Ua hÉicnecháin)* suggests that these forms may perhaps represent *Dromainn* (or *Droim) Eí(gh) neacháin.*

29)   ISLANDEADY (B Burrishoole, 36; B Carra 65), *Oilén Éadaí* ('the island of ——?).

Oleayn Edayn in Visit., 1565; *Ellaneden* in Straff., 1635, and a similar form in BSD. The late medieval Betha Chellaigh mentions *Oilén Etgair* in *Claenloch,* a lake which, according to other sources, lay in the vicinity of Castlebar. It is tempting to equate *Claenloch* with Islandeady Lake and *Oilén Etgair* (mod. *Oileán Éadghair,* 'Edgar's Island') with Islandeady. The Saxon name Edgar would not be particularly unusual in an area so close to *Mag nÉo na Sachsan* (see *Mayo,* no. 59 below).The other forms cited would point to a form such as *Oileán Éadain* or *Oileán Eadáin,* while the form in use among Irish-speakers in the last century was *Oileán Éadaí* (or *Oileán Éadaigh).* Whatever the original form of the name, and whatever its meaning, these had obviously been long forgotten.

30)   KILBEAGH (B Costello, 131; + Co. Roscommon), *Cill Bheitheach* ('birchen church').

Killbegh in a Fiant dated 1592; *Killbeagh* in an Inquisition from 1625. The local Irish form recorded in the Namebook was *Cille Beitheach.*

31)   KILBELFAD (B Tirawley, 54), *Cill Bhéalad* ('the church of *Béalad').*

The form *Kildeleth* in Tax., 1302, appears to be a garbled version of the name. The correct original form occurs in the Book of Leinster (later 12th cent.), *Cell Belfhota;* the forms in BSD include *Killbelody* and *Kilbealfadda.* The truncated version *Cill Belad* is found in the Book of Lecan (c. 1400), while in the recension of the same text in Mac Fhirbhisigh's Book of Genealogies (c. 1650) the name is rendered *Cill Bhéulad. Béalfhada* is a personal name which obviously originated as an epithet or nickname meaning 'long-mouthed'.

32)   KILBRIDE (B Tirawley, 18), *Cill Bhríde ('Bríd's* church', i.e. the church of St. Brigid).

Cellbrigdi in Pont. Hib., 1199; 17th-cent. forms include *Kilbridy, Kilbride* and *Killbreedy.*

33)   *KILCOLMAN (B Clanmorris, 96), Cill Cholmáin ('Colmán's* church').

Kil-colman in Tax., 1302, and *Killcolman* and *Killcollman* in 17th-cent. sources.

34)   KILCOLMAN (B Costello, [now in Co. Roscommon] 44) *Cill Cholmáin ('Colman's* church').

Caislen Cille Calman in Annals of Four Masters, *sub anno* 1270; *caislén Cille Colmáin* in same annals at the year 1284; *Kellcalman* in Tax., 1302; *Cille Colmain* (genitive) *.i. baile mc. Rúghraide Mc. Gosdelb* in AConn, 1536; *Killcollmane* in Straff., 1635.

35) KILCOMMON (B Erris, 823), *Cill Chomáin, ('Comán's* church').

Cellchoman in Pont. Hib., 1199; *Kilcoman* in CBC, 1585. *Cill Chomáin* in Annals of Four Masters, *sub anno* 1180, and in Mac Fhirbhisigh's Book of Genealogies, in a passage written in 1664. (Kilcommon is the largest parish in Ireland.)

36) KILCOMMON (B Kilmaine,707), *Cill Chomáin* ('*Comán's* church').

Kyllcomayn in Annates, 1440, and in Visit., 1565; *Cillchoman* in Annates, 1492; *Kylcomen* in a Fiant dated 1568; *Killcomen* in 17th-cent. sources.

37) KILCONDUFF (B Gallen, 67), *Cill Chon Duibh* ('*Cú Dubh's* church').

Garbled from *Kelcomdilk* in Tax., 1302; *Cill-Conduibh* in Annals of Ulster, *sub anno* 1384; *Killconduibh* in surviving extract from lost Annals of Lecan, *sub anno* 1385; *Killconduffe* in BSD. (Note the occurrence in the vicinity of Kilconduff of the surname *Cunniffe/Ó Conduibh*.)

38) KILCUMMIN (B Tirawley, 17), *Cill Chuimín* ('*Cuimín's* church').

Cellcummin in Pont. Hib., 1199; *Kilcomyn* in Tax., 1302; *Killcomyn* in Straff., 1635; *Killcomen* and *Killcomin* in BSD.

39) KILDACOMMOGE (B Carra, 12; B Gallen 18), *Cill Dachomóg* ('*Dachomóg's* church').

Cilla Kamog in Annates, 1442; *Kylldacomoch* in Visit., 1565; *Kildacamoge* in BSD. (The prefixes *Do* — or, as here, *Da* — and *Mo* and the ending *-óg* indicate hypocoristic forms — or 'pet-forms' — of personal names; a better-known form of the name in question here is *Comán*. See also *Kilmolara*, no. 50, and *Kilmovee*, no. 53, below).

40) KILFIAN (B Tirawley, 117), *Cill Aodháin* ('*Aodhán's* church'?).

The name is not attested in anything resembling its present anglicised form before c. 1655 when *Killfian* appears on the Down Survey Barony Map of Tirawley. The BSD also has the form *Killfyan*. The Namebook gives the form in use among Irish-speakers in the locality around 1838 as *Cill Fhidheáin/Fhiáin*. The second element puzzled John O'Donovan and, rather characteristically, he plumped for a personal name, and a saint's name at that, *Cella Sancti Fiani,* thus adding yet another name to the list of otherwise unattested Irish saints! If the Irish form given in the Namebook were correct, it would be difficult to avoid translating it 'wild church', however improbable that might seem. The Mayo historian H. T. Knox, however, made a suggestion which could very well solve the problem. In an appendix to his *History of the County of Mayo,* 1908, he published a translation of the text called the 'Senchus Búrcach' (or 'Historia et genealogia familiae de Burgo') which seems to date from about 1578. In this there is mention of *baile Chille hAodháin,* which Knox identifies with the cryptic note 'The same as Kilfian'. This might seem rather unlikely, until one considers that in Connacht Irish *Cill Fhiáin* (or even *Cill Fhidheáin)* and *Cill Aodháin* are virtually identical in pronunciation. It could very well have happened that the original form, and meaning, of the name had been forgotten by the time it came to be written in anglicised form in the mid-17th cent., and that the 'f' was 'restored' by way of over-compensation. A rather similar process occured in the case of a number of other placenames in which the relevant element began with a vowel, an 'f', or an 'n' preceded by the article — notably in certain instances of the name *An Nuachongbháil* which is found in several counties (see no. 63 below): this became *An Uachongbháil (gen. Na Fuachongbhála).* If Knox's suggestion is correct, the question then arises: does a form corresponding to *Cill Aodháin* (earlier *Cell Áedáin*) occur in any pre-17th cent. source? Turning to the Annates for the diocese of Killala, we find, *sub annis* 1476 and 1494, the respective forms *Kyllidgayn* and *Killigan* which might be interpreted as *Cill Aodhagáin* (a variant of *Cill Aodháin*?) or even as *Cill Aodháin* itself but with the lenited 'd' not yet quite silent as in Modern Irish pronunciation. It must be admitted, however, that the identification in this case is far from certain. But there is another form in the Annates for Killala, at the year 1493, which with very slight emendation would appear to correspond very closely to *Cill Aodháin: ecclesia de Kyllcayn* (recté *Kylleayn?*). Moreover, there is corroboration of this identification in the very next line with a reference to *rectorie de Bridac;* this latter represents an ancient territory called *An Bhréadach* which, we are told, comprised the parish of Moygawnagh and *part of Kilfian.*

41) KILGARVAN (B Gallen, 80), *Cill na nGarbhán* ('the church of the *Garbháns',* i.e. people named *Garbhán*).

Cellnagaruan in Pont. Hib., 1199; *Kelnangarnan* in Tax., 1302; *cethraimi Chilli na nGarban* in a late (15th or even 16th-cent.?) addition of the Book of Lecan; *Killnogarvan* and *Killnagarvane* in Staff., 1635. (Placenames of this structure — noun + personal name in genitive plural — are quite rare; probably the most notable example is *Doire na bhFlann,* Co. Tipperary, where some valuable objects from the early Christian period were discovered early in 1980.)

42) KILGEEVER (B Murrisk, 236), *Cill Ghaobhair* ('the church of ——?').

Kilgonir in Tax., 1302 (the 'n' being obviously a mistake for 'v'); *Kyllgayuayr* in Visit., 1565; *Killgeever* in BSD. The word *gaobhar* means 'contiguity, proximity'. Whether that is in fact the word represented by the latter part of the present name is uncertain. Once again, O'Donovan took it to be a personal name, translating 'Geever's church'!

43)   KILLALA (B Tirawley, 23), *Cill Ala* ('the varicoloured church'?).

Cill Alaid (dative) and *Cill nAlaid* (accusative) in early 10-11th-cent. Tripartite Life of Patrick; *Cellalad* in Pont. Hib., 1199; Latin form *ecclesia etc. Aladensis* in Tax., 1302, Annates, 1419, 1427, etc.; *Cilli hElaid* and *Cilli hAlaich* (both in genitive) in Book of Lecan, c. 1400; *Killale* in Browne's Map, 1584; *Killalow, Killal(l)o* and *Killala* in CBC, 1585. The adjective *alad* — if that is what is in fact represented by the second element of this name — means 'variegated, piebald', etc. The nominative form in Old Irish would have been *Cell Alad.* — as in Pont. Hib.

44)   KILLASSER (B Gallen, 80), *Cill Lasrach* ('the church of *Lasair'*).

Cill Lasrach i nGaileanguibh in the late Middle Irish *Betha Lasrach* which is preserved in a MS written in 1670. The present-day anglicised form appears in a Fiant dated 1593 and also, as well as the form *Killassir,* in Straff., 1635.

45)   KILLEDAN (B Gallen, 58), *Cill Liadáin* ('*Liadán's* church').

Kelualydan in Tax., 1302; *Killudeyn* in Annates, 1477; *Killedane* in CBC, 1585, and BSD; *Killidan* in Inquisition dated 1617; *Killedan* in Straff., 1635. The form in the Namebook, recorded from Irish-speakers in the locality in 1838, is *Cill Liadáin.* There is no basis for the form *Cill Aodáin* which gained currency from its use by Douglas Hyde in his edition (1903) of the poems and songs of blind Anthony Raftery. (One of the latter's most popular compositions was of course his song in praise of his native Killedan). If the second element in fact represented the Old Irish name *Áedán,* its more modern form would be *Aodhán,* with the lenited medial 'd' virtually silent — as in the case of *Kilfian* (see no. 40 above), if the identification made there with the form *Cill Aodháin* found in a late-16th-cent. source be correct. (Incidentally, the name *Aidan* is a 19th-cent. revival based on the Latinised form *Aidanus* — just as *Brendan* is based on *Brendanus* rather than on the living Irish *Bréanainn.*) Turning to the alternative name which, it is suggested, may occur in the second element of *Killedan,* it may be noted that at least one churchman named *Liotán* (modern *Liodán*) appears in the Annals — he was an abbot of Tuam who died in 900. The same name gives the Connacht surname *Ó Liodáin* (also *Ó Loideáin*), anglicised *Lydon* and *Leyden.* Indeed, Hyde in his edition of Raftery's works, when referring to people named Lydon from the Kiltamagh area, renders the name *Ó Liadáin.* It seems reasonable to suggest, therefore, that *Liadán* (or perhaps *Líodán*) was a local variant of *Litán/Liodán.* The form in the Taxation of 1302 appears to indicate a form of the placename involving the surname (as *Cell Ua Litáin,* later *Cill Ó Liodáin, or Cill Ó Liadáin*), but this is not supported by the rest of the evidence.

46)   KILMACLASSER (B Burrishoole, 27), *Cill Mhic Laisre* ('*Mac-Laisre's* church').

Kilmalasser in Tax., 1302, *Kyllmcclacer* in Visit., 1565; *Kilmaglasse* (and the rather garbled *Kilmackash*) in CBC, 1585; *Killmaclasser* in Straff., 1635. The first form cited from CBC corresponds remarkably closely to the forms recorded in the Namebook, 1838, *Cill Mhig Laise* and *Cill Mhic Glaise*. *Mac-Laisre* is an Early Irish personal name (a forename, not a surname) meaning 'son of flame'.

47) KILMAINEBEG (B Kilmaine, 14), *Cill Mheáin Bheag* ('middle church little').

Kilmedon (Church of the Apostles), Tax., 1302; *Kyllmeaynbech,* Visit., 1565; *Killmainbeg,* BSD.

48) KILMAINEMORE (B Kilmaine, 56), *Cill Mheáin Mhór* ('middle church great').

Cellola Media in Tírechán (late 7th cent.); *Kellmedoin* in Pont. Hib., 1199; *Cill* (and *Qill*) *Meodoin* in AConn, 1225; *Kil-medhon (Church of St. Patrick)* in Tax., 1302; *Kylmain* in Annates, 1478; *Kyllmeaynmor* in Visit., 1565; *Kilmaine* in CBC, 1585.

49) KILMEENA (B Burrishoole, 44), *Cill Mhíone* ('Míona's church').

Kellmidoni in Pont. Hib., 1199; *Kilmayn* in Tax., 1302; ?*Kyllmynan* in Visit., 1565; *Killmine* in Straff., 1635; *Killveeny* and *Killveeney* in BSD. *Mío(dh)na* (or *Míodhain*?) appears to represent an otherwise unattested personal name.

50) KILMOLARA (B Kilmaine, 15.5), *Cill Molára* ('Molára's church').

Kyllmolara in Visit., 1565; *Kilvolarra* in an Inquisition dated 1616; *Killmolare* in BSD. *Kellnagiglara* in Tax., 1302, may represent a garbled version of the name.

51) KILMORE (B Erris, 119), *An Chill Mhór* ('the big church').

Killmore in Straff., 1635, and BSD. This may be the place referred to as *Kylmore in Tyreawle* in a Fiant dated 1568, and the *Kilmorry Parish* in an Inquisition from 1623 may be the same place. The forms recorded in the Namebook as being in use among Irish-speakers around 1838 are *Cill Mhaithios* and *Cill Mhór Mhathas;* the latter was interpreted by John O'Donovan as meaning 'great church of Matthias'.

52) KILMOREMOY (B Tirawley, 18; Tireragh, 32), *Cill Mhór Mhuaidhe* ('great church of the *Muaidh*/Moy').

Cellola Magna Muaide in Tírechán, late 7th cent.; *Cell Mór, Cell Mór Huachtir Muadi* and *Cill Móir Óchtair Múade* in the Tripartite Life of Patrick, c. 900; *Cellmor* in Pont. Hib., 1199; *Kilmormoy* in Tax., 1302; *o Chill Moir Muaidi* (dative) in Book of Lecan, c. 1400, and *ó Chill Mhóir M(h)uaidhe* in version of same text in Mac Fhirbhisigh's Book of Genealogies, c. 1650.

71

Co. Mayo Civil Parishes.

Included here are Castlemore, Kilcolman, and part of Kilbeagh - all in the barony of Costello - which were transferred to Co. Roscommon in 1898. Thin lines within parishes indicate barony-boundaries which do not coincide with parish-boundaries, e.g. when a parish is divided between two or more baronies.

53) KILMOVEE (B Costello, 83), *Cill Mobhí* ('Mobhí's church').

Kelmoby in Tax., 1302; *Killmovy* in Straff., 1635; present-day anglicised form in BSD. *Mobhí* is a pet form of *Brénainn.*

54) KILTURRA (B Costello, 14 + Co. Sligo), *Cill Tora* ('church of ——?').

There is an entry headed *Cell toraidhi* — said to be from a MS in Trinity College, Dublin, and identified as 'Kilturra townland and parish in Co. Sligo' — in Fr. Edmund Hogan's great *Onomasticon Goidelicum* (a dictionary of names of places and tribes found in a wide variety of Gaelic sources, both manuscript and printed), published in 1910. The manuscript-text in question is a copy of the 'Annals of Tigernach' and the name cited by the *Onomasticon* occurs in the entry for the year 621 — not, however, as *Cell toraidhi,* but as *ecluia* (presumably a corruption of *ecclesia*) *toraidhi.*

There is, moreover, nothing whatever in the entry to suggest that this place might have been located on the borders of the present-day counties of Mayo and Sligo. Rather does it seem from the general context that the place in question was a church on Tory Island, off the coast of Co. Donegal. Kilturra, then, does not seem to be attested before the 17th cent.; the form *Killturroe* appears on the Down Survey Barony Map, Corran Barony, Co. Sligo, c. 1655, and *Killturragh* in the BSD. (A form similar to the latter also appears in the Royal Visitation of the diocese of Achonry, 1633.) What the second element in the name represents is uncertain.

55) KILVINE (B Clanmorris, 22), *Cill Mhiáin,* ('*Mián's* church').

Killmyanas vel Kyllmyannd in Annates, 1432; *Kylerina vel Kilvina* in Annates, 1511; *Kilmeyn* and *Kyllmeyn* in Visit., 1565; *Cill Midáin* in Annals of Loch Cé sub anno 1584; *Killveyne* and *Killvyne* in Straff., 1635. *Kilfina* in Tax., 1302, may also refer to this place. The Namebook records that at that period (c. 1838) the parish was 'frequently called also *Killmine Parish*'.

56) KNOCK (B Clanmorris, 6; B Costello, 40), *An Cnoc* ('the hill').

Knocke in Inquisitions dated 1625 and 1629; *Knock* in BSD. The name does not seem to be unambiguously attested prior to 1625, although it has been suggested that the form *Enocdrumchaba,* in a letter dated 1466 (catalogued in the Calendar of Papal Letters), should be emended to read *Cnocdrumchalra;* similarly *Drumugakarg* in the same source (1460) might be read as *Druimgalraig.* Both these forms correspond quite closely to the name of the Church of Ireland vicarage which appears as *Knockdrumcalry* and *Knockdrumcally* in a variety of 18th and 19th-cent. sources. The form *Knockdrimcallry* does appear in the Inquisition of 1625 (cited above) in which there is quite a separate mention of *Knocke;* the name occurs at the end of a list of townlands located between Ballyhaunis and the Roscommon border — 'Levallyroe, Knockenarry, Tonregie, Garran, Reban et Knockdrimcallry'. If, however, *Reban* is a mistake for *Bekan* (see no. 17 above), *Knockdrimcallry* could very well represent Knock. It may be worthy of note that the townland in which the present parish-church of Knock is situated — and adjacent to the fragment of a ruined church in the old graveyard — is called *Drum;* it appears in the Inquisition of 1625 as *Carrowenedroma (= Ceathrú an Droma).* The historian H. T. Knox suggested more than three quarters of a century ago that *Druggulragi* in Tax., 1302, represented a garbled version of *Droim Calraigi.* From the context, the names *Dumchakuin* and *Dumkakuyn* in the Annates, 1492, appear to represent still more garbled versions. The name *Cnoc Droma Chalraighe* (mod. *Chalraí*) means 'the hill of the ridge of the Calraige'; the latter were an ancient people who in Connacht were particularly associated with the Crossmolina area and with part of Co. Sligo where they gave their name to the parish of *Calry.* Knock, of course, is nowadays commonly known as *Cnoc Mhuire* ('Mary's Hill') among Irish-speakers as a result of the apparition of August 1879.

57)   LACKAN (B Tirawley, 30), *Leacain* ('a hillside').

Lecu in Pont. Hib., 1199; *Lecor* ('r' being a mistake for 'n'?) in Tax., 1302; *Lachayn* in Annates, 1441, and *de Leacain* in same source, 1535; *Lacka* in Browne's Map, 1584, and *Lacca* in a letter written by Browne to Walsingham the following year; *Lackan* and *Leckan* in BSD. *Leacain* is originally the dative of *Leaca* (earlier *Lecu,* precisely the form from 1199), a word which basically means 'a cheek' and, by extension, 'a hillside, or slope'.

58)   MANULLA (B Carra, 22), *Maigh Nulla* ('the plain of *Nulla*').

Magh-enculi (sic) in Tax., 1302. The Book of Lecan, c. 1400, has *Tuath Muigi Indalb* and *Tuath Muigi hIndalb,* while Dubhaltach Mac Fhirbhisigh's version (c. 1650) of the same passages reads *Tuath Mhuighe Fhiondalba* and *Tuath Muighe hIondailb* respectively. There is a wide variety of forms in the Annates: *Magfindealba,* 1492, *Magemuildr vel Magennuldr,* 1442, *Magumdelba,* 1447, *Maynnala,* 1482, *Manulla,* 1492, *Magfinalud,* 1510. *Maynnulu* in Calendar of Papal Letters, 1475; *Mayinalam* in Visit., 1565; *Moyonly* and *Moynollie* in CBC, 1585, *Moynulla* in Straff., 1635; *Minola* in Bald's Map of Mayo, 1830. The second element in the name may be a personal name such as *Find-delb* ('fair shape') or, possibly, *Find-dalb.* (*Dalb* on its own appears to have been a rare female name; it is also a word meaning 'lie, deceit, sorcery'.) The development of the name from *Mag Find-delbae* (or, in more modern dress, *Magh Fionndealbha*), or some such form, to *Manulla/Maigh Nulla* may have been by way of forms such as *Maigh Fhionnalbha, Maigh Ionnalla, Maigh Nalla,* and so to *Maigh Nulla.*

59)   MAYO (B Clanmorris, 39; B Kilmaine, 8), *Maigh Eo* ('plain of yew-trees').

Pontifex Maigo hEu Saxonum in Annals of Ulster, *sub anno* 731; *episcopus Maigh hEu* in same annals at the year 773, and *espuc Maighi-Éo* at 1183. Among the occurrences of the name in AConn are *Mag nEo,* 1225, *Magh nEo na Sachsan,* 1230, *epscop Moige hEo na Saxan,* 1478. *Archidiaconum Maionensium* in Pont. Hib., 1216; *de Magio* in Tax., 1302, and in Annates, 1471. Other examples in the Annates include *de Mayo,* 1431, *Mageonensis diocesis,* 1441, *monasterium Sancti Michaelis de Mayo, 1462, ecclesia Sancti Geraldi de Mayo,* 1476. *Maio* in Visit., 1565; the '*abby of Mayo*' and '*towne of Mayo*' in CBC, 1585. In BSD the part of the parish in the barony of Kilmaine is called *Templemurry alias Mayo Parish* while that in Clanmorris barony is called *Temple Garret.*

60)   MEELICK (B Gallen, 32), *Míleac* ('low-lying marshy land' *or* 'an isolated piece of land').

co Miliuc (dative) in AConn, 1225; *Milio* (recté *Milic*?) in Tax., 1302; *Milick* in Straff., 1635; *Meelick* in BSD. Of the two meanings suggested above for the word *míleac* (it does not appear in any of the standard dictionaries), the first is that given by P. W. Joyce in his *Irish Names of Places,* vol. 1, while the second is that normally given by John O'Donovan.

61) MOORGAGAGH (B Kilmaine, 7), *An Múr Gágach* ('the split or cracked wall or rampart').

Moregagagh in Inquisition dated 1616 and in Straff., 1635; *Morgagagh* in BSD. The older name seems to have been *Cillín Bhréanainn,* 'the little church of *Bréanainn': Cyllynbrenyn alias Sancti Brendani* in Annates, 1492, *Kyllynbrenayn* in Visit., 1565, and *abbey of Killenbrenan* in Straff., 1635.

62) MOYGAWNAGH (B Tirawley, 82), *Maigh Ghamhnach* ('plain of strippers').

Maggamnach in Pont. Hib., 1199; *Monganenath* in Tax., 1302; *Magh Gamnach* in Book of Ballymote and *o Muig Gamnuch* (dative) in Book of Lecan (both from late 14th cent.); *o Muigh Gamhnach* in Mac Fhirbhisigh's Book of Genealogies, c. 1650; *Moygawnagh* and *Magawnagh* in BSD.

63) OUGHAVAL (B Murrisk, 52½), *An Nuachabháil* ('the new foundation').

Uchongal in Tax., 1302; *Ucauayll* in Visit., 1565; *Aghavale* in BSD. The name appears in a 14th-cent. MS of the so-called 'Annals of Tigernach' in the phrase *a ndamlíag nahaachongbala* (recté *na hUachongbala'*), 'in the stone church of *An (N)uachongbáil;* the same phrase occurs in a related set of annals called the *Chronicum Scotorum* (at the year 1131) as *i ndomlíag na Nuacongbala.* There are several other places of the name throughout Ireland and many of them exhibit the tendency, seen here, of words beginning in 'n', when preceded by the definite article, to drop the 'n' in certain cases, due to confusion with the 'n' of the article. The reduction of the medial *ong* in *An (N)uachongbháil* exemplifies a fairly common phonetic development in Irish, of which several instances may be found in placenames, namely the tendency of *ong* to change to *ú.* A further tendency (illustrated by Oughaval and by other instances of the name, such as Noughaval in Clare and Westmeath, Nohoval in Cork and Oughaval in Laois) is for the middle syllable to be shortened, due no doubt to the presence of long syllables both before and after it, and thus we arrive at forms such as *Oughaval* and *An Nuachabháil.* (*Congbháil* means 'a holding, a settlement, an establishment, a foundation', particularly one of ecclesiastical origin.)

64) RATHREAGH (B Tirawley, 17), *An Ráth Riabhach* ('the grey, or striped, rath').

Rathreth in Tax., 1302; *Rathreagh* and *Rathriegh* in Straff., 1635; *Rareogh* and *Rathreagh* in BSD.

65) ROBEEN (B Kilmaine, 44), *Róibín* ('little Róba').

Rodbin in Tax., 1302; *Roibin Beag* (rather tautologous!) in Book of Lecan, c. 1400; *Robyn* in Visit., 1565; *Robin* and *Robyn* in Straff., 1635;

Robin and Any Parish in BSD. *Róibín* (or *Roidhbín*) is essentially meaningless, being merely a diminutive of the name of the neighbouring larger parish of *Ballinrobe,* known in earlier times (see no. 11 above) as the 'parish of *Rodhba'.*

66)   ROSLEE (B Carra, 15.5), *Ros Lao* ('(the) height of (the) calves').

Rosselowe in Tax., 1302; *Ros laeg* in Book of Lecan, c. 1400; *Roslee* in BSD. The forms *Rossleghane* and *Rosleaghane* in Straff., 1635, seem to refer to Roslee, but the endings are rather puzzling.

67)   ROSS (B Ross 44; + Co. Galway), *Ros* ('a height').

Ros' in Tax., 1302; *Rosse* in CBC, 1585, in an Inquisition dated 1617, and in BSD. The word *ros* originally meant a piece of elevated ground, and by extension came to mean a headland or promontory, especially a wooded one.

68)   SHRULE (B Kilmaine, 47), *Sruthair* ('a stream or current').

Sruthra (genitive) in AConn, 1271. *Struthir* in Tax., 1302; *Strutyr* in Annates, 1487; *Scruyr* in Visit., 1565; *Shrower* in Browne's Map, 1584; *Shruell* in CBC, 1585; *Sruher* in Straff., 1635; *Shroule* in BSD. *Sruthair* seems to be virtually identical in meaning to *sruth,* from which it derives. The change from 'r' to 'l' (or vice versa) is a phonetic development of which there are numerous examples in Irish.

69)   TAGHEEN (B Clanmorris, 27), *Teach Chaoin* ('fair house'?).

Theachin in Tax., 1302; *Teaghkeyne* and *Tecayn* in Visit., 1565; *Taghkin* and *Taghine* in Staff., 1635; *Teaghkeene* in BSD. The recommended Irish form follows that recorded in the Namebook as the version in use among Irish-speakers in the locality around 1838; John O'Donovan considered it to mean 'beautiful house'. The second element in the name is, however, somewhat problematical. The name could conceivably have originally been *Teach Caín* (mod. *Teach Caoin*), the second element (meaning 'fair, smooth, pleasant, gentle', etc.) being one which occurs quite frequently in Irish placenames — Achadh Caoin, Cluain Caoin, Droim Caoin, etc. The lenition of the initial 'c' — of which there would appear to be some evidence in the form from 1302, and in one of the forms in Straff. — might have come about through the influence of the preceding 'ch', but this is by no means certain. It is indeed possible that the word which has been interpreted as 'chaoin' might represent some other word entirely — perhaps a personal name?

70)   TEMPLEMORE (B Gallen, 39), *An Teampall Mór* ('the big church').

The name does not appear to be attested prior to the 17th cent. when *Templemore* appears in an Inquisition dated 1625, while the BSD has the present anglicised form. The 'great church' in question was no doubt associated with the noted abbey, originally Franciscan but later Dominican, founded at Strade *(An tSráid)* in this parish some time before the mid-13th cent.

71)   TEMPLEMURRY (B Tirawley 9), *Teampall Muire* (Mary's church').

First attested, as *Tamplemurry,* in an Inquisition dated 1625; the present anglicised form appears in BSD.

72)   TOOMORE (B Gallen, 27), *Tuaim Mhór* ('big mound').

Rather poorly attested, *Thuamore* in Tax., 1302; *Towmore* in BSD; and *Tuaim Mór* and *Tuaim Mhór* in the Namebook as the forms in use among local Irish-speakers around 1838. The Ordnance Survey Letters, 1838, suggest yet another form — *Tuath Mór,* 'large country' (or tribe-land). John O'Donovan thought the name was represented by *Tuaim Da Bodar* in the Book of Lecan, c. 1400, and *Tuaim Da Bhodhar* and *Tuaim Dha Odhar* in Mac Fhirbhisigh's Book of Genealogies, c. 1650, but this is not altogether certain. There is nothing intrinsically improbable in the identification, but, unfortunately, the other names in the relevant passages from the Book of Lecan — which should help establish the general location of *Tuaim Da (B)odar* — are themselves more or less problematical as to identification and location. Besides, the more clearly and unambiguously attested forms of the parish-name (though admittedly rather scanty) do not seem to offer much corroboration for the suggestion that *Tuaim Dhá (Bh)odhar* was at one time the name used to designate this place.

73)   TOUAGHTY (B Carra, 13), *Tuath Aitheachta* ('tributary tribe, or tribe-land').

The form *Termehathyn* in Tax., 1302, if indeed it refers to this place, is extremely garbled. The name does not appear to be attested again until the early 17th cent. when *Towaghty* appears in an Inquisition dated 1616; *Towght* and *Towaght* in BSD, and *Toughta* in *Hiberniae Delineatio* ('Petty's Atlas'), 1685; *Tuath Eachta* in the Namebook as the form in use among Irish-speakers around 1838. The second element is somewhat uncertain, but the Irish form suggested by John O'Donovan, and adopted here, is quite plausible. There is a single annalistic reference, in the Annals of the Four Masters *sub anno* 938, to a people called the *Uí Aitheachda* who were no doubt identical to the *Tuath Aitheachta* who — we assume — gave their name to the parish.

74)   TURLOUGH (B Carra, 100), *Turlach* ('winter-lake').

Turlacha (probably genitive) in Pont. Hib., 1199; *Turlach* and *muinter Turlocha* in AConn, 1236; *Tirlagh* in Tax., 1302; *Torlach* in Visit., 1565; *Turlo* in Browne's Map 1584; *Torleigh, Torlagh* and *Turlagh* in CBC, 1585; *Turlaigh* (genitive) in part of Dubhaltach Mac Fhirbhisigh's Book of Genealogies written in 1664. (*Turlach* is of course a compound of *tur* + *loch* and means literally 'dry lake'.)

(Population, according to 1971 Census, given in brackets).

1)   BALLA (293), *Balla:* see parish-name, Section II, no. 9. Pop. *1841* 562; *1851* 389; *1871* 453; *1891* 429; *1911* 323.

*2)   BALLAGHADERREEN (1,121), *Bealach an Doirín,* ('the pass of the little oak-wood'). (* In Co. Roscommon since 1898.)

Bealach an dairín in Annals of Loch Cé, *sub anno* 1548; *Dirin alias Ballaghdirrin* in BSD. Pop. *1841* 1,341; *1851* 1,197; *1871* 1,496; *1891* 1,266; *1911* 1,317.

3)   BALLINA (6,063), *Béal an Átha* ('the mouth of the ford').

'Founded 1729 by O'Hara, Lord Tyrawley, originally named Belleek', Lewis's *Topographical Dictionary,* 1837.The name which later became the town-name occurs in various 17th-cent. sources: *Carowvellanaha* in an Inquisition dated 1617; *Bealeake alias Ballanahe* in BSD; *Ballina* in *Hib. Del.* 1685. *Bel atha in fhedha* (modern *Béal Átha an Fheá*) in a late (15th, or perhaps 16th, cent.) addition to the Book of Lecan may represent an earlier form of the name, but the absolutely identity of the place mentioned in the great Sligo manuscript with *Ballina/Béal an Átha* is not altogether certain. Pop. *1841* 5,313; *1851* 4,635 (+747 in workhouse); *1871* 4,307; *1891* 4,846; *1911* 4,662. (These figures are rendered somewhat unsatisfactory for purposes of comparison by periodic changes in the extent of the urban district — as in 1881, when Ardnaree and Bunree were incorporated in the U.D.)

4)   BALLINDINE (232), *Baile an Daighin* ('the town of the stronghold').

Ballindangin in an Inquisition dated 1609 and (in addition to *Ballendangen*) in BSD. The form *daighin,* instead of *daingin,* reflects the reduction of *ng* to *gh* which is a fairly general feature of northern dialects of Irish. Pop. *1841* 448; *1851* 191; *1871* 271; *1891* 222; *1911* 221.

5)   BALLINROBE (1,272), *Baile an Róba:* see par.-name, Sect. II, no. 11. Pop. *1841* 2,678; *1851* 2,161 (+2,301 in workhouse); *1871* 2,408; *1891* 1,852; *1911* 1,585.

6)   BALLYHAUNIS (1,093), *Béal Átha hAmhnais* ('ford-mouth of strife').

Bealahawnish is a Fiant dated 1586; *Bellahawnis* in Straff., 1635. The form *Bellahaunes,* as a name for the barony now known as Costello, is found in one of the State Papers dated 1570, and the form *Hanahannassa* found in a document in the Augustinian archives dating from 1432 may represent a particularly garbled version of the name. 'Beul Ath hAmhnuis' is the title of a song by the famous 18th-cent. vagabond poet, sometime Augustinian friar, sometime soldier in various Continental armies, Tomás Ó Caiside, better-known as 'An Caisideach Bán'. And the town-name appears in the name of another popular Irish love-song, 'Máire Bhéal Átha hAmhnais'. Pop. *1841* 353; *1851* 378; *1871* 542; *1891* 911; *1911* 1,149.

7) BELMULLET (744), *Beal an Mhuirthead* ('the mouth of the Mullet').

Although the town itself only dates from 1825, when it was founded by Major Bingham (who over the previous thirty years had built Bingham's Castle and founded Binghamstown), the name is attested, as *Ballimolitt, in Hiberniae Delineatio* ('Petty's Atlas'), 1685. The word *mullet* is English, but whether it refers to the fish of that name or to the five-pointed star called by that name in heraldry (and perhaps suggested by the shape of the peninsula?) is uncertain. The original name of the town in Irish was probably *Béal an Mhuileat,* a form that still survives to some extent. A change from 'l' to 'r', which is quite common in Irish (see *Shrule,* Section II, no. 68, above) may have given *Béal an Mhuireat* which in turn became *Béal an Mhuirthead.* Pop. *1841* 637; *1851* 935; (+400 in workhouse); *1871* 849; *1891* 652; *1911* 681.

8) CASTLEBAR (5,979), *Caisleán an Bharraigh* ('*de Barra*/Barry's castle').

Caslen an Barraig in AConn, 1412; *Caslanevarre* in a Fiant from the reign of Edward VI, 1553; *Castelbarra* in a Fiant dated 1585; *Castlebarr* in Straff., 1635. Pop. *1841* 5,137; *1851* 4027 (+1,584 in workhouse and 359 in gaol); *1871* 3,571; *1891* 3,588; *1911* 3,698.

9) CHARLESTOWN (529), *Baile Chathail* ('Charles's town').

The town was built at the time of the Great Famine (c. 1846) by Lord Dillon's agent, Charles Strickland. It borders the village of *Bellahy (Béal Lathaí,* 'a mouth or entrance to a muddy place') which lies in Co. Sligo. Originally named *Newtown Dillon,* the present name was appended in the 1860s — giving the official form *Charlestown or Newtown Dillon.* Whether the later name derived from the apparently popular Charles Strickland, as local tradition would have it (it seems he was that *rara avis,* a lenient and even benevolent land-agent), or from Charles Henry, 14th Viscount Dillon, who held the title from 1832 until his death in 1865, is not altogether clear. The Irish form of the name, given above, was that used by Irish-speakers in the locality from the end of the last century. Pop. *1841*----; *1851* 119; *1871* 709; *1891* 779; *1911* 669.

10) CLAREMORRIS (1,718) *Clár Chlainne Mhuiris* ('the plain of *Clann Mhuiris';* for the latter name see Section I, no. 3, above).

The form *Claremorris* does not seem to have appeared on a map until about 1868; the form on the first edition of the Ordnance Survey Map, 1839, and in a number of other sources from the late 18th and early 19th cents., is *Clare*; the latter form, which is the name of the townland which gave its name to the town, appears in Hib. Del., 1685, and also in the records of the sale of Forfeited Estates, 1703. There is some evidence, however, that — despite the general use of *Clare* as an abbreviated form of the name — the form *Claremorris* was regarded, from the 18th cent. at least, as the 'more correct' form of the name. The Irish form of the name occurs of course in Raftery's song 'Cill Liadáin'; a copy of the song in a manuscript dated 1835 has *Clárr Chloinne Muiris,* while the Namebook, 1838, has *Clár Chlann Muiris* and *Clár Chlann Muiris na mBrigh* (i.e. of *Brees,* or 'Brize'). Pop. *1841* 2,256; *1851* 1,562 (+500 in workhouse); *1871* 1,103; *1891* 1,259; *1911* 1,069.

11)   CONG (208), *Conga:* see parish-name, Sect. II, no. 24. Pop. *1841* 364; *1851* 519; *1871* 364; *1891* 227; *1911* 145.

12)   CROSSMOLINA (1,077), *Crois Mhaoilíona:* see par.-name, Sect. II, no. 26. Pop. *1841* 1,672; *1851* 1,225; *1871* 852; *1891* 662; *1911* 529.

13)   FOXFORD (868), *Béal Easa* ('mouth of (the) waterfall').

The earliest mention of Foxford appears to be that by Robert Downing in a survey of Co. Mayo for William Molyneux, c. 1682; he refers to 'a new plantation of English and Scots, and Iron works called now *Foxford olim Bellasea'.* John O'Donovan's assistant in the Ordnance Survey, Thomas O'Conor, was told locally in 1838 that the name derived from *Béal Átha Sionnaigh* ('the mouth of the ford of (the) fox') which in turn derived from 'a stone presenting to the eye a form apparently like that of a fox . . . near the eel-weir, in the river to the north of Foxford bridge', but O'Conor considered this a piece of folk etymology, specially invented to account for the name. *Foxford alias Carrownahine* appears in the records of the sale of Forfeited Estates, 1703. The Irish form of the name, *Béal Easa,* is attested in Straff., 1635, as *Bellasse* and *Bellassa,* and in the BSD, as *Ballasse alias Bellassa.* The name still survives, as *Bellass,* the name of a townland on the opposite bank of the Moy to Foxford — in the parish of Ballynahaglish. Pop. *1841* 680; *1851* 681; *1871* 540; *1891* 585; *1911* 621.

14)   KILKELLY (225), *Cill Cheallaigh* ('*Ceallach's* church').

This may be the *Cill Cellaigh* mentioned as the scene of a minor affray under the year 1224 in the Annals of Loch Cé; the incident is recounted again, in rather more detail, under the following year in the same annals, and also in AConn. If the identification is correct, however, it is somewhat strange that there appears to be no further mention of the place until *Killkelly Rd.* appears on maps of Ballaghaderreen and Swinford in Taylor and Skinner's *Maps of the Roads of Ireland,* 1778. The village itself appears, as *Killkelly,* on William Bald's Map of Co. Mayo, 1830. Pop. *1841* 142; *1851* 204; *1871* 259; *1891* 262; *1911* 208.

15)   KILLALA (368), *Cill Ala:* see parish-name, Section II, no. 43. Pop. *1841* 1,446; *1851* 970; (1,079 in workhouse) *1871* 654; *1891* 588; *1911* 503.

16)   KILTAMAGH (978), *Coillte Mach* (' (the) woods of ——?').

The earliest attestation appears to be as *Koillmagh* in an Inquisition dated 1617. *Cullenagh* and *Cullinagh* in BSD and *Hiberniae Delineatio,* 1685, respectively appear to be scribal, or engraver's, errors for *Cull(e)magh,* and this and the form *Cullemagh* in the Acts of Settlement and Explanation, 1684, suggest that the initial element may at that time have been in the singular — *Coill* rather than *Coillte*. However, Straff., 1635, has *Kiltemagh*. Bald's County Map, 1830, has *Kultamaugh or Newtown Browne*. The earliest manuscript copy of Raftery's song 'Cill Liadáin', dating from 1835, has 'go *Coillti Mach* rachfad', while the Ordnance Survey Namebook gives *Coillte amach* as the form in use among local Irish-speakers, and suggests the meaning 'out-woods'. While the form *Coillte Amach* can immediately be discounted as impossible, it and the other Irish form mentioned tend to support the evidence from the 17th-cent. forms, and from present-day speech, that the 'a' in the second element is short. This conflicts with the form *Coillte Mághach* which gained some currency as a result of its use by Douglas Hyde in his edition of Raftery's poems and songs, 1903. Hyde was no doubt influenced by the well-known Old Irish tale of Mac-Dathó's pig in which one of the principal characters is the Connacht hero *Cet mac Mágach* – *Mága* (or *Mágu*) is said to have been his mother's name. If we turn to the early Irish genealogies, however, we find *Mágu* to have been a rare *male* personal name, but we also find in the same source that the mother of *Cett* and his six brothers was named not *Mágu* but *Máta* (or *Máta Muirisci,* 'M. of Murrisk'). Whatever the second element in *Coillte Mach* represents, it is most unlikely to be the name of Cett's mother! One possiblility is that it was originally the word *macha,* 'a milking enclosure', or, perhaps, 'a field , a plain' (similar to *machaire*), and that the final syllable had been lost by the time of its first attestation in 1617. (This would be similar to what happened in the case of *Ard Mhacha/Armagh,* where the second element is identical to that which has been suggested as underlying *Coillte Mach* — although *Macha* in the case of Armagh is said to have been a personal name.) In support of the suggestion that Coillte Mach may in fact represent Coillte Macha, 'woods of (the) milking place', we may cite that N.E. of the town is the rather similarly named townland called Cuiltybo — Coillte Bó, 'woods of (the) cows'. Pop. *1841* 650; *1851* 658; *1871* 907; *1891* 921; *1911* 1,019.

17) LOUISBURGH (310), *Cluain Cearbán* ('the meadow of (the) buttercups').

The village is named from one Louisa Browne, a sister of the man who founded the place in the 18th cent. The name *Louisburg* appears in a document in the Public Records Office dated 1796. The Irish name appears in Straff., 1635, as *Clooncarbane;* it still survives as that of the townland of *Clooncarrabaun. Pop. 1841* 448; *1851* 403; *1871* 549; *1891* 400; *1911* 375.

18) NEWPORT (420), *Baile Uí Fhiacháin* ('the town of *Ó Fiacháin*').

Called *Newport-Pratt* in William Seward's *Topographia Hibernica,* 1795 — from the former Treasury official named Pratt who founded the town early in the 18th cent. The older form of the Irish name was *Baile Ó bhFiacháin* ('the town of the *Uí Fhiacháin*'), which appears in the *Senchus Búrcach,* c. 1578, and in anglicised form, as *Ballyovighan,* in the Calendar

81

of Ormond Deeds, 1576, as *Ballyveaghane* in CBC, 1585, and in Straff., 1635. In latterday Irish speech, in the Gaeltacht and Breac-Ghaeltacht areas of Achill and around Ballycroy, the form *Baile Ó bhFiacháin* has become corrupted to the nonsensical *Baile Uí bhFiacháin,* and also to *Bail' Fhiacháin* which represents a much more common structure in Irish placenames, namely *Baile* (or some such element) plus the genitive singular of a surname — thus *Baile Uí Fhiacháin* which has been recommended as the official Irish form. Pop. *1841* 1,091; *1851* 984 (+1,035 in workhouse); *1871* 851; *1891* 598; *1911* 467.

19) SHRULE (288), *Sruthair:* see parish-name, Section II, no. 68. Pop. *1841* 729; *1851* 590; *1871* 330; *1891* 246; *1911* 205.

20) SWINEFORD (1,105), *Béal Átha na Muice* ('the ford-mouth of the pig').

What appears to be the earliest attestation of the name, as *Swinford* — which is still the more commonly-used form — occurs in Taylor and Skinner's *Maps of the Roads of Ireland,* 1778. Despite the very satisfactory Irish form, which was recorded in the Namebook as being in use among Irish-speakers around 1838, the name is originally English. The town was built in the latter part of the 18th cent. by the Brabazons who had received land in the barony of Gallen at the time of the Cromwellian settlement. The family had come originally from Leicestershire where, near one of the family seats, is a village called Swinford, and it seems more than likely that it was this which inspired the naming of their new town in the parish of Kilconduff. That some already-existing local name such as *Áth na Muice,* or *Cloch (na) Muice* — for which there is some slight evidence — may have helped suggest the name is a distinct possibility, but there is no clear indication that this was in fact the case. Pop. *1841* 1,016; *1851* 991 (+942 in workhouse); *1871* 1,366 (including workhouse); *1891* 1,473; *1911* 1,302.

21) WESTPORT (3,023), *Cathair na Mart* ('the stone fort of the beeves').
The town (designed by James Wyatt) and its English name date from around 1780, but the Irish name is attested a good two centuries earlier, for example, as *Cathair na mart,* in the Annals of the Four Masters, sub anno 1583, as *Cahernamart* in a letter from Sir Richard Bingham, 1592, and as *Cahernamarte* in Straff., 1635; the name is also still represented by the townland of *Cahernamart,* which was the site of an O'Malley castle in the 16th cent. Pop. *1841* 4,365; *1851* 4,121 (+2,991 in workhouse); *1871* 4,378 (including workhouse, etc.); *1891* 4,070; *1911* 3,674.

OTHER MAYO VILLAGES

BALLYCASTLE *Baile an Chaisil.* Pop. *1841* 798; *1851* 372; *1871* 372; *1891* 311; *1911* 299.

HOLLYMOUNT— *Maolla.* Pop. *1841* 454; *1851* 431; *1871* 278; *1891* 249; *1911* 152.

KILMAINE *Cill Mheáin.* Pop. *1841* 421; *1851* 331; *1871* 214; *1891* 162; *1911* 118.

NEALE *An Éill.* Pop. *1841* 196; *1851* 151; *1871* 130; *1891* 89; *1911*--.

Footnote: (I am grateful to my superiors who have kindly permitted me to make use of material from the archives of the Placenames Office and of the Ordnance Survey in preparing these notes. I am also thankful to my colleagues in the Placenames Office and in the Archaeological Branch of the Ordnance Survey for their comments and suggestions when I was working on this article and on the 'Outline History of Mayo'.)

THE PRINCIPAL SURNAMES OF MAYO
by *Nollaig Ó Muraíle*

The figures after each name denote the number of entries under that surname in the births index of 1890; the first figure in each case refers to County Mayo, the second to Connacht (C) and the third to Ireland (I) as a whole. Anglicised names in italics are of Norman origin. (MacHale, however, appears to represent both Gaelic *Mac Céile* and Welsh *Hywel* or *Howell*). Note that some anglicised forms may have a number of variants (e.g. Burke/Bourke, Connor/O'Connor, etc.), and that a number of quite distinct Gaelic surnames may be represented by a single anglicised form (e.g. Conway).

    Walsh – Breathnach 134 (out of 249 in C. and 932 in I.).
    Gallagher — *Ó Gallchóir* 92 (144 in C.; 488 in I.).
    Kelly — *Ó Ceallaigh* 89 (329 in C.; 1,242 in I.).
    Malley/O'Malley — *Ó Máille* 78 (96 in C.; 115 in I.).
 5 Moran — *Ó Móráin* 77 (132 in C.; 265 in I.).
    Duffy — *Ó Dufaigh* 55 (95 in C.; 305 in I.).
    McHale — *Mac Héil* 50 (50 in C.; 51 in I.).
    Gibbons – Mac Giobúin 47 (57 in C.; 78 in I.).
    Joyce – Seoigh(e) 46 (131 in C.; 164 in I.).
10 Connor/O'Connor — *Ó Conchúir* 45 (121 in C.; 698 in I.).
    Conway — *Ó Conbhuidhe, Ó Connmhacháin, Ó Connmhaigh* 40 (58 in C.;169 in I.).
    Higgins — *Ó hUiginn* 39 (105 in C.; 205 in I.).
    Murphy — *Ó Murchú* 39 (110 in C.; 1,386 in I.).
    Burke/Bourke - de Búrca 36 (174 in C.; 397 in I.).
15 Reilly/O'Reilly — *Ó Raghailligh* 36 (85 in C.; 648 in I.).
    Durkan — *Mac Duarcáin, Ó Duarcáin* 35 (58 in C.; 62 in I.).
    Doherty — *Ó Dochartaigh* 34 (58 in C.; 457 in I.).
    McHugh — *Mac Aodha* 34 (81 in C.; 176 in I.).
    Sweeney — *Mac Suibhne* 33 (73 in C.; 254 in I.).
20 Lyons — *Ó Laighin* 32 (71 in C.; 210 in I.).

(The above list is based, in part, on Sir Robert E. Matheson, *Special report on surnames in Ireland* (Dublin 1909), p. 34.)

ULSTER MIGRATION TO MAYO
1795 - 1796

by Desmond O'Neill

"Go to Hell, Connacht will not receive you;
Fire and Faggot (Signed) Will Thresham and John Thrustout".

That threat, or "notice to get out", was well known to Catholics in north Co. Armagh after the infamous "Battle of the Diamond", fought at a crossroads half-way between Loughgall and Portadown, on 21 September 1795. That battle was the culmination of a thirty year period of increasing economic rivalry in the flax and linen business, but it was not the end of the "war", between Catholics and Protestants. Flax growing and weaving were introduced about the year 1740. The export value of linen, and its products, was such that, about 1800, it far exceeded the combined export value of all other Irish-farm products. Catholics, like their Protestant neighbours, had benefited from the boom, but many forces were not satisfied! There was a chronic shortage of land and housing available for leasing. Catholics were in a minority in many areas, and their property was the focus of attack, mostly at night, by gangs of armed Protestants. Local landlords and magistrates, with the tacit support of the authorities in Dublin, turned a blind eye to the growing depredation. These gangs organised themselves into a special society called "Peep-o-Day Boys". The raids became more systematic, and Catholics fled the growing danger in greater numbers, but not before uniting themselves into a secret defensive organisation — "The Defenders". Jimmy Hope, who was a United Irish organiser among Ulster refugees in Connacht, and a sufferer at the hands of the Peep-o-Day Boys, stated that he heard the Peep-o-Day men boasting of "the indulgence they got from magistrates for wrecking and beating Papists, and the snug bits of land that their friends got when the Papists fled to Connacht, and the fun they had in committing depredations". Catholics, or "Papists", as the Protestants contemptuously called them, were not allowed to have arms. Protestants, on the other hand, could bear arms, and they certainly used them against Papists with impunity. The Irish Volunteers, in the Armagh town area, with their boast, "Ireland Awoke, Dungannon Spoke, with fear was England shaken", were soon to dash the hopes of peace and security of Catholics. On Mid-Summer Eve, 1789, a Volunteer company, led by John Moore of Drumbanagher, shot down harmless boys making merry around the traditional bonfire. A serious outbreak of violence, between the Peep-o-Day Boys and the Defenders, was inevitable. Challenges and counter-challenges, insults and

84

counter-insults, jibes and jeers, beatings and murders were commonplace. Some efforts were made to resolve differences but they did not succeed.

THE BATTLE OF THE DIAMOND

The first explosion occurred after an anti-Papist sermon by Rector George Mansell, in Portadown Episcopalian Church on 12 July 1795, from which the congregation emerged seeking to chastise every Papist on their journey home. Apart from houses being wrecked, and people seriously beaten, two Catholics engaged in cutting turf were beaten to death. Challenges for a musketry battle between the two parties were common knowledge, and certainly gossip among militia-men stationed in Dublin and Westport. It seems incredible that the Government was unaware that preparations for such a fight were being made. The Defenders took up positions on a hill at the Diamond crossroads in the heart of a largely Protestant area, on Thursday 17 September 1795. The Peep-o-Day Boys did likewise on another hill nearby. A force of indifferently-armed Defenders, numbering about 300 men, faced a lesser number of Peep-o-Day Boys, who were better led and armed with Volunteer muskets, supplemented by contributions from local squires. Sporadic fire took place on Saturday 19th; Sunday was quiet. On Monday morning heavy musket fire began; the Defenders attacked on foot against entrenched Peep-o-Day Boys. Poor leadership and ineffective arms resulted in at least 30 Defenders being killed, and victory going to the Protestants, who reputedly suffered no losses. The outcome of the Diamond fight was professed by the victors to be "a godly conquest, construed as a sanction for spoliation of the homes of the Philistines", first in the vicinity of the fight, and then in the other Ulster counties. On the evening of the fight, the "Peep-o-Day Boys", who wore orange cockades on their hats, changed their society's name to "Orangemen".

For the Catholics, the situation was indeed grim:

"Their jails they are filled with your nearest relations,
Your wives and your children are sorely oppressed;
Your houses are burned, your lands desolated,
By a band of ruffians with orange cockades".

The inactivity of the magistrates was likewise recorded:

"The clergy and landlords they have oppressed you,
Because that poor Ireland they wished to keep slaves;
They bribed your own neighbours to ruin your labours,
Says they you are Papists, and so must be knaves".

After the Battle of the Diamond, the newly-named "Orangemen", in mobs as large as 300 men, wrecked havoc on Catholic families. The anguish of fathers and mothers awaiting the mob, which at any time was likely to burst into their homes, was impossible to bear. It was easier, safer and wiser to sell one's possessions and leave. An estimated 20,000 refugees went to Scotland, 5,000 to America, 1,000 to Co. Galway and 4,000 to County Mayo.

MAYO

The "Northerns" who came to Mayo were an economic boom to the landlords, but were also looked upon as a potential political threat. Most newcomers from the northern counties had "recommendations of behaviour", which they presented to their new landlords. Ulster refugees were "noted" as far as possible upon their arrival in Mayo; most zealous in keeping records of "northerners" were landlord and magistrate Denis Browne and his brother, Earl Altamont, Westport House, and James Cuffe Esq., Deel Castle, Crossmolina. The Earl of Moira "noted" tenants who vacated his estates in Co. Down on a townland basis. Those who left the parish of Tullylish, Co. Down, on 19 October 1796 were "noted" by James Cuffe on 22 December 1796 in the Ballina and Foxford areas.

James Cuffe stated that most of his refugees were weavers. The same was true for settlers in other parts of Mayo. Castlebar, Westport, Ballaghaderreen and Newport had thriving linen industries. There were few houses in the Louisburgh area that did not have one or two looms. The Castlebar linen industry had a turnover of £500 weekly, and Newry Market was supplied with woven woollens from Connacht. Thomas Reid of Eglish, Clonfeakle, on his way through Westport in 1822 found "a smart linen market attended chiefly by emigrants from the County Armagh", *(Travels in Ireland in 1822)*. Northern refugees settled all around Mayo, especially in the Aughagower, Ballina, Castlebar, Crossmolina, Foxford, Louisburgh, Newport and Westport areas. Many descendants of those families are happily with us in Mayo today, while others have emigrated. The names of most of the refugees who came to Mayo during that period, and the townlands and parishes they left, can be found in the State Paper Office, Dublin Castle. Tables 1 and 2 shows two such lists.

Northern refugees continued to settle in Mayo until 1822. It is hoped that these lists will encourage interested Mayo families, with North of Ireland origin, to conduct research and trace their family trees.

Table 1　"Northerns" who settled in **Crossmolina and its Environs**

Settlers' Name	Total No. in Household	Diocese	Parish	Townland	County
			From		
Gettings, Hugh	x	Dromore	Aghaderg	Aghaderg	Down
Hendrick, Jas.	x	Dromore	Aghaderg	Aghaderg	Down
McDeatt, Jn.	x	Dromore	Aghaderg	Drummiller	Down
O'Neill, Jn.	x	Dromore	Aghaderg	Drummiller	Down
O'Neill, Hy.	x	Dromore	Aghaderg	Drummiller	Down
Fall, Samuel	x	Dromore	x	Drumlark	Armagh
Toal, Chas.	x	Dromore	Seagoe	Silverwood	Armagh
Tool, Chas. Jn.	x	Dromore	Seagoe	Silverwood	Armagh
Tool, Fras.	x	Dromore	Seagoe	Silverwood	Armagh
Tool, Wm.	x	Dromore	Seagoe	Silverwood	Armagh
Quin, Fras.	x	Armagh	Kilmore	Brackagh	Armagh
McDonnell, Myles	x	Armagh	Loughgall	Annaghmore	Armagh
Kain, Jn.	x	Clogher	Clogher	Bolies	Tyrone
Mynah, Robert	x	Clogher	Clogher	Bolies	Tyrone
McQuort, Jas.	x	Clogher	Clogher	Bolies	Tyrone
Rafferty, Jas.	x	Clogher	Clogher	Bolies	Tyrone

Table 2   "Northerns" who settled in **Foxford and its Environs**

Settlers' Name	Total No. in Household	Diocese	From Parish	Townland	County
McConvill, Chas.	5	Dromore	Tullylish	Ballydugan	Down
McConvill, Paul	8	Dromore	Tullylish	Ballydugan	Down
Devlin, Jn.	9	Dromore	Seagoe	"Balimanas"	Armagh
Cunningham, Thos.	4	Dromore	Seagoe	Edenderry	Armagh
Ryans, Ned.	9	Dromore	Seagoe	Edenderry	Armagh
McConville, Jn.	5	Dromore	Seagoe	"Hacknahay"	Armagh
McConvill, Jn.	6	Dromore	Seagoe	x	Armagh
McCan, Chas.	x	Dromore	Seagoe	Lurgan	Armagh
Whitelock, Ed.	x	Armagh	Kilmore	x	Armagh
Fox, Jas.	8	Armagh	Killyman	Derrycorry	Armagh
McCann, Pat.	4	Armagh	Killyman	Derrycorry	Armagh
McNeas, Fras.	5	Armagh	Tartaraghan	x	Armagh
McNeas, Hy.	5	Armagh	Tartaraghan	x	Armagh
McNeas, Jn.	3	Armagh	Tartaraghan	x	Armagh
McNeas, Patt.	7	Armagh	Tartaraghan	x	Armagh
Brannagan, Jn.	9	Armagh	Tynan	"Nall"	Armagh
Brannagan, Pat.	8	Armagh	Tynan	Drum	Armagh
Smith, Wm.	5	Clogher	Ballyscullion	Leitrim	L'Derry
Togher, Phil.	x	Dromore	Tyllylish	Ballydugan	Down

SOURCES

1.   Patrick Tohall "The Diamond Fight of 1795 and the Resultant Expulsions" in "Seanchas Ardmhacha" Vol. 3 No. 1. 1958.

2. Patrick Hogan "The Migration of Ulster Catholics to Connaught 1795-'96" in "Seanchas Ardmhacha" Vol. 9 No. 2. 1979.

3.   W. E. H. Lecky *The History of Ireland in the Eighteenth Century"*.

4.   Keeper of State Papers, State Paper Office, Dublin Castle. State Paper Office Sources S.O.C.   3046/3,   12/9/1796.   S.O.C.   1015/21,   27/6/1796.   620/26/145,   22/12/1796. 620/26/183, Dec. 1796.

"THE YEAR OF THE FRENCH"

by Gabriel Colleran

The publication of Thomas Flanagan's epic novel "The Year of the French", in 1979, has focussed attention on County Mayo, and the activities which took place there after the French landed at Kilcummin Strand on 22 August 1798.

The influence of the French Revolution (1789-1795) spread around Europe, undermining the positions of the rulers of many states and challenging feudalism and absolutism everywhere. In 1792 the National Assembly of Paris pledged the help of the French nation to all people seeking liberty. Theobold Wolfe Tone (1763-1798) went to France in search of French help for Ireland. His efforts were rewarded and, in December 1796, 15,000 men under General Hoche sailed for Bantry Bay, but the fleet was scattered by storms and returned to France. After the May 1798 rising in Ireland, Wolfe Tone again pleaded with the French authorities for assistance. The French Directory decided to help. An expedition of 1,100 men under General Humbert left La Rochelle on 6 August 1798 for Ireland with a supply of ammunition and 1,000 uniforms for Irish recruits. There were four Irishmen on the expedition: Bartholomew Teeling, an officer in the French army, who was made aide-de-camp to General Humbert, Fr. Henry O'Kane, a native of the Killala area who was made official interpreter, Matthew Tone, brother of Wolfe Tone, and a man named O'Sullivan. General Humbert got strict instructions that his soldiers were to uphold the highest standards of discipline. Other expeditions were planned, but only one other sailed for Ireland, the one which arrived in Lough Swilly in September of that year and was captured by the British. As a result, General Humbert went on an impossible mission, and a high price was paid, in places like Mayo, for that folly. On 22 August 1798 three large white ships, the Concorde, the Franchise, and the Medeé, sailed into Killala Bay with English colours flying from the mast heads. The Protestant Bishop of Killala at that time was Dr. James Stock. His two sons, Edwin and Arthur, rowed out to welcome their visitors and invite the officers to their father's house. They were taken into custody, and the three ships finally halted in Kilcummin Bay, about eight kilometres north of Killala. The English flags were quickly hauled down.

KILLALA

As soon as the French soldiers began to disembark the local people went out to meet them with open arms. One of the first to disembark was Fr. Henry O'Kane, the priest from Killala. He spoke to the local people in

Irish, the majority of whom had very little English at that time. The disembarkation was completed by about 7 p.m. General Sarrazin, the second in command, set out for Killala with Captain Fr. Henry O'Kane at the head of three hundred men. He addressed the people who met them, along the route, in Irish. On the outskirts of the town, approximately eighty yeomen and regulars were drawn up to oppose the advance of the French. They were greatly outnumbered and retreated when the French came into view. Captain O'Kane went to Killala on horseback to survey the town. He was fired on by an English detachment from a side street. He was not hit, and drove into the market place, where he was challenged by a yeoman. Captain O'Kane drew his pistol and shot the yeoman dead.

Sarrazin and his men arrived in Killala and were met with a volley from the enemy, to which they did not reply. Instead they charged with their bayonets. The yeomen fled in disorder, some into the castle, and the remainder out the road towards Ballina. The French soldiers followed the former to the castle, where they surrendered to the French and were made prisoners. General Humbert, who had joined Sarrazin on the outskirts of Killala, accompanied by his aide-de-camp Bartholomew Teeling and his staff officers, went forward and spoke to Bishop Stock, whose residence was then made the headquarters of General Humbert. This quick encounter left the town of Killala completely in the hands of the French. On the evening of 22 August a French soldier climbed to the top of the episcopal palace and lowered the English flag. It was replaced by a green and gold flag, bearing the words "Erin-Go-Bragh", to the cheers of local

The French Landing in Killala Bay: painting by William Sadler II.
(National Gallery of Ireland)

89

people. One French soldier was injured and two English killed that day. The Protestant Rector of Castlebar, who was in Killala for a visit to Bishop Stock, was also injured. The arrival of the French at Killala caused panic among the English and their supporters. It was rumoured that several landings had taken place in different parts of the country. It was even reported that Bonaparte himself had arrived. The English military commander of Mayo sent a dispatch to Lord Castlereagh in Dublin Castle. The local Irish leaders sent messages for help throughout counties Mayo and Sligo. The most important of those who answered the call was Colonel Matthew Bellew, a former officer in the Austrian army and a brother of the Catholic Bishop of Killala. He was appointed general of the insurgent auxiliaries. Many priests arrived with recruits from their parishes, including Fr. David Kelly, Ballycroy, Fr. James Conroy, Addergoole, Fr. Monnelly, Backs, and Fr. Owen Cowley. Local leaders were given army commissions and placed in charge of groups of recruits.

BALLINA

General Humbert sent General Sarrazin, with fifty men, to Ballina. He found Ballina well protected and returned to Killala. The British garrison in Ballina believed that the French had returned in panic and followed them. General Humbert and his dragoons met the challenge near Moyne friary, and the British retreated. That evening two French/Irish groups, led by General Sarrazin and General Fontaine, set out from Killala with the intention of capturing Ballina in a surprise night attack. On their journey they came unexpectedly upon a four hundred enemy patrol, who broke and fled after slight resistance. Later that same night the entire garrison from Ballina began a further advance on Killala. They were challenged by General Sarrazin at Rosserk friary, where both sides fought bravely, but the second Irish/French group, under General Fontaine, moved in behind the English forces, and poured an unexpected volley into their ranks. Believing that they were being attacked by a different group the British fled back to Ballina in utter confusion. The French/Irish troops waited until morning and then marched unopposed into Ballina. The British forces had received such a shock the previous night that they fled from Ballina to Foxford. Before the French/Irish entered Ballina that morning, they sent a small advance party under cover of darkness by the old Rosserk road to ensure the safety of the troops. The people in the row of cottages outside Ballina heard the French galloping past and lit small amounts of straw to show them the way. This road has been known since as Bóthar-na-Sop. On entering Ballina the French/Irish soldiers saw the body of Patrick Walsh, a native of the Crossmolina area, who was given a commission in Killala the previous day and went to Ballina to prepare for the arrival of the French. He was arrested, shortly after entering the town, and hanged. General Humbert joined Sarrazin at Ballina the following day, and received a tumultuous reception. There was a colony of Ulster weavers in Ballina at that time, 500 of whom joined the insurrection, and were put under the command of Captain Bartholomew Teeling. Shortly afterwards other groups of volunteers arrived in Ballina. General Blake replaced Colonel Matthew Bellew as chief in command of the auxiliary forces, due to the poor state of Bellew's health.

CASTLEBAR

General Humbert decided to attack the British garrison at Castlebar. Fr. James Conroy of Addergoole, a fluent French speaker, got an interview with Humbert, and persuaded him to attack Castlebar by the Crossmolina road, instead of the Foxford road. There was a strong force of British troops in Foxford. General Humbert left Ballina on 26 August for Castlebar with a force of about 700 French soldiers and an equal number of Irish auxiliaries. In order to deceive the British spies, Humbert led his army towards Foxford for a few kilometres, and then turned westward via Crossmolina. The British supporters at Ballina were informed. They sent word at once to their counterparts at Castlebar. The job was given to a local Catholic, Lieutenant William Burke, who was a member of the British Forces. On his journey through Lahardaun he met Fr. Conroy, who persuaded him not to deliver the message. Fr. Conroy and Lieutenant Burke were to pay for this incident later with their lives. When Humbert's Irish/French soldiers reached Lahardaun about midnight, they were supplied with bread, milk and chicken. They then continued on their march over Barnageeha and on to Castlebar. At that time, the province of Connacht was under the command of General Hutchinson. He was based in Galway, but had moved to Castlebar on Saturday 25 August. He immediately surveyed the area from the Foxford direction and chose a hill from which to attack the enemy. General Trench, with two hundred horsemen, was sent on a reconnoitring mission by General Hutchinson early the following morning. General Trench had only reached Mount Burren when he saw the advance-guard of Humbert's army approaching. Captain Mangan was riding at the head of the Irish/French army and his men fired at Trench's troops. Trench retreated quickly to Castlebar and prepared for an encounter. The British force under General Lake took up position on Sion Hill, just north of Castlebar.

"THE RACES OF CASTLEBAR"

Humbert decided to attack the enemy and divided his forces into five groups under Colonel Defour, General Blake, General Sarrazin and Colonel Ardouin. The battle for Castlebar started on Monday morning 27 August in the area between Tucker's Lake and Rathbawn Lake. The French/Irish at one stage drove a herd of cattle in front of them, but the cattle became frightened and retreated causing some confusion. The French/Irish made an effective bayonet charge through the centre and caused panic in the British ranks. There were many casualties on both sides at Sion Hill. The English retreated towards the town of Castlebar and most of them ran away towards Tuam. There was some bitter fighting at various

91

places in and around Castlebar. A squadron of French cavalry under Fontaine attacked an English group at the bridge in Castlebar. Many defenders jumped into the river to escape capture. While this was happening a small group of Ardouin's men had reached the western side of the town unobserved, where they placed themselves in a commanding position to fire on the remaining defenders at a critical time. This they did, which coincided with Fontaine's cavalry charge, and the capture of Castlebar was complete, with the French/Irish troops in possession. Most of the British forces ran away towards Tuam and Athlone. Some were captured and imprisoned. The event has since been known as "The Races of Castlebar". It is believed that the British lost four hundred soldiers, and the French one hundred and eighty. There was no roll-call for the Irish, but as they were involved mainly in the front lines and were exceptionally brave, we can assume that their losses were very heavy. In order to save further bloodshed, Humbert sent his aide-de-camp, Teeling, with a small escort and a flag of truce to General Lake, offering him honourable terms on capitulation. Teeling overtook the British rearguard about five kilometres outside the town. Lord Roden was in charge of them, and one of his men suddenly fired on the flag, killed one of the escort and captured Teeling. Teeling demanded an interview with General Lake, which was eventually given. The tone of Humbert's proposal made Lake very angry. He said to Teeling: "You Sir are an Irishman, I shall treat you as a rebel", but Teeling replied that British officers were still prisoners at Castlebar. Shortly afterwards Hutchinson came and apologised for the shooting, and asked that there be no reprisals. Teeling's flag was restored to him, and late that evening he arrived back to Humbert in Castlebar. It took great persuasion by Teeling to stop Humbert from killing British officers as a reprisal. A municipal council was appointed in Castlebar to keep order, and John Moore of Moore Hall was appointed President of the Provisional Republic of Connacht on 31 August.

Some men from west Mayo joined the French in Castlebar. Humbert decided to wait for expected French assistance before going further. His intention was to travel north, secure assistance and attack Dublin from that end. On 3 September news reached Humbert that Lord Cornwallis was within a day's march of the town with a large army. Humbert realised that he had made a mistake in not following the enemy. He called a meeting with his officers, where it was decided to set out at once towards Sligo, with the intention of travelling through Counties Leitrim and Longford, where he was promised recruits. On 3 September General Humbert marched out of Castlebar for Dublin. He left behind one hundred wounded men, a few French officers, and a detachment of insurgents to maintain order. A number of prisoners, including the local parson, Rev. Ellison, were set free. Rev. Ellison informed Colonel Crawford, who had a reconnoitring party at Partry, about the French evacuation. Colonel Crawford and his men went to Castlebar without delay, and placed John Moore and the French officers under arrest.

BALLINAMUCK

Humbert and his men travelled forty kilometres to Bellaghy, where they received information that General Lake was at Ballaghaderreen with 16,000 men. The English Commander at Sligo sent a regiment to Tobercurry under the charge of Captain O'Hara. On entering the village they shot a man named McGuire for wearing a green neck-cloth. When Humbert's advance guard reached Tobercurry they were attacked by O'Hara's regiment, and a stiff encounter took place. Three British soldiers were killed and a number taken prisoner. The remainder fled back to Sligo. Shortly after this encounter, Humbert was joined by insurgents from Ballina, under Captain O'Dowd.

On the morning of 5 September, as Humbert's men were having breakfast after passing through Collooney, they were attacked by Colonel Vereker and men of the Limerick militia. Humbert divided his forces in two, and sent one group to surround Vereker's forces while the other was to advance slowly. This they did, but one cannon, manned by an English gunner named Whittier, inflicted heavy casualties on the insurgents. Teeling suddenly galloped out from the French ranks, pulled up beside the cannon and shot Whittier dead. The Limerick militia then retreated in disorder to Sligo and gave a victory to Humbert. Humbert turned towards Dromahair, in the hope of recruiting the United Irishmen in the counties of Longford and Westmeath. When General Humbert and his men were resting in Drumkeeran, an English officer, Colonel Crawford, demanded to see him. Humbert sent Sarrazin to meet the Colonel who stated: "Lord Cornwallis recognises your worth and will treat you with all the honour due to brave men, if you will place your trust in him". Sarrazin replied: "we cannot, without dishonouring ourselves, accept his proposals".

On 7 September Humbert crossed the Shannon, something Cornwallis had hoped to prevent. He was soon overtaken by Colonel Crawford's cavalry and a fierce engagement took place. Crawford retreated after losing many of his men. General Humbert marched to Ballinamuck, Co. Longford, where he was attacked by a force under General Lake and Lord Cornwallis. Humbert surrendered easily. He and a small group of French soldiers were treated as prisoners of war, with full honour, while about 500 Irish insurgents were slaughtered on the hillside of Shanmullagh. Those who escaped were soon re-captured, and slaughtered.

SLAUGHTER IN MAYO

On hearing of the surrender at Ballinamuck, the insurgent troops at Ballina and Killala decided to continue the fight. On 11 September, Colonel Patrick Barrett and Captain Henry O'Kane set out with six hundred men from Killala to retake Castlebar, on the same road that Humbert had previously travelled. When they reached the outskirts of Castlebar, they met stiff resistance from a British garrison. After some fierce fighting, Captain O'Kane was able to enter the town from the northern end when the defenders on that side retreated before him. Fighting continued in the town until mid-day. When the Irish officers realised that they could not retake the town, they retreated to Ballina. A number of the insurgents, who had been imprisoned in Castlebar, were ill-treated, and some put to death. This caused resentment among the Irish troops at Killala, and it was suggested that a number of English Loyalists should be imprisoned as a retaliatory measure. The proposal did not succeed, as the cunning Protestant Bishop of Killala, Dr. Stock, suggested that two representatives, one representing the Protestants and the other the Catholics, should be sent under a flag of truce to the British commander at Castlebar. The Catholic representative, Roger McGuire, was taken prisoner for a while, and the other representative made secret arrangements with the British for the final assault on Killala. The two then returned to Killala with a letter, from the British officer General Trench, promising that the prisoners would be treated "with all possible tenderness and humanity".

General Trench immediately decided to surround Killala, by sending troops under Lord Portarlington from Sligo to Killala via Ballina. Portarlington left Sligo on Friday 21 September with 1,000 men. On 22 September Colonel Patrick Barrett and Captain Henry O'Kane, with a battalion of pikemen, left Ballina to challenge Portarlington's advance. They met and fought at Scurmore, but were forced to retreat. Not far from Scurmore is the village of Carrowcarden, which at that time was almost entirely Protestant and Loyalist, but a local Irish officer, McDonagh, had earlier ordered a number of local residents to fall in behind his small band of insurgents. They did through fear, but when the retreat began, these men ran back to their houses in Carrowcarden. They were followed by Portarlington's soldiers and many were slaughtered. Portarlington's forces entered Ballina unopposed, as Captain O'Kane and his men had left earlier for Killala. General Trench left Castlebar for Killala. As Portarlington advanced from Ballina towards Killala, his troops plundered and burnt farmhouses on the way, leaving nothing but misery and destruction behind them.

Killala was taken by General Trench on Sunday 23 September, during which day three hundred lost their lives. Some were slaughtered on the streets of Killala, and the rest were drowned in the Owenmore river. The latter group fled from Killala towards Palmerstown, but the bridge was held by British troops. The fugitives then ran towards Rathfran, with bullets whistling by them, but on arrival at the Owenmore river plunged into a full tide and were drowned. Any survivor was soon slaughtered. In Killala the last days of September 1798 were days of bloodshed as insurgents were captured and massacred. Isolated incidents took place for some time around Mayo, but they were quickly crushed and the participants massacred. The aftermath in Mayo was a "reign of terror," with arrests of suspected rebels, trials, and executions. It has been estimated that approximately six hundred people were killed in Mayo in the weeks following the defeat of the French/Irish at Ballinamuck. Humbert returned to France and later went to Mexico, where he was killed in a rebellion against the Spaniards. "The Year of the French" left a legacy of human suffering and bitterness in Mayo, which took years to forget.

SOURCES

1. *The Last Invasion of Ireland* by Richard Hayes.
2. *The Year of Liberty* by Thomas Pakenham.
3. Rev. Fr. E. Mac Hale P.P. Killala.

MAYO ELECTIONS 1801 — 1982

by Bernard O'Hara

There were fifty two general elections and sixteen by-elections in County Mayo during the period 1801-1982. Under the Act of Union, Ireland became part of the United Kingdom with effect from 1 January 1801. The two Mayo members of the Irish parliament in 1800, the Rt. Hon. Denis Browne and George Jackson, transferred to the British House of Commons in 1801, under the terms of the union agreement. There was no general election in 1801. All members of parliament from Mayo sat in the House of Commons from 1801 to 1918.

Mayo elected four Sinn Féin members of parliament in the 1918 general election, Dr. John Crowley, Joseph McBride, Éamon De Valéra and William Smears. They and sixty nine other Sinn Féin members of parliament refused to go to Westminister, and established a parliament in Dublin on 21 January 1919, the First Dáil as it came to be called. After the Anglo-Irish Treaty, which was signed in London on 6 December 1921, all members of parliament for the twenty six counties sat in Dáil Éireann.

CONSTITUENCIES

County Mayo was one constituency from 1801 to 1885, and elected two M.P.s. The county consisted of four constituencies from 1885 to 1920, North, South, East and West, and elected one member each. Mayo was divided into three constituencies in 1921, Mayo North and West (four seats), South Mayo and South Roscommon (four seats), and Mayo East and Sligo (five seats). Mayo became two constituencies in 1923, North Mayo with four seats and South Mayo with five. The boundary between the constituencies was adjusted in 1935, and North Mayo lost one seat with effect from the 1937 general election. There was another revision in 1947, under which South Mayo lost one seat with effect from the 1948 election. County Mayo had seven T.D.s from 1948 until 1969. In the 1961 revision of constituencies a part of County Roscommon was added to Mayo. County Mayo was divided into two constituencies in 1969, East Mayo and West Mayo, with three seats each. A part of County Roscommon was added to East Mayo in 1974. Following the implementation of the Walsh Commission recommendations in 1980 County Mayo alone became two constituencies, East Mayo and West Mayo, with a slight change in the boundary between each. Mayo had six Dáil deputies in 1982, Seán Calleary (Ballina), Pádraig Flynn (Castlebar), Denis Gallagher (Achill), Enda Kenny (Derrycoosh, Castlebar), Patrick J. Morley (Bekan) and Patrick J. O'Toole (Ballina).

96

THE ELECTORATE

The composition of the electorate changed radically from 1801 to 1982. From 1801 to 1918 the right to vote was confined to male adults only, provided they satisfied the required property qualification. The property qualification from 1801 to 1829 was possession of a 40s freehold. Under the Irish Parliament Act 1829, following Catholic Emancipation, the qualification became £10 freehold. The Representation of the People (Ireland) Act (1832) extended the franchise to some leaseholders. The Parliamentary Voters (Ireland) Act 1850 gave the franchise to occupiers of property with a rateable valuation of £12 or more. Voting was done publicly until 1872, and in most cases under landlord duress. The landlords told voters who to vote for, and refusal to obey often resulted in eviction. The secret ballot was made obligatory by the Ballot Act of 1872.

The Representation of the People Act 1918 gave the right to vote to all adult males and to women aged thirty or over. Proportional Representation was introduced in place of the straight vote in 1921. Section one of the Electoral Act 1923 gave women the right to vote at the age of twenty one, a right men had since 1918. The Third Amendment of the Constitution Act 1972 and the resulting referendum gave all persons aged eighteen or over the right to vote.

The electorate of county Mayo in five random years was as follows:

Year	Electorate	Population (at nearest Census date)
1832	1,350	367,956
1881	3,087	245,212
1911	31,023	192,610
1973	68,916	109,525
1981	83,332	114,019

MAYO MEMBERS OF PARLIAMENT

The following is a list of persons elected members of Parliament for County Mayo from 1801-1982.

The political affiliation of members is shown by an abbreviation as follows:

APN	Anti-Parnellite Nationalist	L	Liberal
C	Conservative	L(R)	Liberal (Repealer)
C na nG	Cumann na nGaedheal	L (Ind)	Liberal (Independent Opposition)
C na T	Clann na Talmhan	Lab	Labour
FF	Fianna Fáil	N	Nationalist
FG	Fine Gael	R	Repealer
HR	Home Ruler	Rep	Republican
Ind.	Independent	SF	Sinn Féin
Ind N (O'B)	O'Brienite		
Ind. Opp.	Independent Opposition		

The year of election means a general election, unless otherwise stated.

PERIOD 1801 — 1885

Year of Election	Names of M.P. s

1801 (Ex Officio) Rt. Hon. Denis Browne, George Jackson.
1802 Rt. Hon. Denis Browne, Hon. Henry A. Dillon.
1806 Rt. Hon Denis Browne, Hon. Henry A. Dillon.
1807 Rt. Hon. Denis Browne, Hon. Henry A. Dillon.
1812 Rt. Hon. Denis Browne, Hon. Henry A. Dillon.
1814 (By-Election) Dominick Browne.
1818 Dominick Browne, James Browne.
1820 Dominick Browne, James Browne.
1826 James Browne, Lord George Charles Bingham.
1830 James Browne, Dominick Browne.
1831 John Browne, Dominick Browne.
1832 John Browne, (L) Dominick Browne (L).
1835 Sir William John Brabazon bt. L(R) Dominick Browne (L).
1836 (By-Election) Robert Dillon Brown L(R).
1837 Sir William John Brabazon bt. L(R) Robert Dillon Browne L(R)
1840 (By-Election) Mark Blake L(R).
1841 Robert Dillon Browne (R) Mark Blake (R).
1846 (By-Election) Joseph Myles McDonnell (R).
1847 George Henry Moore (L) Robert Dillon Byrne (R).
1850 (By-Election) George Gore Ouseley Higgins (L).
1852 George Henry Moore L(Ind.) George G. O. Higgins L(Ind.).
1857 Capt. Roger William H. Palmer (C), George Henry Moore (Ind. Opp)
      (On petition Moore was unseated and a new writ issued).
1857 (By-Election) Lord John Thomas Browne (L).
1859 Capt. Roger W. H. Palmer (C) Lord John Thomas Browne (L).
1865 Lord John Thomas Browne (L) Lord George Bingham (C).
1868 Lord George Bingham (C) George Henry Moore (L).
1870 (By-Election) George Ekins Browne (L).
1874 George Ekins Browne (HR) Thomas Tighe (HR).
1874 (By-Election) (On Petition Browne & Tighe unseated and a new writ issued).
      George Ekins Browne (HR) John O'Connor Power (HR).
1880 John O'Connor Power (HR) Charles Stewart Parnell (HR).
1880 (By-Election) (Parnell opted for Cork City). Rev. Isaac Nelson (HR).

PERIOD 1885 — 1918

	North Mayo	West Mayo	East Mayo	South Mayo
1885	Daniel Crilly (N)	John Deasy (N)	John Dillon (N)	James Francis Xavier O'Brien (N)
1886	Daniel Crilly (N)	John Deasy (N)	John Dillon (N)	James Francis Xavier O'Brien (N)
1892	Daniel Crilly (APN)	John Deasy (APN)	John Dillon (APN)	James Francis Xavier O'Brien (APN)
1893 By-Election		Dr. Robert Ambrose (APN)		
1895	Daniel Crilly (APN)	Dr. Robert Ambrose (APN)	John Dillon (APN)	Michael Davitt (APN)
1900 By-Election				(Davitt resigned) John O'Donnell (N)
1900	Conor O'Kelly (N)	Dr. Robert Ambrose (N)	John Dillon (N)	John O'Donnell (N)
1906	Conor O'Kelly (N)	Dr. Robert Ambrose (N)	John Dillon (N)	John O'Donnell (N)
1910	Daniel Boyle (N)	William Doris (N)	John Dillon (N)	John O'Donnell Ind. N (O'B)

1910	Daniel Boyle (N)	William Doris (N)	John Dillon (N)	John Fitzgibbon (N)
1918	Dr. John Crowley (SF)	Joseph McBride (SF)	Éamon De Valéra (SF)	William Smears (SF)

PERIOD 1921 — 1922

Mayo North and West	South Mayo and South Roscommon	Mayo East and Sligo
1921 (June) Dr. John Crowley (SF)	Liam Sears (SF)	Dr. Francis Ferran (SF)
Joseph McBride (SF)	Thomas Maguire (SF)	Alex. McCabe (SF)
Thomas Derrig (SF)	Dan O'Rourke (SF)	Francis Carty (SF)
Patrick Ruddledge (SF)	Harry Boland (SF)	Thomas O'Donnell (SF) J. Devins (SF)
1922 (June) Dr. John Crowley (SF)	Liam Sears (SF)	Dr. Francis Ferran (SF)
Joseph McBride (SF)	Thomas Maguire (SF)	Alex. McCabe (SF)
Thomas Derrig (SF)	Dan O'Rourke (SF)	Francis Carty (SF)
Patrick Ruddledge (SF)	Harry Boland (SF)	Thomas O'Donnell (SF) J. Devins (SF)
	(H. Boland was killed in July 1922,D. O'Rourke resigned 1/12/1922,but no By-Election was held for either vacancy).	

PERIOD 1923 — 1969

	North Mayo (4)	South Mayo (5)
1923	P. J. Ruttledge (Rep)	W. Sears (C na nG)
	J. McGrath (C na nG)	T. Maguire (Rep)
	H. Coyle (C na nG)	J. McBride (C na nG)
	J. Crowley (Rep)	M. Kilroy (Rep)
		M. M. Nally (C na nG)
1924 By-Election 18th Nov.	(H. Coyle vacated seat) Dr. John A. Madden (SF)	
1925 By-Election 18th March	(J. McGrath resigned) Michael Tierney (C na nG)	
1927 (June)	M. Davis (C na nG)	T. J. O'Connell (Lab)
	P. J. Ruttledge (FF)	M. Kilroy (FF)
	M. Henry (C na nG)	M. M. Nally (C na nG)
	J. A. Madden (SF)	E. Mullen (FF)
		J. Fitzgerald Kenny (C na nG)
1927 (September)	P. J. Ruttledge (FF)	R. Walsh (FF)
	M. Davis (C na nG)	M. Kilroy (FF)
	M. Henry (C na nG)	J. Fitzgerald Kenny (C na nG)
	M. O Clery (FF)	M. M. Nally (C na nG)
		T. J. O'Connell (Lab)
1932	P. J. Ruttledge (FF)	J. Fitzgerald Kenny (C na nG)
	P. O'Hara (C na nG)	R. Walsh (FF)
	M. Davis (C na nG)	M. Kilroy (FF)
	M. O'Clery (FF)	E. Moane (FF)
		M. Nally (C na nG)
1933	P. J. Ruttledge (FF)	M. Kilroy (FF)
	M. O'Clery (FF)	R. Walsh (FF)
	M. Davis (C na nG)	E. Moane (FF)
	J. Morrisroe (C na nG)	J. Fitzgerald Kenny (C na nG)
		M. Nally (C na nG)

1937	P. J. Ruttledge (FF)	M. O'Cleary (FF)
	J. Munnelly (FF)	R. Walsh (FF)
	P. Browne (FG)	J. Fitzgerald Kenny (FG)
		E. Moane (FF)
		M. Nally (FG)
1938	P. J. Ruttledge (FF)	M. O'Cleary (FF)
	P. Browne (FG)	R. Walsh (FF)
	J. Munnelly (FF)	J. Fitzgerald Kenny (FG)
	(J. Munnelly d.	M. Moran (FF)
	1941, no by-election	M. Nally (FG)
	was held)	
1943	P. J. Ruttledge (FF)	M. O'Clery (FF)
	J. Kilroy (FF)	D. Cafferky (Far)
	P. Browne (FG)	J. Blowick (Far)
		J. Fitzgerald Kenny (FG)
		M. Moran (FF)
1944	P. J. Ruttledge (FF)	M. O'Clery (FF)
	P. Browne (FG)	D. Cafferky (C na T)
	J. Kilroy (FF)	R. Walsh (FF)
		M. Moran (FF)
		J. Blowick (C na T)
1945 By-Election		(M. O'Cleary resigned)
4th December		B. Commons (C na T)
1948	P. Browne (FG)	R. Walsh (FF)
	P. J. Ruttledge (FF)	B. Commons (C na T)
	J. Kilroy (FF)	M. Moran (FF)
		J. Blowick (C na T)
1951	P. Browne (FG)	J. Blowick (C na T)
	T. O'Hara (C na T)	D. Cafferty (C na T)
	P. J. Ruttledge (FF)	M. Moran (FF)
		S. Flanagan (FF)
1952 By-Election	(Death of P. J. Ruttledge)	
26th June	P. A. Calleary (FF)	
1954	P. A. Calleary (FF)	J. Blowick (C na T)
	P. J. Lindsay (FG)	S. Flanagan (FF)
	T. O'Hara (C na T)	M. Moran (FF)
		H. Kenny (FG)
1957	P. A. Calleary (FF)	M. Moran (FF)
	S. Doherty (FF)	J. Blowick (C na T)
	P. Lindsay (FG)	S. Flanagan (FF)
		H. Kenny (FG)
1961	P. A. Calleary (FF)	M. Moran (FF)
	M. Browne (FG)	H. Kenny (FG)
	J. R. Leneghan (Ind)	S. Flanagan (FF)
		J. Blowick (C na T)
1965	P. A. Calleary (FF)	M. Moran (FF)
	P. J. Lindsay (FG)	H. Kenny (FG)
	T. O'Hara (FG)	S. Flanagan (FF)
		M. D. Lyons (FG)

100

PERIOD 1969 — 1982

	Mayo West	Mayo East
1969	H. Kenny (FG) M. Moran (FF) J. Leneghan (FF)	S. Flanagan (FF) T. O'Hara (FG) M. Finn (FG)
1973	M. Staunton (FG) D. Gallagher (FF) H. Kenny (FG)	S. Calleary (FF) M. Finn (FG) S. Flanagan (FF)
1975 By-Election 12th November	(Death of H. Kenny) E. Kenny (FG)	
1977	E. Kenny (FG) D. Gallagher (FF) P. Flynn (FF)	S. Calleary (FF) P. J. Morley (FF) P. O'Toole (FG)
1981	E. Kenny (FG) D. Gallagher (FF) P. Flynn (FF)	S. Calleary (FF) P. J. Morley (FF) P. O'Toole (FG)
1982	E. Kenny (FG) D. Gallagher (FF) P. Flynn (FF)	S. Calleary (FF) P. J. Morley (FF) P. O'Toole (FG)

SOURCES

1. *Magill Book of Irish Politics* 1981. Edited by Vincent Browne.

2. *Parliamentary Election Results in Ireland 1801-1922.* Edited by Brian M. Walker.

3. *Ireland: A Parliamentary Directory* 1973, 1977, 1981. Ted Nealon.

4. T. P. O'Neill, History Dept., U.C.G.

THE 1857 MAYO ELECTION

by Rev. Jarlath Waldron

The 1857 election was one of the most controversial elections ever held in County Mayo. Bear with me, and, with a little bias perhaps, I will tell you the story behind that election, which so excited my great-grandfather one hundred and twenty five years ago. What about great-grandma? Was she not interested at all? Indeed she was, but the poor creature had no vote (no woman had); she was not supposed to have a brain in her head, never mind be interested in politics! Let me be honest and admit that great-grandfather, with all his big talk, had no vote either — he had not a rateable valuation over £12, but that, I assure you, did not prevent him from getting hot around the collar about this particular event. Not one of the four candidates for the two (straight vote) seats promised one penny more in great-grandfather's pocket; neither could one of them promise to remove his greatest millstone i.e. his landlord, for the simple reason that all four were landlords themselves. Anyway, if he ever laid eyes on them, he could not understand very much of what the candidates were gassing about, because for all practical purposes, he had only 'The Irish' tá fhios agat, and the landlords, tá fhios agat aríst, had only 'the English'!

THE POLITICAL SITUATION

You heard of course of the Ecclesiastical Titles Bill 1851? Bored with the lack of some good issue to arouse the lethargic English public, the Prime Minister, Lord John Russell, decided to introduce what proved to be a monumental red herring. The Pope unwittingly provided the excuse for it. In appointing Archbishop (later Cardinal) Wiseman to Canterbury Pio Nono had directed that he use his full title 'Archbishop of Westminister'. Lord John Russell, in his famous letter to the Bishop of Durham conceded that this constituted an unwarranted intrusion by an outside power in the internal affairs of a sovereign state, an attack upon the Established Church of England, and specifically, an aggression against the Protestant Bishop of Lambeth, who alone had the right to be so designated. All hell broke loose. The English press, with *The Times* to the fore, hoisted a kite of 'No Popery'; the whole population became incensed with self-righteous indignation, and there was a disgraceful attack upon a (Catholic) Eucharistic procession at Stockport. Riding on the crest of a wave of popular support, Russell introduced his infamous Ecclesiastical Titles Bill. Under the Bill, which became law in February 1851, Catholic Bishops were forbidden from using their full Ecclesiastical Titles i.e. Archbishop Wiseman could not describe himself as 'Archbishop of Westminister'! The penalty was a fine of £100 and imprisonment for a second offence.

102

What has all this to do with the Mayo election of 1857 ? Fan ort. Were the militant 'Big' Catholics of Ireland going to take this lying down? Beag a' baol. With the blessing of Archbishop Cullen of Dublin (later Cardinal) and most of the bishops, the big Catholics kicked back; John Sadleir, M.P. (Carlow) and William Keogh M.P. (Athlone) formed the C.D.A. — the Catholic Defence Association. This grouping of Catholic M.P.'s, who pledged themselves never to support any English government which would not withdraw the obnoxious measure, became known as the "Pope's Brass Band". Our own Archbishop, John Mac Hale, gave the C.D.A. his blessing and indeed it was he himself who drove "a coach and four" right through Russell's Act by — within a week — publicly signing himself +"John Archbishop of Tuam". Even in the very chambers of the House of Commons itself he brazenly broke the law, by insisting on using his full title. This effectively ridiculed and subverted Russell's infamous Act. This Mac Hale well knew and thereafter lost interest in the C.D.A. He had one other compelling reason for this — it was taken over completely by his arch-rival, Archbishop Cullen. Never one to espouse causes advocated by "the castle Bishop of Dublin", our own 'Lion of the Fold' gave his support and blessing to the rival Tenant's Defence League. Largely, of course, a Catholic movement it concerned itself with the practical needs of the poor peasant, great-grandfather. The three Fs, Fair Rent, Free Sale, and Fixity of Tenure, encapsulated their demands.

Archbishop Cullen, equally suspicious of all Archbishop Mac Hale's projects, hated the Tenant League — the policy of the unspeakable Young Irelanders. Predictably too, he veered off Mac Hale's long and cherished Independent Opposition Policy. The Archbishop had been advocating this even before O'Connell launched the Repeal Movement. The essential idea of Independent Opposition was to vote against the Government of the day, whichever it might be, on party measures, and by throwing its weight from side to side, render party government impossible. It would then become necessary, if the government of the British Empire were to be carried on at all, for one party in the State to conciliate the Irish members, by one means or another. Considering the chronic "hung" state of the British Parliament such a policy was bound to benefit Ireland; the Independent Irish Parliamentary Party, if it stuck to its pledges, could not fail to acquire Repeal, or Home Rule of some variety, plus the three F s. Whatever about the failures of the past, after the 1852 election the Independent Opposition Policy had a party; approximately fifty of the Irish M.P.'s at Westminister were committed to it. The "Brigadeers" pledged themselves to abstain from identifying with either of the two great parties, or accepting their whip, but to judge each issue on its merits, and to promise their support to whichever party would give to Ireland's starving poor most crumbs from the master's table. Certainly no party would get their votes until what the Telegraph *(The Mayo Telegraph or Connaught Ranger)* called "this galling, unholy obnoxious measure", the Ecclesiastical Titles Act, was withdrawn.

A very vital element of Independent Opposition was the solemn pledging before the Election of 1852 by each candidate that he would refuse every blandishment, or offer of preferment, for himself, friend, or family, certain to be made by the British Government. This had ever been their approach — appeal to the natural greed of Irishmen — each one has his price, they are easily broken. Divide et impera — divide and conquer.

JOBS FOR THE BOYS

No two candidates had been more vociferous with their pledges during the 1852 election than the two 'Big' Catholics, Sadleir and Keogh — with the possible exception of a certain Mayo man. Of him much more anon.

Imagine the consternation of the country when the news broke on 17 December 1852 that the incorruptibles had proved very corrupt, the very citadel of Independent Opposition had capitulated: William Keogh had become Solicitor General, and John Sadleir, Lord of the Treasury. Lesser luminaries — among them our Mayo M.P. also succumbed to the blandishments and bribes of Lord Aberdeen, the new Prime Minister. The defection of the Catholic Mayo Brigadier to the ranks of the Liberal Party was the sole issue of this celebrated Mayo Election of 1857, the first time the defector had to face his constituents after the great betrayal.

The brass-banders, the Johnny-come-lately Whigs, were condemned by every true patriot in the land and by none more violently than "a certain Archbishop in the West of Ireland". However, the leading churchman in the country, Archbishop Paul Cullen failed to join Archbishop MacHale's censure of the Sadleirites. This sinister silence was widely and correctly construed as implicit support for the latter. This was the final parting of the ways for Archbishop Paul Cullen, the converted Whig, and Archbishop John MacHale, "the unapologetic Nationalist". Gavan-Duffy, one of the great bastions of support for Independent Opposition and Tenant Right, left the country in complete dejection. Frederick Lucas, the converted Englishman, editor of *The Tablet,* and an equally committed propagandist of the same policies, had died. That left only one of the original leaders of the Independent Irish Party to keep the Nationalist flag flying. He was a Mayo man, George Henry Moore.

GEORGE HENRY MOORE

The popular (or priests') candidate was Mister Mayo himself, George Henry Moore M.P. of Moore Hall. He was leader of the 15 M.P.'s still faithful to the creed of Independent Opposition and Tenant Right: latterly indeed they tended to be called Moorites. Moore himself had therefore to campaign in other vital constituencies such as Tipperary and Dublin, and felt quite certain of re-election in Mayo.

Nomination Day was fixed for Friday, 3 April, and Polling Day for Monday 6 April. Moore did not return to Mayo until Monday 30th of March— leaving himself with only four days in which to defend his seat. Still in those four days of frightful weather he addressed meetings in

Castlebar, Swinford, Ballyhaunis, Claremorris, Ballinrobe, Belmullet and Ballina. Everywhere the crowds were large and indulged in vociferous 'groaning' every time the name of the opposition candidate was mentioned. Great-grandfather, a Moore man, hated him: "Gooseley" Higgins he called him or occasionally "Mister Useless Higgins".

GEORGE GORE OUSELEY HIGGINS

"The unpopular candidate", was Lieut-Col. George Gore Ouseley Higgins M.P. from Glencorrib. Whence this unpopularity? He was the Mayo man who had defected to the hated Whigs. Along with Sadleir, Keogh et al, Ouseley Higgins had joined the Liberal Party thus breaking his solemn pledge to remain aloof in Independent Opposition and, as you suspect, had in the process feathered his own nest to no small degree.

If the Irish group of fifty members had remained together in Independent Opposition they would have held the whole Parliament in their hands. The breakdown of members was:

Whigs	150	Tories	292
Radicals	130	Irish	50
Peelites	40		**342**
Total	**320**		

Mammon won of course, jobs were offered and the greedy succumbed. George Henry Moore refused to accept any post. His "carrott" was the post of Chief Secretaryship of Ireland.

After his defection in January 1853 Higgins had received "the patronage of the county", which was a euphemism for "the job appointer" for all County Mayo. Every position in the country, from the highest to the lowest, was at his disposal, he named the sheriffs of the county, (his own father Capt. Fitzgerald Higgins he made High Sheriff), and no one could hope for a job such as postmaster, ganger, pensions officer, etc. except through him. Promotions in the police were given to his nominees, and the grand jury was packed so that he could name the road contractors and county officials. Higgins had Mayo sewn up. Because of his patronage Higgins did not lack support in the election, even though it came largely from the second-class ("squireen") Catholic landlords, business men, professional men, and strange to say, many of the Protestant Clergymen of the county, a motley crew, one castigated by Moore as being "the confederated dishonesty of Mayo". In his book *"The Independent Irish Party"* James Whyte saw in this the emergence of a completely new element in Irish politics — the bourgeoisie.

I described Ouseley Higgins as "the unpopular candidate". This was usually a euphemism for the candidate whom the priests opposed. Generally it was the Protestant (and landlord) candidate they took on, but what made the 1857 Election particularly juicy for many was that "the unpopular candidate" was a Catholic! Ouseley had three sisters Mercy

Nuns, one of whom had served as a nurse in the Crimea with Florence Nightingale, the second was also in Westport and the third in Swinford. Notwithstanding this very clerical background, only two priests in the diocese openly supported him, Dean Burke, the parish priest of Westport, and the Rev. Michael Phew P.P. Shrule. Higgins was connected with both places — he was born in Westport, indeed I suspect he was baptised by the Dean, and he resided in Glencorrib in the parish of Shrule. He also had a place in Mountpleasant where he frequently stayed, this connected him with the parish of Carrownacon. Moral courage was required to oppose the Archbiship and support Higgins. When it accidentally became clear on Nomination day that the pastor of Carrownacon, Rev. James Browne, was also going to support Higgins, Archbishop Mac Hale cuttingly remarked to him in front of some of his colleagues: "An open enemy I respect, but I detest a secret foe". The Rev. James changed his mind and plumped for Moore!

Ouseley Higgins was a confirmed social climber and his ambitions in this regard were not confined to the big-wigs of Mayo. No! His sights were set on the more rarefied heights of English aristocratic society; the Mayo seat at Westminister was only the spring-board from which to take off into those heady regions. His very title 'Colonel' was somewhat spurious; Lord Lucan, who did not like him, refused him a commission in the Mayo Militia — the Local Defence Force of the day. However, when he became a Whig, with the Brass Banders, and was handed, as we saw, 'the patronage of the county', this included even the Lord Lieutenancy thereof. To this post he appointed another Derbyite, Sir Richard O'Donnell of Newport; the latter promptly obliged with the desired quid pro quo — the slightly bogus title of Lieut. Col. 'Ouse' had arrived in society!

ROGER W. H. PALMER

The third candidate was Captain Roger W. H. Palmer of Keenagh Lodge, Crossmolina, a Tory. The Palmer estates extended from Newport to Belmullet and to the boundaries of Sligo, near Swinford. Captain Palmer had distinguished himself in the Crimea and specifically at the Cavalry Charge of the Light Brigade at Balaclava in association with his fellow Mayo man, Lord Lucan of Castlebar. Although the son of an absentee, evicting landlord, the dashing young officer was himself of moderate views politically — dar leis féin. Palmer was supported by the bigger landlords and by the Tory Mayo newspaper "The Mayo Constitution", Castlebar. Mayo constantly rejected Tories, and furthermore because of non-residence, and military service, Roger Palmer was practically unknown in the county. Nevertheless he was virtually assured of a seat in Mayo. Why? Mayo had two seats, as we saw. Now in order to oust Ouseley, Moore and his canvassing priests were asking their voters to give their number 2 to Palmer. (Archbishop Cullen described this confederation of priests and Orangemen as "an Unholy Alliance"). Higgins too sought plumpers, or, that the second vote should go to the Tory. Palmer then was expected to take the first seat, leaving a head on clash between the two sitting Catholic M.P.s for the second seat. (For the statistician the result of the 1852 election was Moore, Independent, 695 elected; Higgins, Independent, 550, elected; Mac Alpine, Conservative, 360.)

The fourth candidate in 1857 was one Alexander C. Lambert of Brookhill, Claremorris. Although he went forward as a Tenant-Righter, he commanded little support, and Moore ditched him early on as a running-mate in favour of the Tory. Lambert withdrew from the election before Nonimation day.

THE MAYO PRIESTS AND THE ELECTION

Ever since O'Connell had coaxed the priests into politics in the heady days of Emancipation and Repeal, electioneering was like a drug to many of them. Being the natural leaders of flocks who were largely illiterate and Gaelic-speaking, they felt it their duty to advise, direct and counsel their few freehold voters. This was particularly necessary because these voters were almost universally coerced to vote for their landlords choice. "I vote for my man's man" was about all the English some voters could muster on election day. In those days voting was public, that is to say, the voter, after being identified and sworn, called out the two candidates names ós cóir an tsaoil, and specifically in front of his landlord standing by; the sub-sheriff then entered the votes in the register.

The landlord 'brought in' his tenants, usually the day before polling, shepherded them to the booth, voted himself first, and then stood aside as his tenants filed past. Should any of those latter dare vote otherwise they were in grave danger of eviction. Granted, by 1857, most voting was done alphabetically and not in tallies. However, it was still public; either the landlord himself, or his agent, or bailiff 'brought up' each freeholder in turn to vote. What galled the priests was that this landlord M.P. was precisely the man who would do untold harm to the tenants' cause in Westminister. Under the leadership of Moore of Mayo, the faithful remnant of the Independents sought basic rights for tenants — that they should not be evicted if they paid their rent, and that if he were evicted they should be compensated for the improvements they had made i.e. that "the Ulster Custom" be extended to the whole of Ireland. On the other hand the landlords and their men in Westminister were determined not to yield an inch to Moore and great-grandfather's demands. To them 'Tenant Right was 'Landlord wrong'.

THE 1857 ELECTION: THE PRIESTS WATERLOO

Even though still fairly considerable, the influence of the priests at elections had been waning for some time.

Because of the spread of education, and the English language, many people could now read the papers and make up their own minds. Correspondingly, more and more priests withdrew entirely from politics.

The hot-heads, who were also often the most concerned priests, still 'operated' and it was the activity of a handful of these that gave this election its peculiar spice! These men were unlikely to be deterred even by the statute of the Synod of Cashel 1850 explicitly forbidding priests from public participation in politics. As Archbishop of Armagh (1849) and Apostolic Delegate (i.e. the Pope's representative), 1851, Paul Cullen, after his arrival in Ireland had steered that motion through the Synod. Gavan Duffy, who hated him, said of Archbishop Cullen "There was to be no priests in politics except Bishops, no Bishops in politics except Archbishops, no Archbishops in politics except the Apostolic Delegate — himself". Apart from this at all, Archbishop Cullen did not approve of priests being associated with populist movements. What he saw in Rome during the Garibaldi — Mazzini riots coloured his subsequent thinking in this regard. He abhorred the Tenant Righters, to him they were Carbonari re-incarnated. Young Ireland was equally as dangerous as Young Italy. Newman says Cullen "always compared the two with the most intense expression of words and countenance. Cullen assured me they never came right — never — he knew from his experiences of Rome".

In Connacht in 1857 — apart from the diocese of Elphin — Archbishop Cullen's writ simply did not run. For, like Moses shepherding the Israelites in the desert, the great Archbishop Mac Hale goaded, guided, and guarded his flocks with undying enthusiasm and care. He was everything Cullen was not; indeed it is almost true to say everything that Cullen was for, he was against. Mac Hale was the people's, the tenants' man, 'agin the Government', 'agin the landlords', an Independent Opposition man and a confirmed Tenant Righter, an Irishman. He was great-grandfather's man.

Archbishop John MacHale.
(Photograph by Lawrence)

Ensured therefore of their Metropolitans support, the priests of Mayo met in James Armstrong's Hotel in Castlebar on Monday 23 March. Priests attended from the dioceses of Achonry, Killala and Tuam. They passed three Resolutions: "That it is the unanimous determination of this meeting that our trusted faithful representative, George Henry Moore, should receive the strenuous and cordial support of the Clergy and people of this great county at the coming election. We deem it an imperative duty imposed upon us, by our relations with our respective flocks, to recommend to them, in the strongest terms, to repudiate the pretensions of Col. Ouseley Higgins, who, by his wholesale and unscrupulous violation of the most solemn pledges has betrayed the interests of a noble, but too confiding, constituency. For the purpose of expelling him from the representation of this county we hereby pledge ourselves to give our strenuous and active support to any other candidate who may solicit the suffrages of the electors, except the same be a notorious and reckless violator of public and solemn engagements".

Signed: Martin Browne A.D., P.P., Chairman. Richard Hosty, R.C.C.; Patrick Greene, R.C.C.; Henry Cahill, R.C.C., Secretaries — all curates in Castlebar.

Moore's clerical support got an even greater boost on 29 March (Passion Sunday) when four of the bishops of the province (Mac Hale of Tuam, Durkan of Achonry, Feeney of Killala, and McEvilly of Galway), present in Tuam for McEvilly's consecration, resolved "that all the energies of the people should be directed towards the rejection of Mr. Ouseley Higgins who has been unfaithful, and to the return of Mr. Moore, who has been their honest, faithful, uncompromising supporter in Parliament". One of the two remaining Connacht bishops who did not sign was Browne, "the Dove of Elphin," as O'Connell called him; he, as we saw, was a lackey of Archbishop Cullen to whom all such political shenanigans were anathema.

THE HIGGINS CAMP

However, not all Catholics were browbeaten or cowed by this considerable clerical commitment. Most Catholic landowners (admittedly, largely 'squireens') supported Higgins. (He dispensed jobs, remember?). These people bitterly resented the priests' interference in a sphere where it was none of their business. They were Liberals by conviction and anti-Moore, because they hated and feared Tenant-Right and, with Archbishop Cullen, could see no future in futile wrangling with the government of the day, who alone could provide badly needed cash for Ireland. Some important Protestant landlords were Liberal by conviction; for instance Colonel Knox "who owned Ballinrobe", Capt. Brabazon "to whom Swinford belonged", Sir Richard O'Donnell of Newport, and its environs, and Lord Dillon whose annual income in Costello came to £150,000, — now surely over a million. These gentlemen were also confirmed Higginsites, except Lord Dillon who, as an absentee, stood committed solely because of the convictions of his agent, Thomas Strickland of Loughglynn, and his son Charles. Some Protestant clergymen also strung along, because they were traditional Liberal supporters, and Higgins was now the official Whig candidate.

Some professional and business people appear on the impressive list of people whose names were published in the local newspapers at the commencement of the campaign, as "gentlemen who were committed to insure the return of Colonel Ouseley Higgins to Parliament". At the end of the list there was the significant aguisín "with power to add to their number".

THE CAMPAIGN

"There is nothing here except those awful elections" reported Dr. Dixon, Archbishop of Armagh, to Rome on 13 April 1857, "and oh, with what uncharitableness, intemperance etc. they have deluged the country." George H. Moore returned home on Passion Sunday (then two weeks before Easter) and five days before Nomination. For it was only then the penny dropped — the penny that his own seat in Mayo was in dire jeopardy; this his frantic friends, especially his priest-friends, had realised for some time and had been passionately urging him to return and direct his own campaign. In the four days remaining he conducted a fantastic whirlwind tour of the major towns of the county — his transport a covered carriage drawn by two horses. (Horses by the way, were the big passion of Moore's life). In all the major population centres he addressed meetings and conducted a quick canvass. In each town he was accompanied by the local clergy who, of course, invariably appeared with him on platforms and always addressed the crowds, at length, on his behalf.

If Moore only spent four days campaigning, his opponent, "the Col." had spent four years assiduously and painstakingly preparing for his first, dreaded, meeting with his constituents, since his dramatic volte-face (when the Brass-banders became Whigs) in January 1853. He had judiciously used his 'patronage' and filled every job in the county, from policeman to road ganger, with a view to his re-election. He was now quite confident that his patronage would pay off at the polls.

The handsome, dashing Crimean, Captain Palmer, had hardly to campaign at all, what with the other two doing the dirty work for him. About the most strenuous thing he did was insert his Election Manifesto in the local newspapers for a few weeks, and waited for the big day, 3 April the day of Nomination.

NOMINATION DAY

"Dr. Mac Hale has very great influence in the County of Mayo" conceded Mr. David Ruttledge J. P. of Barberfort, Ballinrobe, in London later that year. It was one of the great understatements of the nineteenth century: the *"Times"* of London described him as "the archiepiscopal dictator of the Western Province". All of this influence was now firmly behind Moore. The priests had opposed Moore on his first venture into politics in 1846, thereafter he became "the priest's man". Archbishop Mac Hale and Moore were close friends and confidants. The Archbishop had officiated at Moore's wedding in 1851 to Mary Blake of Ballinafad, and in the 1852 Election had personally nominated him. Indeed on the Friday of Passion Week, Nomination Day, Archbishop Mac Hale travelled to Castlebar once more to do Moore the honour of nominating him, but just before he entered the Courthouse he found, to his embarrassment, that he had no vote. A certain suspicion arose that Ouseley, through the good offices of his father, the High Sheriff, ensured just that. (Moore himself was to be similarly embarrassed the following Monday when he entered the Carra booth, in Castlebar, to find he had no vote either!). Geoffrey Martin Esq. J. P. of Curraghmore, Ballinrobe, at short notice, took the place of the Archbishop and, accompanied by wild-cheering inside the packed Courthouse, re-echoed by the vast throng outside, proposed G. H. Moore "as a fit and proper person to represent this great county in the Imperial Parliament". Archdeacon Browne, P.P. Balla, seconded in a long speech declaring that Moore had laboured long and perseveringly that Ireland might have "happy homes and altars free". Sir Richard A. O'Donnell (Newport), amid a storm of cheers and hisses rose to propose Col. Higgins. He met with such sustained noise, hissing, hooting and groaning that it took him nearly an hour to utter eight or ten audible sentences, in which he attacked George Moore, Archbishop Mac Hale and the priests. Dean Burke P.P. Westport, who was no lover of his Archbishop, seconded Higgins. He too sailed on stormy seas and came in for "shouts, cheers, whistling, laughter, and many a handsome joke". Colonel Gore (Sligo) proposed W. H. Palmer and he was seconded by Sir Robert Lynch-Blosse (Athavallie), Balla, and, as one would expect, Captain Palmer's exploits in the Crimea came in for glowing tributes.

The candidates then spoke. Moore was heckled and abused. Higgins had hired a crowd of Castlebar corner-boys to heckle and shout down the opposition. The hecklers each were to receive five shillings a day. Despite a hostile reception also, Colonel Higgins made a manful defence, denying that he ever broke a pledge and recounting all the Bills he had voted for. Moore conceded that after the dissolution was announced Higgins had consistently voted with them; "indeed at that stage had I proposed the abolition of Christianity he would have supported me without a moments hesitation". Were it not that Moore then appealed to the crowd to give Higgins a hearing it is doubtful if one audible sentence would have been heard apart from his first three words "Electors of Mayo."

Palmer got a quiet hearing.

The drama was not quite over with the speeches. Mr. Ruttledge (a Higginsite), then sub-sheriff, stood up and coolly demanded £200 from Moore (as a Nomination deposit) and added, with a sinister sneer, that no cheque would be accepted from Mr. Moore, or from any of his supporters. It was useless for Moore to protest at this unprecedented and deplorable chicanery, and state that he had not that amount of money on his person. They were absolutely proceeding to take the show of hands to declare the two nominated candidates elected, when in a tense, subdued, but wildly excited atmosphere, a quick whip-around amongst Moore's supporters produced the required sum. It was a race against time and Moore just beat the clock.

SUPPORT FOR MOORE

In its last editorial before the election *"The Telegraph"* shrieked, "vote for Moore and Palmer and down with Traitors! and Whig jobbers!! and Situation Beggars!!! It then concluded with dark forebodings, "To your tents, O Israel; for if Moses cannot lead in the battle, Joshua will!" Was the allusion prophetic? Who, in the context, was Joshua, and who Moses?

Archbishop Mac Hale decided to give further help to George H. Moore. He issued a special pastoral urging support for Moore and 'rejection of the renegade'. On this Palm Sunday morning hardly a Catholic Church in Mayo failed to hear an impassioned appeal from the altar in support of Moore, along with some caustic comments about Ouseley Higgins. I would love to give you some of them but let me be content with one celebrated remark by the Rev. Luke Ryan, Administrator of Kilmeena (then a mensal parish). Pointing down the aisle of Kilmeena Church he said "If the devil appeared there now I would as soon vote for him as for Ouseley Higgins." According to one eye witness he thumped the altar simultaneously to indicate conviction.

From the reaction of some of the English papers (who evidently took the devil very seriously) one visualised some kind of bizzare instant beauty contest in Kilmeena Church between Ould Nick and Our Ouseley, with the administrator as adjudicator; having received the nod from their priest, His Nibs had done a kind of a lap of honour up and down the aisle to the tumultuous acclaim of the worshipful Kilmeenas. A Dhiabhail!

BRINGING IN THE VOTERS

Palm Sunday was spent bringing in voters. This was the duty of the landlord and his first step towards "delivering" them. Supporters of the unpopular candidate always needed protection in Mayo. The county had been literally deluged with dragoons and other military for the polling. Let us, for instance, follow the fortunes of just one such group of voters in the 1857 Mayo election. By arrangement a hundred or so of Higgins's voters had gathered in Claremorris town at 10.00 a.m. on Palm Sunday morning, outside the old Imperial Hotel. From there they were to be taken, under guard, to Ballinrobe, for the voting. The baronies of Clanmorris and Kilmaine generally polled (in separate booths) in Ballinrobe. A magistrate, David Ruttledge, resident of Co. Galway, but a voter in Mayo, had,brought, by order of the High Sheriff, a company of dragoons to protect the voters. About fifty of the latter, mounted on their own horses, were anxious to get away out of Claremorris while the people were still at ten o'clock Mass. Suddenly, before they were ready to depart for Ballinrobe, the congregation began to teem down the narrow lane from the old Catholic Church, sited where the Town Hall now stands. (Catholic churches were then and down to our own day generally called 'Chapels' — Protestant edifices alone were called Churches). The voters were immediately assailed by the disgorging congregation, who had palms in one hand and stones in the other. "We got a tremendous pelting with stones. I never saw anything like it myself", protested Ruttledge. Were it not for the dragoons some voters would have been killed. While approaching Ballinrobe they heard that troops were sent out to provide further protection. Even then they feared to enter the town through the Main Street, but approached their destination, Monaghan's Hotel, from another route, Chapel Lane.

CHAPEL LANE

The bush telegraph had alerted Fr. Peter Conway of their approach and at the end of twelve o'clock Mass he told his congregation, "you have a perfect legal right to show your dis-approbation of his (Higgins) conduct by shouting and hooting after every one who comes to support him. But take care, do not molest or maltreat any of the soldiers or police". He then gave them his blessing.

Before the convoy of Higginsites could escape into Monahan's, Fr. Conway's worshippers, duly blessed, dispersed, and highly motivated debouched into the narrow lane to extend to them the kind of welcome indicated by their curate. A fracas occurred but no one was injured. When the excitement was at its height 'Father Peter' himself appeared. He told the Higginsites what he thought of them bilingually. One of them, Joseph Burke of Ower, produced a pistol, pointed it at Fr. Conway and said "I am determined, if any man flings a stone at my men, I will give him the content of this pistol". This was the coup de grace which finished the battle of Chapel Lane. Fr. Peter quickly disappeared and the mob dispersed.

I would not like in any way to belittle Fr. Conway. Indeed, he was one of the most remarkable priests of nineteenth century Ireland, one of the country's unsung Famine priests who built no less than four churches in Tuam diocese, including Partry (1844), and according to Moore saved thousands of lives in those awful days. Unquestionably Fr. Peter was not strong in discretion, and undeniably he let his enthusiasm for the cause of his friend, Moore, get the better of him. He was the very first voter in the Kilmaine Barony booth after it opened on Monday morning and was so active the first two days of polling in bringing up voters and canvassing that the sub-sheriff, Mr. Sharkey, threatened to arrest him.

Monday was market day in Ballinrobe and consequently the town was thronged ó mhaidin. It was in a state of ferment all day and the Riot Act was read a few times in the hope of quietening things down. Ruttledge discontinued the polling around one, closed the booth, and ordered a

113

cavalry charge to clear the streets. We have the evidence of several Protestant landed gentlemen, solid citizens, not supporters of Moore, who stated that all of those measures were totally unnecessary, but would be good window dressing for a petition. Polling commenced on Monday 7th April, the second day of Holy Week, and continued for three days. As it entailed individual identification and swearing of every voter before his public statement of support, it was a lengthy business.

RESULT

Unlike elections today, the result of the Election of 1857 was known even before the nine sheriffs came to Castlebar with their polling books. Because of the public voting the tally men could tell you exactly, at any moment, how many votes each candidate had received. However, on Holy Thursday, the Sheriff officially declared a result; Palmer 1,238; Moore 1,169; Higgins 1,041, adding a sinister remark that he had reserved his future proceedings in this matter for a petition in the House of Commons. (Incidentally his son had 800 plumpers). So after all the shouting, travelling, canvassing, threatening, cursing and coercing, Moore had only a majority of 128. Higgins was beaten. There was great jubilation and rejoicing throughout the county, amongst the clergy, and the tenantry. "Let us lift up our hearts and rejoice" editorialised *The Telegraph,* "for this great County of Mayo has won the victory". "This glorious county has redeemend itself, and Mr. Ouseley Higgins has been taught a sober lesson of morality and truth". Amongst the victory celebrations was a big banquet in Castlebar. The Archbishop did not attend, although he did send a letter to be read. Nearly all the priests of the county were there. For some reason Fr. Peter Conway did not attend. They drank ten toasts that night, including one "To the Queen" — "loyalty having ever been the characteristic of the Irish people". Still, somehow, one felt they were all conscious that the sword of Damocles hung over all the festivities, and finally the blow did fall.

THE PETITION

After some short vacillation Higgins decided to go ahead and petition the House of Commons to annul Moore's Election. He left for London to prepare the petition. Under the heading "Higgins versus his own Church" *"The Telegraph"* (of Wednesday 13th May) informed its readers that "the petition is in reality a masterly invective against the Catholic clergy, and the Archbishop of the West. It is a strange document coming from one who professes allegiance to the Faith. The Col. brings his action on the grounds of undue influence, bribery, threatening, and want of qualification, " but for the system of violence, threats, denunciations, intimidation your petitioner would have been returned at the said election to serve in the Parliament for the said county". Rest assured the Col. got no respite from attack, innuendo, ridicule, abuse etc. from the said *Telegraph* for the next few months. In the first week of June 1857 all the Mayo newspapers printed in full "the humble petition of Lieut. Col. G. G. O. Higgins". It ran to approximately 8,000 words, and was really a cri de coeur to his peers "Please, lads, throw out George, and let me in".

MAYO AND THE HOUSE OF COMMONS

The year 1857 was by no means the first time that Mayo brought its post-election rows to the sacred portals of St. Stephen's, Westminister. After the 1852 election the defeated Tory, Col. Mac Alpine, petitioned alleging undue clerical influence. The petition did not change the result. So both protagonists had been over the course before and both knew it to be a costly exercise in democracy. To prevent Moore being out of pocket in defending his case the priests, and other friends of Moore, organised a "Moore Indemnity Fund". This naturally received the fulsome blessing of *"The Telegraph"* and the scornful ridicule of *"The Constitution"*. It was warmly subscribed to all-over the county, with indeed many contributions from outside. In appointing 'select' committees to deal with election petitions it was customary to select five M.P.'s from among the members of Parliament, two from each side of the House with a neutral chairman. George Moore had few friends in the House of Commons. He was sarcastic in debate and intolerant of mediocrity and sham, a supporter of Tenant Right and Independent Opposition. There was no question of Moore getting an unbiased committee. The members of this committee were, Sir John Hammer Bart, Col. North, Christopher Puller Esq., George Tomline Esq., and the chairman William Scholefield Esq. Great grandfather, when he read their names, scoffed "I'll bet none of them buckoos came from Carrabehy and nee'r a wan o' them ever heard tell of Crocsbolgadán".

The entire proceedings were a facade. The House of Commons did not want Moore. British justice must be done and be seen to be done. Archbishop Mac Hale, himself, and half Mayo were subpoenaed to appear before the House of Commons, to give evidence. During the sixteen days of taking evidence, the committee examined fifty-three witnesses, asking them 13,172 questions. Archbishop Mac Hale was questioned for one and a half days and emerged with honour. The depositions of those examined fill 465 foolscap pages of "Minutes of Evidence before the Select Committee". It makes fascinating reading.

RESULT OF THE PETITION

The findings of the Select Committee were: "That G. H. Moore was by his agents guilty of undue influence at the last election for the Co. of Mayo — that he was therefore unworthy to represent the shire in the Mother of Parliaments." The committee exonerated Moore himself of any conspiracy with the priests and "reported" the Rev.s Peter Conway and Luke Ryan to the House. There was very moderate jubilation in the Higgins camp, whereas *The Telegraph,* et al, nearly blew a gasket. Did this result mean that Higgins was automatically in as M.P. for Mayo?

Far from it, Is minic a bhain duine slat a bhuail é féin. *The Telegraph* commented, "The unseating of his opponent has been the death of him".

After a few months hesitation, Higgins got the message — the petition had turned everyone against him — his political life in Mayo was ended. The chairman, Scholefield, objected to the release of the Mayo Writ until 'Priest Conway and Priest Ryan' would be arraigned and suitably chastised. However, the Lord John Thomas Browne, threw his hat in the ring immediately after the Petition finished, and the Independent Party decided to support him. So, with the support of the priests, his triumph was assured. Nomination day was fixed for 30 December and, as expected, there was no opposition. So irony of ironies, Mayo for the first time ever, was represented by two non Catholic landlords.

THE TRIAL OF TWO PRIESTS

The House of Commons decided by a small majority to prosecute the two Mayo priests, who were "reported" in the Select Committee's report, Rev. Peter Conway and Rev. Luke Ryan. The curtain was up for the last act of the 1857 Mayo election. The decision to prosecute was a major political blunder, and illustrated once again the insensitivity of English public opinion to the temperament and soul of Ireland. It stirred up a veritable hornet's nest. The country exploded with wrath, and the story became an international issue within a few days with articles in the press of France and America. As in the case of Moore and the petition, once more came the inevitable Indemnity Fund to help the priests defend their case. Money flowed in from all over the country — it finally totalled £1,165,,17,,11. Fr. Ryan's health was poor and he was unable to attend for trial that winter, but Rev. Peter Conway was there. Aware of Rev. Peter Conway's popularity in the nation at large, and alarmed lest there be a public demonstration at his arrest, the Crown dispatched "troops of dragoons and police by the hundred" by special train from Broadstone Terminus to Athenry and then proceeded by forced marches to Ballinrobe. When they arrived there, they found the bird had flown. Where was he? He was in Dublin, where he calmly walked into the Crown Office with his solicitor and counsel to stand his trial. So "the Storming of Ballinrobe" became another source of merriment and ridicule throughout the land.

Rev. Peter Conway's trial was a farce, if a sinister one. Under the Corrupt Practices Prevention Act he was indicted on thirty four counts, the last reading just "Riot in Cong". They filled two hundred and forty-six office sheets, and the trial was followed with intense interest, not merely in Ireland, but throughout the world, not of course forgetting the Vatican. What added insult to injury was the 'ex-officio' form of trial the Government ordered — one unheard of now in England and abandoned in Ireland for over thirty years — that and the fact that the frightful election riots in Kidderminster, England went totally unpunished.

Even though O'Hagan, the defence counsel, had only four days in which to prepare after receiving the indictment, he was able to answer all thirty-four counts. When the jury disagreed, Rev. Peter was discharged; this was hailed as a victory but, to placate the Orangemen, the Whigs needed blood.

In January and February 1858 he was arraigned again. "They are now on the country," wailed *The Telegraph*, "and God defend the right".

The judge himself, a Mr. Perrin, was aware of the national revulsion at this 'priest-hunting' and failed to see how a county like Mayo, boasting of one hundred and fifty nobility and gentry — one hundred and twenty of whom were magistrates — that twelve men could not be found who could give a fair and impartial verdict. A jury was found, and at the end of the trial Fr. Conway was acquitted. He returned to Ballinrobe, and a huge crowd gathered to welcome him. Fr. Luke's case was heard the following March. He too was acquitted.

THE AFTERMATH

The Whig Government fell in 1858, and, of course, leaving office with them were all the Irish Sadleirite "hacks" whose appointment caused all our trouble in Mayo. The country was overjoyed. Heaven was on its side for a change. Even Mac Hale commented on "the singular coincidence between the moment of the fall of the prosecuting ministry and the liberation of the persecuted clergy."

Moore, of course, was out of a job; and slow horses did not help his precarious financial position. He remained out of Parliament until 1868, when he sold all his horses, in order to put together enough cash to enable him to run again for Mayo. This time he was successful but sadly his term in Westminister was short; he died, after a stroke, in the year 1870.

Archbishop Cullen forwarded all the evidence of the commission to Rome. Despite the Archbishop's eloquent appeal to have Propaganda denounce Rev.s Peter Conway and Luke Ryan, and their Archbishop, Mac Hale, "who is to blame for this scandal," Cardinal Barnardo of Propaganda diluted his criticism by writing on 28 September to all four Archbishops of Ireland, complaining about the political activity of the Mayo clergy and labelling it reprehensible. "They appear in Rome", bewailed Archbishop Cullen, "to be afraid of the Lion, and he knows that".

Ouseley Higgins went to England and died there, without heirs.

With George Henry Moore removed from Parliament after 1857 the Tenant Right Movement (and Independent Opposition) received a body blow which it did not survive. The landlord once more reigned supreme. Evictions commenced in a big way, which, in turn, led to the growth of secret societies, agrarian 'outrages' and atrocities, Coercion Acts, the Fenian Movement and later Land League troubles. Parliament had failed the people.

A clerical comment. To be brutally honest we must consider the victory of Fathers Conway and Ryan as a pyrrhic one. For, let's face it, although they won, they lost. What priest in Ireland would throw himself headlong into electioneering again, have himself hauled before the courts, and ridiculed throughout the English speaking world? What Irish politician wanted to suffer the fate of Moore, because he had a few hot-headed clergymen tagging along at his coat tails? No. Fr. Conway's trial had underlined the stark truth that 'Spiritual Intimidation' equals Undue Influence equals Automatic Loss of Seat. All Ireland got the clear message. The 1857 Mayo Election did not mark the end of the priest in politics in Ireland, but it, quite definitely, marked the beginning of that end. Both politicians and priests saw the writing on the wall.

ARCHBISHOP PAUL CULLEN

I myself have a hunch — just a hunch — that the State Trials of Frs. Peter Conway and Luke Ryan received the secret blessing of Archbishop Paul Cullen. More and more, the latter had become "an Irish Whig", "a Castle Bishop," a "law and order" man. (But who made the laws? and for whom must order be maintained?) B'shin í an fhaidhb. To maintain 'law and order' for the establishment, it was essential to quieten, to subdue, and crush the tenant serfs of Ireland. To protect 'the rights of property' (which included the right to the tenant vote) the last remaining bulwark of defence of the tenant had to be removed — the priests. This then was the thinking of Palmerston and his Ministry — the basic reason for the petition to unseat Moore and the State Trials of Fr. Conway and Fr. Ryan.

The tragedy of Paul Cardinal Cullen — Ireland's first Cardinal — was that, although he sincerely loved Ireland and was concerned for her oppressed poor, he was so conditioned by his instincts, his background, and his obsession with Law (Civil and Ecclesiastical), that he actually delivered Ireland, holus polus, to the whims of "the base Whigs" and her defenceless tenants into the hands of greedy and merciless landlords. As a man Paul Cullen was able, saintly, charitable to a degree, and extremely hard-working, but also a victim to his own (sometimes narrow) prejudices. How ironical that two of the great Constitutionalists who dominated Irish politics during two thirds of the nineteenth century should have their attitudes to resurgent Ireland crystallised by two revolutions they witnessed on the European mainland: O'Connell spancelled by his revulsion to the bloodshed he witnessed in France during 1789-90, and Cullen horrified and frightened by the violence of the Mazzini-Garibaldi riots in Rome 1849. It is interesting to speculate how much these two held up the onward march of Ireland's self-development. How much further advanced would she have been by century's end, if Mac Hale had been listened to. With his unique combination of gifts — ability, courage, Irish Nationalist background and yet Royalist convictions, how much of the subsequent mistakes and trauma could have been avoided.

And after all the shouts of victory died down, it was clear that once again — as usual — Archbishop Cullen had won. We know that his attitude to the tenants of Ireland was one of the basic dividing points between himself and Archbishop Mac Hale. This confrontation will, I feel sure, remind you of the situation in South America today. I submit that in his stand on these issues Archbishop Mac Hale was over a hundred years ahead of his time. The emotional and intellectual response to John Mac Hale's centenary, in 1981, in contrast to the poor response to Archbishop Cullen's a few years previously (1978) speaks for itself.

For the great Archbishop of the West the 1857 Election represented another round lost to Archbishop Cullen in their on-going battle for supremacy. It certainly was a political waterloo for Archbishop John of Tuam. He clearly saw the profound effect it had on the morale of his priests. He suffered further defeats in the rejection of his candidates in Galway and Sligo. Dismay and depression assailed him. Apart from the Galway Election of 1872 he never actively interfered in politics again.

The 1857 Election was not so much then between Moore and Higgins, between Westminister and the plain people of Ireland, between the Whigs and Rev. Peter Conway, but rather between Archbishop Mac Hale and Archbishop Cullen. Indeed we could almost regard it as the penultimate round of the Ecclesiastical heavy-weight championship of Ireland. Maybe the prize was not the dominance of the Irish Church, but at least the two were locked in a ferocious battle for the soul of the Irish Church. The issue between them in 1857 clearly was: should the local curate go on taking an interest in Irish politics, and direct and lead his people in the vital bread and butter problems of their lives? (In other words, souls do not exist without bodies, and can a concerned priest then ignore his people's bodies? cf. today's Liberation Theology trauma). Should then the priest continue to protect the defenceless tenant from his endemic enemy, the landlord? For him "the coercion of the clergy was necessary to counteract the coercion of the landlords." That was Archbishop Mac Hale's Gospel. Or rather, should the priest withdraw from politics entirely, seclude himself in his sacristy and obey the Synods of Cashel and Dublin by not taking sides between tenant and landlord, but let the law take its course? If the tenant is evicted, too bad, but fiat lex. That was Archbishop Cullen's sincere belief, the direction the Irish Church should take. "The business of a priest is to confine himself to his spiritual duties and in the intervals of these to devote himself to reading and meditation."

GREAT-GRANDFATHER

So where did this leave great-grandfather? Locked as he was in a life or death struggle with his landlord, harassed by an unseeing and unfeeling foreign government, who had he now to support him? To whom could he turn for leadership and direction? The priests, after 1857, had willy-nilly to desert him. He knew he had their sympathy, but sympathy was no use at eviction time. There he needed their commitment and their presence in there fighting shoulder to shoulder with him. This great-grandfather knew he would never have again, even in Archbishop Mac Hale's Mayo. It was a bitter pill to swallow. If the priest was not for him, he was against him.

119

Archbishop Cullen's priest would advise him to pay his rent, to respect his landlord's property, and to obey the laws of perfidious Albion. This new breed of priest, therefore, to great-grandfather was an establishment man, the landlord's lackey, a West Briton. It was more than he could take. Although he knew his wife was violently anti-Fenian, secretly he sympathised with his son's nocturnal drillings. (The Fenians were founded in 1858; his son John joined them). The hostility of Honor Waldron (née Waldron) to the Fenians was predictable, reflecting very much the attitude of the priests. (She had two brothers and two cousins who were priests in the diocese). For John Waldron to join the Fenians was quite a turn-around for such a 'safe', conservative family like the Waldrons, but it speaks volumes for the disillusion and dejection of the times.

Secret societies were not active or widespread in Tuam diocese in 1857. Archbishop Mac Hale always held that this was due to the involvement of his priests with their parishioners. The Pope's representative in Ireland, Paul Cullen, had now 'settled' the Meath priests, equivalently silenced the Callan Curates, and he had done his utmost to have the two pestilential priests of Mayo quietened for ever.

He had unwittingly done exactly what George Henry Moore so dreaded in 1854: "I believe that to place an interdict upon the clergy — in their efforts to vindicate the social and religious rights of their people — would be the most subtle and dangerous of all the penal laws by which it has been sought to damn and degrade us".

Listen finally to one sentence from Gavan Duffy on the same occasion: "Let laymen understand this, that our national cause has prospered in exact proportion to the interest taken in it by the priesthood".

The tragedy of our story is that a few priests had taken too much interest in a secular affair. 'Too far East is West'. Some priests had gone so far that they almost finished forever 'Priests in Politics'.

All Ireland had got the clear message from the Mayo Election of 1857.

SOURCES

1. *The Telegraph or Connaught Ranger.* Weekly newspaper published in Castlebar.
2. *The Mayo Constitution.* Weekly newspaper published in Castlebar.
3. Mayo Election 1857: Minutes of Evidence before Select Committee.
4. Mayo Election 1852: Election Petition. Minutes of Evidence.
5. *An Irish Gentleman George Henry Moore. His travel, his racing, his politics* by Colonel Maurice George Moore.
6. *Troubled Times in Irish Politics* – T. D. Sullivan.
7. *Life of John Mac Hale Archbishop of Tuam* (2 vols.) — Rt. Rev. Bernard O'Reilly.
8. *Paul Cullen and his Contemporaries 1820-1902* (5 vols.) — Peadar Mac Suibhne.
9. *The Making of the Roman Catholic Church in Ireland* (1850-60) — Emmet Larkin.
10. *Land and The National Question in Ireland* (1858-82) — Paul Bew.
11. *New Ireland* – A. M. Sullivan.

12. *History of Archdiocese of Tuam* – E. A. D'Alton.

13. *Ireland Since The Union* – Justin McCarthy.

14. *The Moores of Moore Hall* – Joseph Hone.

15. *The Independent Irish Party 1850-9* – J. H. Whyte.

16. *The Times (London).*

17. *The Freeman's Journal* (Dublin).

JOHN MacHALE

The following verses were written by Timothy D. Sullivan (1827-1914), the author of "God Save Ireland", which he sang at the banquet in Tuam, in 1875, to celebrate Archbishop John MacHale's golden jubilee in the episcopacy:

"In our Green Isle of old renown
   In many a bygone age,
Full pure and clear the stream runs down
   Of soldier, saint and sage.
But high amid these glories bright
   That shine on Inisfail
Be ours to write in lines of light
   The name of John MacHale.

A pastor true and brave is he;
   Beloved by rich and poor,
A patriot spirit, bold and free
   To dare and to endure.
No traitor's wile, no force or guile
   With him can e'er prevail
Whose watch and ward, whose guide and guard
   Is noble John MacHale.

Oh, men will come and pass away
   Like raindrops in the sea,
And thrones will crumble to decay
   And kings forgotten be,
But through all time, in every clime
   The children of the Gael
Will hear the name and sound the fame
   Of glorious John MacHale.

Long may he live to guide our land
   And glad our hearts as now,
The crozier in his manly hand
   The mitre on his brow.
And when God's love calls him above
   For us there ne'er will fail
The gracious cares, the potent prayers
   Of noble John MacHale."

Source: *History of the Archdiocese of Tuam* by Right Rev. Monsignor D'Alton, P.P. 87, 88.

Seán Mac Éil Ardeaspag

le Máirtín Ó Direáin

Scéal do thréada is léir
San aghaidh chrua sin ort,
Ach trua is taise is follas
Fós san aghaidh sin ort.

Ní géilleadh ach déine
A chím san aghaidh sin ort
I láthair do náimhde féin
Is náimhde do thréada bhoicht,
Ach do shúil ghéar ag faire
Is go síor san airdeall
Ar gach claonbheart bréan
Dár cheap clann an oilc.

Ba tú d'aithin na bréaga
Go rí-shoiléir á gcur
I bhfoirm na firinne féin,
Is dhiúltaigh gach uair
Gach siolla ó chuain an fhill.

Ba léir duit baol do thréada
Is níor leor leat do dhícheall
Idir chorp is anam á gcaomhnú
Ba léir duit nead an dochair
Láthair na spíde, Máthair an Oilbhéis
Is ní dheachaigh ort iamh
Ná foras, a charraig fhir,
Ach ag iarraidh do thréad
A thabhairt slán as lár na tubaiste.

Níorbh aon sceach a sheas
I mbearna an dúshláin
Ach carraig dhaingean
Is daigéad déanta fir:
Is níor pheaca mar ainm ort
Leon Tréada Iúda mhóir,
A easpaig chóir cheart,
A shagairt óir bhí docht
Gan dochar dod' dhaonnacht.

A Thobair na bhFiann
As a n-ólaidís na Fianna uisce,
Ní mór ár laoch a roinnt
Ar Chonnacht aoibhinn féin
Is ar Éirinn uile;
Go scáirdí uisce na nGrást
Ar anam Sheáin Ardeaspaig.

122

GAELTACHT MHAIGH EO

Nollaig Ó Gadhra

Chomh fada siar leis an mbliain 1367, ar a laghad, daoradh an Ghaeilge chun báis.[1] Cé gur iomaí forógra agus beart namhadach a cuireadh sa timpeall sna tréimhsí éagsúla de stair na tíre ó shin i leith, tá na cuntais oifigiúla chomh breac céanna le fianaise a thugann le tuiscint gur mhair an Ghaeilge mar theanga na gnáthmhuintire ar fud an chuid is mó d'Éirinn anuas go dtí an céad seo caite.[2] Ba sa dara leath den 19ú céad — sa ghlúin tar éis an Ghorta — a thit saol na bpobal Gaeilge as a chéile ar fad. Bhí na pobail sin chomh lag, tráite tanaí, buailte faoi dheireadh an chéid, agus chomh scaipthe ar fud na tíre, gur baineadh brí nua as an bhfocal "Gaeltacht" anseo in Éirinn le hais na húsáide a bhaintí (a bhaintear?) as an téarma in Albain.

Tá an scéal ar fad inste arís is arís eile, mar shampla ag Dúghlas de hÍde sa léacht cáiliúil úd *"The Necessity for de-Anglicizing Ireland"*[3], a thug sé don National Literary Society of Dublin sa bhliain 1892 agus go háirithe sa leabhar *Mise agus an Connradh*[4] ina bhfuil an clár figiúirí seo a leanas i gcló sna Nótaí aige ó na Daonáirimh éagsúla a tógadh ó aimsir an Ghorta Mhóir anuas go dtí an Chéad Chogadh Mór:

Bliain	Gaeilge Amháin	Gaeilge agus Béarla
1851	319,602	1,204,684
1861	163,275	942,261
1871	103,562	714,313
1881	64,167	885,765
1891	38,192	642,053
1901	20,953	620,189
1911	16,873	565,573

Ar ndóigh, b'ábhar conspóideach é scéal na bhfigiúirí Daonáirimh faoi staid na Gaeilge riamh anall, agus is ea fós. Seans go léiríonn an mhoill a tháinig ar an meath ag deireadh na tréimhse atá clúdaithe thuas, mar shampla, dea-thionchar Chonradh na Gaeilge agus an athbheochan sa chuisle náisiúnta a d'fhág go raibh níos mó daoine sásta a rá go raibh Gaeilge acu ná mar a bhí ag pointe níos luaithe, nuair atá gach uile sheans go raibh Gaeilge níos fearr, agus ó dhúchas, fiú amháin, ag go leor daoine nach ligfeadh an náire dóibh a admháil go raibh an scéal amhlaidh. Éiríonn le de hÍde a áiteamh orainn go raibh úsáid na Gaeilge mar ghnáthnós coitianta ar fud na tíre go léir nach mór go dtí a aimsir féin. Ach léiríonn an tagairt a bhí aige ina léacht don "little admixture of Saxon blood in the north-east corner" gur thuig de hÍde go raibh éagsúlachtaí

123

tábhachtacha ó réigiún go réigiún, agus go deimhin, ó pharóiste go paróiste maidir le staid na Gaeilge an uair úd. Agus tá fós inniu. Sin é an fáth gur mhol An Craoibhín Aoibhinn ag an am sin, bliain sar ar bhunaigh sé féin agus roinnt bheag daoine eile Conradh na Gaeilge "nothing less than a house to house visitation and exhortation of the people themselves — in order to keep the language alive where it is still spoken — which is the utmost we can at present aspire to". Agus cé gur leag An Craoibhín a mhéar ar chroí na ceiste, b'fhéidir, nuair a mhol sé, chomh maith, go raibh sé riachtanach "to bring pressure on the politicians not to snuff it (an teanga Ghaeilge) out by their tacit discouragement, because they do not happen themselves to understand it . . . ."[5] cuireann líon na nGaeilgeoirí ar fud na tíre — gach aon chuid den tír ainneoin na bhfórsaí go léir a bhí ag obiar ina coinne leis na céadta — alltacht agus náire orainn inniu. Tá a fhios againn go raibh pobail Ghaeltachta le fáil i gCo. Chill Cnainnigh nuair a bhí Amhlaoibh Ó Súilleabháin i mbun pinn,[6] agus tá léargas an-bhreá tugtha ag an Ollamh Breandán Ó Madagáin ar conas mar a bhí an scéal i mo chontae dúchais féin ina leabhar *An Ghaeilge i Luimneach* anuas go dtí tús an chéid seo.[7] Mar sin féin, is deacair dúinn fíricí na fianaise a shamhlú dúinn féin, go háirithe nuair a léiríonn staidéir den chineál seo an fhírinne lom scanrúil gur féidir deireadh a chur le traidisiún beo Gaeltachta i gcontae ar bith, agus gur chuma cé chomh díograiseach is a bhíonn lucht athbheochana ar ball — mar atá i Luimneach mar shampla — nach bhfuil rud ar bith is féidir a dhéanamh faoin slabhra gan bhriseadh, idir na glúinte, chomh luath agus a bhristear é. Ní bheidh an t-athshnadhmadh cosúil leis an gceangal leanúnach go deo. Sin é an fáth gur leagadh an oireadh sin béime ar an "Ghaeltacht", ó thús ré na hathbheochana náisiúnta, agus sin é an fáth gur leag an Stát Éireannach béim ar leith ar an "Ghaeltacht" nuair a ghalc sé cúram slándála na Gaeilge air féin chomh maith.

BUNÚ AN tSAORSTÁIT

Níl sé i gceist agam dul siar ar an stair go léir anseo, ach amháin lena mheabhrú do léitheoirí gur lean an meath ar na ceantair a aithníodh mar cheantair oifigiúla Ghaeltachta de bharr obair Choimisiúin na Gaeltachta 1925-27 in Acht na dTithe Gaeltachta, 1929. Mhol an Coimisiún sin gur cheart idirdhealú a dhéanamh idir "Fíor-Ghaeltachtaí" (an teanga ag 80% den phobal nó os a chionn) agus "Breac-Ghaeltachtaí" (an Ghaeilge ag idir 25—79% den phobal).[8] Bhí go leor áiteanna i gCo. Mhaigh Eo nach bhfuil cáil na Gaeilge orthu inniu ina mBreac-Ghaeltachtaí sna 1920aí. Bhí an cuma ar an scéal, más fíor do Dhúghlás de hÍde agus daoine eile, go raibh bonn éigin leis an maíomh, fiú más fíor gur seandaoine is mó a raibh Gaeilge acu sna ceantair "bhreaca" ag an am a rinneadh an t-áireamh, agus má tá sé rí-shoiléir nach raibh an Ghaeilge á seoladh ar aghaidh go dtí an chéad glúin eile ná á labhairt mar ghnáth-theanga sa phobal níos mó. Ach faoin am a rinneadh na ceantair "Ghaeltachta" oifigiúla a leagan amach arís, in Ordú na Limistéirí Gaeltachta, 1956,[9] ba léir go raibh an t-ádh ar na ceantair a áiríodh mar "Fhíor-Ghaeltachtaí" i lár na bhfichidí a bheith fós i dteideal aitheantais mar "Ghaeltachtaí" faoi chóras nua Roinn na Gaeltachta nach ndearna idirhealú docht dlíúil idir "Fíor" agus "Breac" a thuilleadh! De réir Ordú na bliana 1956, aithníodh na Toghranna Ceantair seo a leanas i gCo. Mhaigh Eo a bheith sa Ghaeltacht Oifigiúil: Abhainn Brain, Acaill, Baile an Chalaidh, Barr Rúscaí, Béal Deirg Mór, Béal an Mhuirthead, An Ceapach Dubh, Cnoc an Daimh, Cnoc na Lobhar, Cnoc na Rátha, Corrán Acla, Dumhach Éige, An Geata Mór Theas, An Geata Mór Thuaidh, Gleann Chaisil, Gleann na Muaídhe, Na Muingí agus Muing na Bó.

Aithníodh bailte fearainn áirithe atá mar choda de na Toghranna Ceantair seo a leanas freisin: Baile Odhbha, Guala Mhór, Pártraí, Tamhnaigh na Groí.

Tá an tOrdú Limistéirí seo míshásuil go maith, agus fillfimid ar an scéal sin arís, go háirithe i gcás Cho. Mhaigh Eo. Is léir ón leagan amach atá ar na ceantair oifigiúla sin thuas go bhfuil deacrachtaí ar leith ag "Gaeltacht Mhaigh Eo" sa mhéid is go bhfuil na ceanatair aitheanta roinnte i dtrí réigiún, i ndeisceart, in iarthar agus in iar-thuaisceart an chontae, atá scartha óna chéile. Tuar Mhic Éadaigh (gur chuid de Ghaeltacht thuaisceart Chonamara í, i ndáiríre, agus a raibh cuid mhaith di istigh le Co. na Gaillimhe go dtí gur athraíodh an teorainn le bunú na gComhairlí Contae sa bhliain 1898)[10], Acaill (leithinis an Chorráin díreach roimh dhul isteach ar an oileán féin, agus oirthear an Oileáin féin) agus Iorras (dhá nó trí cinn de phobail ag pointí triantáin is féidir a tharraingt anuas ar an mbarúntacht: is fada ó bhí Iorras ar fad ina Ghaeltacht) — sin agaibh na trí phóca is láidre dá bhfuil fágtha de Ghaeltacht mhór Mhaigh Eo. Tá siad scartha óna chéile, agus tá a dtréithe féin ag gach aon cheann acu — rud a fhágann go gcaithfear scrúdú ar leith a dhéanamh ar gach ceann acu ar ball.

DE RÉIR NA mBARÚNTACHTAÍ

Maidir le staid na Gaeilge ar fud Cho. Mhaigh Eo trí chéile, tar éis scrios an Ghorta fiú amháin, is fiú breathnú, b'fhéidir, ar na figiúirí seo a leanas, don bhliain 1851 agus 1891, atá le fáil de réir bharúntachtaí, sna Daonáirimh:[11]

		1851	1891	
Barony	Irish Only	Total No. of Irish Speakers and these as %	Irish Only	Total No. of Irish Speakers and these as %
Burrishoole	4,654	16,516 (66.8%)	612	9,523 (51.2%)
Carra	3,943	23,041 (70.5%)	229	12,228 (47.2%)
Clanmorris	1,881	11,618 (58.7%)	71	6,938 (43.8%)
Costello	5,309	21,310 (49.3%)	113	18,513 (43.2%)
Erris	8,510	17,216 (87.7%)	1,766	12,530 (75.9%)
Gallen	6,289	25,847 (75.3%)	362	19,070 (54.9%)
Kilmaine	10,425	20,333 (65.6%)	743	12,897 (70.4%)
Murrisk	1,548	16,094 (64.4%)	43	5,703 (37.7%)
Tirawley	7,084	28,103 (63.6%)	295	12,963 (41.6%)
TOTAL	**49,643**	**180,078 (65.6%)**	**4,234**	**110,365 (50.4%)**

Seans go gcuirfidh cuid de na figiúirí sin iontas ar dhaoine. Is léir, mar shampla, gur chúlú réasúnta cothrom a tharla ar úsáid na Gaeilge ar fud an chontae go léir agus gur lú an bhearna a bhí idir na "ceantair laidre" agus na "ceantair laga" ná in go leor contaetha eile. Bhí Gaeilge ag leath phobal an chontae go fóill in 1891, díreach roimh bhunú Chonradh na Gaeilge agus tús na bolscaireachta a thug ar dhaoine a mhaíomh, glúin ina dhiadh sin, go raibh Gaeilge acu nuair nach raibh aon ghreim acu ar an teanga i ndáiríre. Cé a shílfeadh, maidir le figiúirí na bliana céanna, gur i Muraisc a bhí an céadchuid Gaeilgeoirí ba lú i measc bharúntachtaí uilig an chontae ag an am (37.7%), agus gurb é sin an t-aon fhigiúr céadchodach ag an am a bhí faoi bhun 40%? Mar sin féin, agus ag an am céanna, níl ach dhá fhigiúr os cionn 60%, sé sin, Cill Mheáin (70.4%) agus Iorras (75.9%). Is léir go raibh greim éigin ag an mBéarla ar Iorras féin faoin bhliain 1891, é sin, nó go raibh dornán maith daoine ann nach ligfidh an náire dóibh a admháil go raibh Gaeilge acu. Tá an figiur sin, thart ar 75-76%, íseal go maith le hais na bhfigiúirí a bhí le fáil ag an am céanna ó Chonamara, agus ó cheantair eile ina bhfuil an Ghaeltacht beo i gcónaí inniu, agus nuair ba mhinic breis is 90% den phobal a bheith cláraithe mar chainteoirí Gaeilge in 1891. Mar sin féin, féach gur laghdaigh líon na gcainteoirí Gaeilge ó 87.7% go 75.9% idir 1851 agus 1891, agus gur thit líon na ndaoine nach raibh acu ach Gaeilge ó 8,510 go 1,766, sa tréimhse chéanna. Tionchar an Ghorta, tionchar an bhochtanais agus na himirce, agus na gcúiseanna ar fad eile a luaitear inniu mar leithscéal leis an gcúl le dúchas a tharla sa tréimhse sin.

Ach cuimhnigh gurb é seo tréimhse Chonradh na Talún agus ré an fhéinmhuinín a chothaigh Mícheál Dáibhéid sna gnáthfheirmeoirí sa ghlúin chéanna, más fíor. Má tá rud ar bith le rá i dtaobh na tréimhse, ní mór a admháil gur le linn na tréimhse áirithe sin, nuair a bhí muintir Mhaigh Eo ag bailiú an mhisnigh, más fíor, i ngnóthaí áirithe den saol, a chaith siad uathu na comharthaí dúchais ba bhunúsaí a bhí acu riamh, agus nár chuir an misneach a ghabh le bua Chogadh na Talún stop leis an meath ach a mhalairt ar fad. Mhair cumhacht an dtiarnaí talún féin píosa níos faide in Iorras, mar shampla, ná in go leor áiteanna.

TUAIRIMÍ UÍ GHAORA

Seo rud a thug Colm Ó Gaora, as Ros Muc, faoi deara nuair a chaith sé tamall ag obair do Chonradh na Gaeilge in gCo. Mhaigh Eo, cúig nó sé de bhlianta roimh thús an Chéid Chogaidh Mhóir. Tá cuntas an-bhreá aige ar na heachtraí a bhain de le linn an ama sin sa chaibidil "In Iorras" ina leabhar *Mise,* agus is fiú go mór do dhuine ar bith a bhfuil spéis aige san ábhar seo é a léamh.[12] Tosaíonn an chaibidil leis an abairt "Bhí baile Bhéal an Mhuirthead chomh gallda an t-am sin le aon bhaile mór in Éirinn" — agus sin maíomh do bhaile atá fós sa "Ghaeltacht oifigiúil", ag cur staid na tíre in aimsir an Réamonnaigh san áireamh! Leanann Ó Gaora lena chuntas mar seo a leanas:

"Is ar an mbaile sin a bhíodh tarraingt mhuintir Iorrais. Bhíodh margadh ann gach uile sheachtain agus aonach uair sa mhí, agus ba Gaeilge a chluintí ó na daoine a thagadh chucu ach ba Béarla a labhraíodh, muintir an bhaile leo. Chuir seo an teanga faoi drámh. Sa bhaile seo a bhí teach na mbocht agus ospidéal an cheantair. Is air a bhíodh triall na gcomhairleoirí ceantair agus lucht polaitíochta na háite. Is ann a théadh lucht soláthar postaí dá muintir, area, is ann a chónaíodh na boic mhóra a raibh cumhacht acu na postaí seo a thabhairt uathu. Ba thart ar Bhéal an Mhuirthead a chonaic an méid d'iarsmaí na dtiarnaí talún a bhí fanta in Iorras. Cé go raibh a gcaol droim lag go leor san am sin féin, bheadh ionadh ag duine an chumhacht a bhí fanta acu anseo. Bhí duine acu ansin fós a raibh seanbhealaí na dtiarnaí aige thart san áit agus gan aon cheann faoi air ach é chomh leitheadach le cat a mbeadh póca air. Níorbh ionadh mór mar sin go mbeadh an tseoiníteacht agus an galldachas bréige seo san áit.

"Ar a shon gur baile gallda a bhí i mBéal an Mhuirthead, is ann a chonaic mé an chéad chóip den pháipéar "Sinn Féin". An cailín a raibh teach an phosta ansin aici san am — Lasarfhíona Ní Shamhraidín — a thug dom é. Gael dúthrachtach a bhí inti agus scriobhadh sí féin sa pháipéar sin anois is arís. Bhí sí ina Rúnaí ag Cumann na nDéantús Gaelach nó go bhfuair sí bás tamall ó shin. Na grásta dá hanam, ba cóir ionneachúil don té a raibh an siúl faoina chois mar a bhí mise san am.

"Dhá bhliain a chaith mé idir Gaoth Sáile, Baile Chruaich agus Bainegar Iorrais. Bhí sé scoil agam le cuairt a thabhairt orthu faoi dhó sa tseachtain, agus dhá chraobh den Chonradh le múineadh gach uile oíche. Ina cheann sin bhíodh ranganna do oidí scoile agam gach uile Shathairn agus craobh tar éis an Aifrinn Dé Domhnaigh. Ní raibh scíth ná suaimhneas i ndán don mhúinteoir taistil. Bhíodh orm an paidrín páirteach a rá tar éis an Aifrinn agus rang san oíche chéanna in áit éigin sa cheantar".[13]

Ní féidir an cuntas fíor-shuimiúil seo ar fad a athchló anseo. Caithfidh sibh féin é a léamh. Ach is léir ón méid sin féin thuas nach é leas na Gaeilge agus leas an dúchais a bhí na sagairt ná na múinteoirí ag déanamh in Iorras ag an am, cé go raibh eisceachtaí mar a léiríonn Ó Gaora ar ball.[14] Tá cur síos aige ar chuid de na raiceanna a tharraing a chuid oibre ar son Chonradh na Gaeilge ag an am, agus cur síos an-bhreá aige freisin ar mheon an phobail ag an am faoi chúrsaí náisiúnachta trí chéile. Mar shampla:

"De réir mar a bhínn ag cur aithne ar na sagairt bhínn ag éirí níos meabhraí ar a ndearcadh náisiúnta. Nuair a d'fheicinn an *"Leader"* nó an *"Freeman"* ina dteach, thugadh seo an-mhisneach dom, agus thiteadh sé isteach i m'intinn go mba Ghaeil dúthrachtacha a bhíodh iontu. Mura mbeadh ach an *"Freeman"* le feiceáil agam, ní bhíodh le fáil agam ach moladh an pháirtí Ghaelaigh, agus an teach anamh ina mbíodh an *"Irish Times"* le feiceáil agam, thiteadh an lug ar an lag orm agus ba bheag a bhínn in ann a rá sa teach sin".[34]

127

Agus maidir le tionchar na dtiarnaí talún, tá an méid seo aige:

"Barr ar cheithre bliana a chaitheas leis an obair in Iorras. Thug mé tuilleadh is dhá bhliain acu sin taobh istigh den Mhuirthead. Sa Gheata Mór a bhíodh cónaí orm. Thaitin an áit agus na daoine thar cionn liom, sé sin an méid acu a bhí Gaelach. Bhí rian na dtiarnaí talún go mór ar an áit san am sin. Go dtí fiú ainm an Gheata Mhóir ba é Baile an Bhiongamnaigh a thugtaí air in onóir nó in easonóir na dtiarnaí ar leo an ceantar sin a baisteadh an t-ainm air. Ba le na Biongamaigh dúicheacha na háite sin tráth. An t-am seo bhí réimse acu ó Chaol an Mhuirtheadh go Fód Dubh — ar feadh d'amharc ar gach aon taobh den bhóthar gan both ná bothán, teach, teallach ná tinte le feiceáil air. É ar féarach ag leathfheirmeoirí agus boicíní na tíre. Togha na bhfear agus plúr na mban ag tabhairt na farraige siar orthu féin, níos luaithe ná chuirfidis de mhúisiam ar an tiarna an talamh seo a iarraidh air ná a bhaint de le láimh láidir.

"In aice an Gheata Mhóir a mhair Riocard Bairéad, an file ba mhó le rá ina am féin. Is ann a cailleadh agus a cuireadh é. Bhí seanchas agus scéalta nár bheag san áit. Scríobh mé mo chion acu an t-am úd ach rinne na Tans luaithreamhán díobh blianta ina dhiaidh sin, nuair a dhódar an teach orainn in Aibreán na bliana 1921.

"Bhí ionadh agam an uair sin, agus tá fós, duine a raibh dearcadh náisiúnta aige, mar a bhí curtha i leith an Bhairéadaigh, gur bheag de spiorad na haimsire sin atá le feiceáil ina chuid filíochta. Deirtear go raibh sé seal i bpríosún i mbliain na bhFrancach, de bhithín a chuid náisiúntachta. Is mó go mór, de dúnghaois lucht tionscailt na talún a bunaíodh i bhfad ina dhiaidh sin, atá ag baint leis ná moladh an chlaímh a bhí i gceist lena linn. Sna bólaí seo freisin a mhair "Eoghan Cóir" a bhain barr ar mísc agus a thug craobh an tíoránaigh leis thar aon bháille dár mhair in Iorras ariamh.

"Bhí níos mó greama ag na daoine san áit seo ar an nGaeilge ná bhí sa taobh tíre deireanach a raibh mé ann. Ní raibh bualadh an Fháil Mhóir le fáil. Focal Béarla ar bith ní chloisfeá ann an uair sin. Ba mhór an t-ionadh liom sin, agus an staighean Galldachais a bhí sa bhFód Dubh agus aniar uaidh sin go dtí Tír Thrá. Bhí tarraingt an-lear coigríoch ón Ioruaidh ar an áit sin, mar bhí monarcha a leáidis míolta móra inti curtha ar bun ar thrá Thír Thrá acu, agus d'fhaigheadh na daoine saothrú ar fónamh ag obair sa mhonarcha sin."[15]

AN CÚLÚ I MAIGH EO

Ar éigean is gá méid na tubaiste a bhain don Ghaelige san 19ú céad a ríomh anseo. If fíor gur sheas an teanga an fód níos fearr i Maigh Eo ná i gcontae ar bith eile i gCúige Chonnacht seachas Gaillimh, ainneoin na mór-imirce, ainneoin an bhochtanais, agus an laghdú ar tháinig ar an daonra ó aimsir an Ghorta i leith. Ní shílim go raibh scéal chúlú na Gaeilge mórán níos éagsúla i gCo. Mhaigh Eo trí chéile ná an rud a bhí ag titim amach ar fud an iarthair go léir, ag deireadh an chéid seo caite. Agus de bharr tionchar agus dea-shampla an Ardeaspaig Mhic Éil i dTuaim, seans go raibh an scéal níos fearr sa chuid sin den chontae a bhí go díreach faoina chúram, ná go leor áiteanna eile. Chuir seasamh ceanndána Mhic Éil moill ar fhorás na "scolaíochta náisiúnta", ní foláir, rud a d'fhág go raibh líon mór daoine ina gcainteoirí dúchais ar fud an chontae go léir, agus fiú amháin in oirthear an chontae, ag an am a bunaíodh Conradh na Gaeilge. Ach ní mór idirdhealú a dhéanamh idir na pobail ina raibh an Ghaeilge fós in uachtar mar theanga an phobail, agus na pobail úd i lár agus in oirthear an chontae, ina raibh an Béarla ag teacht i réim, go háirithe ó 1870 ar aghaidh, le linn Chogadh na Talún agus tús na himirce rialta go Meiriceá. Níor chabhraigh forás na n-iarnród leis an scéal go léir, ná dearcadh Gallda lucht na mbailte móra sa chontae ach an oiread. Féach go bhfuil nuachtán Béarla againn i gCaisleán an Bharraigh i gcónaí, an *Connaught Telegraph,* a bunaíodh chomh fada siar le 1829. Níl a fhios agam cé mhéad den ghnáthphobal i lár chontae Mhaigh Eo a raibh léamh an Bhearla acu ag an am sin? Bhí an taobh eile leis an scéal chomh maith, agus ní féidir dearmad a dhéanamh, mar shampla den éacht a rinne leithéid an Chanónaigh Uilleog de Búrca (1829-1887), an té a scríobh *"The College Irish Grammar,"* agus a thuill an teideal "Athair na hAthbheochana" dar leis an té a scríobh scéal a bheatha le gairid, Proinsias Ó Maolmhuaidh, i ngeall ar a chuid oibre ar son na teanga.[16]

FOILSEACHÁIN NÁISIÚNTA TEO.

Foilseacháin Náisiúnta Teoranta (FNT) a d'fhoilsigh an leabhar ague cé go bhfuil oifigí acu ag 29 Sráid Uí Chonaill Íocht., i mBaile Átha Cliath is i gCathair na Mart atá clólann FNT, rud a fhágann gur i gCo. Mhaigh Eo a foilsíodh go leor den liosta fada leabhar Gaeilge atá curtha ar fáil ag an gcomhlacht seo le dhá scór bliain anuas.[17] Bhí an chéad eagrán de *Chré na Cille*[18], úrscéal mór Mháirtín Uí Chadhain i measc na leabhar tábhachtach ar cuireadh cló air i gCathair na Mart, faoi láimh oilte Joe Kenny, ag deireadh na 1940aí, agus tá forás ag teacht ar an obair ó shin. I measc na n-údar a d'fhoilsigh FNT ó shin tá Mícheál Ó hOdhráin (Rúnaí Uachtarán na hÉireann) a rugadh i bPártraí agus a scríob an bailiúchán gearrscéalta *Sléibhte Mhaigh Eo* i measc saothair eile.[19] Tá tábhacht an-bhunúsach leis na nua-eagráin de shaothair Ghaeilge cháiliúla atá curtha amach sa litriú nua agus i gcruth an lae inniu ag FNT thar na blianta. Leithéid *Imeacht na nIarlaí* le gan ach teideal amháin a lua.[20] Pádraig de Barra a rinne eagarthóireacht agus cóiriú ar an saothar seo agus an Cairdinéal Tomás Ó Fiaich, nuair a bhí sé fós ina Ollamh Staire i gColáiste Phádraig, Maigh Nuad, a scríobh an Réamhrá fada fíor-úsáideach a chabhraíonn leis an ngnáthléitheoir an saothar a thuiscint sa chomhthéacs stairiúil ceart. Corcaíoch is ea Pádraig de Barra agus tá sé ina Bhainisteoir ar Chlólann FNT i gCathair na Mart i gcónaí. Tá ardcháil air mar eagarthóir nua-Ghaeilge agua tá sé ag obair leis i gcónaí, ag cóiriú eagrán nua de mhórshaothair na Gaeilge agus á réiteach in eagráin nua. Deirtear liom, agus seo á scríobh, mar shampla, gur ghearr go mbeidh eagráin nua ar fáil ó FNT a chuirfidh ar chumas pobal Gaeilge na linne seo, den chéad uair riamh b'fhéidir, *Foras Feasa ar Éirinn* agus *Agallamh an Seanórach* a léamh i ngnáth-Ghaeilge ár linne. Rud a fhágann gur féidir a rá go bhfuil réabhlóid fhoilsitheoireachta dá gcuid féin curtha i gcríoch ag FNT ina gClólann i gCathair na Mart le glúin anuas, fiú mura bhfuil eolas ag gach éinne i gCo. Mhaigh Eo faoin ghaisce seo.

INNIU AGUS AN "MAYO NEWS"

Muintir FNT a fhoilsíonn INNIU freisin agus ní minic a thuigeann gach éinne i gCo. Mhaigh Eo b'fhéidir, go bhfuil an nuachtán seachtainiúil seo i nGaeilge, a mbeidh dhá scór bliain slánaithe aige faoi Lá le Pádraig seo chugainn (17 Márta, 1983), á chlóbhualadh go rialta gan bhearna gan bhriseadh i gcló-theach an *Mayo News* ó cheannaigh muintir Ghlúin na Bua é i 1948. Tá éacht dá chuid féin curtha i gcríoch ag lucht foilsithe INNIU le glúin anuas a bhfuil tionchar do-chreidte tar éis a bheith aige ar stair na Gaeilge — mura mbeadh ann ach an bealach inar chabhraigh an páipéar, tríd an chéad Eagarthóir, Ciarán Ó Nualláin, agua a chomrádaí, Tarlach Ó hUid, atá ina Eagarthóir anois, le forbairt na nua-théarmaíochta trína húsáid go rialta ar mheán a léití go forleathan sna scoileanna, gan trácht ar an bpáirt mhór a bhí ag muintir INNIU san iarracht chun léamh na Gaeilge sa Chló Rómhánach a bhunú mar nós.

Níl scéal na Gaeilge ar pháipéir áitiúla Mhaigh Eo sásúil go fóill agus ní raibh riamh, ainneoin díol mór a bheith orthu i measc na bpobal Gaeltachta sa chontae sin. Cé gur cheannaigh dream Gaeilge i mBaile Átha Cliath an *Mayo News* agus gur choinnigh siad ag imeacht ó shin é le linn dóibh a bheith ag forbairt FNT agus INNIU, agus cé gurb í an fhoilsitheoireacht Ghaeilge ba bhunchúis le ceannach na clólainne i gCathair na Mart an chéad lá riamh, níor éirigh leo mórán níos mó a dhéanamh d'usaid na Gaeilge sa nuachtán áitiúil seo atá ina Bhíobla in Acaill ach go háirithe, ná na nuachtáin Bhéarla eile. Cinnte, ba ghnách alt nó dhó agus fiu amháin míreanna nuachta a chur i gcló i nGaeilge, ach minic go leor, ní bhíodh ann ach píosa éigin a cuireadh i gcló cheana féin ar INNIU, nó a réitíodh le haghaidh an pháipéir Ghaeilge sin, agus nach mbíodh bainteach go minic leis na rudaí áitiúla a mbeadh spéis ar leith ag léitheoirí Gaeltachta Mhaigh Eo iontu. Ní shin le rá nár dearnadh iarrachtaí ó am go chéile. Scríobh mé féin colún "Scéalta ón bPríomhchathair" don *Mayo News* le linn dom a bheith ag obair mar iriseoir i mBaile Átha Cliath idir 1966 agus 1968, agus scríobhadh Risteárd Ó Glaisne agus Seosamh Ó Cuaig agus daoine eile ailt i nGaeilge don pháipéar ag tréimhsí éagsúla, a bhí dírithe go sonrach ar riachtanais léitheoirí an *Mayo News* féin. Mar sin féin is dóigh liom go bhfeádfaí a rá nár éirigh riamh leis an iarracht chun soláthar maith míreanna i nGaeilge a chur sa pháipéar, ainneoin na dea-thola agus iarrachtaí go leor.[21]

Muintir Ghaeltacht Mhaigh Eo a bheith gan taithí ar bith ar ábhar a léamh go rialta i nGaeilge, go háirithe sa Chló Rómhánach, an deacracht is mó a bhí ann, dhéarfainn.

CNOC MHUIRE

I nGaeilge a tugadh cuid den bhfianaise a bhain leis an bhfiosrúchán a rinneadh faoi nochtadh na Maighdine Muire i gCnoc Mhuire, deirtear, ach tá sé suntasach a thabhairt faoi deara gurb iad na daoine aosta a roghnaigh an Ghaeilge mar theanga fianaise sa chás seo.[22] Arís, cainteoir dúchais Gaeilge a bhí i Mícheál Daibhéid, a rugadh sa tSráid, idir Caisleán an Bharraigh agus Béal an Átha, sa bhliain 1846, agus a labhair Gaeilge le linn a óige sa phobal Éireannach i Haslington i Sasana mar ar lonnaigh a mhuintir ó 1851 ar aghaidh.[23] Bhí greim chomh docht sin ag an nGaeilge ar chlann an Dáibhéidigh i gcónaí, de réir cosúlachta, go raibh blas láidir Lancashire ar an mBearla d'fhoghlaim bunaitheoir Chonradh na Talún, agus gur fhan an blas úd ar a chuid Béarla leis go deireadh a shaoil. Mar sin féin bhí an Ghaeilge ag imeacht i léig ar fud Mhaigh Eo chomh maith le go leor áiteanna eile, ó aimsir an Ghorta go dtí deireadh an chéid, agus cé go raibh líon ard cainteoirí Gaeilge le feiceáil ag gach Daonáireamh a rinneadh isteach sa chéad seo, ní mór a bheith cúramach faoin chiall is ceart a bhaint astu. Taobh amuigh ar fad de cheist chruinnis, agus den náire a bhí ar dhaoine áirithe a admháil go raibh Gaeilge acu fiú amháin (rud a d'aistrigh ina ábhar maíte, ar ball, faoi thionchar na hathbheochana i gcásanna áirithe), ní hionann ar chor ar bith Gaeilge a bheith ag daoine fásta agus cinnteacht go mbeidh sí ag an gcéad ghlúin eile, nó go deimhin, go bhfuil sí á labhairt mar theanga an phobail.[24] Is cinnte go raibh glúin ag fás aníos a bhí á tógáil le "Béarla," cé go raibh an bheirt thuismitheoir cláraithe ina gcainteoirí dúchais Gaeilge. Is cinnte freisin, gur minic a bhíodh gnóthaí poiblí á ndéanamh trí "Bhéarla" ag daoine a raibh Gaeilge ó dhúchas acu. Tá sé ar siúl i gcónaí faoin nós aisteach Éireannach úd, a deir gur leor Béarlóir amháin i gcomhluadar, i gcumann nó i dteach tabhairne leis an slua ar fad a chasadh i dtreo an Bhéarla. Rinne teaghlaigh áirithe a gcuid socruithe dátheangachais féin. Mar shampla, ba nós le teaghlaigh i Maigh Eo go dtí le fíordhéanaí an paidrín agus paidreacha eile an tí a rá i nGaeilge, go ceann na mblianta, tar éis don athair agus don mháthair a bheith éirithe as úsáid na Gaeilge mar ghnáth-urlabhra, agus gan aon eolas ar an nGaeilge a bheith seolta ar aghaidh go dtí an chéad ghlúin eile, taobh amuigh de na paidreacha. Thug mé féin an scéal seo faoi deara i Maigh Eo i dtosach, sa bhliain 1966, nuair a chaith mé tamall in Ospidéal an Chontae i gCaisleán an Bharraigh tar éis timpist ghluaisteáin a bheith agam láimh le Béal an Mhuirthead, ar mo chéad turas go hIorras, agus go Gaeltacht na hEach Léime agus an Fhóid Dhuibh.[25] (Bhí an Ghaeltacht seo, ag ceann leithinis an Mhuirthead, beo go maith ag an am sin, agus bhí cuairt á tabhairt againn ar an áit le socruithe a dhéanamh le haghaidh Chomhdháil shamhraidh lucht ollscoile an Chomhchaidrimh an samhradh ina dhiaidh sin. D'éirigh linn, ainneoin na ndeacrachtaí, breis is 100 duine fásta a mhealladh ar saoire seachtaine go dtí an ceantar, ag deireadh mhí Iúil 1967 — an chéad Chomhdháil dá leithéid a bhí riamh ag an gceantar, agus go bhfios dom, an t-aon cheann a bhí ann ó shin — ach sin scéal eile do lá éigin eile!)

GAEILGE AG DIA?

Bhí fear, sean-Óglach de réir mar a thuigim, as Acaill sa bharda i gCaisleán an Bharraigh le linn dom a bheith ann. Cainteoir dúchais Gaeilge a bhí ann, seanfhear cráifeach de réir gach cosúlachta. Gach tráthnóna, tar éis an tae, thosaíodh sé ag rá an phaidrín amach os ard sa bharda, i nGaeilge ar ndóigh. Rud a thaitin liom féin, agus a thug dóchas áirithe dom nach raibh cluiche na Gaeilge caillte ar fad in Acaill ach an oiread, fiú má thuig mé go raibh ceithre scór bliain nach mór ag an bhfear seo, agus nár lean sé go mbeadh eolas ar na paidreacha féin ag an gcéad ghlúin eile. Ach an rud ba shuimiúla a thug mé faoi deara ná go raibh gach fear eile, ó gach cúinne de Chontae Mhaigh Eo nach mór, a bhí sa bharda mór in éineacht linn, in ann na paidreacha a rá i nGaeilge chomh maith. Go deimhin, dúirt cúpla fear a bhí in aice liom gur fearr a bhí na paidreacha coitianta ar eolas acu i nGaeilge, ná i mBéarla, mar go ndeirtí an choróin Mhuire i nGaeilge sa bhaile i gcónaí — mar chuirtéis do mhamó nó daideo. Cuimhnigh nach raibh úsáid na gnáth-theanga san Aifreann ach díreach ag teacht isteach thart faoin am sin. Cuimhnigh freisin nach raibh na daoine seo in ann gnáthchomhrá Gaeilge a choinneáil, ná a thuiscint, cé go raibh an teanga sin mar mheán cumarsáide le Dia agus lena Mháthair bheannaithe i gcónaí acu.

Ba lú, b'fheidir, an tionchar a bhí ag úsáid na gnáth-theanga i searmanais eaglasta na hEaglaise Caitlicí i nGaeltachtaí Mhaigh Eo ná áit ar bith eile sa tír. Mar shampla, cé gur tugadh an Ghaeilge isteach mar ghnáth-urlabhra san Aifreann ar fud na Gaeltachta i lár na 1960aí, fiú amháin i bpobail laga ar nós na Rinne, Oileán Chléire agus Chúil Aodha (mar a rinneadh an fhorbairt cháiliúil ar an liotúirge dúchasach faoi threoir Sheáin Uí Riada agus an chóir áitiúil), ar éigin má ceadaíodh úsáid na Gaeilge mar ghnáthnós ag Aifrinn i nGaeltachtaí Mhaigh Eo go ceann na mblianta ina dhiadh sin. Cheadaítí Aifreann i nGaeilge anseo agus ansiúd, agus má bhí sagart "díograiseach" ann, ba ghnách leis Aifreann a léamh i nGaeilge — agus gan mórán a rá ós ard i dtaobh an scéil lasmuigh! Ach ní fhéadfaí a rá, ag tús na 1970aí féin, go raibh an Ghaeilge á húsáid ná an dúchas á fhorbairt i gceantar Gaeltachta ar bith i Maigh Eo, mar a bhí i nGaeltachtaí laga na Mumhan, le linn na 1970aí féin. Bhí "mionlach" Béarla le cur san áireamh i ngach pobal, de réir cosúlachta, a raibh aird níos mó air ná éileamh an dúchais, agus fágadh na daoine a labhraíodh Gaeilge sa bhaile nó a thoilíodh do mhúineadh an traidisiúin Ghaelaigh trí na scoileanna, ina strainséirí i gcúrsaí eaglasta i gcónaí i Maigh Eo — mura bhfuil athrú ar an scéal le fíordhéanaí? Tharla sé, mar sin, nach léití Aifreann Domhnaigh i nGaeilge ar an Each Léim mar ghnáthois, nuair a thug muid Comhdháil an Chomhchaidrimh go dtí an ait i samhradh na blaina 1967. Tugadh cead dúinn, ar ndóigh, Aifreann a bheith i nGaeilge againn le linn dúinn a bheith ar saoire sa chomharsanacht. Chaithfí freastal ar na turasóirí, cé go mba léir gur ghealaigh an ócáid croithe mhuintir na háite chomh maith. Iarradh ormsa, mar Uachtarán ar an gComhchaidreamh ag an am, na ceachtanna a léamh ag an Aifreann Gaeilge sin. Nós eile a tháinig isteach le Vatacáin II, ná páirt a thabhairt don phobal tuatach i gcás mar seo. Ach ó tharla nár ghnách an tAifreann a léamh i nGaeilge sa chomharsanacht seo ó cheadaigh Vatacáin II a leithéid, is cosúil gurb é Aifreann seo an Chomhchaidrimh an chéad cheann a léadh i nGaeilge ó aimsir Phádraig Naofa i leith.

SA CHÉAD SEO

Rud a thugann go croí na ceiste muid — staid na bpobal Gaeltachta i gCo. Mhaigh Eo san aois seo, agus an scéal mar atá sé faoi láthair. Cé go ndearna lucht na hathbheochana faillí mhór i dtaobh Ghaeltacht Mhaigh Eo agus nach raibh an traidisiún liteartha chomh láidir agus a bhí i bpócaí Gaeltachta níos lú i gcontaetha eile, is léir gurb é an saibhreas is luachmhaire a fágadh, gan áireamh, ó dheireadh an chéid seo caite, ná an líon mór cainteoirí breátha ó dhúchas a bhí beo i gcónaí sa chontae, agus an oidhreacht bhreá chanúna glaine a bhí ar fáil do lucht foghlamtha agus léinn ach iad a bheith sásta í a shaothrú.

Mar a tharlaíonn, tá saothair foilsithe faoi na canúintí éagsúla sna pócaí éagsúla Gaeltachta i Maigh Eo ar fáil anois nach raibh ar fáil scór bliain ó shin. Agus cé gur bailíodh an t-eolas ar a bhfuil siad bunaithe blianta fada roimhe sin arís, tugann siad léargas luachmhar dúinn ar staid na teanga sna ceantair éagsúla Ghaeltachta sa chéad seo. Is léir ó na staidéir acadúla seo go léir, agus ón méid a scríobh daoine eile ag tús an chéid, gur mar thrí phóca ar leith a bhí scaipthe óna chéile, a mhair an Ghaeltacht i Maigh Eo isteach sa ghlúin seo i.e. thart faoi Thuar Mhic Éadaigh i ndeisceart an chontae, Acaill, (agus an leithinis díreach roimh dhul isteach ar an oileán duit, san áireamh) agus Iorras. Ceantar fairsing scéirdiúil, atá gearrtha amach ón chuid eile d'Éirinn ag na mílte portaigh is ea Iorras, agus ní hiontas ar bith é go bhfuil traidisiún Gaeltachta an cheantair seo briste bearnaithe freisin. Taobh amuigh den iargúltacht agus den droch-chóras cumarsáide leis an gcuid eile den tír, ní minic a ritheann sé le daoine, b'fheidir, go bhfuil barúntacht Iorrais beagnach chomh mór le Co. Lú ar fad. Ní iontas ar bith é, mar sin, go mbeadh a thraidisiún Gaelach féin ag roinnt leis san am atá caite. Mar a deir Éamonn Mac an Fhailigh ina Réamhrá le *"The Irish of Erris Co. Mayo"*:

"Erris has had its poet in Riocard Bairéad, familiarly known in the district as Dick Buiréad, who lived in the latter half of the 18th century and the early part of the 19th century. The year of his death, very probably, was 1819. He composed many ballads, topical, bright and light of touch, and his ironic satire is still savoured by Errismen. Knight, in 1836, wrote of him: 'One man of real genius died about sixteen or eighteen years ago!' He goes on to describe him as 'sweet, correct, mellifluous in his language and verse . . . his songs were sung and listened to'. He 'seemed to follow the style of Swift . . . . . was an enthusiastic admirer of his.'"[26]

RIOCARD BAIRÉAD

Níl fúm anseo, ach an oiread, léirmheas a dhéanamh ar údar "Eoghan Cóir", "Preab san Ól" agus go leor de na dánta eile a d'fhoghlaim muid b'fheidir, ar scoil. Ach tá bunleabhar ar Riocard Bairéad agus a shaothar ar fáil ó Nicholas Williams againn, anois, agus is fiú go mór do dhuine ar bith gur spéis leis oidhreacht Iorrais agus oidhreacht Ghaeltacht Mhaigh Eo é a léamh.[27] Ar ndóigh, bhí aird na tíre dírithe ar Thuar Mhic Éadaigh, ag tús an chéid, nuair a bunaíodh Coláiste Gaeilge in áit ina raibh an Ghaeilge go láidir i réim i gcónaí, más fíor. Nó an raibh? Cuimhnigh go raibh greim faighte ag an mBéarla i mBéal Átha an Ghaorthaidh faoin am a bunaíodh an chéad Choláiste Gaeilge ar an sráidbhaile sin in iarthar Chorcaí sa bhliain 1904. Deirtear go mbeadh an Ghaeilge imithe as an áit ar fád, dhá ghlúin ó shin, murach an Coláiste céanna, agus an cháil a thuill sé don áit. Mar an gcéanna, le Tuar Mhic Éadaigh b'fhéidir, agus fiú amháin an Spidéal, nach bhfuil ach 12 mhíle ó chathair na Gaillimhe?

TUAR MHIC ÉADAIGH

Is cinnte gur chabhraigh suíomh na sráidbhailte seo, faoi bhun scór míle ón stáisiún traenach ba ghaire, i Maigh Chromtha, i nGaillimh agus i gCaisleán an Bharraigh, leis an gcinneadh chun Coláiste Gaeilge a bhunú iontu, oiread is a chabhraigh staid na Gaeilge sna pobail sin ag an am. Agus cé gur chabhraigh an Coláiste Gaeilge, agus an Coláiste Ullmhúcháin ar ball, gan amhras, le Tuar Mhic Éadaigh, níl sé leath chomh cinnte gur cuireadh stop leis an meath, ná gur chabhraigh na beartais thionscail éagsúla a bhunaíodh san áit, ar ball, leis an scéal. Tá saothar breá scoláiriúil againn anois ó Sheán de Búrca, *"The Irish of Tourmakeady, Co. Mayo"* ina bhfuil an méid seo le rá aige:

"Tourmakeady itself, although the scene of strong anglicizing efforts by landlords and others in the 19th century, was entirely Irish-speaking at the beginning of this century, when an Irish college was established there. Irish is still a living language there, though the circumstances accompanying its use are changing at an onimous rate: many customs, pastimes, and beliefs, that were once part and parcel of the Irish speaker's world are now moribund; and the innovations that replace them frequently involve foreign phrases and an alien vocabulary. The fact that it remains an economically under-developed area, with a high rate of emigration, has the twofold effect of reducing the numbers of speakers and increasing the import of English".[28]

Ní ceart a cheapadh áfach gur torthaí diúlacha amháin a bhí ar iarrachtaí an stáit féin ar na Gaeltachtaí, Gaeltacht Thuar Mhic Éadaigh san áireamh. Mar shampla, nuair a bhunaigh Earnán de Blaghd na Coláistí Ullmhúcháin sna 1920aí bhí Tuar Mhic Éadaigh i measc na n-áiteanna a roghnaíodh le haghaidh scoile do chaillíní agus tá traidisiún fada cáiliúil ag baint le Coláiste Mhuire ó shin i leith a raibh tionchar nach beag aige ar chúrsaí oideachais an cheantair.

Fiú amháin nuair a dúnadh na Coláistí Ullmhúcháin chéanna sna 1960aí, lean Coláiste Mhuire air mar mheánscoil den scoth ina múintear na hábhair trí mheán na Gaeilge agus tá sé ina áis tábhachtach oideachais i gcónai ní amháin do na scoláirí cónaithe ach freisin do lucht iarbhunscoile an cheantair.

I measc na n-iarscoláirí cáiliúla atá ag an gColáiste tá Máire Geoghegan-Uí Chuinn, de bhunadh Charna, atá ina hAire Stáit sa Roinn Oideachais faoi láthair, agus a bhain áit amach sa stair di féin mar Aire Gaeltachta idir mí na Nollag, 1979 agus lár na bliana 1981 — an chéad bhean a bhí ina comhalta den Rialtas ó aimsir na Cuntaoise Markievicz a bhí ina hAire Saothair sa Chéad Dáil.

ACAILL

An rud atá ráite faoi Thuar Mhic Éadaigh thuas, is féidir é a rá freisin faoi Acaill agus faoi gach blúire eile den Ghaeltacht Mhaigh Eo. Níl an imirce chomh tréan, ar ndóigh, agus a bhíodh. Níl scéal na fostaíochta chomh dona i dTuar Mhic Éadaigh ach an oiread.[29] Is cinnte gur chaith an stát, trí Ghaeltarra, pingin nach beag leis an áit thar na blianta, i bhfad níos mó ná mar a caitheadh i nGaeltachtaí níos laidre, agus níos tábhachtaí in áiteanna eile. Ach ní raibh bonn an réasúin riamh faoin teoiric nach raibh le déanamh ach fostaíocht sa bhaile a chur ar fáil agus go mairfeadh na pobail mar phobail Ghaeltachta. Tá go leor leor samplaí againn ó Ghaeltachtaí Mhaigh Eo féin a bhréagnaíonn an teoiric chéanna, Acaill ina measc. Tá staidéar breá eile déanta ag Gearóid Stockman ar Ghaeilge Acla curtha i gcló le cúpla bliain anuas.[30] Ach b'éigean dúinn fanacht go dtí 1980 sar a bhfuair muid an chéad leabhar i nGaeilge ón oileán mór cáiliúil céanna a bhfuil tarraingt lucht léinn agus ealaíne air leis na cianta. Sin é *Diabhal Smid Bhréige Ann!* le Pádraic Seoighthe, duine de laochra teanga an cheantair a choinnigh an teanga beo faoi dhíon a thí féin nuair nach raibh mórán eile san áit á dhéanamh. Mar sin féin, féach go ndeir sé ina réamhrá: "Faraor géar go dtig a rá go bhfuil an bás ag bagairt ar Ghaeltacht Acla — loic ar an chineál ungadóireachta ar dúradh faoi go bhfeicfí 'cosa crainn faoi na cearca'. Tá saibhreas Gaeilge i dtalamh".[31]

SEÁN Ó RUADHÁIN

Ach ar eagla an lagmhisnigh ar fad, breathnaímis, más ea, ar an saibhreas a tháinig slán i Maigh Eo, agus go háirithe in Acaill agus in Iorras, ainneoin na n-ainneoin — an saibhreas úd atá le fáil i scríbhinní leithéid Sheáin Uí Ruadháin.

Rugadh Seán Ó Ruadháin i nDúloch, láimh le Gaoth Sáile in Iorras sa bhliain 1883 agus cailleadh é i mBaile Átha Cliath sa bhliain 1966. Cara le Dúghlas de hÍde a bhí ann, bhí baint aige le Conradh na Gaeilge ó thús an chéid agus chaith sé tamall ag taisteal ar fud an iarthair mar Mhúinteoir Taistil. Ceapadh ina Ollamh le Gaeilge i gColáiste Oiliúna Dhún an Chéirigh, sa Charraig Dhubh i mBaile Átha Cliath é, ar ball, agus bhí rian a chumais le feiceáil ar na céadta bun-oidí a raibh máistreacht ar Ghaeilge agus ar mhúineadh na Gaeilge acu ar fud na tíre glúin ó shin. B'e Seán Ó Ruadháin a scríobh an t-úrscéal *Pádraic Máire Bán* a foilsíodh sa bhliain 1932 agus ar cuireadh athchló air i 1934, 1935, 1937 agus 1938. D'aistrigh sé saothar Dickens agus Stevenson go Gaeilge sna tríochadaí agus is fiú go mór leithéid *Mé Féin is M'Asal* — leagan Gaeilge de *Travels With a Donkey* le Robert Louis Stevenson a foilsíodh sa bhliain 1937 — a léamh i gcónaí mar shampla den saibhreas teanga agus cumas aistriúcháin a bhí ag baint leis an bhfear seo a raibh Gaeilge Mhaigh Eo go ceolmhar aige.[32] Bhí spéis ar leith ag Ó Ruadháin i nglaineacht chanúna agus i bhforbairt cheart na Gaeilge ag am nuair a bhí an teanga á forbairt agus á cur in úsáid ar bhealaí nach mbíodh i gceist riamh roimhe sin, mar is léir d'éinne a léann an colún "Ceart nó Mícheart?" a bhíodh aige ar *Feasta* ar feadh na mblianta. Scríobh sé gearrscéalta freisin. Mar shampla *Grinn-Sgéalta* a foilsíodh i mBaile Átha Cliath sa bhliain 1929.

Mhair deirfiúr le Seán Ó Ruadháin ina ceantar dúchais féin i nDúloch go dtí le fíorghairid. Bhuail mé féin léi cúpla uair nuair a chuir mé aithne ar an gceantar, thart ar lár na 1960aí. Faoin am sin bhí an Ghaeilge ag dul ar chúl go tréan sa cheantar, rud a ghoill uirthi. Dúnadh na bunscoile i nDúloch an rud ba mhó a bhuail buile ar an gceantar Gaeltachta seo dar léi.[33]

Cé go bhfuil Gaeltachtaí Iorrais agus Acla gar go maith dá chéile ó thaobh tíreolais de, tá difríochtaí spéisiúla teanga idir na pócaí éagsúla a mhaireann beo agus de réir gach cosúlachta, téann na difríochtaí sin siar i bhfad sa stair.

Deir na húdair go léir linn go raibh siad bunaithe sar ar scaradh na pócaí éagsúla Gaeltachta óna chéile ag rabharta an Bhéarla.

TIONCHAR THÍR CHONAILL?

De réir dealraimh, is gaire Gaeilge Acla, ar bhealaí, do Ghaeilge Thír Chonaill ná do "mheánchanúint" Iorrais féin, rud a thug Colm Ó Gaora faoi deara le linn dó a bheith ag obair do Chonradh na Gaeilge sa cheantar ag tús an chéid.[34] Tá Gaeilge Acla tráite go mór ó shin i leith, ach rinne Gearóid Stockman staidéar cumasach ar an teanga nuair a bhí beocht éigin sa chanúint í gcónaí, fiche bliain ó shin. Sa Réamhrá lena shaothar *The Irish of Achill, Co. Mayo* tá an méid seo le rá aige inter alia:

"Irish is still spoken in many villages in the western half of Curraun and the eastern half of Achill Island but, as is the unfortunate case in most Gaeltacht areas, it is rapidly dying . . .

"To the dialectologist Achill Irish is of immense interest because of the influence of Ulster Irish on the dialect. Wagner in his Introduction to *A Linguistic Atlas and Survey of Irish Dialects* mentions the strong Ulster superstratum combined with a North Connaught substratum in the Achill and Ballycroy area . . .

"There is still an awareness of Ulster origins among the inhabitants of Upper Achill and Curraun but there is no feeling of kinship. Donegal people are considered as rapid speakers of Irish who have strange words like *tábla, bealach mór* and *plaincéidí*, whereas Connemara people are respected as having excellent Irish and being more like themselves.

"Yet after spending a short time in Curraun, I became aware of a feeling of distinction between the people of Lower Achill and those of the rest of the area. 'If you are going to Lower Achill, bring a lunch with you', I was advised by a Curraun man; 'you'll get nothing to eat from the "Gráidhíní". When I asked who the 'Gráidhíní' were I was informed that this was a nickname given to the people of Lower Achill because they addressed one another as 'a ghrádh', a term which was not used in the eastern side; they were a different type of people altogether, I was told, mean and inhospitable".[36]

Ní mór dúinn a bheith buíoch do Stockman agus do lucht an Léinn Éireannaigh in Ollscoil na Banríona, Béal Feirste as ucht an tsaothair seo. Bhí dua nach beag ag baint leis agus léiríonn an t-údar ceann de na deacrachtaí aisteacha is gnách a bheith ag lucht bailithe an bhéil bheo i gcomhluadair thuaithe, anuas go dtí ár linn féin fiú amháin, nuair a deir sé i bhfonóta lena Réamhrá faoi chuid de na daoine a labhair leis:

"Some speakers were reluctant to have their voices recorded and Sp. 10 expressed the wish that neither her voice nor her name should live after her. Sp. 1 informed me that a photographer once persuaded a few Achill people to pose for a photograph. The photograph, to their dismay, appeared on post-cards. Since then people are wary and fear that their recorded voice might be used on radio or played in neighbours' houses to be laughed at. Where informants asked me to conceal their identity, I have tried to respect their wishes."

TUAIRIM UÍ RATHAILLE

Maidir leis an tionchar a bhí ag na hUltaigh, agus dá bhrí sin ag Gaeilge Uladh, ar Mhaigh Eo, seo mar a scríobh Tomás Ó Rathaille faoin scéal, sa bhliain 1931:

"On the other hand, a certain amount of Ulster influence is to be observed a long way from the Ulster border, in the northern half of Co. Mayo. This is, doubtless, to be attributed mainly to the transplantation of the Cromwellian period. The Cromwellian scheme was to transport the Irish of Ulster to Mayo, and to part of Galway (mainly the western side of that county). To the Ballycroy district in W. Mayo (N.E. of Achill Island) a considerable number of Ulster inhabitants were removed, among them a grandson of Niall Garbh Ó Domhnaill. This particular Ulster colony long preserved its individuality and the memory of it still survives. P. Knight, writing in 1836, says: "Ballycroy and Achill have been for an undetermined number of years inhabited by a colony from the North of Ireland, who are called by their neighbours 'Ultagh' or 'Ulster men'. He adds that they intermarry almost exclusively with one another, and still retain the ancient dialect of language used in the North. Two years later O'Donovan wrote that the Ballycroy people still speak the Ultonian dialect of Irish. In 1896 a writer says of them: The dialect they speak is somewhat different from that of other peoples of Erris, though not so much as formerly, and has most of the characters (sic) of Ulster Irish. Natives of Ulster were of course transplanted to many other parts of Mayo besides Ballycroy, which is chiefly remarkable in that its Ulster colony, held together for so many generations as a separate community".[37]

In dhá cheann de na trí fhonóta leis an méid sin thuas, deir an Rathallach: "Among the eight commonest surnames in the district a generation ago were five Ulster names, Cafferky, Sweeny, Mc Manomon, Kane and McGinty. Other Ulster surnames like Campbell, O'Donnell, Boyle and Gallagher were also represented," agus ansin arís, "In a list, compiled in 1894, of the commonest surnames in the districts of the Mullet and Portacloy, in N.W. Mayo, I note that the commonest surname, but one, is the Cavan name, Reilly".[38]

IORRAS INNIU

Bhí sé de mhí-ádh ag Gaeltacht Mhaigh Eo freisin nár foilsíodh an bunsaothar tábhachtach "The Irish of Erris, Co. Mayo" le Éamonn Mhac an Fhailigh go dtí 1968, cé gur bailíodh go leor den ábhar ar a bhfuil an leabhar bunaithe chomh fada siar le lár na dtríochadaí. Is fíor, mar a deir an t-udár, gur bhailigh sé ábhar breise thart faoin bhFál Mór sna blianta 1961-'62, agus glacann sé buíochas leis na daoine seo a leanas sa réamhrá: Liam Ó hEimhrín, a cailleadh ar 17 Samhain, 1962, Seán Bhilín Ó Maolfhábhaill (John Lavelle) "in his seventies", Mícheál Mhac a' tSaoir (Michael MacIntyre) "about seventy" agus Mícheál Ó Coradhuibh (Michael Corduff) "somewhat over seventy".[39] Níl a fhios agam an bhfuil na daoine seo beo inniu, ach is léir go raibh pobal beo Gaeltachta in Iorras anuas go dtí ár linn féin. Ní miste, mar sin, b'fhéidir, breathnú ar a bhfuil le rá ag Éamonn Mhac an Fhailigh ina réamhrá faoi bheocht na hoidhreachta Gaeltachta seo lenár linn féin, sar a thosóimid ar scagadh a dhéanamh ar an dearcadh oifigiúil faoin "Ghaeltacht oifigiúil" — cluiche eile ar fad a tháinig chun cinn chomh luath agus a thosaigh an stát Éireannach ag plé le polasaithe a raibh sé mar aidhm leo, más fíor, an Ghaeltacht a neartú agus a chaomnadh. Deirtear sa réamhrá:

"The barony of Erris occupies the north-west corner of the Co. Mayo. Broadhaven from the North and Blacksod Bay from the South, penetrate to meet at the isthmus of Belmullet and cut off from the rest of the Mullet penninsual to the West. On the east Erris adjoins the barony of Tirawly. The term Erris in the language of the older inhabitants of Dú Chaocháin, is of restricted meaning and applies to the Mullet penninsula only. P. Knight, at p 4 of his book (*Erris in the Irish Highlands,* Dublin, 1836) writes: 'Erris means western penninsula and strictly speaking should be confined to the portion within the isthmus of the Mullet . . . . the natives call all beyond that 'the mountains'."

"At two points in the barony I found Irish in full vigour as the vernacular: (1) Faulmore and adjacent townlands to the west; (2) Dú Chaocháin, comprising Kilgalligan, Carateigue, Stonefield and Cornboy in the north of the barony, beside Beinn Bhuí Head. At these two places, Irish was, in 1936, the everyday speech of old and young and the majority of the children acquired their first knowledge of English on attending school. Many of the older people knew Irish only.

"The entire people of the two islands of Inishkea had been accomodated in new holdings by the Irish Land Commission at Glosh and Nakil on the opposite mainland soon after 1930. In their new homes on the mainland these migrants from Iniskea formed a compact community whose main pursuit continued to be fishing. They have always been entirely Irish-speaking.

"Faulmore was, before the Land Commission's scheme of consolidation there was completed in 1936-'37, an old-world rural village or 'baile', made up of a score or more of thatched houses built close to one another. The main harvest of the community was from the sea. With the coming of consolidation each household acquired additional land and a new dwelling on its own holding. The old village was demolished. In the past Faulmore had considerable contact with the Iniskea islands, and intermarriage between members of the two communities was not uncommon.

"Doohoma is on the southern coast of the small penninsula or headland south-west of Geesala village, and has its extension in Ceann Reamhar Head pointing in the direction of Achill. In Doohoma in 1935, those of the older generation were fluent Irish speakers but English was fast replacing Irish as the everyday speech of the younger generation and those of school age. There has been heavy emigration to Scotland and to England for many years from the Doohoma district.

"Phonetically and in its accidence Erris Irish is in marked contrast with the Irish of Ballycroy and Achill, where Donegal influence is much in evidence. Doohoma people used to quote the Ballycroy version of the proverb 'cat after kind' viz. *siúl a' chuit ag a' phisín,* for which Doohoma people said *siúl a' chait ag a' bpisín.* They contrasted too, *ar a' phortach, insa bhád, ar a' bheithíoch* for Ballycroy, with their own *ar a' bportach, insa mbád, ar a' mbeithíoch.* They also adverted to the Achill and Ballycroy pronunciation of *déanamh* as *déanú,* for which they in Doohoma would say *díonú.*

"The Irish of Erris seems to be typical of Mayo Irish in general; it is conservative in its sounds, as also in its declensional patterns, and has not gravely disgressed from Classical Irish, though there are some features in which it shows a striking departure from classical forms. Two scholars in the past have had observations to make which are apposite here, and may be quoted. John Mac Neill in *Clare Island Survey* Section I, part 3, p. 7, says of the local dialect of Clare Island: 'Its phoentic system is the best preserved of all the extant Irish dialects known to me, that is to say, is the most fully in conformity with the orthography of Early Modern Irish'. T. F. O'Rahilly in his *Irish Dialects,* p. 246, remarks: 'On the whole, it would seem that the Irish of N. Connacht has the fewest deviations from the older pronunciation'. These remarks would appear to be equally applicable to the Irish of Erris today".[40]

Sin agaibh é, más ea, tuairimí na scoláirí ar thábhacht oidhreacht Ghaeilge Mhaigh Eo, agus ar an staid a bhí uirthí glúin nó dhó ó shin. Bhí an oidhreacht sin ag imeacht le sruth an uair úd, mar a bhí le blianta fada roimhe sin. Is baolach nach bhfuil mórán athrú mór ar an scéal faoi láthair, ainneoin tuiscint níos fearr a bheith ag daoine, b'fhéidir, ar thábhacht agus ar phráinn na ceiste, tar éis a raibh d'Airí Gaeltachta de bhunadh Mhaigh Eo le 25 bliana anuas.[41] Le scrúdú a dhéanamh ar an scéal reatha, áfach, agus leis an tionchar a bhí ag an athbheochan náisiúnta, Cogadh na Saoirse agus polasaithe oifigiúla an stáit ar son na Gaeltachta, a mheas, ní mór dul ag plé le figiúirí agus le toscaí eile ar fad seachas na cinn a raibh spéis ag na scoláirí iontu. Tosaíonn an obair sin, is dócha, leis an Saorstát agus leis an gCoimisiún Gaeltachta.

COIMISIÚN GAELTACHTA

Ar an 27 Eanáir, 1925, bhunaigh Coiste Feidhmiúcháin Shaorstát Éireann "a Commission of Inquiry into the Preservation of the Gaeltacht", ag raibh na téarmaí tagartha seo a leanas:

"To inquire and report to the Executive Council as to the percentage of Irish speakers in a district which would warrant its being regarded as (a) an Irish speaking district or (b) a partly Irish speaking district, and the present extent and location of such districts".

"To inquire and make recommendations as to the use of Irish in the administration of such districts, the educational facilities therein, and any steps that should be taken to improve the economic conditions of the inhabitants."[42]

Is léir ón méid sin thuas go raibh ré na bhFíor-Ghaeltachtaí agus na mBreac-Ghaeltachtaí oifigiúla buailte linn cheana féin, go mbeadh brú áitiúil agus polaitíocht áirithe ag baint le leagan amach na gceantar feasta, agus go mbeadh cibé scéimeanna forbartha ar leith a chuirfí ar bun don Ghaeltacht ceangailte feasta le stádas oifigiúil mar cheantair Ghaeltachta. Shocraigh an Coimisiún ar cheantair ina raibh an Ghaeilge ar eolas ag 80% den phobal nó os a chionn a áireamh mar "Fhíor-Ghaeltacht", agus go n-áireofaí mar "Bhreac-Ghaeltacht" aon cheantar ina raibh Gaeilge ag idir 25% agus 79% den phobal. Ba ar an mbonn sin a leagadh amach na ceantair fhairsinge "Ghaeltachta" a cuireadh le chéile ar bhonn Dhaonáireamh na bliana 1926, agus ba ar an mbonn sin a leagadh amach an chéad liosta de cheantair oifigiúla Ghaeltachta in Acht na dTithe Gaeltachta, 1929.[43] Cúis mhagaidh dúinn inniu an ró-dhóchas a léirigh an Coimisiún sin agus cúis bhróin dúinn freisin, b'fhéidir, a laghad airde a tugadh i ndeireadh na dála ar na moltaí fiúntacha go léir a rinne an Coimisiún, faoi Chathaoirleacht an Ghinearáil Risteaird Uí Mhaolchatha, chun feabhas a chur ar shaol na Gaeltachta. Mar sin féin, ba léir gur thuig ceann an rialtais ag an am, Liam T. Mac Cosgair, croí na faidhbe, mar is léir ón méid seo a leanas sa litir a scríobh sé, ar an 4 Márta, 1925, chuig an Ginearál Ó Maolchatha, nuair a bhí sé féin agus an Coimisiún díreach ag dul i mbun oibre:

"We recognise also that the future of the Irish language and its part in the future of the Irish nation depend, more than on anything else, on its continuing in an unbroken tradition as the

139

language of Irish homes. This tradition is the living root from which alone organic growth is possible. For this reason the Irish people rightly value as a national asset their 'Gaeltacht', the scattered range of districts in which Irish is the home language".[44] Focail bhreátha, ach ba mhór ar fad an difríocht a bhí idir port dóchasach an Choimisiúin agus na ceantair mhóra a áiríodh mar "Ghaeltacht", idir Fhíor agus Bhreac, ag deireadh na 1920aí, agus an scéal fírinneach fiche bliain níos déanaí, ná ó shin. Sa bhliain 1950, rinne an tOllamh Brian Ó Cuív léirmheas an-ghéar ar an gcur i gcéill nuair a dúirt sé, agus é ag tagairt do scéal na Gaeltachta in Éirinn trí chéile:

"Today Census Returns may lead unthinking people to believe that great strides are being made in the preservation of our language but the facts are that Irish is no longer the every-day language of even one electoral division in Counties Cork, Waterford or Clare; that in Kerry the only area where it is extensively used is the western part of the Dingle penninsula; while in Galway, Mayo and Donegal, the districts where Irish is ordinarily used have been greatly reduced".

"I do not mean to imply that many people in the so-called Fíor-Ghaeltacht areas are not able to speak Irish but it is an undoubted fact that many of those who can speak it no longer do, and this is a condition that is spreading . . . . All of us have had experience of those homes where the grand-parents are native Irish speakers, one or both of the parents English speakers, and the children, in spite of the work done in the schools, also English speakers. We get a revealing picture of the position in details published last year in connection with the Department of Education's £5.00 grant for children from Irish-speaking homes. There is no doubt that this scheme has been a help in many areas, and this is reflected in the fact that about 75% of the children on the rolls in Fíor-Ghaeltacht schools qualified for the grant in 1947-'48. In the Breac-Ghaeltacht however, less than 3% of the children qualified. In other words, less than 3% of the homes with children of a school-going age have Irish as the home language, although according to the 1936 Census, in those areas 41% of the people were Irish speakers".[45]

GAELTACHTAÍ "OIFIGIÚLA"

Sin agaibh guth na fírinne mar sin a lucht léite! Is léir nach raibh ciall ar bith leis an "Bhreac-Ghaeltacht" chomh fada siar leis an Dara Cogadh Mór, má bhí riamh. Cuireadh deireadh leis an miotas a chum Coimisiún na Gaeltachta agus Acht na dTithe Gaeltachta, 1929, nuair a bunaíodh Roinn na Gaeltachta i 1956.[46] Comhrialtas ina raibh Fine Gael mar phríomhpháirtí a bhunaigh, agus an Ginerál Ó Maolchatha, a bhí ina Aire Oideachais ag an am a stiúraigh an obair chun cinn faoi cheannas Rúnaí Párlaiminte Gaeltachta as Maigh Eo, Pádraig Mac Loinsigh. Cuireadh deireadh leis an idirdhealú a bhíodh ann idir "Gaeltacht" agus "Breac-Ghaeltacht" agus áiríodh mar "Gaeltacht oifigiúil" ceantair ainmnithe i gcontaetha Phort Láirge, Chorcaí, Chiarraí, na Gaillimhe, Mhaigh Eo agus Dhún na nGall, ina measc aon áit ina raibh Gaeilge ag tromlach an phobail.[47] Ina measc freisin áfach bhí áiteanna ina raibh Gaeilge ag daoine, cé nach raibh siad á lábhairt níos mó, agus fiú amháin bailte cosúil le Béal an Mhuirthead i gCo. Mhaigh Eo, áit nach raibh an Ghaeilge ar eolas ag mionlach agus nár usáideadh an teanga mar ghnáthmheán cumarsáide sa phobal le fada an lá — má úsáideadh riamh. Ní miste a rá gur caitheadh go flaithiúil le Co. Mhaigh Eo nuair a bhí an leagan-amach nua seo á dhéanamh ar na ceantair oifigiúla Ghaeltachta — níos falithiúla, mar shampla, ná Co. an Chláir, b'fhéidir.

Is cinnte go raibh áiteanna i Maigh Eo nach raibh an Ghaeilge leath chomh láidir iontu agus a bhí sí i measc na gcóilíneachtaí a bunaíodh i gCo. na Mí ó lár na 1930aí ar aghaidh, agus nach bhfuair aitheansas iomlán mar Ghaeltacht go dtí lár na 1960aí.

Ba leir ón méid a scriobh Brian Ó Cuív i 1950 nach raibh morán céille le staitistíocht na Gaeltachta le fada, agus nach raibh ciall ar bith, ó thaobh na glúine a bhí ag fás aníos, le figiúirí ar bith seachas na bhfigiúirí a bhí le fáil ó scéim an deontais labhartha Gaeilge (£5.00 in aghaidh na bliana a bhí i gceist ag an am agus bhí an scéim á riaradh ag an Roinn Oideachais) mar gur thug siad léargas éigin ar líon agus neart na n-áiteanna san "Fhíor-Ghaeltact" ina raibh an teanga á seoladh ar aghaidh i gcónaí go dtí an chéad ghlúin eile.

IMNÍ NA COMHDHALA, 1953

I meamram a scríobh Comhdháil Náisiúnta na Gaeilge chuig an Taoiseach i mí Dheireadh Fómhair na bliana 1953, tá an tuairim chéanna le fáil san athchoimre réadúil a tugadh ar staid na Gaeltachta. Dúradh:

"The only reliable statistical information as to the number of traditional Irish speakers in the Gaeltacht is provided by the scheme under which the Department of Education pays grants of £5.00 a year for Irish-speaking children attending school in the Gaeltacht. The following table shows the number of Fíor-Ghaeltacht children attending national schools in each county which qualified for the grant for the year 1949-'50, and the corresponding traditional Irish-speaking population of the county calculated on the assumption that it bears the same relationship to the number of grant-earning children as the total population of the county bears to the number of children aged 5 to 14 in the county. The table also shows, for comparison purposes, the number of Irish-speakers in the Fíor-Ghaeltacht in 1925 as ascertained by the Gaeltacht Commission:

County	No. of N.S. children who got £5 grant 1949-'50	Corresponding traditional Irish-speaking population in 1950	Commission's No. of Fíor-Ghaeltacht Irish-speakers in 1925
Galway	3,505	17,525	46,380
Donegal	2,302	12,116	38,653
Mayo	610	3,050	23,186
Kerry	516	2,867	17,520
Cork	259	1,524	5,812
Waterford	99	550	5,113
Meath	54	284	—
Clare	—	—	2,007
TOTAL	7,345	37,916	138,671

The figure of 38,000 as representing the number of traditional Irish-speakers in the Fíor-Ghaeltacht is almost certainly too high as Irish is falling into disuse in some bilingual households, to which the £5.00 grants are being paid, and others are so scattered among habitual English-speakers that their districts could not be classified as Fíor-Ghaeltacht".[48]

Dhá phointe is gá a dhéanamh faoin méid sin. Féach go bhfuil Maigh Eo fós chun tosaigh ar Chiarraí sa liosta sin thuas. Ach is fearr a mhair an pobal Gaeltachta, i gCorca Dhuibhne ar aon nós, ó shin i leith, i ngeall ar obair na scoileanna, i ngeall ar an spéis a chuir lucht na hathbheochana san áit mar ionad saoire agus foghlamtha Gaeilge, i ngeall ar an dearcadh níos deimhnithí a bhí ag lucht riaracháin, lucht údaráis agus fiú ag cuid den lucht gnó agus forbartha, ar úsáid na Gaeilge agus go háirithe, dar liom, toisc bunús níos dlúithe a bheith faoin bpobal Gaeltachta féin laistiar den Daingean — baile ina raibh seasamh níos fearr ag an teanga ná mar a bhí i mbaile ar bith ar imeall Ghaeltacht Mhaigh Eo mar shampla.

Tá tábhacht ar leith leis an bpointe a rinne meamram na Comhdhála faoin leagan amach scaipthe a bhí ar theaghlaigh le Gaeilge, i nGaeltacht Mhaigh Eo. D'imigh na mílte leo ag obair go Sasana. Phós go leor acu mná nach raibh Gaeilge acu agus fiú má d'fhill siad arís leis an gclann a thógáil sa bhaile, ní raibh an brú céanna ón bpobal, agus a bhí i gcuid mhór de Thír Chonaill, mar shampla, leis na "strainséirí" seo a shliogadh isteach i gcultúr dúchasach an phobail — fiú amháin sa chás go raibh an Ghaeilge in uachtar sa chultúr sin i gcónaí agus fiú amháin sa chás go raibh fonn ar an mbean strainséara luí isteach le gnás na háite. Sin é an rud a bhí i gceist agam nuair a luaigh mé, ag tús na haiste seo, go raibh gá níos mó le Radio na Gaeltachta chun an pobal a cheangal le chéile i Maigh Eo ná in áit ar bith eile sa tír. Níl ceangal ar bith eile ag obair ar son na Gaeilge i gcás go leor de na bailte, na leathpharóistí, agus go deimhin na tithe scaipthe féin, faoi láthair.

I gcás mheamram na bliana 1953 thug an Chomhdháil Náisiúnta athchoimre ar chúlú na Gaeltachta ó aimsir bhunaithe an stáit. Níl a fhios agam go cinnte cé scríobh, ná cé réitigh na mapaí de na contaetha éagsúla. Ach is léir go raibh an Ghaeltacht mar a bhí sí ag deireadh na 1940aí, nó tús na 1950aí, siúlta ag an údar agus cé nach bhfuil ann ach buile faoi thuairim agam, brathaim macántacht agus dáiríreacht Sheáin S. Uí Éigeartaigh, beannacht Dé leis, ar an gcuntas seo a leanas:

"The deterioration between 1925 and 1950 remains startling after every possible allowance is made for inaccuracies in the comparative figures. The Gaeltacht Commission may have been anxious to record as many Irish-speakers as possible, but enumeration (which was carried out by the Garda Síochána and included persons under 3) tallies with the Census results for 1926, which recorded 128,440 Irish-speakers aged 3 or over in the areas designated Fíor-Ghaeltacht by the Commission. Even if it is assumed that half the Irish-speakers found by the Commission had, in fact, abandoned the use of Irish as their ordinary language, the number of traditional Irish speakers must have shrunk from 69,000 to less than 38,000 in 25 years, a decline of well over 1,000 a year. If this decline continues it is clear that the Gaeltacht will disappear entirely before the end of the century. In fact the rate of decline is likely to increase as the traditional patterns of life are destroyed by modern civilisation, and the Gaeltacht will have vanished in much less than 40 years, unless adequate corrective measures are taken.

"The statistical conclusions are borne out by the practical experience of all who are familiar with the Gaeltacht. There are no longer any appreciable areas in Clare, Waterford or Cork in which Irish may be heard as the ordinary language, and for practical purposes the Fíor-Ghaeltacht now consists of most of 11 parishes, and part of 13 others, situated west of Lough Corrib in Co. Galway, northwest of a line from Killybegs to Carrigart in Co. Donegal, along the northwest coast of Co. Mayo and in the Dingle penninsula in Co. Kerry".

Athchoimre an-chruinn go deo a bhí ansin ag an am, agus cé gur féidir a rá go raibh dul amú áirithe ar an údar faoina bhfuil tite amach i bPort Láirge agus i gCorcaigh ó shin, tá an t-ádh orainn má tá staid na Gaeltachta faoi láthair chomh tréan leis an 11 pharóiste úd, agus an 13 leathpharóiste a bhí ina bpobail nádúrtha Gaeltachta glúin ó shin.

ROINN NA GAELTACHTA, 1956.
De bharr obair na Comhdhála Náisiúnta agus nithe éagsúla eile, bhunaigh an Rialtas Oifig na Gaeltachta agus na gCeantracha gCúng sa bhliain 1951 leis na tionscail "thraidisiúnta" ó aimsir Bhord na gCeantar

Cung a stiúradh agus le hiarrachtaí forbartha an rialtais sa Ghaeltacht a chomhordú. Ba léir nár leor an iarracht agus sa bhliain 1956, bhunaigh an dara Comhrialtas Roinn na Gaeltachta le freagracht chinnte as leas na Gaeltachta a leagan ar bhall éigin den rialtas.

Rinneadh na ceantair oifigiúla Ghaeltachta a leagan amach as an nua ar fad, de réir Ordú na Limistéirí Gaeltachta, 1956, faoi stiúr an Ghinearáil Risteaird Uí Mhaolchatha — an leagan amach bunúsach céanna agus atá ar an nGaeltacht "oifigiúil" riamh ó shin. Bhí an Maolchathach ina Aire Oideachais freisin ag an am agus ceapadh Pádraig Mac Loinsigh, Teachta Dála de chuid Fhine Gael don sean-Dáilcheantar Mhaigh Eo Thuaidh mar Aire na Gaeltachta, 1956-'57, go dtí gur briseadh an dara Comhrialtas i mí Mhárta, 1957. B'é seo an chéad Aire de bhunadh Mhaigh Eo a raibh cúram na Roinne nua Gaeltachta air — agus a rian sin le feiceáil, dar le go leor daoine, ar an bhflaithiúlacht a léiríodh i leagan amach na gceantar oifigiúil "Gaeltachta" ina chontae dúchais féin! Nuair a tháinig Fianna Fáil ar ais i mbun rialtais in earrach na bliana 1957, thug an Taoiseach nua, Éamon de Valera a chéad ghluaisteán stáit do Theachta óg mar Rúnaí Párlaiminte a bheadh freagrach as Roinn na Gaeltachta. Loinseach eile, Seán Ó Loinsigh, as Corcaigh, a bhí anseo, a raibh ainm in airde air go háirithe sa Chumann Lúthchleas Gael, agus a raibh post Dev mar Thaoiseach bainte amach aige laistigh de dheich mbliana eile. Cad d'imigh ar an nGaeilge agus ar an nGaeltacht sa ghlúin sin? Má ghlactar le Ordú na Limistéirí Gaeltachta, 1956, agus le Roinn na Gaeltachta díreach mar bhonn comparáide, tá an t-eolas seo a leanas le fáil i dtaobh na gceantar Gaeltachta i gcontaetha éagsúla ó *Dhaonáireamh na hÉireann, 1961.*
Imleabhar IX – An Ghaeilge: Tábla 10: Daonra Iomlán (Gach aois) i 1956 agus 1961: Na Coda de gach contae a áirítear mar limistéar Gaeltachta in Ordú na Limistéirí Gaeltachta, 1956.

Contae	1956	Daoine 1961
Dún na nGall	28,878	26,357
Gaillimh	24,584	22,877
Maigh Eo	18,229	16,275
Ciarraí	9,367	8,736
Corcaigh	3,697	3,487
Port Láirge	948	792
An tIomlán	**85,703**	**78,524**

Ar Tábla II den Imleabhar Daonáirimh céanna, tugtar líon na nGaeilgeoirí agus na neamh-Ghaeilgeoirí, 3 bliain d'aois, agus ós a chionn, i 1961, sa chuid de gach contae a áirítear ina Limistéar Gaeltachta in Ordú na Limistéirí Gaeltachta, 1956, mar seo a leanas:

	Gaeilgeoirí	Neamh-Ghaeilgeoirí	Gaeilgeoirí mar % den iomlán
Port Láirge	689	49	(93.4%)
Gaillimh	19,895	1,608	(92.5%)
Dún na nGall	22,096	2,946	(88.2%)
Ciarraí	7,207	7,108	(86.7%)
Corcaigh	2,789	497	(84.9%)
MAIGH EO	11,599	3,778	(75.4%)
An tiomlán	**64,275**	**9,986**	**(86.6%)**

Is léir ón dá thábla seo cé go bhfuil líon ard cainteoirí dúchais ag Maigh Eo i gcónaí, tá an céadchuid (75.4%) cuid mhaith níos ísle ná an meánuimhir (86.6%) agus níos ílse ná mar atá an sceál i bpocaí beaga Gaeltachta i gCorcaigh agus i bPort Láirge abair, nó i nGaeltachtaí láidre cosúil le Gaillimh agus Dún na nGall.

AN SCÉAL FAOI LÁTHAIR?

Conas tá an scéal inniu i Maigh Eo? Is léir gur thuig Comhdháil Náisiúnta na Gaeilge, mar a thuig an tOllamh Ó Cuív, agus Éamonn Mhac an Fhailigh, glúin ó shin, go gcaithfí dul i mbun na ceiste seo ar bhonn paróistí agus na leathpharóistí féin agus nach raibh mórán céille i ndáiríre le staitistic ar bith a bhí mórán níos forleithne ná an ceantar bunscoile agus scéim an Deontais £5.00 a bhíodh á riaradh ag an Roinn Oideachais tráth dá saol. Ardaíodh an deontas seo go £10.00 i lár na 1960aí agus — rud níos tábhachtaí ar fad — aistríodh feidhmiú na scéime ó Roinn an Oideachais go dtí Roinn na Gaeltachta, rud a d'fhág, i measc rudaí eile, nach iad cigirí an oideachais a dhéanann scrúdú na bpáistí níos mó. Deontas Labhartha na Gaeilge a thugtar ar an scéim sin agus cé nach bhfuil aon tábhacht leis an £10.00 féin san lá atá inniu ann, tá sé á húsáid mar shlat tomhais ag Roinn na Gaeltachta i gcónaí le aitheantas a thabhairt do na teaghlaigh ar fud na "Gaeltachta oifigiúla" a mheasann lucht na Roinne dualgas ar leith a bheith orthu ina dtaobh maidir le feidhmiú scéimeanna eile. Rud a fhágann scéim labhartha na Gaeilge ina hábhar aighnis agus ina hábhar conspóide in áiteanna go leor i gcónaí, go háirithe i gcás na dteaghlach úd nach n-éiríonn leo í a bhaint, nó má mheasann bunmhúinteoirí go bhfuil an tuarastal breise is féidir a thuilleamh trí scoil a mhúineadh trí Ghaeilge sa Ghaeltacht i mbaol sa chás go bhfuil líon lucht na £10.00 ag titim. Ar ndóigh, tá an taobh eile den scéal ann chomh maith. Tá aithne agam ar dhaoine sa Ghaeltacht agus go deimhin i nGaeltachtaí laga Mhaigh Eo féin, a thóg clann mhór le Gaeilge agus a dhiúltaigh aon bhaint a bheith acu leis an scéim labhartha Gaeilge riamh, ar bhonn prionsabail. Ta sin ceart go leor freisin ar ndóigh, ach amháin go gcuireann sé líon na n-óganach atá á dtógáil le Gaeilge i gceantar ar bith ó riocht beagán. Rud a chothaíonn an t-éadóchas, go háirithe nuair is cinnte gur ar thaobh an "dóchais" is gnách le cigirí Roinn na Gaeltachta an botún a dhéanamh.

Ag breathnú dúinn, ar fhíricí fuara an lae inniu, faoi Gaeltacht Iorrais agus Gaeltacht Mhaigh Eo trí chéile, is iontach ar bhealach go bhfuil bonn éigin fírinne leis an scéal mar a fuair Colm Ó Gaora é, 70 éigin bliain ó shin, roimh an Cheád Chogadh Mór, agus roimh Éirí Amach na Cásca, 1916, san lá atá inniu ann. Nó bhí, go dtí le gairid ar aon nós. Is cinnte go bhfuil an saol imithe i bhfeabhas go mór idir an dá linn. Is cinnte freisin go ndeachaigh scéal na Gaeilge ar chúl, mura mbeadh i gceist ach líon na ndaoine óga a d'fhág na ceantair ar thóir oibre, agus líon na seandaoine a thug scoth na Gaeilge chun na cille leo. Mar sin féin, ní scéal éadóchais ar fad é. Tharraing agóidí Anraí Uí Chorradhuibh agus a chairde ag deireadh na 1950aí aird ar an áit, agus má tá obair mhór le déanamh ar na bóithre i gcónaí, bhí toradh maith amháin, ar a laghad, ar an iarracht nuair a bhunaigh Gael-Linn meánscoil i Ros Dumhach sa bhliain 1962. Rinne Seán Ó hÉalaí, fear as Acaill, a d'fhill ó Shasana le dul ag obair do Chonradh na Gaeilge sa bhliain 1966, obair nach beag sa Ghaeltacht féin agus — rud a bhí díreach chomh tábhachtach ar bhealach b'fhéidir — tharraing sé aird na mbailte móra agus coinsias an lucht riaracháin oifigiúil ar an bhfaillí a bhí déanta ag Maigh Eo dá Gaeltacht féin. Bhí moladh agus cáineadh tuillte ag Roinn na Gaeltachta agus Gaeltarra riamh i Maigh Eo, i ngeall ar na scéimeanna forbartha agus oibre a chuir siad ar bun. Ach tá athrú mór ar na deiseanna oibre, agus ar an saol a bhíonn i ndán do lucht fágála na scoileanna le fiche bliain anuas. Cuireadh cúpla comharchumann ar bun a raibh ráth orthu, cuid acu a raibh i bhfad níos mó céille ag baint leo ná comharchumainn i nGaeltachtaí eile, sa mhéid is go mbíonn siad ag plé le ábhar dúchasach amháin de ghnáth — caoire, iascaireacht, talmhaíocht — agus le príomhghnó amháin, ach níl a fhios agam an fearr an tionchar atá ag na hiarrachtaí seo ar scéal na teanga ná cuid de na tionscail eile a bhunaigh an stát go díreach. Níl gnó na gcoláistí samhraidh chomh trean i Maigh Eo agus atá i nGaeltachtaí móra eile. Arís, níl a fhios agam an maith an rud é seo nó nach ea. Tá cúpla cúrsa den scoth ar fáil i nGaeltachtaí Mhaigh Eo anois gach samhradh agus b'fhiú go mór do lucht foghlamtha na Gaeilge i Maigh Eo féin tacaíocht níos fearr a thabhairt dóibh agus a gcuid gasúir a cheangal le leas na nGaeltachtaí is gaire dóibh. Ar an taobh eile den scéal, deir cuid de na daoine atá dáiríre faoi chúrsaí Gaeilge agus a chuireann páistí go Conamara mar shampla gach samhradh, nach bhfuil an Ghaeilge sách láidir mar theanga an phobail i gcuid mhór de "Ghaeltacht" Mhaigh Eo inniu chun go mbeidis sásta páistí a chur ann. An freagra gairid air sin ar ndóigh ná gur laige fós a bheas an teanga i Maigh Eo amach anseo mura seasann Gaeilgeoirí an chontae trí chéile leis an dream a choinnigh beo an fad seo í.[50] Agus ní miste a mheabhrú do gach uile dhuine go bhfuil cuid de na coláistí Gaeilge is fearr sa tír á rith i lár na Galltachta agus i mbailte móra agus cathracha fiú amháin, ag daoine atá dáiríre faoin scéal. Nílim ag rá gur féidir brath ar ghairmiúlacht mhúinteoireachta lucht coláistí Gaeilge leis an "nGaeltacht" lag i Maigh Eo a shlánú. Ach chabhrgigh cúrsaí Gaeilge le Gaeltachtaí eile a bhí ag geata na reilige a thabhairt ar ais, píosa den bhóthar ar aon chaoi, agus de bharr an cheangail a nascadh idir dreamanna áirithe agus ceantair Ghaeltachta áirithe thar na blianta, go bhfuil seans ann ag an bpointe seo go mairfidh siad chomh fada is a bhíonn Gaeltacht ar bith in Éirinn beo. Tá dualgas ar leith ar ghluaiseacht dheonach na Gaeilge sa ghnó seo. Rinneadh beagán, go háirithe sna 1960aí, agus ní mór tógáil air anois. Ach ní féidir tada a dhéanamh mura bhfuil muintir na bpobal sa Ghaeltacht féin i Maigh Eo sásta tús a chur leis an iarracht, comhoibriú a lorg agus a fhógairt don saol mór go bhfuil rún acu a bpobal Ghaeltachta féin a neartú *mar Ghaeltachtaí* agus ní mar cheantair saoire nach bhfuil de shaintréithe ag baint leo ach an iascaireacht, agus uaigneas na hiargúltachta.

145

Fear as Gaeltacht Acla, Donncha Ó Gallchóir, a thug Údarás na Gaeltachta ar an saol i ndeireadh thiar. Fear a d'fhéach chuige go bhfaigheadh a Ghaeltacht lag féin gach uile chúnamh agus cothrom na féinne i structúr an Údaráis, ar bhonn na limistéar a leag Pádraig Mac Loinsigh amach i 1956. Thuig Ó Gallchóir go maith go raibh cur i gcéill ag baint leis an leagan amach sin, ach ó tharla béim ar leith a bheith leagtha ar an bhforbairt shóisialta agus ar chothú an dúchais agus na teanga san reachtaíocht nua, seans gur shíl sé go mb'fhiú an seans deireanach seo a ghlacadh. Labhair sé amach go macánta ag an am céanna faoi dhrochstaid na Gaeltachta, ar an gcúlú a tharla ina cheantar féin lena linn féin, agus ar an mbaol go bhféadfadh an rud céanna a tharlú in áiteanna eile ar fud na Gaeltachta go léir mura gcuirfí athrú ar chúrsaí.

AIRE EILE AS MAIGH EO

Tá Aire Gaeltachta eile as Maigh Eo, Pádraig Ó Floinn againn faoi láthair, agus fear de bhunadh Ghaeltacht Mhaigh Eo, Pádraig Ó Tuathail a bhí ina Aire Gaeltachta sa Chomhrialtas deireanach. Níl a fhios agam cén tuairimí atá acu faoi cheist seo na gcumhachtaí breise don Údarás, ná faoi fhadhbanna go leor eile, go háirithe i Maigh Eo. Ní féidir leo a rá go deo nach bhfuil eolas ar an bpráinn acu. Is gearr go mbeidh orainn a bheith ag cur ceisteanna arís faoi chuid de na fadhbanna is práinní acu agus faoi cé atá freagrach as iarrachtaí réitigh. Níl an chumhacht ag an Údarás faoi láthair. Agus chomh fada agus is léir, níl aon dream eile ag obair ar an scéal, nó fiú amháin ag iarraidh comhordú a dhéanamh ar bhealach a thabharfadh dóchas breise don am atá le teacht.

POLASAÍ GAELTACHTA

Nuair a bhí mé mar Chathaoirleach ar Choiste Gaeltachta Chonradh na Gaeilge, i lár na 1970aí, d'fhoilsigh muid doiciméad *"Polasaí Gaeltachta"* ina raibh go leor le rá i dtaobh an Údaráis ar mhaith linn a fheiceáil, agus faoin obair phráinneach a bhí le déanamh sna ceantair Ghaeltachta ba laige.[51] Ní miste a rá, freisin, gur fhoilsigh Coiste Dúiche Mhaigh Eo de Chonradh na Gaeilge polasaí d'Acaill agus d'Iorras ag deireadh na 1960aí agus gur leanadh d'fheachtas cosanta do na Gaeltachtaí sin go dtí gur thosaigh an chaint faoi bhunú an Údaráis.[52] Chomh maith leis sin, d'eagraigh an Conradh i gCaisleán an Bharraigh, ar an 2 Bealtaine, 1981, seimineár lae ar Ghaeltacht Mhaigh Eo sna 1980aí, ag ar labhair Donncha Ó Gallchóir agus Pádraig Ó Tuathail i measc daoine eile. Ní deas an scéal a bhí le hinsint ag Seán Ó hÉalaí, Cathaoirleach Choiste Gaeltachta na craoibhe, sa cháipéis a chuir sé ar fáil ar an lá sin, agus cé go raibh geallúintí go leor san aer réamh-Olltoghcháin úd, níl sé soiléir cé chomh fada ar aghaidh is atáimid, tar éis go raibh dhá Olltoghchán agus beirt Mhaigh Eoch ina nAirí Gaeltachta ó shin!

Ag an seimineár ar "Ghaeltacht Mhaigh Eo sna hOchtódaí", i gCaisleán an Bharraigh, bhí an méid seo a leanas le rá ag Seán Ó hÉalaí,

Cathaoirleach na Craoibhe de Chonradh na Gaeilge, faoin seasamh a bhí ag Gaeil an chontae sin ag an am:

"Maidir le seasamh agus tionchar, tá sé le maíomh ag Maigh Eo

* Gur duine de bhunadh Thuar Mhic Éadaigh, agus Bainisteoir an Chontae, atá ina Chathaoirleach ar Údarás na Gaeltachta.

* Go bhfuil seal caite ag duine de bhunadh Acla mar Aire na Gaeltachta; go bhfuil beirt de bhunadh Dháilcheantair Mhaigh Eo Thiar ina nAirí Stáit faoi láthair — duine sa Roinn Tionscail agus Tráchtála agus an duine eile sa Roinn Iompair.

* Gurb é an tríú Teachta Dála i nDáilcheantar Mhaigh Eo Thiar atá ainmnithe mar urlabhraí ar Chúrsaí Forbartha an Iarthair ag príomhpháirtí na freasúra.

* Gur duine de bhunadh Bhéal an Átha atá mar Phríomh-Stiúrthóir ar Radio Teilfís Éireann.

* Go bhfuil triúr ball ainmnithe ó Mhaigh Eo Thiar ar Chomhairle Radio na Gaeltachta, agus go bhfuil seal caite ag duine acu siúd mar Chathaoirleach ar an gComhairle.

* Go bhfuil ionadaí tofa ag Maigh Eo Thiar ar Údarás na Gaeltachta agus go raibh sé ainmnithe roimhe sin ar bhord Ghaeltarra Éireann.

* Gur i gCaisleán an Bharraigh a saolaíodh Taoiseach na tíre, Cathal Ó hEachaidh."[53]

AN BÉAL BEO

Rud amháin atá lárnach don ghnó ar fad dar liom. Tá scéal na Gaeilge sa Ghaeltacht féin ainnis go maith, fiú amháin i gcuid de na háiteanna a bhí láidir glúin ó shin, agus murar féidir an taoide sin a chasadh sna 1980í, tá sé chomh maith againn ár hataí a chaitheamh leis an iarracht ar fad. Ní mhaithfidh an ghlúin atá le teacht, i Maigh Eo, ar fud na hÉireann, gan trácht ar scoláirí na hEorpa agus lucht sibhialtachta an domhain go deo dúinn é. Fúinn féin atá sé an rogha a dhéanamh. Níl aon éalú ón dúshlán ná ón dualgas.

Luaigh muid níos luaithe san aiste seo nach raibh ciall ar bith leis na figiúirí éagsúla don Ghaeltacht le blianta anuas ach amháin, b'fhéidir, líon na ndaltaí scoile a bhí i dteideal an Deontais Labhartha Ghaeilge. Luaigh muid freisin go raibh planda na Gaeltachta chomh lag sin inniu, go háirithe i Maigh Eo, nach foláir figiúirí a fháil do gach bunscoil i ngach paróiste agus sna leathpharóistí féin. Fiú amháin sa chás sin, mar a dúirt muid cheana, tá seans go bhfuil cuma an ró-dhóchais ar an scéal, arís, go háirithe i Maigh Eo, mar a bhfuil trí limistéar ar leith atá scartha óna chéile, aitheanta mar "Ghaeltacht Oifigiúil", go bhfuil a fhios againn an Béarla a bheith bunaithe le fada i mbailte áirithe istigh i lár na gceantar seo, agus nach bhfuil fiú amháin na socruithe riaracháin is simplí déanta ag lucht oideachais, lucht dlí is cirt srl. le stádas na bpobal Gaeltachta a aithint mar Ghaeltachtaí i ngnóthaí laethúla poiblí. Ghlac muid leis an dearcadh seo freisin nuair a bhí "Polasaí Gaeltachta" an Chonartha á réiteach againn i lár na 1970aí.[54] Mhol muid gur cheart teorainneacha na Gaeltachta a bhunú ar na haonaid bhunscoile (bhí an paróiste féin ró-mhór dar linn) agus gan aithteantas mar Ghaeltacht a thabhairt ach amháin do cheantair ina raibh an Deontas Labhartha Gaeilge le fáil ag breis is 50%

147

de na daltaí, ar a laghad, faoi láthair. Bheifí ag súil go n-ardófaí an figiúr sin go 80% de dhaonra na scoile taobh istigh de chúig bliana. Maidir leis na ceantair nach raibh labhairt na Gaeilge sa bhaile ag 50% de na daltaí, bheadh cúig bliana ag na pobail sin a shocrú ina n-intiní féin ar theastaigh uathu luí isteach ar an iarracht tharrthála seo ar an nGaeltacht nó ar theastaigh uathu géilleadh don rud a bhí ag titim amach ar aon chaoi. Ní le leatrom a dhéanamh ar aon phobal a bhí an méid seo á mholadh. Dúirt muid nach raibh tada in aghaidh cabhrú le "ceantair neamhfhorbartha" ar scála chomh flúirseach le cibé rud a bhí ar fáil don Ghaeltacht, ach nár cheart a bheith ar cur airgid a vótáladh don Ghaeltacht, amú ar cheantair nach raibh ina nGaeltachtaí níos mó agus ó tharla nach raibh na pobail seo sásta cloí le gnás na Gaeltachta go bh'fhearr iad a scaradh ón dualgas a bhí ar an Roinn agus ar an Údarás ina leith mar nach raibh siad ach ag cur isteach ar na hiarrachtaí chun córas ceart trí mheán na Gaeilge a chur ar fáil do na pobail fhírinneacha Ghaeltachta faoi láthair.

Ba ar bhonn na réasúnaíochta sin a rinne muid iarracht sa *"Pholasaí Gaeltachta"* eolas éigin a chur ar fáil faoi staid na Gaeilge i measc na n-ógánach i Maigh Eo agus i ngach Gaeltacht eile le linn dúinn a bheith ag fanacht leis an Údarás a bhí geallta. Chuige sin d'fhoilsigh muid staitistíocht na Scéime Labhartha Gaeilge chomh cruinn agus a bhí ar ár gcumas do na blianta 1969-'70 agus arís 1973-'74, le céadchuid garbh faoi líon na bpáistí i ngach scoil a bhí ag fáil an deontais, le go bhféadfaí comparáid éigin a dhéanamh idir an dá shraith figiúirí, agus treo na gaoithe, a fheiceáil mar a déarfá. Ní pictiúr ró-mhaith a fuair muid, cé go raibh cúpla póca Gaeltachta láidir go maith i gcónaí. Bhí deacrachtaí eile ann chomh maith, mar shampla, maidir le bunscoileanna a dúnadh nó a bhí le dúnadh, maidir le daoine nach raibh sásta cur isteach ar an scéim ar chor ar bith, agus maidir leis an gcaoi ina bhfuil nó nach bhfuil leagan amach na scoileanna i bparóistí éagsúla ag freastal do riachtanais teanga na bpobal áitiúil. Mar sin féin foilsimid anseo an t-eolas a chuir Conradh na Gaeilge ar fáil do na blianta 1969-'70 agus 1973-'74:[55]

	1969-'70		1973-'74	
	Líon ar an rolla	Líon (agus %) a thuill an Deontas	Líon ar an rolla	Líon (agus %) a thuill an Deontas
Each Léim	121	68 (57%)	73	37 (50%)
Sraith	80	4 (5%)	70	5 (7%)
Poll an Tómais	127	6 (4.5%)	120	1 (0.8%)
Ros Dumhach	54	9 (16%)	75	16 (21%)
Ceathrú Thaidhg	76	70 (92%)	79	70 (87%)
Gaoth Sáile	61	13 (21%)	60	11 (18%)
Tóin Ré Gaoth	39	1 (2%)	49	12 (25%)
Bun an Churraigh	53	12 (22%)	68	9 (13%)
Sáile	41	8 (20%)	35	6 (17%)
Gob an Choire	60	3 (5%)	68	3 (4%)
Gleann Sáil	22	15 (68%)	20	9 (45%)
Coill an tSiáin	28	21 (75%)	40	18 (45%)
An tSraith	37	2 (5%)	40	9 (22%)

ÚDARÁS AGUS VÓTÁIL

Ba cheart a rá nár dearnadh aon leagan amach nua ar na ceantair oifigiúla Ghaeltachta nuair a bunaíodh an tÚdarás i 1979, agus cé gur léir ón méid sin thuas, go bhfuil an-difríochtaí i gcónaí idir neart na Gaeilge i bpócaí éagsúla den "Ghaeltacht oifigiúil" sin i Maigh Eo, gur ar bhonn ordú na Limistéir, Gaeltachta, 1956, a tionóladh an chéad toghchán don Údarás i mí na Nollag, 1979. Cuireadh Gaillimh, Maigh Eo agus an Mhí le chéile mar cheantar trí shuíochán agus toghadh Pól Ó Foighil (Fine Gael) agus Seán Ó Neachtain (Fianna Fáil), beirt as Conamara, mar aon le Tadhg Ó Cuinn (Fianna Fáil) ó Bhéal an Mhuirthead. Tá Tadhg ina Bhainisteoir ar Chomhar Iorrais Teo. ar an mbaile sin, agus is cinnte go dtuigeann sé an dúshlán atá roimhe mar bhall den Údarás má tá feabhas éigin le cur ar na figiúirí thuas ar bhealach a fhágfaidh go mbeadh ciall ar bith leis an gcéad toghchán Údaráis eile, agus má tá a bhunáit thacaíochta le choinneáil aige in ait a raibh droch-cháil cheart air mar bhaile Gallda in aimsir Choilm Uí Ghaora féin! Maidir leis an gcuid eile de Ghaeltacht Mhaigh Eo, cá bhfios? Deirtear gur dream láidir creidimh iad muintir Mhaigh Eo, agus go gcreideann siad i miorúiltí fiú amháin. Is maith sin, an fad is a bhíonn an dóchas agus an grá agus an gníomh réadúil crua-oibre ceangailte isteach le chéile chomh maith. Níl áit ar bith don bhréag agus don chur i gcéill afach i gcás mar seo, mar is cuma an miorúilt nó obair dhian atá in gceist agat — nó an dá rud i detannta a chéile más fearr leat! — ní féidir tada a thógáil ar an mbonn bréagach níos mó. Tá muid ró-ghar do gheata na reilige cheana féin, mura bhfuil muid ag bhruach na huagha féin. Tá a leagan féin cumtha ag Pádraig Ó Floinn le cur síos a dhéanamh ar an scéal ó ceapadh inar Aire Gaeltachta é. Deir sé go bhfuil "an bunlíne scroichte againn".[56] Tús leighis aithint, b'fhéidir?

NÓTAÍ

1. Reachtanna cáiliúla Chill Chainnigh, a dhréachtaigh Párlaimint Angla-Éireannach sa chathair sin sa bhliain 1366 mar fhreagra ar an ngearán go raibh go leor de na Gaill ó chéadionradh na Normanach in 1169 i leith tar éis cúl a thabhairt le "teanga, dlithe agus nósanna" na Sasanach agus iad féin a chomhshamhlú in oidhreacht na nGael. Ní minic a ritheann sé le daoine b'fhéidir nach i mBéarla ach i bhFraincis na Normanach a bhí na Reachtanna céanna scríofa!

2. Féach, mar shampla, an chéad léacht in *Irish Dialects and Irish-Speaking Districts* le Brian Ó Cuív. Dublin Institute for Advanced Studies, Baile Átha Cliath 4. 1971.

3. Sliochta as an léacht *"The Necessity for de-Anglicizing Ireland"* i gcló (leathanaigh 617-618) in *A History of Ireland Under the Union, 1800-1922* le P. S. O'Hegarty. Methuen & Co. Ltd., London 1952.

4. *Mise agus an Connradh* le Dúbhglas de hÍde. An Gúm, 1937, ina bhfuil cuntas an-bhreá ar chúrsaí na Gaeilge le linn na 19ú aois anuas go dtí bunú Chonradh na Gaeilge féin, in 1893.

5. P. S. O'Hegarty, op. cit. 6. *Cin Lae Amhlaoibh,* Eagarthóir Tomás de Bhaldraithe. An Clóchomhar, Baile Átha Cliath, 1970. 7. *An Ghaeilge i Luimneach 1700-1900* le Breandán Ó Madagáin. An Clóchomhar, Baile Átha Cliath, 1974.

8. Féach *A Board for the Gaeltacht – Memorandum for the Taoiseach* a d'fhoilsigh Comhdháil Náisiúnta na Gaeilge i mí Dheireadh Fómhair, 1953. Táthar buíoch don Chomhdháil as ucht cead athfhoilsithe.

9. Ordú na Limistéirí Gaeltachta, 1956, (Ionstraimí Reachtúla I.R. Uimh. 245 de 1956) lenar

cinneadh "limistéirí Gaeltachta chun críocha ailt den Acht Airí agus Rnaithe (Leasú), 1956 (Uimh. 21 de 1956). Foilsíodh fógra san *Iris Oifigiúil,* an 28 Meán Fómhair, 1956, á rá gur dearnadh an Ionstraim Reachtúil seo. Foilsithe ag Oifig an Soláthair, Baile Átha Cliath.

10. Ina Réamhrá le *"The Irish of Tourmakeady, Co. Mayo"* scriobhann Seán de Búrca: "The present work deals with the spoken Irish of a narrow tract extending along the west side of Lough Mask, between it and the mountains, from its Northern tip to the border of Co. Galway. Part of the area was included in Co. Galway until the boundary was adjusted in 1898".

11. I gcló ag Ó Cuív. op. cit. Leathanach 92. 12. *Mise* le Colm Ó Gaora. An Gúm, 1943. 13. Ó Gaora. op. cit.

14. Léiríonn an blúire seo a leanas chomh maith an easpa measa a bhí ag ceannairí an phobail ar an nGaeilge go minic sa chéad seo caite agus mar ba ghnách leis an ngnáthphobal aithris a dhéanamh ar an sampla a thug a gcuid ceannairí dóibh, go háirithe i gcúrsaí teanga agus cultúir. Ina chuntas "In Iorras" deir sé:

"Chomh tráthúil is chonaic tú ariamh, mar a chuirfeadh Dia ó neamh chugainn é, tháinig sagart Gaelach don Gheata Mór. Fear óg — at tAthair Pádraic Mac Aodha, a bhí tar éis Maigh Nuad a fhágáil, a bhí ann. Bhí a chroí i nGluaiseacht na Gaeilge agus in éineacht le bheith ina chainteoir líofa dó, ba thogha scríbhneora é sa teanga sin freisin. Níorbh fhada dó sa Gheata Mór go raibh sé féin agus mé féin mar a bheadh cuingir ann. Riar sé ar chás i gcúis na ndrámaí de. Scríobh sé dráma dúinn — "An tÁdh agus an Mí-Ádh" — agus léiríomar sa Gheata Mór agus ina dhiaidh sin i dTeach na mBocht i mBéal an Mhuirthead, é. Thug foireann as Poll an Tómais léargas don cheantar sin air ina dhiadh sin. D'éirigh thar fheara bacall leis. Ó ba é an sagart a scríobh an dráma, agus ó bhí sé i mbun an ruda, ní raibh boicín i mBéal an Mhuirthead nach dtáinig ag féachaint air. Chuir seo meas ar an oíche agus bhíomar sásta go leor linn féin go bhfanfadh acu seo a bhí ina ndris chosáin romhainn roimhe sin".

15. Ó Gaora *Mise* op. cit. 16. *'Athair na hAthbheochana' – Uilleog de Búrca* le Proinsias Ó Maolmhuaidh, FNT, Baile Átha Cliath, 1981.

17. Tá catalóg na dteideal atá i gcló i gcónaí le fáil ó FNT féin. Nó feach *Catalóg Leabhar Gaeilge* Bhord na Gaeilge (1978).

18. Sáirséal agus Dill ar ndóigh a d'fhiolsigh *Cré na Cille* ach deirtear i ndeireadh an leabhair "Arna chur i gcló do Sháirséal agus Dill Teo. ag Foilseacháin Náisiúnta Teo., Cathair na Mart, idir Lá Fhéile Muire sa bhFómhar agus Lá Nollag, 1949".

19. *Sléibhte Mhaigh Eo,* Mícheál Ó hOdhráin, FNT, 1964. 20. *Imeacht na nIarlaí.* Eag. Pádraig de Barra, FNT, 1971.

21. Feách trodán an *Mayo News* do na blianta éagsúla. Le linn dó a bheith fostaithe ag INNIU agus ar ball ag FNT, bhíodh colún ag Seosamh Ó Cuaig, "Seo Siúd . . . . ." i ndeireadh na 1960aí ina mbíodh cuid mhaith den soiscéalaíocht faoi chearta sibhialta don Ghaeltacht a bhíodh ar bun aige ag an am, le fáil. Ach ní léir gur thug Gaeltacht lag Mhaigh Eo mórán airde. D'fhill Seosamh ar Chonamara (Iar-Chonnachta mar a thugtaí ar Ghaeltacht na Gaillimhe ag an am sin!) mar a raibh pobail níos báúla agus ardáin níos oiriúnaí le fáil.

22. Deir an tAthair Michael Walsh ina leabhar "The Apparition at Knock" (sa chéad eagrán a foilsíodh i 1959) i dtaobh na fianaise a thóg an Coimisiún fiosraithe in 1879:

"While the dispositions are not a verbatim report, it will be conceded that in them the witnesses, at least the principal ones, speak in character. Patrick Hill speaks true to type as a boy of thirteen. His sentences are short and animated. He is the first of the group to cross the wall. He has no inhibitions about going right up to the figures, so that he can see everything and miss nothing. He is observant; he sees details that others do not see."

"The evidence of Mrs. Trench, who was 'three score and fifteen years' has its own characteristic charm. It is to be regretted that her story as told in Irish was not preserved in that tongue. But even the translation reflects the piety and devotion typical of an old Irish woman".Féach freisin *Venerable Archdeacon Cavanagh, Pastor of Knock (1867-1897)* le Liam Ua Cadhain. Knock Shrine Society, 1953."

23. *Davitt and Irish Revolution 1846-'82* le T. W. Moody. Oxford University Press, 1981.

24. Is cosúil gurb í an Ghaeilge an teanga a bhí in uachtar i measc na n-ógfhear ar fud Chonnacht thart faoin bhliain 1865, nuair a thug Diarmaid Ó Donnabháin Rosa dhá thuras ar an gCúige ag eagrú na bhFíniní. Seán Ó Lúing (*Ó Donnabháin Rosa I,* Sáirséal agus Dill, 1969).

150

25. Féach "Seal i Maigh Eo" sraith cheithre alt a foilsíodh sa mhíosachán Gaeilge, *Agus,* i míonna Bealtaine, Meitheamh, Iúil agus Lúnasa, 1967, faoi mo chuid imeachtaí, ag an am sin. Féach freisin "Gaeltacht Iorrais" le Nollaig Ó Gadhra ar an *Irish Independent* den 6 Deireadh Fómhair, 1967, agus go háirithe alt i mBéarla "Mayo leads Munster in native speakers" leis an údar céanna ar an *Irish Press* den 14 Nollaig, 1966.

26. *The Irish of Erris, Co. Mayo* le Éamonn Mhac an Fhailigh. The Dublin Institute for Advanced Studies, Baile Átha Cliath. 1968.

27. *Riocard Bairéad: Amhráin.* Nicholas Williams a chuir in eagar. An Clóchomhar Tta., Baile Átha Cliath. 1978.

28. *The Irish of Tourmakeady, Co. Mayo* le Seán de Búrca. Dublin Institute for Advanced Studies. 1970.

29. Mar sin féin, níor cheart a cheapadh go raibh an scéal i Maigh Eo sásuil ar fad ná go raibh an scéal ag dul i bhfeidhas, mar a léirigh Seán Ó hÉalaí, Cathaoirleach Chraobh Chaisleán an Bharraigh de Chonradh na Gaeilge, ag seimineár ar an mbaile sin, faoi thodhchaí Ghaeltacht Mhaigh Eo, a tionóladh ar an 2 Bealtaine, 1981. I measc na nithe a bhí sa cháipéis a réithigh Mac Uí Éalaí agus lucht an Chonartha don ócáid, bhí na figiriúirí seo a leanas faoi na ceantair Ghaeltachta sna contaetha éagsúla ina raibh "ceantair Ghaeltachta" aitheanta:

	Daonra			Fostaíocht lán-ama a chruthaigh an tÚdarás/Gaeltarra			
	1961	1979	±%	31.12.'78	31.12.'79	30.6.'88	±%
Dún na nGall	26,375	25,238	(-4.24%)	1,679	1,694	1,722	+2.56%
Gaillimh	22,877	24,163	(+5.62%)	1,279	1,286	1,291	+0.94%
Maigh Eo*	16,275	13,402	(-17.65%)	858	745	694	-19.11%
Ciarraí	8,736	8,322	(-4.74%)	230	259	262	+13.91%
Corcaigh	3,487	3,485	(-0.06%)	283	290	310	+9.54%
Port Láirge	792	1,383	(+74.62%)	7	8	3	?
An Mhí	Gan Chuntas	961	—	230	190	149	—

* Bhí an daonra 13,402 i gCo. Mhaigh Eo roinnte mar seo a leanas idir na trí cheantar:

Iorras	8,870
Acaill (cuid de)	3,015
Tuar Mhic Éadaigh	1,517
An tIomlán	13,402

30. *The Irish of Achill, Co. Mayo,* Gearóid Stockman, QUB, Belfast 1974.

31. Pádraig Seoighthe. *Diabhal Smid Bhréige!* FNT, Baile Átha Cliath 1980.

32. Robert Louis Stevenson *Mé Féin is M'Asal.* Seán Ó Ruadháin do chuir Gaeilge air. An Gúm, Baile Átha Cliath. 1937.

33. Féach "Mayo Leads Munster in Native Speakers" le Nollaig Ó Gadhra. *Irish Press,* 14 Nollaig, 1966.

34. Ó Gaora. op cit. 35. Stockman opp. cit. 36. Stockman ibid.

37. Thomas F. O'Rahilly. *Irish Dialects Past and Present.* Dublin Institute for Advanced Studies. 1970. Leathanaigh 189-190.

38. Ibid. 39. Mac an Fhailigh. op. cit. Réamhrá. 40. Ibid.

41. Tar éis Phádraig Mhic Loinsigh sa dara comhrialtas (1956-'57) tháinig Mícheál Ó Móráin mar Rúnaí Párlaiminte (1959-'61) mar Aire Tailte agus Aire Gaeltachta idir 1961 agus 1968. Bhí Pádraig Ó Fachtna mar Rúnaí Párlaiminte Gaeltachta don Móránach, sna trí bliana deireanacha den tréimhse sin. Ceapadh Donncha Ó Gallchóir mar Aire na Gaeltachta i lár na bliana 1977, go dtí Nollaig 1979, agus be é a thug an reachtaíocht isteach leis an Údarás a bhunú. Nuair a tháinig Gearóid Mac Gearailt i gceannas ar Chomhrialtas i mí Iúil, 1981, cheap sé Pádraig Ó Tuathail ina Aire Gaeltachta agus nuair a tháinig Cathal Ó hEachaidh ar ais i mbun oifige mar Thaoiseach i mí Mhárta, 1982, cheap sé Pádraig Ó Floinn mar Aire Gaeltachta.

42. *Irish Dialects and Irish-Speaking Districts.* Three Lectures by Brian Ó Cuív. Dublin Institute for Advanced Studies. 1971.

43. De réir Acht na dTithe (Gaeltachta) 1929, de bhreis ar na contaetha ina bhfuil aithbeantas

ag limistéirí oifigiúla Gaeltachta inniu — Dún na nGall, Maigh Eo, Gaillimh, Ciarraí, Corcaigh, Port Láirge agus an Mhí — agus Co. an Chláir, tugadh aitheantas do na Togharanna. Ceantair seo a leanas sna contaetha seo a leanas mar "cheantair a háirítear sa Ghaeltacht chun crícheanna an Achta seo" chomh maith:

I gCo. na Chabháin: Doire Leathan. Doire na Neannta, Dún Mhac Íomhair.

I gCo. Liatroma: Drom Caorthain. Drom Railghneach Thoir.

I gCo. Luimnigh: Mainistir na Féile, Cathair, Drom Treasna, Conc Uí Choileáin, Uíbh Rosa, Seanadh Ghualann.

I gCo. Lú: Druim Mullach.

I gCo. Ros Comáin: Bealach an Doirín, Ceathrú Riabhach, Crannach, Críoch, Díseart, Cill Caradh, Teach Mac Chonaill.

I gCo. Shligigh: Cliathmhuine Theas, Drom Colm, Lios an Doill, Thoir, Lios an Doill Thuaidh, Ros Inbhear Thiar, Baile Idir Dhá Abhainn, Achadh Conaire Thoir, Achadh Conaire Thiar, Áth Cláir, Beann Fhada, Cill Mac Taidhg.

I gCo. Thiobraid Árann Theas: Baile Uí Phéacháin, An Caisleán Nua.

44. Ó Cuív op. cit. 45. Ibid. 46. Ordú na Limistéirí Gaeltachta, 1956.

47. Níor tugadh aitheantas do na "coilíneachtaí" i gCo. na Mí go dtí 1967, cé go raibh scéim Labhartha na Gaeilge agus cúpla scéim eile a raibh tábhacht leo, ó thaobh na bpobal mar Ghaeltachtaí, i bhfeidhm ón tús.

48. *A Board for the Gaeltacht – Memorandum for the Taoiseach.* Comhdháil Náisiúnta na Gaeilge (comh-eagras ina raibh Conradh na Gaeilge, Glúin na Bua agus an Comhchaidreamh páirteach ag an am) a d'eisigh ar an 22 Deireadh Fómhair, 1953, i riocht leabhráin ina raibh freisin léarscáileanna de na contaetha Gaeltachta ag léiriú (i) Breac-Ghaeltacht, 1925 (ii) Fíor-Ghaeltacht, 1925 agus (iii) meastachán na Comhdhála den Fhíor-Ghaeltacht thart faoi 1953. 49. Ibid.

50. Go Co. na Gaillimhe a chuireann tromlach lucht na Gaeilge ar fud Chontae Mhaigh Eo a gcuid páistí leis an teanga a fhoghlaim le linn an tsamhraidh. Cé go bhfuil feabhas áirithe ar úsáid na Gaeilge i gcúrsaí eaglasta i ndeoisí éagsúla an chontae le cúpla bliain anuas, sé an Béarla atá in uachtar i gcónaí ar an altóir Dé Dohmnaigh, fiú i gcás chuid de na pobail atá tar éis cur isteach ar chomórtas forbartha pobail Údarás na Gaeltachta.

51. *Polasaí Gaeltachta* Coiste Gaeltachta Chonradh na Gaeilge. Clódhanna Teo, Baile Átha Cliath. 1976.

52. *Coiste Cosanta Acla/Iorrais, 1971.* Bunaíodh an Coiste Cosanta faoi choimirce Choiste Diúiche Mhaigh Eo de Chonradh na Gaeilge sa bhliain 1968 agus leanadh den bhfeachtas ar son na gceantar Gaeltachta a bhí aitheanta sa chontae go dtí gur bunaíodh Údarás na Gaeltachta.

53. *Gaeltacht Mhaigh Eo sna hOchtódaí* — Réamhrá le Seán Ó hÉalaí, Cathaoirleach Fochoiste Gaeltachta den Chonradh i gCo. Mhaigh Eo, leis an doiciméad a réitíodh le haghaidh an tseimineáir a tionóladh i gCaistleán an Bharraigh, ar an 2 Bealtaine, 1981.

54. *Polasaí Gaeltachta,* 1976. op cit. 55. Ibid.

56. Óráid an Aire ag oscailt oifigiúil Ardfheis Chonradh na Gaeilge i nDún an Óir, Baile an Fheirtéaraigh, Trá Lí, Co. Chiarraí ar an 7 Bealtaine, 1982.

COUNTY MAYO IN GAELIC FOLKSONG

by Brian O'Rourke

An essay on "Gaelic Folksong in County Mayo" would presumably document the tradition of Irish-language folksong as it existed in that county from, say, the eighteenth to the present century; that tradition would be exemplified not only in the songs indigenous to Mayo, but also in numerous other widely-sung songs of uncertain provenance of which some indeed might have flourished with particular vigour, or survived solely — or in some unique or distinctive form — in that part of the country. (1) The title of the present essay, however, is different, and signifies a more modest purpose than that just outlined; my intention it to comment on some of the songs which originated certainly or probably in Mayo, and on a few others which refer to Mayo place-names, and to show how they illustrate some typical features of the folksong tradition generally.

RAFTERY

Mayo cannot claim to have contributed much to the classical bardic poetry of Ireland in the period c. 1200-1600, when court poets composed their elaborate verses in praise of chieftains. Indeed the first Mayo poet whose name springs readily to most people's minds is Raftery — (Antoine Ó Raifterí nó Ó Reachtúire, c. 1784-1835) — who lived at a time when the bardic tradition was scarcely any longer even represented vestigially by the work of the 'learned' eighteenth-century poets of Munster and South-East Ulster, and when the efforts of individual versifiers tended to merge with the great body of mostly anonymous folk poetry and song. Indeed Raftery can be said to have added to this patrimony insofar as a number of his compositions, wedded to traditional airs, entered the repertoire of the common people and so 'became' folksongs.

Though his home county figures less prominently in the blind poet's work than Galway (where he spent most of his adult life), it is interesting and fitting that the first Irish song ever noted down by Douglas Hyde, who was later to do so much to preserve the songs of Connacht, was most likely Raftery's "Condae Mhaigh Eo" or "Cill Aodáin". (2) When, thirty years later, he brought out the first edition of Raftery's poems, Hyde described how he had first heard this song: "I had risen out of a fine frosty day in winter, my little dog at heel and gun on shoulder, and it was not long I had gone until I heard the old man at the door of his cottage and he singing sweetly to himself:

'Anois teacht an Earraigh, beidh an lá dul chun síneadh,
Is tar éis na Féil' Bhríde ardóidh mé mo sheól,
Ó chuir mé i mo cheann é ní stopfaidh mé choíche,
Go seasfaidh mé síos i lár Chontae Mhaigh Eo.

Ó fágaim le huacht é go n-éiríonn mo chroí-se,
Mar éiríos an ghaoth nó mar scaipeas an ceo,
Nuair smaoiním ar Chearra nó ar Bhalla taobh thíos de,
Ar Sceathach a' Mhíle nó ar phlána Mhaigh Eo.'

The words pleased me greatly. I moved over to the old man, and 'Would
you learn me that song?' says I. He taught it to me, and I went home and
with me a great part of "The County Mayo" by heart. That was my first
meeting with the wave that Raftery left behind him. I did not hear his name
at that time, and I did not know for many years afterwards that it was he
who had composed the piece which had pleased me so well". (3)

In his book, Hyde also gives popular accounts of the circumstances of
the song's composition: some said it was meant to appease Frank Taafe,
who had banished the poet from Cill Aodáin, others maintained that it
resulted from a competition with a Galway poet, who, on hearing Raftery
extol his native place as a natural paradise, exclaimed "Bad luck to you,
Raftery, you have left nothing at all for the county Galway!" (4) A
prominent feature of the song is, of course, the exaggerated praise lavished
on Mayo for its natural abundance and social prosperity; much more likely
to appeal to the singer or listener, however, are the more homely lines
which briefly evoke and celebrate such places as Claremorris, Balla, Carra
and Kiltamagh. There is one quatrain which seems to me to hold the
extravagant and the sincere in fine balance; the first two lines reflect, in
muted form, the hyperbole that characterises the bulk of the verses; the
second two, for all their element of wish-fulfilment, are such as many a
person would feelingly make his own:

Cill Aodáin an baile a bhfásann gach ní ann,
Ta sméara 's subhchraobh ann, is meas ar gach sórt,
Is dá mbeinnse im sheasamh i gceartlár mo dhaoine,
D'imeodh an aois díom, is bheinn arís óg. (5)

(Cill Aodáin is the town in which everything grows,
Blackberries and raspberries and fruit of all sorts,
And if I were standing among my own people,
My age would go from me and I'd be young once more.)

One of the most famous of the love-songs ascribed to Raftery — 'Brídín
Vesey' — is said to have been composed about a servant-girl from
Castlebar, who saddened the poet by leaving her employment in Loughrea
(perhaps in the parish priest's house) to work for a Protestant minister who
moved to Killaloe. Parts of the song are tiresome, as when the poet
indulges in a litany of learned allusions — to Virgil, Mercury, Pluto,
Jupiter, Hercules, Cerberus, Charon, Calvin, Cromwell, Henry VIII,
Luther, Rhadamanthus, Vulcan, Minos, Fionn Mac Cumhaill, Oscar, Goll
Mac Morna, Cuchulain, the children of Uisneach, Hector and Mentor!
Assuredly it is not such elements which have kept 'Brídín Vesey' popular,

but rather those other features it shares with so many of our best folksongs; a simplicity and frankness in the expression of admiration and love; a capacity for fashioning fresh images from conventional elements, and a homelines deriving — in part — from localisation:

Phósfainn Brídín Vesey
Gan cóta, bróg ná léine,
A stór mo chroí dá bhféadfainn,
Do throscfainn duit naoi dtráth.
Gan bhia, gan deoch, gan aon chuid,
Ar oileán i Loch Éirne,
D'fhonn mé is tú bheith in éineacht,
Go réiteoimis ár gcás.

Dá bhfaighinn amach do thuairisc,
Dá dtéitheá go bonn Cruaiche,
Rachadh an scéal ro-chruaidh orm
Nó leanfainn de mo ghrá;
'S go m'bfhearr liom sínte suas leat
'S gan fúinn ach fraoch is luachair,
Ná bheith ag éisteacht leis na cuacha
'Bhíos ar siúl roimh éirí lá.

Da bhfeicfeá réalt an eolais,
'S í ag teacht i mbéal an bhóthair,
Déarfá go mba seod uait
Do thógfadh ceo is draíocht;
A grua dearg mar rósaí
'S a súil mar drúcht an fhomhair,
A béilín tanaí ró-dheas
'S a bráid ar dhath an aoil.

Bhí a dá chíoch corra comh-cruinn
Mhol me iad 's ní mór liom,
'Na seasamh ag déanamh lóchráinn,
'S iad ceaptha os comhair a croí.
Tá mé i mbrón 's i ndeor-chaoi,
Ó sciorr tú uaim thar teorainn,
Cé gur fada ó fuair mé comhairle
Go ngiorrofá ar mo shaol.

Ba mhilse blas a póige
Ná mil na mbeach 's í reoite,
Ba dheas a seasamh i mbróig
'S a cúilfhionn fáinneach fionn;
Is dá mbeinn-se is bláth na h-óige
I mBalla nó i mBothóla,
Ní fhágfaimis go deireadh fomhair é
Ach ag spórt 's ag déanamh grinn.   (6)

Hyde provides a translation of the entire poem in his *Songs Ascribed to Raftery* and gives besides a metrical English version of the earlier parts of it in his *Love-Songs of Connacht* (7); however, I should prefer to quote here an adaptation by Donagh MacDonagh (even though it does not correspond exactly to the verses given above), since it is a fine poem in its own right:

I would marry Brídín Vesey
Without a shoe or petticoat,
A comb. a cloak or dowry
Or even one clean shift;

155

And I would make novena
Or imitate the hermits
Who spend their lives in fasting
All for a Christmas gift.
O cheek like dogwood fruiting,
O cuckoo of the mountain,
I would send darkness packing
If you would rise and go
Against the ban of clergy
And the sour lips of your parents
And take me at an altar-stone
In spite of all Mayo.

That was the sullen morning
They told the cruel story,
How scorning word or token
You rose and went away.
'Twas then my hands remembered,
My ears still heard you calling,
I smelt the gorse and heather
Where you first learned to pray.
What could they know, who named you,
Of jug and bed and table,
Hours slipping through our fingers,
Time banished from the room?
Or what of all the secrets
We knew among the rushes
Under the Reek when cuckoos
Brightened against the moon?

You are my first and last song,
The harp that lilts my fingers,
Your lips like frozen honey,
Eyes like the mountain pool,
Shaped like the Reek your breast is,
Whiter than milk from Nephin,
And he who never saw you
Has lived and died a fool.
Oh, gone across the mearing
Dividing hope from sadness
What happy townland holds you?
In what country do you reign?
In spite of all the grinning lads
At corner and in haybarn,
I'll search all Ireland over
And bring you home again.   (8)

FAIR CASSIDY

Raftery left Mayo and came back — or at least desired to — and to that we owe his 'Condae Mhaigh Eo'; Tomás Ó Casaide (c. 1705-1775) came to Mayo and left again, and this gave us 'An Caisideach Bán' and 'Máire Bhéal Átha hAmhnais'. Ó Casaide was born in Roscommon, and entered the Augustinian monastery at Ballyhaunis. He was, it seems, ordained a priest, but, as he tells in his autobiography, he had to leave his Order 'fá phósadh dona gan bhrí' (9) — because of a bad marriage. Was he guilty of some irregularity in performing a marriage ceremony? More likely the 'pósadh dona' was his own, for 'An Caisideach Bán' is heavy with the guilt of illicit love. The autobiography is silent on the details of the affair, but all the indications are that its course did not run smooth. Ó Casaide relates

156

how he was kidnapped and pressed into service in the French army; he fought in Poland in 1733 before deserting, and later joined the Prussian army, from which he also escaped, to make his way back to Ireland. He asked to be re-admitted to his Order, and was put on probation, but kicked over the traces and took to the road as a singer and entertainer. Recounting his story in song from town to town, he seems to have retained some sense of spiritual mission: 'Mise píobaire Chríost' (10) — I am Christ's piper — he comments in a tantalising phrase. And the people lent him their ears; his story was remembered and retold. The 'troubled friar' became a figure of folklore, and in the several recorded versions of his songs, it is difficult to distinguish what is his own from what is the product of defective transmission and sympathetic reconstruction by people who took his drama to their hearts.

A very beautiful version of 'Máire Bhéal Átha hAmhnais' appears in *Nua-Dhuanaire III* (11); the following stanzas, however, are from a related version which — though somewhat less coherent and less musical — I prefer for the poignancy of its images of departure:

Ar a dhul 'n a' chuain domh is mé bhí go h-uaibhreach,
Tinn lag buartha im intinn;
Bhi mé 'féachaint uaim ar a' spéir aduaidh
'S í ag éalú uaim ina trealltaí.
Ach faraor géar géar, 's mé an ceann gan chéill,
Níor ghlac mé comhairle mo mháithrín féin,
Is gur dúirt sí liom tríd chomhrá grinn,
Go Béal (Áth)a hAmhnais ná triall ann.

Bá mhór a thug mé grá do mo chúilfhionn bán
An lá breá ar chúl a 'gharraí,
'Sdo do bhéilín tláith mar chubhar na trá
'Sdo do ghrua chomh dearg leis na caorthainn.
Chuir mé lámh ar an chuan 's bhí mo chroí lán gruaim
Ag ceiliúr caoin na n-éanlaith,
'Snach trua gan mise ag éalú leat
Faoi rópaí is seoltaí séidte.

Óró 'chuid 'sa rúin nach ngluaisfeá ar siúl
Go tír na long as Éirinn:
Níl tuirse croí ná tinneas cinn
Nach leigheasfaí ann gan amhras.
Nó ba tú mo rogha inniu is inné
Agus coinnigh agat féin ón bhás mé,
Nó gan grásta Dé ní mhairfidh mé
Ar a' tsráid seo i mBéal Átha h-Amhnais.

(Going down to the harbour I was sad and weary,
Looking at the Northern sky receding from me.
Am I not the foolish man who did not take my mother's advice
When she told me wisely not to go to Ballyhaunis.

What love I gave you that day in the garden,
Your beautiful mouth pure as sea-foam, and your cheek
    like the rowan berry,
I put my hand on the quay, my heart full of sorrow, listening to the bird song —
What a pity you and I are not speeding away full-sail together.

Come away darling to the land of ships, away from Ireland.
There is no pain of heart or head that won't be cured there.
My own love, keep me from death —
Without God's grace there is no life for me here in Ballyhaunis.) (12)

"I think there is hardly any song better known in North Connacht than the Caisideach Bán", writes Douglas Hyde, who adds that "there are two songs, or even three, mixed up together" (13) in the version he published, even though this lacks some of the most commonly-sung verses, including the second of the following two:

Thug mé an ruaig údaí ó mhullach na Cruaiche
Chugat anuas chun an tSléibhe Bháin,
Ar thuairisc mo chailín d'fhág m'intinn buartha
Agus rinne sí gual dubh de mo chroí im lár.
Ó d'at mo ghuaillí go sniuch mo chluasaí
Agus fuair mé fuagra glan géar ón mbás,
'S dheamhan an duine dhá gcuala mo scéal an uair sin
Nár dhúirt go mba trua bocht an Caisideach Bán.

'S bhí mé i gcoláiste go ham mo bhearrtha
Agus ins an ardscoil ar feadh chúig mblian,
Nó go bhfuair mé oideachas agus comhairle ón Eaglais,
Agus faraor cráite, a bhris mé thríd.
Is rí-mhór m'fhaitíos roimh Rí na nGrásta
Nach bhfuil sé i ndán dom go dtiocfad saor,
Mar is mó mo pheaca ná leath Chruach Phádraig,
I ngeall ar an ghrá a thug mé dho iníon maoir. (14)

(I came tearing down from the top of the Reek,
Down towards you, to the White Mountain,
Seeking my girl who left my mind troubled,
And made a black coal of my heart inside.
Oh, my shoulders swelled up to my ears,
And I got a clean sharp warning from death,
And there was no-one who heard my story that time
Who didn't say fair Cassidy was to be pitied.

And I was in college till the time of my shaving
And in the high school for five years,
Till I got learning and advice from the Church,
But, my bitter regret, I broke out through it.
Great is my fear before the King of Graces,
That it's not in store for me to get off free,
For greater is my sin than half Croagh Patrick,
Because of the love I gave to the steward's daughter.)

It is obvious that with the passing of time, Ó Casaide's circumstances were variously interpreted and the song several times reshaped; thus, while the keynotes of guilt and suffering are always struck, the precise details of his plight are presented in a variety of ways. Hyde collected a verse which purports to outline the circumstances of the friar's fall:

Lá dár éiríos faoin gcoill chraobhaigh,
Do casadh orm spéir-bhean is í 'baint cnó;
D'aithris mé léi go mba bráthair Dé mé
'S go ndéanfainn a h-éisteacht ar chúpla póg.

D'umhlaigh an cúilfhionn dom ar a glúna,
Agus faraor, rinneas an ní nár chóir,
Óir b'é an breithiúnas aithrí bhí ar an gcúis sin,
Gur ghoid mise uaithí siúcra a póg. (15)

(One day as I happened in the branching wood
I met a sky-woman gathering nuts;
I told her I was a friar of God
And that I would hear her for a couple of kisses.
The fair one bowed down to me on her knees,
And alas! I did a thing that was not right,
For the penance that I judged for her case,
Was that I stole from her the sugar of her kisses.)

Another verse recorded from the same source indicates that Ó Casaide married the girl, and regretted it:

Do bhí bean uasal seal dá luadh liom
Agus chuir me suas di, céad faraor géar!
Agus phós mé an stuaic-bhean na mala gruama
Do rinne gual díom, i lár mo chléibh.
Dá mbeadh an *chance* sin ar tharsainn an teampaill,
Bheinn san am sin ar mo chomhairle féin,
Ach anois tá mé caillte is níl gar i gcaint orm
Agus beidh mo chlann bhocht ag gol im dhéidh.

(There was a lady once on a time betrothed to me (i.e. the Virgin),
And I gave her up, a hundred times bitter alas!
And I married the hard (?) woman of the gloomy brow,
Who has made a coal of me in the middle of my breast.
If that chance had happened at the threshold of the Church
        (i.e. *before I was ordained a friar*)
I would have been at my own disposal,
But now I am lost, and there is no use in talking about me,
And my poor children shall be weeping after me.) (16)

However, a different version stresses the hopelessness of his wish to marry:

Och ochón ó, 'sé mo chroí atá brónach,
Go mbeidh an lá seo romhainn is sinn pósta seal;
Níl, dar ndóigh, is ní bheidh go deo deo,
'S a mhíle stóirín, mo bheannacht leat. (17)

(Alas, alas, it is my heart that is sad
Till the day before us when we are married awhile;
We are not, of course, and we never, ever will be,
And, my thousand treasures, my blessing on you.)

One might gather from certain verses that the extent of the priest's involvement with the girl — whether or not it entailed marriage — was sufficient to occasion his downfall, but not to induce her to leave, with him, the scene of his disgrace:

'Gus a chúilín donn-deas ar chaill mé na grádhaimh leat,
Nár fhaghaidh tú na grástai mura n-éalair liom.

And my pretty girl for whose sake I lost my degree,
May you not get grace if you don't come away with me. (18)

Hyde's main version of the song suggests that he failed to win her love:

Nár shuarach 'na h-éamais dá bhfaighinn Éire
Agus mé am shéanadh ag mo chairde gaoil,
Is tú am mharú le do ghean, a spéirbhean,
A chuaigh mé dá h-éileamh agus nach bhfaighinn.

Were it not miserable without her, if I should get (all) Ireland,
And I being denied by my friends and relatives,
And you killing me with your love, o sky-woman,
Whom I went to ask for and might not get. (19)

It is further suggested — in a plausible variant of a quatrain found elsewhere — that the girl was turned against him by others:

Nach bradach bréagach cuireadh i gcéill di
Nach bhfásann féar insan áit a mbím,
Nach dtigh ón ngealaigh a soillse bréige
'S nach lasann réalt ann ar feadh na h-oíche!

Oh! false and cruel the things they told her,
That where I rove no grass will grow;
That the moon keeps back her borrowed light
And the stars of the night refuse to glow!* (20)

The theme of persecution sometimes crystallises into a depiction of Ó Casaide as a hunted man, wandering in lonely places:

A dhaoine, an trua libh an Bráithrín Buartha
Atá dá ruaigeadh anonn 's anall,
I measc gleannta dorcha agus sléibhte uaigneach . . . .?

O people, do ye think him a pity, the troubled friar,
Who is being routed backwards and forwards
Amidst dark valleys and lonely mountains . . .? (21)

There is a variant of this verse which I am tempted to interpret as referring symbolically to the poet's loss of his priestly privileges:

Bráthair buartha mé atá ar fuadhradh,
Is cuireadh an ruaig orm anonn is anall;
Ó ní cruaidhe na sléibhte fuara,
Agus thógadar anuas mé ó bharr an tSléibhe Bháin. (22)

(A troubled friar I am, who is wandering,
I have been hunted from place to place;
Oh, the cold mountains are not harder,
And they took me down from the top of the White Mountain.)

In the earliest surviving manuscript version of 'Máire Bhéal Átha h-Amhais', Ó Casaide's invitation to the girl to come away with him is placed in the context of his desire to be free of the clergy's condemnations (23), but a verse of 'An Caisideach Bán' given by Hyde suggests that he met with further criticism as he travelled and sang his songs:

Níl coir ná cáin im' aghaidh san áit seo
Ach súgradh is meidhir, is go ngabhaim foinn;
A phobail chataigh, fíafraím tráth dhíbh,
An milleann grás bheith (ag) déanamh grinn?

(Ah! men have nothing to say against me
Except my mirth and my gift of song;
Tell me, good people, is grace made little
By things like these — that ye make them wrong?)* (24)

Ó Casaide may well have made merry as he wandered, but there are some fine lines which contrast his earlier status with his subsequent hardship:

Agus bhí me sealad ag foghlaim Béarla,
Agus dúirt an chléir go mba mhaith mo chaint;

160

An fhad úd eile gan onnsa céille
Ach mar na h-éiníní faoi bharr na gcrann;
Amuigh san oíche gan fascadh na dídean,
Agus sneachta dhá shíor-chur fo íochtar gleann. (25)

(I spent a time learning the English language,
And the clergy told me my accent was good;
For another long while I was without an ounce of sense,
But like the birds on the tops of the trees;
Out at night without shelter or cover,
And snow falling heavily in the valley below.)

And what of Ó Casaide's feelings for the girl? There are lines in which —
in the manner of several other songs — he swears fidelity to her till the
impossible happens:

Níl brí ná spreacadh i dteas na gréine,
Is go snámha na h-éisc ar an muir gan braon,
Is go n-éirí na tuilte chomh hard leis na sléibthe,
Go deo ni thréigfidh mé grá mo chroí. (26)

(There is no strength or vigour in the heat of the sun;
And until the fish shall swim in a waterless sea,
And the floods shall rise as high as the mountains,
I will never desert the love of my heart.)

The most powerful and complex verse of all, to my mind, however, is one
which gives expression to the several emotions that clashed in Ó Casaide's
soul. The juxtaposition of disparate elements may well result from a
corruption of the text, but as this stands, I think it bears the following
reading: a tranquil, admiring evocation of the lady's beauty gives way of a
sudden to a curse-like outburst born of desperation; this is followed by a
bewildered admission of love's enduring power to enslave, which is finally
resolved into a plea for God's pity:

Siúd í tharainn í an eala bhán-deas,
Agus í chomh gléasta le bean ar bith;
Trua mar geineadh í i mbroinn a máthar,
Mar is le haghaidh mo bháis a rugadh í.
Níl bun cíbe ná tulán timpeall,
Ná gleanntán aoibhinn a mbíonn mo ghrá,
Nach bhfuil ceol dá sheinnm ann de ló is d'oíche,
Is go bhfóire Críost ar an gCaisideach Bán! (27)

(There she is going past us, the pretty white swan,
And she as well dressed as any woman;
A pity she was conceived in her mother's womb,
For it was to cause my death that she was born.
There is no marsh or hillock around,
Or any pleasant valley that my love frequents,
In which music is not playing by day and by night,
And may Christ help fair-haired Cassidy.)

In my comments on 'An Caisideach Bán', I have wandered from version
to version, neglected the usual order of the verses, omitted several, and
quoted translations by various hands. It may be appropriate, before
leaving Ó Casaide, to present his song in more unified fashion, by quoting
again a spirited adaptation by Donagh MacDonagh:

I left my prayers and the kneeling pilgrims
And went wild running down the Holy Reek

161

And all who saw me said: 'That is Cassidy
Who adandoned God for a girl's cheek.'

The first time I saw her I was a student
Reading my prayerbook, I raised my eyes
But they betrayed me, raced to embrace her,
And I had not slept at the next sunrise.

When I was at College they taught me English
And praised my accent, but with that first sight
The only language that I knew was love-talk
And all my thoughts were turned to birds in flight.

I have no land, no stock nor money
To win that girl to me, I cannot pray,
But I'd mount the Reek on my bleeding knees
If I could have her on my wedding-day.

She could cheat my heart to believe in marvels,
That no grass would grow, that no moon would shine,
That the stars are lightless, that she could love me;
And oh! Christ in Heaven that she were mine.

The sun will cool and the moon will darken
And the fishes swim in an empty sea,
The floods will rise above the mountains
And Cassidy still be in slavery.

She passes by and I curse the mother
Who bore that daughter to torture me —
Ah sweet, if we could elope together
I'd risk my neck on the gallows tree.

There is no hill and there's no valley,
No road, no bog that she passes by
But is filled with music, heart-breaking music,
And may Christ have mercy on Cassidy. (27a)

THE SHADOW OF CROAGH PATRICK

Croagh Patrick looms large in Cassidy's mind and art, and it figures
prominently too in the verses of a much lesser-known figure, whose
situation resembles is some respects that of 'the troubled friar'. Malachy
('Lacky') Ó Máile, from Partry, is the author of two separate songs entitled
'Leaicí an Chúil Bháin', both referring to his expulsion from a seminary for
rakish behaviour. The priest responsible for his expulsion was a cousin of
his own, probably the Athair Maolmhuire referred to in the following
verse:

Grá an Athar Maolmhuire ní rachaidh i mo chroí-se,
Ó chuir sé mé ag íoc na pianach,
Turas na Cruaiche, thart timpeall naoi n-uaire,
Gan aon duine liom ach mé in m'aonraic.
D'at sin mo ghlúiní le tuirse is le crúiteacht,
Mar bhí mé lách umhal don chléireach,
Ach ar chomhairle an tsaoil ní rachaidh mé arís
Mar gheall ar aon mhnaoi dá fhéachaint. (28)

(The love of Father Maolmhuire will not enter my heart
Since he put me paying the punishment,
A pilgrimage to the Reek, nine times all round it,
And no-one with me, but I on my own.

162

That swelled up my knees with tiredness and oppressiveness,
Because I was gentle and obedient to the clergy,
But no-one could prevail on me to go there again
On account of looking at any woman.)

The fifth line here may echo the corresponding line of 'An Caisideach Bán', just as the following quatrain recalls other lines from that poem:

Níl uachtarán tuaithe as seo go bun Cruaiche
Ná chugad go mbuailidh sé Gaillimh,
A chluinfeadh mo thuairisc gan áireamh ar mo shuairceas
Nach ndéanfadh ansin truaighe do Leaicí. (29)

(There's no country ruler from here to the foot of the Reek
Or from there to Galway,
Who on hearing an account of me, not to mention my gaiety
Would not then take pity on Lacky.)

What Lacky particularly resented, it seems, was that, despite his readiness to confess and do penance, his name was blackened:

Dhéanfainn ann faoistín agus aithrí ghlan díreach,
Is níor chóir mo chraobhscaoileadh faoin bpobal. (30).

His attempt to clear his character by specifying the only fault of which he was guilty indicates his inadequate ideas on the proper preparation for priesthood:

Ach ag mealladh 's ag pógadh na gcailíní óg,
Is nach 'in í a d'oirfeadh do mo shamhail? (31)

(Only coaxing and kissing the young girls,
And isn't that what would suit the likes of me?)

It seems also that this practice survived his marriage to a widow (a Mrs. Badger, who ran an inn near Partry); one of his songs indicates that she was not entirely happy with the attention he paid to other women.

While the Reek may have had painful associations for both Cassidy and Lacky, another clerical song-writer, Father Liam a Búrc, wrote of it in sadness only because he missed it so much when he was transferred from Murrisk to Claremorris, where he found the people less kindly:

Is nuair a éirím féin ar maidin agus feicim i bhfad uaim siar an Chruach,
Bíonn mo chroí istigh ar mire agus m'aigne go buan. (32)

(And when I rise in the morning and I see the Reek from me in the West,
My heart within me, and my mind, are always agitated.)

A Claremorris man, Seán Ó Móráin, took umbrage at Fr. Burke's lack of enthusiasm for his new appointment, and in an answering song, outlined some of the climatic and dietary disadvantages of life beside the Reek:

Bíonn fraoch cruaidh casta thiar ar an gCruaich,
Bíonn sioc uirthi, fearthainn, gaoth, sneachta agus fuacht;
Ní faochain a chleachtamar-ne ná bárnaigh cladaigh chruaidh,
Ach arán sleamhain cruithneachta, 's ní raibh sú na heorna uainn. (33)

(There is hard twisted heather west on the Reek,
There is frost on it, rain, wind, snow and cold;
It's not periwinkles we're used to here or limpets from the hard shore,
But fine wheaten bread, and we never lacked the juice of the barley.)

163

It is natural, of course, that Croagh Patrick should feature in songs of definite Mayo origin, and it is hardly surprising, given its uniqueness, to find it referred to in songs that cannot be pinned down to that part of the country: like Lough Erne, the Reek appears in songs that could have been composed anywhere, evoked fleetingly as an immediately recognisable landmark. In 'Sé Fáth mo Bhuartha', for example, (one of our most beautiful folk-songs), the young man lists among the advantages of the natural paradise in which his true love dwells, the fact that "níl turas na Cruaiche ann" (34) ("there's no pilgrimage to the Reek in it"). And in some versions of 'Múirnín na Gruaige Báine' — of which one is, admittedly, attributed to a Mayo-born poet, Micheál Mac Suibhne (35) — Croagh Patrick is named as one of the places where the young man has sought his beloved in vain. This song, incidentally, in a few different versions, contains what must be the most imaginative compliment ever paid to a girl:

'S go bhfásann níl ina diaidh,
Ar lorg a cos san tsliabh
Dá fhuaire an uair 'réis na Samhna.)
(And, sure, honey grows after her,
On the track of her feet on the mountains,
No matter how cold the time after November.) (36)

"ON THE SIDES OF NEIFIN, WHEN THE NIGHT IS DOWN"
Apart from Croagh Patrick, the other Mayo mountain which seems to have caught the song-writers' fancy is Nephin. 'Mala Néifinn' is one of the very many songs that express the sadness of a man in love:

Dá mbeinnse ar mhala Néifinn 's mo chéadghrá le mo thaoibh,
's lách a chodlóimis in éineacht mar an t-éinín ar an gcraoibh;
's é do bhéilín binn-bhréithreach a mhéadaigh ar mo phian,
's codladh ciúin ní fhéadaim go n-éagad, faighíor! (37)

If I were to be on the Brow of Neifin and my hundred loves by my side,
it is pleasantly we would sleep together like the little bird upon the bough.
It is your melodious wordy little mouth that increased my pain,
and a quiet sleep I cannot (get) until I shall die, alas! (38)

Hyde, who also published this song in his *Love-Songs of Connacht*, commented: "No doubt it was a peasant who was neither poet or bard who composed it, but there are few songs of the great bards themselves that are in my opinion as sweet as it." (39)

John Millington Synge, of course, made Hyde's book his Bible, and there are echoes of the songs in several passages of *The Playboy of the Western World;* perhaps the song just quoted contributed something to this declaration which Christy makes to Pegeen in their famous love-duet: "... and when the airs is warming, in four months or five, it's then yourself and me should be pacing Neifin in the dews of night, the times sweet smells do be rising, and you'd see a little shiny, new moon, maybe sinking on the hills". (40)

'Cuaichín Ghleann Néifin' ("The little Cuckoo of Glen Nephin") is the name of two quite unrelated songs, both of which again express a man's fruitless love for a beautiful girl. One of these songs (41) describes the man's intention to flee into the mountains, far from women, until he hears the cuckoo calling; it makes no mention of Nephin, however, and may have borrowed its title from the other song, in which 'the little cuckoo of Glen Nephin' is a pet-name for the girl. This second song is one I find particularly attractive, not only for its plaintive air, but also for the music of its striking words: here are four of its verses:

Is tá smúit ar na réalta, ar an ngréin is ar an ngealaigh,
Is ar amharc mo shúl féin is ní léir dhom na bealaigh,
I ndiaidh cuaichín Ghleann Néifin nachar fhéad mé riamh a mhealladh;
Is, a stóirín, tabhair ón bpéin mé, ó sí do mhéin bhreá atá dho mo lagan.

Is dá mba liomsa oileán Éireann tré chéile 'gus an Bhreatain,
Nó a bhfuil den ór craobhach ag Séarlas Ó Fatha,
Ó is duitse a bhéarfainn as ucht mo chéadsearc bheith agam,
I ngleanntán Bhinn Néifin nó i mBéal an Átha Fhada.

Is tá cailín óg deas ar bharr an tsléibhe, is deas an féirín í le mealladh,
Agus chaith mé féin an oíche aréir léi le súil is go bhféadfainn í thabhairt abhaile,
Gur chúitíos le Seán Seoighe le góil romhamsa ar mo bhealach,
Is gur bhain sé coróin díom ar mo lóistín 'gus sé pínne ar mo leaba.

If fágfa mise an áit seo mar tá sé an-uaigneach
Is racha mé ag tóraíocht mo mhíle stoirín ins gach áit a bhfuighidh mé a tuairisc.
Ní léir dhom na crosa-bhóithrí, is tá na deora dho mo dhalladh,
Is sé mo léan géar gan teach mo lóistín an áit a gcóiríonn tú do leaba.

(And the stars, the sun and the moon are clouded over,
And the sight of my eyes likewise, and the paths I can't see,
On account of the little cuckoo of Glen Nephin whom I never could win,
O treasure, relieve me from pain; it's your beauty is weakening me.

If I owned the island of Ireland entirely and Britain as well,
Or all of the branching gold that Charles Fahy possesses,
It's to you I would give it, to have my first love with me
In a little valley on Ben Nephin or in Ballinafad.

There's a pretty young girl on the mountain, and she's a nice present to woo,
And I spent last night with her, in hope that I might bring her home.
I paid back John Joyce for going before me on my way,
And he charged me a crown for my lodging and sixpence for my bed.

And I shall leave this place, for lonely it is,
And search for my thousand treasures wherever I hear of her.
I cannot see the cross roads, and the tears are blinding me,
My bitter grief that my lodging house is not where you make your bed.) (42)

We have here some of the main features which characterise Irish men's love-songs: the young man is sick with love, would give everything to obtain the girl, and is weeping in grief at not being able to have her. Such elements are to be found in dozens of Irish songs, and their origins can be traced back to the twelfth-century *chansons d'amour* of Provence in southern France, which gave expression to the exalted notions of 'courtly love' — a new convention which described a man's love for a woman (generally of a higher station) as both an illness (or madness) and an ennobling force. These ideas spread throughout Europe and reached Ireland through the contact with France which followed on the coming of the Normans. What is particularly interesting is that while few genuine men's love-songs have survived in the French and English folk tradition — and those which have contain almost nothing of the courtly love ideas — Ireland is particularly rich in this type of song. (43)

However, for me, the appeal of 'Cuaichín Ghleann Néifin' lies less in the occurrence of these typical elements than in their juxtaposition with the particularised detail which gives them 'a local habitation and a name', — the references to Glen Nephin and Ballinafad, to Séarlas Ó Fatha and Seán Seoighe. Who, incidentally, one may wonder, were these men? Doubtless the first audience of the song recognised the names, and took pleasure in witnessing the universal experience anchored in the local milieu, the familiar knowledge transfigured, enshrined in art. Our pleasure is necessarily different, since our knowledge is incomplete; it partakes, I feel, of the joy of contemplating that tantalising attraction which time can confer on fragments. And if the survival, for perhaps two centuries, of a song containing ideas which go back six centuries more, is an impressive testimony to the conservative nature of the folk culture, it is also, in my view, a tribute to the aesthetic sensibilities of the people who have kept it alive, that they could continue to find beauty in such relics that, detached from their original moorings, have floated their humble mystery down the years.

This song, of course, is by no means unique in this respect: there is, in fact, a delightful fragmentariness about a great many of our folk compositions. One of the reasons for this is that, unlike the ballads of England and Scotland, Irish songs do not tell a story; they consist rather of reflections or comments on an event or situation; in some cases, they may not be understood unless one is already familiar with the background (44), and the necessary information may not always be available. Then, perhaps because there was no story to thread the verses together in strict sequence, several songs have lost verses in transmission. And the fact that the verses are comments, rather than narrative units, has facilitated another process that contributes to a generalised patchwork effect: the migration of lines or verses between songs of similar words. — 'Cuaichín Ghleann Néifin', for example, shares lines with another man's love-song, 'Dúiche Sheoigheach', ('The Joyce Country'), (a song which in the admirable savagery of one of its lines reveals the intensity of passion the folk-poets were capable of expressing: "Is más í do mháithrín atá i do dhiaidh orm, fuil a croí amuigh ar leic an teallaigh!" "And if it's your mother who begrudges you to me, may her heart's blood be (spilled) out on the hearthstone!") (45)

"LOVE, FAREWELL"

This song, 'Dúiche Sheoigheach', in turn shares a verse with another song which mentions Mayo: 'Tá na páipéir á saighneáil'; ('The papers are being signed'). This is a *chanson de jeune fille,* an abandoned girl's song, (a type considerably older than the man's song), and it portrays the plight of a girl whose beloved has joined the English army:

166

Tá na páipéir á saighneáil 's na saighdiúirí ag gabháil anonn,
tá dromadóirí aoibhinn aerach ag Clanna Gael ag gabháil go Tír na Long;
dá mbeadh agam, 's duit a bhéarfainn céad is dhá mhíle bó,
ar chúntar thú a bheith i t'fhéirín liom go Contae Mhaigh Eo. (46)

(The papers are being signed, and the soldiers are going abroad,
The Irish have fine lively drummers going to the Land of the Ships (England);
If I had them, it's to you I'd give a hundred and two thousand cows,
On condition that I had you as a prize with me in County Mayo.)

The plaintive air to which this song is sung is well suited to the pathos of
the thoughts expressed; these are typical of the *chanson de jeune fille*, —
even the final lines of each of the following verses, which show that
murderous curses are not a monopoly of the men:

Nuair éirím amach go huaigneach 's bhreathnaím uaim an cnoc úd thall,
bím ag smaoineamh ar do chúilín dualach d'fhág crua-arraing thrí mo lár;
tá mo chroí 'stigh 'na leac de ghual dubh 's fear mo thruaí níl ach Rí na nGrást,
's pé'r bith cailín óg bhéarfas uaim thú, go síntear suas í i gcónra chláir!

Tá fhios ag Dia dílis gurab iomaí smaoineamh crua deacrach
ag dul treasna thrí mo chroí istigh mar gheall ortsa le fada;
dá mbeadh bliain ar fad san oíche, is leat ba mhian liom í a chaitheamh,
agus diomú na naomh dhuit má ní tú mo mhalairt. (47)

(When I rise out, lonely, and look from me at the hill beyond,
I think about your ringleted head that left a severe pain in my breast;
My heart inside is a lump of black coal and there is no man to pity me but
    the King of Graces,
And any young girl who takes you from me, may she be stretched out in a wooden
    coffin!
The dear God knows that it's many a hard troublesome thought
Is piercing through my heart inside on account of you this long time;
If there was a whole year in the night, it's with you I'd like to spend it,
And the displeasure of the saints on you if you exchange me for another.)

"A MAID AGAIN I NE'ER WILL BE"

Just as the version of 'Cuaichín Ghleann Néifin' commented on above is
linked — via 'Dúiche Sheoigheach' — with 'Tá na páipéir á saighneáil', so
too the 'first' 'Cuaichín Ghleann Néifin' (the one which does not mention
the mountain) is linked by several verses with another abandoned girl's
song, 'Mainistir na Búille', ('Boyle'); the two songs are also sung to the
same very beautiful air. 'Mainistir na Búille' evokes the despair, and the
hopes, of a girl who has been forsaken by the young man who, in all
likelihood, has left her pregnant:

Chaith mé seacht seachtainí i Mainistir na Búille,
Ar mo luí ar mo leaba, ní 'mo chodhladh ach 'mo dhúiseacht,
Ag súil leat chuile leath-uair go dtiúrfá an sagart faoi rún leat;
Ó bhí tú dho mo mhealladh is gur chaill mé mo chliú leat.

(I spent seven weeks in Boyle,
Lying on my bed not asleep but awake,
Expecting every half-hour you'd bring the priest in secret.
Oh, you were deceiving me, and I lost my honour by you.) (48)

The Mayo connection is in the following haunting verse:

Chuaidh mo mhuintir go Baile an Róba ag cur mo chónra dhá déanamh,
Is chuaigh an chuid eile acu go coillte Eochaill ag baint mo chróchair de bharra
    géaga;

Tá súil le Rí na Glóire a'm go bhfuil siad uileag bréagach,
Is go mbeidh mise 's mo mhíle stóirín seal ag ól lena chéile.

(My people went to Ballinrobe to order my coffin,
And the rest of them went to the woods of Youghal to cut my bier from the
    tops of the branches,
I hope to the God of Glory that they are all lying,
And I and my thousand treasures will be drinking together for a while.) (49)

"NEVER WED AN OLD MAN"

Ballinrobe features also in a version of another widely-sung song, 'An Seanduine Dóite' ('The Withered Old Man'). This belongs to a type known as the *chanson de la malmariée,* (the song of the unhappily married woman), which probably also originated in Provence, and which flourished in France and Northern Italy in the twelfth and thirteenth centuries; at least fourteen songs of this kind survive in Irish. (50) The *chanson de la malmariée* expresses a young woman's regret at having married an unsatisfactory husband, who is old, impotent, jealous, mean or cruel; in many instances she is unfaithful to him. 'An Seanduine Dóite' is a lighthearted example of the type:

Dá mbíodh a fhios ag an seanduine ó, mar a bhímse
ag ól is ag imirt le hógfhir na tíre,
le héirí na gealaí go mbrisfeadh sé a phíopa
agus bhuailfeadh sé faic dena bhuig ins an ghríosaigh. (51)

(If the old fellow knew the way I carry on,
Drinking and playing with the young men of the countryside,
At the rising of the moon he'd smash his pipe
And give a whack with his wig in the ashes).

The reference to Ballinrobe is as follows:

Chuir mé mo sheanduine go Sráidbhaile an Róba,
Cleite ina hata agus búclaí ar a bhróga,
bhí triúr á mhealladh is ceathrar á phógadh —
Chuala mé i nGaillimh gur imigh sé leotha. (52)

(I sent my old husband to Ballinrobe,
With a feather in his hat and buckles on his shoes;
There were three (women) courting him and four kissing him,
And I heard in Galway that he went away with them.)

The mention of a particular place in a song like this which does not derive from a specific historical incident is, of course, no indication that the song originated in or near that place; the most one can say is that it was sung at some stage in areas where the place-name in question would be recognised; in the present instance, it is likely that, in a Connacht context, 'Baile an Róba' is mentioned largely because the words suit the rhythm and sound-pattern of the song. It is obvious that 'An Seanduine Dóite' must have undergone many transformations and adaptations in different places: a version collected in Monaghan, having the same lighthearted treatment of the theme, the same rhythm, a similar chorus and a similar use of an ó sound in the penultimate syllable of most lines, has only one line which almost coincides with a line in the version I have quoted from; and the difference here concerns precisely the place mentioned:

Chuir mise mo sheanduine go Tír na hÓige (53).

Another *chanson de la malmariée* containing references to places in Mayo is 'Bean an tSeanduine', a more 'serious' song than the previous one:

Ó, (ag) tíocht aniar ó Bhalla dhom, dhá mhíle amach ón gClár,
Cé casadh orm ach cailín deas, agus í ar a diallait ard.
"An tusa bean an tseanduine?" "Is mé, mo chreach 's mo chrá!
'S dá mbeinn-se bliain 'mo chónaí leis, ní thabharfainn dó-san grá".

"Brón ar mo mhuintir a phós mé chomh h-óg;
Phós siad leis an seanduine mé mar gheall ar chúpla bó.
Míle b'fhearr liom agam buachaillín deas óg,
A thiocfadh isteach ar maidin agus bhéarfadh domhsa póg."

(Coming over from the town of Balla, just two miles outside Clare (morris?),
Whom should I meet but a pretty girl, seated on her saddle high?
"Are you the wife of the old man?" "I am, 'tis my grief and woe,
And if I were living a year with him, I would give him love no more.

Sorrow be on my people who married me so young,
They wedded me to the old man for the sake of a couple of cows.
A thousand times I'd rather to have a nice young boy,
Who would come to me in the morning and greet me with a kiss".) (54)

The references to Balla and Claremorris here quite possibly have the same explanation — suitability to geographical context and to sound-pattern — as that suggested above with regard to the mention of Ballinrobe in 'An Seanduine Dóite'; they do not prove that 'Bean an tSeanduine' originated in Mayo. The same can be said of the next four songs to be discussed.

"AS I ROVED OUT"

'An Binsín Luachra' ('The Little Bunch of Rushes') belongs to the category of 'pastourelle', — a type of song which recounts the attempt of a young nobleman to gain the favours of a country girl. This type may also have originated in Provence, but it acquired some definite new emphases in the North of France in the twelfth and thirteenth centuries; the girl was now described as a shepherdess ('pastourelle') and, more often than not, she yielded to the young man's request. The Irish language has scores of songs which loosely conform to the general outline of the pastourelle, and a handful which follow the French and Provençal models in some detail. (55)

'An Binsín Luachra' is quite a good example of the type, containing some of the key pastourelle elements: though the girl is not a shepherdess, she is engaged in a rural occupation — cutting rushes, for thatch or for carpet making (56) —; the man accosts the girl and a dialogue ensues; though in some versions his proposal is met with a scathing rejection, in most it is eventually accepted. (In this latter case there is a nice use of symbolism, insofar as the scattering of the rushes is a metaphor for the loss of the girl's virginity.) In the many variants of the song, one of the features which changes is, not surprisingly, the location of the encounter. In some cases, the rural setting is sketched in very general terms:

Ó! maidin aoibhinn uaibhreach/ Ar bhruach na coille is glaise bláth
(On a delightful gay morning by the fringe of the wood of greenest blossom) (57),
or: Do bhíos-sa maidin drúchta go huaigneach a' siúl cois trá (58)
(One dewy morning I was walking lonely by the beach.)

In other cases a specific place is mentioned:

Is lá go raibh mé go huaigneach/Ag dul suas dom go h-ínnse Chláir (59).

A Mayo setting is specified in another version:

Ar maidin bhreágh shamhraidh dhom ar chois na Moighe ghlaise bláith,
(On a fine summer's morning as I was beside the flowering green banks
of the Moy . . .) (60)

The song itself was actually claimed for Mayo by James Hardiman (61);
the version he published, however, begins:

Lá dár éirigh mé go h-uaigneach/A' dul suas dam go Condae an Chláir (62)
(One day I rose out, lonely, going up to the County Clare.)

'An Binsín Luachra' was evidently an extremely popular song, possibly
because the air to which it is usually sung is a most attractive one; the great
eighteenth-century poet, Eoin Rua Ó Súilleabháin, used it for one of his
aisling-poems, 'I'm Aonar Seal', and some anonymous devotee of
Napoleon later took it up when composing a song whose title is thereby
easily accounted for: 'The Bonny Bunch of Roses'. (63)

"SUMMER IS ICUMEN IN"

One of the best-known Irish song-lines is 'Thugamar féin an samhradh
linn' ('We have brought the summer with us'), which occurs as the chorus
of a number of songs celebrating the coming of summer. (64) Such songs,
from medieval times, were associated with a type of dance which
celebrated an old custom whereby young girls went to the woods on May-
day and cut branches which they presented to their lovers. (65) In some
versions of a song called 'Thugamar féin an samhradh linn', the only place-
name mentioned occurs in a verse specifying the different kinds of
branches being carried:

Cuileann is coll is trom is cárthain,
Thugamar féin an samhradh linn,
Is fuinnseog ghléigheal Bhéil an Átha,
Thugamar féin an samhradh linn. (66)

(Holly and hazel and elder and rowan,
We have brought the summer with us,
And sparkling bright ash from Ballina,
We have brought the summer with us.)

"THERE'S TORMENT IN THE SPLENDOUR OF HER LIKE"

Ballina is mentioned too in some versions of 'An Sceilpín Droighneach',
('The Thorny Cliff'), a song which contains strong traces of a type known
as the 'reverdie'. This is similar to the pastourelle; the main difference,
however, is that, instead of the poet accosting a shepherdess, he is suddenly
approached by a beautiful woman, a dreamlike personification of spring
or love. (67) (It was from the reverdie that the eighteenth-century political

170

aisling ultimately developed.) (68) In 'An Sceilpín Droighneach' the poet tells how he has been struck by the arrow of love at the sight of such an unattainable beauty; there is no cure for his wound, and he has decided to emigrate — to Egypt or America (69) or to Flanders and Spain (70); alternatively he will walk the country up and down until he finds his love:

> Go Corcaigh is go Beinn Éadair
> 'S go Baile Áth' Cliath 'na dhéidh sin,
> Go Droichead Bhaile 'n Léime
> Is go Béal an Átha síos. (71)

A third song which mentions Ballina also concerns incurable love and a woman not of this world. 'Tá mé 'mo shuí' ('I am sitting up') describes the plight of a man so lovestruck that he is unable to sleep by night or enjoy the hunt by day. In his misery he consults a 'bean sí':

> Casadh bean-tsí dom thíos ag Lios Bhéal an Átha;
> D'fhiafraigh mé di an scaoilfeadh glas ar bith grá;
> Is é dúirt sí gos íseal i mbriathra soineanta sáimh:
> "An grá a théid fán chroí ní scaoiltear as é go bráth".

> (I met a fairy woman at the Rath of Béal an Átha;
> I asked her would any key unlock the love in my heart;
> And she said in soft simple language:
> "When love enters the heart it will never be driven from it". (72)

There is, of course, in Fermanagh, a place called Lios Béal Átha, (Lisbellaw) which could be intended here; however, a version of the song (collected in Armagh) which almost coincides with that quoted from, in all but half a line, refers to "lag Bhéal an Áth" (73) — the hollow of Béal an Átha — so that Mayo may maintain a claim to the mention.

"DESTROYED TRAVELLING"

With 'Tá mé 'mo shuí' we are back in the domain of the 'chanson d'amour'; most of the love-songs with a Mayo setting are of this type, expressing a man's — generally hopeless — love for a beautiful woman. One simple but attractive example is 'Máirín Parcer', which begins in a very conventional way with a list of places the young man has travelled through without ever meeting the match of the girl he loves:

> Shiúil mé Gaillimh agus Baile an Róba,
> Thart Dúiche Sheoigheach agus Conamara,
> Páirt de Achill, an Stáca Mór,
> Thart bun Chruaiche agus Inis Leacan. (74)

The final verse has much of that touching 'naiveté' which accounts for part of the appeal of many songs:

> Ag dul aníos dom ag Cloich an Dá Mhíle,
> Tháinig buaireamh orm agus tuirse;
> Shuig mé síos ar thulán cíbe
> Agus rinneas smaoiteamh ar a thíocht abhaile;
> Fuair mé tuairisc go raibh sí pósta
> Le buachaill óg as an mBaile Raithní,
> Is más é Donnghaile nó Seáinín óg é,
> Go deo deo ní fhillfidh abhaile. (75)

171

(As I came up by Two-mile-stone,
Sadness and tiredness came over me;
I sat down on a sedgy hillock
And thought about coming home;
I got news that she was married
To a young lad from Mulranny (?)
And if it is Donnelly or young Seáinín,
I will never ever go home.)

In many songs the man in love is depicted as travelling — in search of his love, or, occasionally, in flight from her; in 'Molaidh Mo Roghain' ('Molly, my choice') he is portrayed as travelling with her, (while yet in pursuit of her):

Níl aon tom glas coilleadh, badhúin, nó sliabh,
Thart siar go Baile an Tobair nó go h-Árainn na Naomh,
Nár shiúil mé gan tuirse le rún searc mo chléibh,
Le súil 's go bhfuighinn le mealladh í, ach sháraigh sí mé." (76)

(There is no green wooded knoll, fenced laneway, or mountain,
Over west to Ballintober or to Aran of the Saints,
That I did not walk without tiredness, with the secret love of my heart,
In hope that I would manage to woo her, but she got the better of me.)

There are, of course, several places called Baile an Tobair, but since the Aran referred to is Galway's rather than Donegal's (though the song was collected in Donegal), the Ballintober is quite likely Mayo's. The song's opening is undeniably stereotyped, but a later verse shows the writer's capacity to communicate standard ideas in beautiful images:

Tráth ghluaiseas an ainnir an taobh seo den tslí,
Músclaíonn an ghealach, agus soillsíonn an ghrian;
Tig ceo breá meala de ló is d'oíche
Ar ghach taoibh den bhealach a siúlann sí. (77)
(When that girl walks this side of the way,
The moon awakens, and the sun gives its light;
A beautiful honey mist rises by day and night
On each side of the road on which she walks.)

Another Mayo song about a travelling lover is 'Nóirín Mo Mhian' ('Noreen My Desire'). The version published by Mrs. Costello obviously incorporates verses of diverse origin (including one normally associated with 'An Chúilfhionn'), and, insofar as any coherent picture emerges, it is that of a man who loses the girl whose affections he had enjoyed. In some shorter versions sung by different singers — with variable order in the verses — coherence gives way to the kind of fragmentariness earlier referred to, and what we get is the wryly humorous, half-resigned attitude of a man whose adventures are perhaps best summarised by saying that he had very little luck with women on the roads and in the inns of Mayo:

Ag dul thrí shráid Bhalla dhom lá Fhéil' Muire Mór,
Ag díol mo chuid earraí is á roinnt le mo stór,
Nuair a fhiafraigh bean na leanna díom: 'Cá bhfuil luach na mbróg?'
"Cuir mé le hanam na marbh é atá in dteampall Mhuigheo."

I gCaisleán a' Bharraigh sea chodail mé aréir,
Bhí mo mhian agam agus níorbh fhada liom é;
Ag cur mo lámha thart dhom go bpógfainn a béal,
Fuair mé an áit folamh is an leaba fúm féin.

172

Ag dul thrí Mhuigheo dhom 's mé a' comhrá le mnaoi,
Shlad sí mo phócaí is níor fhág sí a'm pinghin,
Tá fhios ag Dia, a stóirín, nach brón atá orm faoi;
'S dá mbeadh fuisgí ar na bóithrí, is dóigh nach bhfuighinn braon. (78)

(As I was going through the street of Balla on Lady-Day,
Selling my goods and sharing them with my love,
When the ale-woman asked me: "Where is the price of the boots?",
"I gave it for the repose of the souls that are in the churchyard of Mayo".

In Castlebar I slept last night;
I had my love with me, and I didn't feel it long,
When I put my hands around, to kiss her mouth,
I found the place empty, and the bed to myself.

As I was going through Mayo, and talking to a woman,
She plundered my pockets and didn't leave me a penny;
God knows, my love, I'm not sorry over that,
And if whiskey ran on the roads , I probably wouldn't get a drop.)

"ITS A GRAND THING TO SEE A YOUNG GIRL WALKING THE ROAD"

A much more coherent song than this is 'Máirín Seoighe' ('Maureen Joyce'), written by Micheál Mac Suibhne (c. 1760-1820), a poet who was born near Cong, and who spent most of his life in Connemara. This song recounting the impression made on the poet by a local beauty could hardly be more conventional, in one sense, and yet it seems to me that it somehow transcends the limitations of the merely formulaic. It begins:

'Gabáil thrí Conga dhom do dhearc mé an chúilfhionn,
Bhí mian na cúige innti de chailín óg,
Bhí a folt a' casadh léi síos go drúchta,
Agus blas a' tsiúcra bhí ar a póig. (79)

(Going through Cong I saw the fair one,
A young girl the whole province could desire;
Her hair hung down to the dew,
And it was the taste of sugar was on her kiss.)

This last detail, if one is to judge by the sequel, was imagined rather than experienced; in any event, he proposes on the spot:

"Ach a chúr na tuinne is a bhláth na n-úll,
Má ghnír mo dhiúltú ní bheidh mé beo." (80)

(But, o foam of the wave, o apple-blossom,
If you refuse me, I will not live".)

The girl's reaction strikes a nice balance between the two extremes of which one or other is generally called forth by such advances; she stopped for a moment, the poet tells us, and:

Las an solas ina brollach líonta,
Agus do gheit mo chroí dhi chomh mear le héan;
Níor dhúirt sí ach "morra dhuit" is a súil a chlaonadh,
Mar bheith sí in imní do lucht na mbréag. (81)

(The light lit up in her shapely breast,
And my heart leaped for her as fast as a bird;
All she said was "good morrow", and she winked her eye,
As if she were worried about the crowd who backbite.)

173

Struck afresh by her beauty, it seems, the poet reels, and just manages a quick prayer for strength; he then asks a neighbour who is the girl, and learns that she is from a good family:

Sé is ainm baiste di-se Máirín Seoighe,
'S tá fir na Fódla go deo 'na diaidh. (82)

(The name she was christened with is Maureen Joyce,
And the men of Ireland are always after her.)

And that is all; 'Mister Sweeney' has met a beautiful girl, and has learned her name. 'Máirín Seoighe' is indeed coherent, but there is so little for it to be coherent about. And yet perhaps it is precisely because less happens here than is usual, that the song makes its peculiar impact; its delightful lightness of touch comes from Sweeney's capacity to make something bright and delicate — like one of those ephemeral iridescent bubbles — out of so little, — out of, one is tempted to say, remembering the lady's complexion, a little soap and water.

"THE LIGHT OF SEVEN HEAVENS"

'Bríd Nic Phádhraic' ('Bridget Patrick') is another song praising a Mayo girl that should be purely conventional: it was, it seems, written (at least partly), by her father, her brother and a neighbour. It is basically a catalogue of exaggerated claims, extolling the beauty, virtues and restorative powers of the girl in question:

Don Ráith Aird choíche má théann tú,
Dearc ar stua na gcraobh-fholt,
Féach Bidí deas na n-aol-chrobh,
Is ní baol duit aon bhás. (83)

(If you ever go to Rahard,
Look on the stately lady of the branching hair,
Look at fair Biddy of the lime-white hands,
And you need never fear death.)

And yet, though one has come across hyperbolic images again and again, it is hard to deny beauty to the likes of the following:

Tá deallradh na gcaora caorthainn
Ar a leacaí is gile mhíne,
Baladh breá na taoime
Go gnáthach ar a póig. (84)

(The shine of the rowan-berry
Is on her cheeks of brightest smoothness,
The fine fragrance of thyme
Is always on her kiss.)

It is as though, for so many of our folk-poets, conventionality was acceptable, but could not mean mediocrity; the common thought had always to be decked out in striking, well-cut dress. And the present song affords, in its final lines, a further example of the capacity to rise above the constraints of convention: having listened to the litany of inflated tributes, we are suddenly told:

Tá sí sínte ar chlártha
Le cur i gcónra amárach,
Is bíodh sin mar údar áthais
Do mhná deasa an tsaoil. (85)

(She is laid out on planks
To be coffined tomorrow,
And let that be cause of gladness
For the fine women of the world.)

One gets the impression that the writer, having demonstrated his inexhaustible ability to mint stereotyped images, felt the need to provide proof, finally, of his freedom from the convention, by breaking the mould of the panegyric, and making this inconsequent sally into the domain of mock-lament.

"AND I WITH MY GOWNS BOUGHT READY"

Another song with a Mayo setting breaks the bounds of convention, insofar as it celebrates success in love — a rare thing in Irish folksong. This is 'An Gaibhrín Donn' ('The Little Brown Goat') which is really a Mayo version of a Donegal song, 'Caisleán na Finne' ('Castlefin') (86). The Donegal version says of the girl:

Ar uaisle na nGall gur bhain sí 'n geall
De mhac rí dealbhtha déid-gheal. (87)

(From among the English nobles she bore her promise
To the well-built king's son with the bright teeth.)

The Mayo version is localised and more specific:

Agus ó uaisle Gall go dtug sí an geall
Go teach Uí Mháille i mBréachmhuigh. (88)

(And from among the English nobles she bore her promise
To the house of O'Malley in Breaffy.)

The Donegal song ends with an observer's comment on the lady's beauty, which could be construed as expressing some sense of loss:

'S níl iasc ar Fhinn nár thóg a gcinn
Tráth chuaidh sí uainn thar sáile. (89)

(And there isn't a fish in the river Finn that didn't lift its head
The time she went from us overseas.)

The Mayo adaptation, thanks to the change of one crucial word, achieves a more personal effect, which is undeniably one of contentment:

Ach níl iasc ar linn nár thóig a cheann
Trá ghluais sí liom thar sáile. (90)

(But there isn't a fish in a lake that didn't lift its head
The time she moved with me overseas.)

"FINE FIERY FELLOWS WITH GREAT RAGES WHEN
THEIR TEMPER'S ROUSED"

There is nothing contented, however, about the young man in another song which mentiones Breaffy: 'Nellí a Charaid' ('Nelly, my friend'). This

175

too is a Mayo version of a song better known under another name, 'An Saighdiúir Tréigthe' ('The Forsaken Soldier'). What is most striking in this song is its abrupt opening: a direct plunge into an account of violent distraction:

Nuair a d'éirigh mé 'r maidín Dia Chéadaoin,
Níor choisreac mé m'éadan, faraor,
Nó gur bheir mé ar an arm a ba ghéire,
Agus chuir mé a bhéal le cloich líomth'.
Chaith mise domh mo chuid éadaigh
'S mo chiall mhaith gur leig mé le gaoth,
'S nuair a chuala mé iomrádh ar mo chéad-searc
Steall mé 'n corr-mhéar ó'n alt díom. (91)

(When I arose on Wednesday morning,
I didn't bless myself, alas;
I grabbed the sharpest weapon
And put its blade to the sharpening-stone.
I stripped off my clothes
And let my good sense go with the wind,
And when I heard talk of my first-love,
I cut off my ring-finger from the joint.)

That is the usual version; in the Mayo version, forensic detail is sacrificed to geography and pious afterthought; it is not an improvement:

Nuair a d'éirigh mé ar maidin Dia Céadaoin,
'S níor choisrigh mé mo éadan, faraor,
Do shiúl mé idir Gaillimh agus Bréachmhaigh,
Nach mairg nach n-umhlaíonn do Dhia!
Bhain mé díom mo chóta 'gus mo léine,
Agus leig mé mo ghéagáin le gaoith;
Nuair a smaoiníos aríst ar mo chéad shearc,
Bhain mé an chorr-mhéar de'n alt díom. (92)

(When I arose on Wednesday morning,
I didn't bless myself, alas;
I walked between Galway and Breaffy,
— Woe to him who does not kneel down to God!
I took off my coat and my shirt,
And let my limbs blow free in the wind;
When I thought again of my first-love,
I ripped off my ring-finger from the joint.)

The 'hero' of 'Siubhán Níg Uidhir' ('Judy Maguire') might also be called a foresaken soldier — there is a verse describing him as a former drummer in the King's Guard, and he is rejected by the young lady of the title. However, there is nothing distracted or despairing in this man's account of a proposal which misfired. He gets a sample of the girl's repartee when he enquires about her concern for his love-sickness:

'Is a Shiubhán Níg Uidhir, an miste leat mé bheith tinn?'
'Mo chrá! más miste liom thusa bheith sínte i gcill,
bróinte agus muilte bheith ag sciligeadh ar thaobh do chinn,
'gus cead a bheith in Iorrus go dtigeadh Síol Éabha ann cruinn!' (93)

('And Judy Maguire, are you sorry to see me sick?'
'My grief! as sorry as if you were stretched in a graveyard,
With querns and mills grinding on the side of your head,
And leave to be in Erris till Eve's children gather there!')

176

He cannot therefore have been too surprised at her spirited reply to his rather cavalier proposal:

Thiar in Iorrus tá searc agus stór mo chléibh,
planda donn linbh a d'eitigh mé a phósadh aréir;
'beir scéala uaim chuici má thug mise póg dá béal,
go dtiúrfainn di tuilleadh dá gcuirfeadh siad bólacht léi!'

'Ó, beir scéala uaim chuige go deimhin nach bpósaim é,
ó chuala mise gur chuir sé le bólacht mé;
má tá buaibh agat ná an iomataidh mórán spré,
bíodh do rogha bean agat 's beidh mise ar mo chomhairle féin!' (94)

(West in Erris is the love and treasure of my heart,
A beautiful brown-haired young girl who refused to marry me last night;
'Bring news to her from me that if I gave her mouth a kiss,
I would give her more if there was a milking-herd going with her!'

'O, bring news to him from me that I certainly won't marry him,
Since I heard that he wants a milking-herd with me;
If you have cows and a large fortune,
Choose any woman you want, but I'll make my own decision!')

The young ex-soldier in 'Siubhán Níg Uidhir' earned his living by buying and selling, and the song's first verse tells us how, after a fair, he drank the price of his boots in the young lady's company. A far more sombre Erris song — 'An Abhainn Mhór' ('The Owenmore': lit. 'The Big River') — was composed by a man whose alehouse merriment in the company of his equally vivacious beloved was terminated by some unspecified trouble between them — perhaps again a row over a dowry? — which forced him to take to the roads, selling hides and begging. Séamus 'ac Cosgair (James Cosgrave) was the man's name; he lived in the early nineteenth century, and according to tradition, he composed this song one evening in Tralee after he had been refused a night's lodging in thirteen houses. As he remembered his native place he must have remembered too one of the great Connacht songs, for his opening line seems modelled on that of 'Caisleán Uí Néill' ('O'Neill's Castle'), to whose air his words are still sung:

Céad slán don Abhainn Mhór, 's é mo bhrón gan mé anocht lena taoibh —
's nach iomaí sin bóithrín caol uaigneach ag dul idir mé is í;
is ann a gheofá an spórt tráthnóna is go mall tíocht na hoích',
gheofá gloinne le n-ól ann is comhluadar geanúil le suí. (95)

(A hundred farewells to the Owenmore, 'tis my grief I'm not beside it tonight —
And there's many a narrow lonely little road going between me and it;
It's there you'd get sport in the evening and at the coming of the night,
You'd get a glass to drink there and very pleasant company to sit with.)

The song, however, is far from being a straightforward exercise in nostalgia: a fine artistic tension is maintained between the ideal and the real:

Bhéarfaidh mé móide is é is dóiche nach mbrisfidh me thríd —
i gcomhluadar ban óg go deo deo ní shuífidh mé síos;
's mé crádh leo i dtús m'óige is i dtosach mo shaoil,
's iad a sheol ón Abhainn Mhór mé is mhúin dom an t-eolas síos go Trá Lí. (96)

(I will make a vow, and it's likely I won't break it —

In the company of young women I will never, never sit down;
It's I was tormented on their account in my early youth at the start of my life,
And it's they sent me away from the Owenmore, and showed me the road to Tralee.)

At one point, self-pity prompts a fine expression of jealous anger:

Tá mo chóta mór stróicthe, óchón, 's é ag sileadh liom síos,
's an té a chuirfeadh cóir air 's é mo bhrón í bheith i bhfad as mo líon;
níl aon fhear a phósfadh mo stórsa is mé bheith ina dhiaidh,
nach mbainfinn an tsrón de, nó ba mhór mhór a chairde sa tír. (97)

(My overcoat is torn, alas, and hanging off me,
And the one who could mend it, 'tis my grief she is far from my reach;
There is no man would marry my love, with me after him,
But I'd knock the nose off him — or he'd need many friends in the country.)

However, this violent emotion subsides into a dispirited recognition of the reality:

ag cuimhniú ar mo mhíle stóirín bhéarfadh ól dom is imirt ar chlár,
bheith ag fear eile póstaí is gur treoraí bocht mise ag imeacht le fán. (98)

(Remembering my thousand treasures, who would give me drink and gaming at
    the table,
Married to another man, while I'm a poor tramp wandering around.)

Folklore has it that Séamus's impromptu outpouring so softened his listeners' hearts that he was given thirteen nights' lodging in Tralee.

"FOR IT'S THAT LAD . . . THAT I'M WEDDING NOW"

Another very fine song about a girl who "has gone to be wed to another" is "Mairéad Nic Shuibhne" ('Margaret Sweeney'), and this too is quite likely of Mayo provenance since the "other" is said to have been a George Brown from Dún na Géige or Brownstown, near Hollymount. (99) It would seem that the song had a very wide appeal, for a version was written down in County Meath in 1853, and a variant collected in Donegal in 1910. (100) There are in fact several versions, none completely self-explanatory, but the account supplied by the Donegal singer appears basically sound: that the song represents the effusions of a young man whose beloved married another and then tried to rescue him from his subsequent depression by pretending that she had not.

In several verses there are vigorous imaginative expressions typical of the 'standard' man's love-song, as, for example, this testimony to the power of a kiss:

Fuair mé póg uait, a stór, is mé ag imeacht i gcéin,
is naoi lá beo gan lón gur bheathaigh sí mé. (101)

(I got a kiss from you, my treasure, and I going away,
And for nine days without food it kept me alive);

or this blend of enthusiasm and bitterness:

Goirim do cheann, do chom, do chiabh, do rosg,
Do bhéilín binn nach ar sheinn ariamh an t-olc;
Do chorp sleamhain slim mar thuinn ag éirí ar loch,
Ó nach mise tá tinn ag ionnsaí an tsléibhe anocht. (102)

178

(I hail your head, your waist, your hair, your eye,
Your sweet little mouth that never spoke a lie;
Your smooth slender body like a lake-wave leaping in light,
Oh 'tis I that am sick as I tackle the hill tonight!)*

Many other verses, however, refer to the specific details of the young man's predicament, and are not altogether clear; one could, I think, interpret some of them as indicating that the young man established the reality of the girl's marriage when he visited her new home, was invited by her husband to spend the night there, and found her, it would seem, unhappy. One verse, containing a striking image, (as well as a variation of a motif already encountered in 'Nóirín mo mhian'), could be taken as symbolically summarising either his discovery of the truth that night or his entire experience of betrayal:

Idir an dair 's a craiceann nach ar chruaidh an céim
Don duine a chuir idir mé is rún mo chléibh;
Chuir mé lámh thairthi le fáinne an lae,
's goidé fuair mé ach an staraí ar leaba lem théagair féin. (103)

(Between the oak and the bark, wasn't it a cruel intrusion
By the man who got between me and the love of my heart?
I put my arm round her at the dawn of the day,
And what did I find but the charmer on the bed with my darling?)

A variant of this verse achieves a different emphasis, expressing his reluctant acceptance of the fait accompli:

Ba é dul idir an daraigh is a craiceann, cé gur mhór an céim,
A dhul eadraibhse feasta, 'sé a mheasaim, a stór mo chléibh;
'Sé a thuigim gur faillíoch atá do scéal, —
Ach mo scaoth beannacht leat, 'ainnirín, cé gur crá liom é. (104)

(It would be like going between the oak and its bark — though it would be a great change —
To go between you from this out; that's what I think, treasure of my heart;
I understand now that your story is false,
But my sincere blessing on you, my girl, though it grieves me sorely.)

Behind the passion and heartbreak of this song, one senses a moving human drama, and, here at least, one would gladly exchange the "charms of fragmentariness" for more detailed information; in its intensity, its pathos, its nobility of diction and its obliqueness, 'Mairéad Nic Shuibhne' is not unworthy of comparison with the great "Úna Bhán".

"STARTING TO SOME GIRL . . . IN FOUR MONTHS OR FIVE"

A somewhat better documented drama than the last is that of Dónal Meirgeach Mac Conmara (Freckled Donal McNamara), an eighteenth century poet from Irrul in south-west Mayo. He was forced by his father to marry a wealthy girl named Síle Ní Mháille from a place called Drumainn, but continued afterwards to frequent a girl of the Fergus family from Carrowmore, with whom he was in love. When this fact was discovered, he went into "exile", to Tipperary. He is credited with the authorship of the well-known song "An Ghaoth Andeas" ("The South Wind"), which asks the wind to carry a kiss from him home to his native province (105), but he

179

also evoked his own personal dilemma in a song bearing his own name. He strikes one, however, as a pragmatic and determined, rather than an overly emotional man, and his song has little or none of that sustained indulgence in the luxuriance of guilt and grief which characterises, for example, 'An Caisideach Bán'. Instead, it proceeds in a businesslike way through quite a comprehensive agenda: in forty-eight short lines, Donal manages to outline the superiority of his previous to his present situation, to evoke the cloud under which he left home, to bid his wife an uncompromising farewell, to comment on the contrast between his accent and that of the Munstermen, to condemn the institution of marriage, to sympathise with his mother's grief, to warn young men not to marry, to describe briefly his own love-sickness, to promise to forswear love of women in future, and, finally, to rebuke his father for pushing him into a marriage of convenience rather than allowing him to spend his life with the girl of his choice. These last lines have about them a ring of genuine feeling:

Narbh fhearr dhuit-se ar dtús mo cheangal go dlúth
Le cailín fada fionn gléigeal,
A d'imreodh a cúig ar chluiche na lúb
Agus a chaithfeadh go subhach saol liom. (106)

(Wouldn't it have been better for you from the start to see me firmly bound
To a tall, fair, shining bright girl,
Who would play her trump card in this tricky game,
And would happily spend her life with me?)

More memorable, perhaps, however, are the lines addressed to his wife; they express in fine balance the blended determination and regret in which his infidelity was accomplished:

Ach a stáid-bhruinneall mhaiseach, chiúin, chiallmhar, chneasta,
Déan tusa do leas más féidir,
Ach slán cáth' fán tseagal fágaim féin agat,
Agus d'fhág sin mo chreach-sa déanta. (107)

(But, o stately, attractive, quiet, sensible, kindly lady,
Make the best of your situation, if you are able,
But the chaff's (lasting) farewell to the rye I bid you,
And that completes my ruination.)

A far more shadowy figure than Dónal Meirgeach is a man named as Dónal Ó Maoláine in some versions of a song, and as Éamon Mhágáine in others. In some of the less complete versions (collected in Mayo and Kerry) his song gives the impression of being a kind of *chanson d'aventure* (adventure song — a type related to the pastourelle), in which he meets a girl who gives him a letter from her father, offering her to him in marriage with a generous dowry; he refuses, saying he is betrothed to another man's daughter, and leaves her lamenting that she ever knew him. The mystery of the girl's forthright proposal is explained by the first verse of a longer version (collected in Donegal) which describes a meeting between the two a year earlier:

Idir an Caiseal agus an Úr-choill thárla orm an cúilfhionn,
Agus í go ró-mhúinte ag dul tharm sa ród;

Bheir me greim gúna uirthi, agus chuir mé ar mo ghlúin í,
Is d'fhág mé a croí brúite aici is í a' sileadh na ndeor. (108)

(Between Cashel and Úr-choill I met the fair-haired beauty,
And she very gracefully going past me on the road;
I took hold of her dress and put her on my knee,
And I left her heartbroken, weeping tears.)

By the time of their second encounter she has already borne his child, as is clear from her grief at his rejection of her:

'A Rí mhór na páirte, goidé dhéanfas mé amárach,
Nó cá bhfaighe mise athair do mo leanbán óg?' (109)

('O great King of love, what will I do tomorrow,
Or where will I get a father for my little child?')

A chailín beag is áille, más fíor a bhfuil tú 'ráidhte,
Ní dhéanfainn-se do áthrach ar dhá mhíle bó,
Munab é tá mé páirteach le bliain is trí ráithe
Leis an iníon sin Sheóin Dáibhís i gConntae Mhuigheó. (110)

(O fairest little girl, if what you say is true,
I would not choose another, even for two thousand cows,
Only I am pledged, this past year and nine months,
To that daughter of John Davis in the County Mayo.)

The girl's retort is in the best tradition of wounded female pride:

Imigh agus déan sin, dheamhan a miste liom fhéin é,
Ní folamh atá Éire, tá fear eile le fáil;
Is fiosach dom céile nach n-iarrfadh pinghin spré liom,
Ach a ghlacfadh mé i mo léine, cé nach folamh atáim. (111)

(Go and marry her then, 'tis little I care about it,
Ireland is not empty, and I'll get another man;
I know a man who wouldn't ask a dowry of a penny with me,
But would take me in my smock, although I'm no pauper.)

In the light of her subsequent reflection on her fatherless child, there would seem to be an element of bravado about this. In any case, she gives no clue that her interpretation of his reference to John Davis coincides with the folklore explanation supplied by Douglas Hyde: that Davis was a tyrant (not from Mayo, but Roscommon, near the Mayo border), who hanged any stranger found near his territory and whose 'daughter' was the tree on which his victims perished. In this interpretation, Dónal (or Éamon) is taken to be a raparee or outlaw; the theory is supported by a verse (collected in Mayo) which mentions the Queen's pardon, and this reference "perhaps indicates that he lived in the reign of Queen Anne (1702-1714), when the raparees flourished as a result of the Williamite wars". (112)

"AND WON'T THERE BE CRYING OUT IN MAYO THE DAY I'M STRETCHED UPON THE ROPE?"

The shadow of the gallows also falls across a young couple's love in another great song of definite Mayo origin, 'Tomás Bán Mac Aodhagáin' ('Fair Thomas Egan'). The story goes that Thomas eloped with the daughter of an English settler named Stanley; the father pursued them, and Thomas was captured, imprisoned, and sentenced to hang. The song gives the girl's point of view. As is the case with many songs, the verses are sung in different order by different singers; however, in the present instance, I feel there is a good case for regarding the particular sequence observed by Tomás Ó Concheanainn in *Nua-Dhuanaire, Cuid III* as the best and possibly the original one. (113) In the translation given below, I have followed this order, and incorporated a verse from *Amhráin Chlainne Gaedheal,* which he omits, at what seems the appropriate point. The translation is not literal, though in aiming at a certain rhyme and rhythm, I have tried to compromise on general accuracy as little as possible; and it is, I think, singable:

On my way home from the wake-house, 'twas my sweetheart stole my sight;
'Tis my sorrow and my woe I never saw my bed last night;
There's a sharp pain piercing through me, and it's lodging in my breast,
And my love, if you forsake me, not a month more will I last.

My fair Thomas came to visit me in a little lonely spot,
And he told me: "Don't be troubled, love, or anything like that;
Your flowing fair hair has snared me, and it's going to hang me too,
And if I'm grieving for my mother, nine times more I pity you."

O fair Thomas, you have my promise, you are the darling of my heart,
'Tis you, Thomas, and no other, I have cherished from the start;
They will hang you, there's no help, unless God spares you by his grace,
And, O Lord, what a vile and foul crime to plough down the prize flower of Ireland's
        race.

O my neighbours and advisers, spare me biting of your tongue,
For exploring the roads of knowledge with my love, through we were young;
I have never heard a bad word of him since God first gave me life:
Only seeing him going the boreen made me wish I was his wife.

I've a summons to Kilkenny (?) and, though I dread it, I must go,
To attend the quarter sessions between the Irish and the foe;
Only two men will be sentenced, and they're dead before they're tried,
And they're fair Thomas Egan and young Whelan by his side.

O they're guarding my heart's darling, standing round him in a ring,
The Fitzgeralds of Clondaly and the army of the King;
There's Major Óg O'Connell and O'Kelly from Cloonee,
And if I'd three men like young Conall, then my true love would go free.

'Twas not robbing of an abbey or a church was his misdeed,
'Twas no victuals fat or lean he thieved, to satisfy his need;
On account of Stanley's milking-cows, they killed my love stone dead,
And the man who pities the English, may the blackguard lose his head!

And o fair Thomas Egan, 'tis my grief you're in the clay;
I don't wonder your poor mother is still mourning night and day;
If she had you on your death-bed, love, what harm that you were sick?
— Instead of hanging from the gallows and the rain against your back.*

If this is the correct order of the verses, then I think the song represents an unusual and remarkable achievement in narrative technique. For it differs from the standard Irish song in that, while not telling the complete story — consider, for example, how much background knowledge is presumed in the line about Stanley's cows —it does involve a definite coherent time-sequence. And yet it does not resemble either the standard English ballad, in which the narration is not only sequential, but is also, ideally, more systematically informative, and is generally delivered in the past tense, after the events, from one fixed, static point in time. The treatment of time here is dynamic, the narrative presentation dramatic; the singer 'moves forward in time' as the song progresses, through a series of distinct 'present moments' separated by intervals. To illustrate: the first verse represents a statement by the girl after a meeting (her first?) with Thomas, before the events justifying the song's composition have taken place; it could well be a verse from an ordinary love-song and not the start of a lament. The girl's position in time as she utters the next three verses is not absolutely determinable, but it is fairly certain that they are 'sung' while Thomas is still alive, and just possible that they are 'situated', respectively, before their elopement, just before Thomas's arrest, and during his imprisonment. The fifth verse is evidently uttered before his trial, the sixth as he is being led to execution, and the last two after his death. — According to folklore, Thomas did not in fact hang: the girl made the song before the sentence was due to be carried out, and the jury was so touched that he was set free. It sounds like wish-fulfilment, but even if it were true, her 'provisional lament' would be no less remarkable, as a dramatic presentation of partly imagined events. — Incidentally, the narrative technique employed is not the only proof of the songwriter's artistic capacity: the last line, for instance, — 'Ach do chrochadh as na sáltrachaí is an bháisteach le do dhroim' (114) — I consider a touch of genius; it is an example of that kind of expressive detail which saves a description from vagueness, rendering it particular and immediate. As the American novelist, Carson McCullers, wrote: 'Always details provoke more ideas than any generality could furnish. When Christ was pierced in his *left* side, it is more moving and evocative than if he were just pierced'. (115)

As to the location of the events in 'Tomás Bán Mac Aodhagáin', the only information I am aware of is that 'Cluain Aoidh is near Partry, Co. Mayo. Major O'Connell was from Newport (Baile Uí bhFiacháin). (116)

We have moved from love-song to lament. Another Mayo song with which we could have managed the transition is 'Sail Óg Rua', 'Young Red-haired Sal'), composed by a man named Seán Mac Aoidh, (John McHugh) from Islandeady, after the death of his young wife, whose maiden name was Ní Mháille (O'Malley). The folklore in respect of this song is less kindly than that associated with the previous one: Mac Aoidh is supposed to have murdered his wife, and according to an account written sometime after 1824, he composed 'Sail Óg Rua', in Castlebar or Dolliwista jail "as a proof of his being innocent of the Crime of Killing her"; another tradition held that some of Sal's family approached his house one night intending to avenge her death, but left again on hearing him composing or singing the song. (117) — All one can say is that if, in addition to being a murderer, Mac Aoidh was a cynical hypocrite, then he was also a brilliant one, for 'Sail Óg Rua' has all the accents of genuine grief:

In Oileán Éadaigh atá mo ghrá is mo chéadsearc,
   an bhean ar lig mé léi mo rún 's mé óg,
a bhfuil triúr an aon-chéill ag gol 'na déidh agam,
is bean a mbréagtha, mo léan, faoin bhfód;
tá mise tréithlag 's níl gar á shéanadh —
   níl mé ar aonchor ach mar an gceo —
is a stór mo chléibh thú, is tú d'fhág liom féin mé,
   is go ndeachaigh tú i gcré uaim 's tú i do chailín óg. (118)

(In Islandeady my love, my first love is (buried),
The woman to whom I gave my love in my youth,
I have three young children crying after her,
And the woman who could quiet them, my grief, is under the sod.
I am weak and worn out, and there's no point in denying it;
I have no more strength in me than the mist;
And, o love of my heart, you left me on my own,
And you went into the clay on me while still a young girl.)

His insistence on his wife's youthfulness is one of the chief sources of the song's pathos:

In aois a sé déag 's ea fuair mé féin í
   is nár lách an féirín í ag fear le fáil . . .
ach an chiúinbhean mhánla a dtug mé grá dhi,
   is gan í ach 'na páiste tráth fuair mé í. (119)

(At the age of sixteen she came to me,
And wasn't she a fine present for a man to get? . . .
But the quiet gentle woman to whom I gave my love,
And she only a child when I got her.)

And the concreteness of the physical detail in the following quatrain seems the expression of an authentic tenderness:

Dá mbeadh fhios ag mo mhuintir leath mar bhím-se,
An tráth do smaoiním ar mo Shail Óg Rua,
Bhíodh sínte síos liom dá fhada an oíche,
'S gur idir á dhá chíoch gheala bhíodh mo lámh. (120)

(If my people only knew half of what I suffer
When I think about my young red-haired Sal,
Who used to be stretched out with me throughout the long nights,
And my hand would be resting between her two bright breasts.)

Whatever about the genuineness of this lament, there is no mistaking the passion of the woman mourning her brother in 'Donncha Bán', ('Fair-haired Denis'), a great song thought to be from the Erris area. It concerns a man who was hanged for a crime committed by his brother-in-law, who, it is said, stole a horse and put it on his (Denis's) land. The fact that the mourning woman is the thief's wife adds an extra dimension of bitterness to her curses:

A mhic Uí Mhaol Chróin, ná raibh séan ort!
ná raibh t'iníon ag iarraidh spré ort!
ná raibh do chlann mhac agat i bhfochair a chéile!
is tú bhain mo dheartháir díom a bhí geal gléigeal. (121)

184

(O, Mulcrone, may you never prosper!
May your daughter never ask a dowry of you!
May you not have your sons together around you!
It was you who robbed me of my shining bright brother.)

One of the most striking things in the song is the following beautiful
example of ellipsis and understatement:

Och, ón ó, nach ciúin í an oíche!
agus ní ciúine ná mná do chaointe;
tá ceann do chónra follamh 's a lár líonta,
is Donncha Bán bocht mo dheartháir sínte. (122)

(Alas and oh, how quiet the night!
But no quieter than your keening women;
The head of your coffin is empty and its centre full,
And fair Denis my brother stretched (dead).)

The keeners' silence is due to shock, most likely: the young man's head
was pulled off by the hanging-rope, and is not in the coffin; the verse is a
good example of the folksong makers' capacity to give expression — albeit,
in this instance, somewhat indirectly — to the most brutal realities. There
is a finely contained violence too in the only verse which mentions specific
places:

Dá mbeadh Donncha Bán san áit ba chóir dhó
idir Caisleán an Bharraigh agus Baile an Róba,
bhrisfí an chroch is ghearrfaí an rópa
agus ligfí Donncha Bán abhaile ar an eolas. (123)

(If fair Denis had been in the right place,
Between Castlebar and Ballinrobe,
The gallows would have been broken and the rope cut,
And fair Denis would have got home safely.)

This, incidentally, is one of the verses which W. B. Yeats adapted from
this song for use in *Cathleen Ní Houlihan,* his famous play on the Year of
the French.

"THUAS SEAL"

The subjects of the laments are generally common folk, but it could happen
that a member of the gentry could also be mourned: there is a song grieving
at the death of one Giorróid Ó Mórdha (Gerald Moore), supposedly a
connection of the Moores of Moore Hall. The story that goes with the song
is that Gerald went to the races of Cnoc Bharúin (Knockbaron?), telling his
wife he would send for her on a given day; the next message she received,
however, was that he had been killed by his horse. The song evokes the
horseman's prowess, and sympathises with his widow, but it begins by
referring to the grief reigning at Moore Hall:

Dá bhfeictheá cúirt Bhalla i lár Chonndae Mhaigh Eo,
Agus a háiléir bhreátha gheala tá le fada faoi bhrón!
Tá an tiarna bocht cráite is ní bheidh sé i bhfad beo,
Faoin a chliamhain a dhul i dtalamh, crann seasta gach spóirt. (124)

(If you saw the court of Balla (i.e. Moore Hall) in the middle of County Mayo,
And its fine bright ceilings which have long been under sorrow!
The poor lord is distracted and he will not be long living,
On account of his kinsman, supporter of every sport, going into the ground.)

185

Now, it happens that an uncle of the novelist George Moore — his father's youngest brother, Augustus — was thrown from his horse at Aintree in March 1845 and died as a result; he has been described as "a fine sportsman" (125), "much loved but somewhat eccentric". (126) Is it possible that this incident underwent a transformation in the popular mind, giving rise to the folklore account referred to above? Or was there another Moore fatality on the turf?

"AND SOME OF THEM WERE FOUND AND SOME OF THEM WERE NOT FOUND"

Not surprisingly, drownings are the subject of several laments in Mayo, as elsewhere. One case, on which no documentation seems to be available, is that of 'Sagart na Cúile Báine' ('The Fair-haired Priest' or 'The Priest of Coolbawn'). The subject of the song is a priest named Joyce, who obviously impressed his flock by his pastoral diligence:

> Go Conndae Mhaigh Eo má théann tú go deo,
> Cuir tuairisc ar fhear de Sheoigheach,
> Agus gheobhaidh tú é ag gabháil chugat an ród
> Mar bheadh aingeal as ríocht na glóire. (127)

> (If you ever go to County Mayo,
> Ask for a man of the Joyces,
> And you will find him coming towards you on the road
> Like an angel from the kingdom of glory.)

As in 'Tomás Bán Mac Aodhagáin', the treatment of time is interesting: the priest is first referred to as if he were still living, and the 'news' of his death breaks rather suddenly:

> Agus éirigí suas go dtéimid chun siúil,
> Go bhfaighimid siúd ón bPápa,
> Is go bhfaighimid léas ar theach phobail Mhaigh Eo
> Do shagart na cúile báine.
> Éirigí suas go dtéimid chun siúil
> Go bhfaighimid sagart na cúile báine,
> A d'imigh aréir is nach bhfillfidh go héag,
> Mar tá sé i Loch Éirne báite. (128)

> (Rise up and let us set out
> To obtain that (man?) from the Pope,
> And to get a lease on a chapel in Mayo
> For the priest of the fair hair.
> Rise up and let us set out
> To get the priest of the fair hair,
> Who went away last night and will not return till death
> For he is in Loch Erne, drowned.)

One wonders if the reference to the oft-mentioned Loch Erne (rather than to some more local place) indicates that the song commemorates an incident of which the precise factual details have become blurred with time. The lament goes on to comment, in fairly standard fashion, on the sadness caused by the priest's decease:

> Tá Conndae Mhaigh Eo faoi leatrom go deo
> Ó cailleadh an t-aonmhac Seoigeach,
> Is go gcuirfeadh sé bród ar aon duine beo
> A d'fheicfeadh é insan éadach Dé Domhnaigh. (129)

186

(County Mayo is griefstricken for ever,
Since that only son of the Joyces died.
And it was a cause of pride to any living person
To see him in his vestments on a Sunday.)

"IT'S THE LIFE OF A YOUNG MAN TO BE GOING ON THE SEA"

A more completely documented drowning is that of Antoine Mac Conmara (Anthony Mac Namara), whose father, Seán, expressed his grief at his death in a fine lament. Seán was born in south-west Mayo and spent most of his life on Inis Bearnan, a small island at the mouth of Killary Harbour. He died some time after 1867, aged about 80, and left a number of compositions on a variety of topics, the most impressive, perhaps, being the song under discussion. — His son, aged 25, and three others, were drowned off the west coast of Mayo, when returning from Inishturk to the mainland. The tragedy probably occurred during the 1840s; whatever the year, it was on the Friday before Lent (130). As to location, the song supplies precise information:

Tá scoith Imligh in imní ó rinne sí an t-ár
. . . fuadaíodh ó thuaidh thú de Charraig Mhic Aodha . . .
. . . sé mo léan géar gur éag tú ar Chaladh Rua 'n Áth'. (131)

(Emlagh Point is anxious since it carried out the destruction . . .
. . . you were swept north of McHugh's Rock . . .
. . . it is my sharp grief that you died at Roonagh Quay . . .)

The lament contains, not surprisingly, several examples of standard reflection and comment, but achieves its own individual character thanks to several specific details; the following verse is a good example of the blend:

Sé mo léan géar nár éag mé sul dá bhfaca mé an t-ár,
An ceathrar in aonacht ag iarraidh reillige ar trá;
Chaill mé mo radharc agus, mo léan géar, tá mo mhisneach ar lár,
Agus arís go lá an tSléibhe ní éileoidh mé eangach ná bád. (132)

(It's my sharp grief I didn't die before I saw the destruction,
The four together seeking burial on a strand;
I lost my sight and, my sharp grief, my courage is gone,
And till judgement day I'll never again look for a net or a boat.)

The cursing of the boatbuilder may not be a unique feature, but the naming of the man in question adds an uncomfortable precision to the convention:

Mo mhallacht-sa féin do Mhac Haeil a rinne an bád,
Nár aithris dom féin go ráibh an t-éag ina chodhladh sa gclár. (133)

(My own curse on McHale who made the boat,
And did not tell me that death was sleeping in the boards.)

The boatbuilder may well have taken no offence, understanding a ritual reference to a superstition that he was supposed to know when one of his boats was fated to be involved in a drowning. Is it likely that Tom Sheáin

187

was likewise untroubled by the frank assertion (and admission) in this next line?

> Sé fuiscí Tom Sheáin a d'fhágaibh mise gan mac. (134)

> (It was Tom Sheáin's whiskey that left me without a son.)

One could hardly ask for more embarrassingly concrete information.

And yet is is perhaps when the poet's statement is at its most general that — such are his sincerity and his gift of expression — his accent attains its most personal tone:

> A Antoine, nach bodhar thú nach gcluineann mo ghlaoidh?
> Agus mé ag ordú thrí mo chodladh bheith leat insan tuinn:
> Fir an domhain agus faighim roghain orthu go dtabharfainn slán
>   thú i dtír,
> Ach táim tuirseach agus ní fhaighim codladh agus tá tusa de mo dhíth. (135)

> (O Anthony, isn't it you that are deaf, that you don't hear my cry?
> And I asking in my sleep to be with you in the water;
> If I had my pick of the men of the world, I would choose to have you safe on land;
> But I am tired, and I cannot sleep, and I miss you.)

"A WEDDING OR A BURIAL, OR THE TWO TOGETHER"

There are two separate Mayo laments expressing the grief of young women widowed on their wedding-day by the sea. One is 'Caoineadh Dhomhnaill Óig' ('Lament for Young Donal'), and concerns a young man named Mhag Fhionntaigh (Ginty or McGinty), from Inishkea, who, it seems, was drowned after leaving some relatives home from his wedding celebration. The song is said to have become mixed up with another written in the same metre and around the same time, on the drowning of a man named Mícheál Bán Ó Maoilfhábhaill (Fair Michael Lavelle). (136) In truth, 'Caoineadh Dhomhnaill Óig' has little enough to make it memorable; it contains a number of standard sentiments, such as the following:

> cé híonadh do do ghaolta bheith buartha de do dhíth?
>   agus, a churacháinín, choíche brón ort! (137)

> (What wonder is it that your relations are saddened by your loss?
> And, little currach, bad luck to you forever!)

There is only one line that may possibly refer to the close tie between the dead man and the mourner:

> 'gus, a Dhomhnaill Óig, nach luath an scaoileadh! (138)

> (And, young Donal, hasn't the separation come soon!)

The whole song, in fact, could well be the statement of any sympathiser. It is a far cry from the beautifully personalised utterance enshrined in the incomparable 'Caoineadh Liam Uí Raghallaigh' ('Lament for William Reilly'). This great song, of which there are Munster as well as Connacht versions, was written by a man named Mícheál Mág Raith; it mourns a young man drowned some time before 1800 in Sruth Fada Con (Sruwaddacon Bay), where the Glenamoy river meets the sea, in north-west Mayo; it seems the accident happened when he was returning home, having rowed the eighty-year-old officiating priest — a Father Peter — back to Kilcommon after the wedding (139). Every verse of this lament sparkles with some gem. Some versions begin — and what an arresting opening it is! — with a magical line which encapsulates the young woman's grief with exquisite economy:

I mo bhaintreach 's 'mo mhaighdean fágadh mé go hóg — (140)
(A widow and a virgin I was left, and I still young.)

The evocation of the wedding itself is marvellously suggestive of the excitement and promise of the occasion:

An cuimhneach libh an lá bhí an tsráid seo lán de mharcaigh,
de shagairt 's de bhráithre ag trácht ar ár mbainis?
Bhí an fhidil ar ceann cláir ann 's an chláirseach á freagairt,
's dháréag de na mná bána ann le mo ghrá-sa chur ar leaba. (141)

(Do ye remember the day this street was full of horsemen,
Of priests and friars coming to our wedding?
The fiddle was at the head of the table and the harp answering it,
And twelve fair women there to bring my love to bed.)

Even in the verse which performs that most standard function of noting the grief of the bereaved, the physical detail provides concreteness, and the contrast between wedding and wake (found also, for example, in 'Donncha Bán' and in Raftery's 'Anach Cuain') gains added impact from the condensed and intimate expression:

Níorbh ait liom scéal cráite bheith amáireach ag t'athair
ná ag banaltra na gcíocha bána a thál ort ' do leanbh,
ní áirím do bhean phósta nár chóirigh riamh do leaba,
is nuair a shíl mé bheith ' do phógadh 's ar do thórramh bhí an bhainis. (142)

(I wouldn't wonder that your father would be mourning tomorrow,
Or the mother of the white breasts that gave you milk as a child,
Not to mention your wedded wife who never made your bed,
And when I thought I'd be kissing you, it was at your wake we had the feast.)

But perhaps the most remarkable verse of all is the one with which the song often concludes: it is again a striking example of the capacity to face up to the most distasteful realities. I quote here from a version somewhat different from that used above, in order to be able to give afterwards what I consider to be the finest verse of the translation done by Seán Ó Riada and Seán Lucy:

Tá do shúile ag na péiste agus do bhéal ag na portáin,
Tá do dhá láimh gheala ghléigeala faoi ghéarsmacht na mbradán;
Cúig phunt a bhéarfainn don té a thógfadh mo dhianghrá,
Ach sé mo léan thú bheith i t'aonraic, a Neilí ghléigeal Nic Shiúrtáin. (143)

(The eels have your eyes / And the crabs have your mouth
Your two shining white arms / Under sway of the salmon;
I'd give five pounds to anyone / Who would lighten my sorrow,
A sad solitary woman / Poor bright Nelly Sheridan.) (144)

THE YEAR OF THE FRENCH

A lament less rich in delightful surprises than 'Caoineadh Liam Uí

Raghallaigh' is 'Aifí Mac Giobúin' ('Aifí Gibbons'), which proceeds systematically, unspectacularly — though, it must be admitted, competently — through a series of common motifs: the sadness of the young man's death far from relatives, the grief which afflicts fauna, flora, sun, moon, stars and friends . . .; ideas, in fact, that could issue from any place at any time. And yet there are elements that imprint on the song the unmistakable stamp of County Mayo and the year of the French:

'''s gurb as Cill Ala a ghluais an dé-smál
a dhíbir sinn ó chéile,
na Francaigh a thíocht go hÉirinn,
mo léan agus mo chrá! (145)'''

(. . . And 'twas out of Killala came that dirty crowd
That sundered us from each other,
The French landing in Ireland,
My sorrow and my anguish!)

For Aifí took part in the events of that fateful year, and had to go on the run to Inishbofin; it was there that he met a violent death at the hands of a man named Coney, as he sat having a drink. (146) (One of the song's editors adds the laconic note: "Níor fágadh an Conghusach i bhfad beo" (147) — "Coney wasn't left long living"). The song-writer — allegedly the victim's uncle — goes on to comment:

An seanfhocal 's ní bréag é,
coidir is ná taobhaigh
an coimhthíoch choích' má fhéadair
's beidh tú níos fearr; (148)

(The old saying is no traitor:
Befriend but never favour
The stranger if you're able,
And thus emerge the gainer.)*

There is such a seanfhocal (149), and it doubtless expresses a national rather than a local caution; yet here, in the context of the young man's death in the wake of his political involvement, it has the ring, not of a received idea, but of a learned lesson.

It would, of course, be strange, if the Year of the French had left no mark on our folksongs, and there are, in fact, a few which deal directly with the happenings of that year. The coming of the French was an event evidently looked forward to by some people, as, for example, the 'Spailpín Fánach' ('Wandering Labourer'):

ní fheicfear corrán im láimh chun bainte,
súist ná feac beag rámhainne,
ach *colours* na bhFrancach os cionn mo leapa
is *pike* agam chun sáite. (150)

(No sickle for reaping will be seen in my hand,
No flail or little spade-handle,
But the colours of the French will be over my bed,
And I'll have a pike for jabbing.)

'An Spailpín Fánach' was originally a Munster song (151), but it travelled, and underwent many transformations; one accretion it acquired in Connacht (probably in Mayo) was this rather optimistic report of the French landing:

Tá na Francaigh anois istigh i gCill Ala,
Agus beimid go leathan láidir;
Tá Bonaparte i gCaisleán an Bharraigh,
Ag iarraidh an dlí a cheap Sáirséal. (152)

(The French are now inside in Killala
And we'll be broad and strong;
Bonaparte is in Castlebar,
Seeking Sarsfield's law.)

A somewhat more realistic account of some of the proceedings is supplied by a song collected in Donegal's Arran Island: 'Na Francaigh Bána' ('The White-Clad French'):

Ar an ceathrú lá fichead de mhí na Lúnasa,
Bhí na Francaigh againne le bánú an lae;
Is an tír ag bogadh le tréan a bpúdair —
Tuilledh sciúirse 'teacht ar Chlann na nGael. (153)

(On the twenty-fourth day of the month of August,
We had the French with us at the dawn of the day;
And the country rocking with the force of their gunpowder —
A further scourge coming on the Irish.)

The first line here contains an apparent inaccuracy: the French landed in fact on the 22nd of August, 1798. It would seem however that it took some time for the news to become widespread. It is interesting that the first reaction of the narrator is one of pessimism; nonetheless he accepts the fait accompli and expresses solidarity with the initial achievements:

Thug muid briseadh ag Cros Maoilfhíona,
Is ag Bealach Gaoithe cuireadh ortha an rotréat;
Ag Caisleán a' Bharra, eadar sin is meán oíche,
Bhí dhá chéad 's trí mhíle le síneadh i gcré. (154)

(We gave them battle at Crossmolina,
And at Windy Gap they were forced to retreat;
At Castlebar, between then and midnight
There were three thousand two hundred to be stretched in the clay.)

The exaggeration in this mention of the 'Races of Castlebar' is quickly followed by a sober account of the defeat of the French. The song ends by sounding once more that old note of hope that characterises so much of our poetry in those troubled times:

Ach tá dúil mhór agam as Rí na Grásta
Is as Bonapartaí nach ndearn ariamh feall,
Go dtiocfaidh ár gcaraid i measc na námhaid,
Is go mbainfidh siad sásamh as Clann na nGall. (155)

(But I have great hope in the King of Glory,
And in Bonaparte who never did wrong,
That our friends will come and rewrite our story,
And take revenge on the English throng.)*

One feels, however, that a more fitting conclusion might have been supplied by the preceding verse, more realistic in its pragmatic considerations:

Mná óga na tíre tá anois gan phósadh,
Tá eagla mhór orm go mbeidh na fir gann,
Á gcur go Sasana leis na Francaigh —
In aghaidh Rí Sheoirse níl gar dóibh ann. (156)

(The young women of Mayo, unwed they will die,
For the young men, I fear, will be in short supply;
Transported to England with the forces of France —
Against King George they haven't a chance.)*

". . . AND THEY RHYMING SONGS AND BALLADS ON THE TERROR OF MY FATE"

And so the dramatic events of the Year of the French resolved themselves ultimately, as always, into the personal dramas and domestic tragedies of individuals and their families — as in the case of Aifí Mac Giobúin, or that of George Chambers. Chambers was a son of the owner of Kilboyne House, a few miles south of Castlebar, and it is said that he fought on the Irish side in 1798, while his brother was a Captain with the English (157). (An account of the events makes the following mention of George's brother: "Captain Chambers, on the British side, fought like a very demon. With his own hand he killed or wounded several Frenchmen, including an officer. Throwing away his sword he seized a musket from a soldier's hands and continued to fight until a grenadier had run a bayonet clear down his throat and out at the side of his neck." (158)) George was arrested, however, not for his part in the fighting, but for other illegal activities. The man responsible for his arrest and conviction was Fr. James Jennings, parish priest of the Neale, who, in the words of Lord Altamont, "seized the leader of the Houghers of Cattle in the County of Mayo" (159), "a villain who styled himself Captain Hough, and under that signature held forth to assassination several of the most respectable gentlemen of the County". (160) Chambers was court-martialled in Castlebar on May 18th, 1799, and "charged with having tendered Unlawful Oaths and with having procured other persons to assist in the Houghing of Cattle" (161). He was sentenced to death, and the sentence was confirmed on June 3rd by Lord Cornwallis; he was subsequently hanged, probably in Ballinrobe, where, it would seem, he was transferred after his trial.

The song, 'Seorsa Sémbers', or 'An Róipín Caol Cnáibe' ('The Little Hempen Rope') expresses the condemned man's thoughts as he awaits execution. Its first verse includes a protestation of his innocence:

Ní raibh mo shleá gléasta, mo chlaidheamh géar, nó m'arm tine,
's a dhaoine uaisle na h-Éireann, narbh olc mo ghléas le dhul a' speireadh! (162)

(My spear wasn't in order, my sharp sword or my firearm,
And, good people of Ireland, wasn't it a poor instrument I had to go houghing!)

The song, as recorded almost a century ago, makes no reference to the role of Father Jennings in George's conviction; it is thought that such a

192

reference may have originally been included, and subsequently allowed to be forgotten. Blame for the young man's fate is attributed instead to a man named Creary, a Protestant minister in Ballinrobe whose relations with Catholics, it seems, were not the happiest:

Tá an Creirí ag cur tréas orm, Dia dár réiteach, agus Muire;
Siad lucht na mbréag a rinne an méid sin, 's dá bhféadfadh, dhéanfadh tuilleadh;
Dá ndéanfainn coir mhór, ní nach ndearna mé ariamh, ná tada,
Ní i bpríosún Bhaile 'n Róba bheadh mo lóistín le bheith feasta. (163)

(Creary is accusing me of treason, God save us, and Mary;
It was the backbiters who did that, and if they could, they would do more;
If I had committed a great crime — a thing I never did, or anything at all,
It's not in Ballinrobe prison my lodging would be from this out.)

Another verse expresses the hope that a Mr. Miller may be able to use his good offices to secure his freedom. A further one coincides almost exactly with a quatrain from 'Príosún Chluain Meala', a song about a man in a similar predicament; it poignantly evokes aspects of his lost liberty. And the song concludes with a motif which is also to be found in that great lament for a hanged man, 'Donncha Bán':

A Sheorsa bháin Shémbers atá ar aon chois i do sheasamh,
Cad chuige nach gcuirir scéala cé'n chaoi a bhfuilir?
Tabhair scéal ag mo mháithrín atá tinn brónach ar a leaba,
Go bhfuil an róipín caol cnáibe le dhul in áit mo charbhata. (164)

(O fair George Chambers, you who are left on one foot standing,
Why don't you send news of the state that you are in?
Take news to my mother who is lying sick and sad on her bed
That the little hempen rope is to go in the place of my cravat.)

I do not know whether this song is ever sung now, but, in 1885, it was still 'a great favourite with the old people of the neighbourhood of where the event transpired'. (165)

Not all the songs referring to the Year of the French are sad ones; at least one light-hearted ditty — given a new lease of life recently by a Clannad recording — has its roots in the Mayo of 1798:

An raibh tú i gCill Ala, nó i gCaisleán a' Bharra',
Nó 'n bhfaca tú 'n campa bhí ag na Francaigh?
Mise 'gus tusa 'gus ruball na muice 'gus bacaigh Shíol Aindí. (166)

(Were you in Killala or in Castlebar,
Or did you see the camp that the French had there?
Myself and yourself and the pig's tail and Andy's crowd's beggars.)

I have heard this described as a nonsense-song; no doubt that is what it is, but I have no doubt either that some, at least, of its nonsense is a secondary growth, nourished by a blurring of outline as history became hearsay: in some people's rendering of the song, Cill Ala became 'Cill Dara' (167) and the 'bacaigh Shíol Aindí' developed a life quite independent of their origin in the phrase 'Bucky Heelander' (168) — a term which refers presumably to the presence of Scottish troops among the forces of the Crown.

GAMES OF LOVE AND DEATH

It should not, I suppose, surprise us that something resembling a nursery-rhyme should owe its existence to an episode of slaughter; after all, 'Ring-a-ring-a-rosy' accompanies a game invented by London children in the seventeenth century to express their reaction to a plague which ravaged their city. Games and humour can be attempts to cope with the facts of death — a fact attested to by the former prevalence of "wake games". A game could take the following form: "one of the gathering simulated the dead man, stretching himself across some chairs and covering himself with a sheet. The others who took part in the game would then gather round and sing verses, for the most part of an impromptu kind, until the seemingly dead man would get tired and come to life again." (169) One song associated with this game was 'Oró Damhnaigh' ('Oró Downey'), which, to judge by some of the placenames mentioned, must have been sung in Mayo:

> Tá Damhnaigh i Lincoln, tá Damhnaigh i Leeds,
> Tá Damhnaigh ina chodladh 's nár éirí sé choíche . . .
> Tá Damhnaigh in Acaill, tá Damhnaigh i gCliar,
> Tá Damhnaigh ina chodladh 's nár éirí sé choiche . . . (170)

> (Downey is in Lincoln, Downey is in Leeds,
> Downey is asleep and may he never get up . . .
> Downey is in Achill, Downey is in Clare (Island)
> Downey is asleep and may he never get up . . .)

Obviously wakes were not the only occasion on which 'game-songs' could be sung; they could accompany work, and thus take their place among the 'songs of occupation', of which relatively few were collected in this country, but which must at one time have been quite common. One can imagine the following lines being tossed to and fro between girls at the spinning-wheel or in the hay-field as they discussed the relative merits of their respective young men:

> 'D'fheicfeá thall i Sasana an lasadh atá ar mo ghrá!' . . .
> 'Tá lasadh buí na heitinne i bpluicín do ghrá.' . . .
> 'Chuaigh mo ghrá an baile seo istigh ina jaunting-car.' . . .
> 'Níor ghabh mo ghrá an baile seo ó ghoid sé an gandal bán.' . . .
> 'Caroline as Ballindine is leggings as an gCláir.' . . .
> 'Up and down the market town and into Johnny Ward's.' . . .
> 'Ghabh do ghrá go Sasana 'failpéireacht ar na mná.' . . . (171)

> ('You'd see beyond in England the radiance of my love' . . .
> 'There is the yellow blush of consumption on the cheeks of your love' . . .
> 'My love went through this town in his jaunting car' . . .
> 'Your love did not pass through this town since he stole the white gander' . . .
> 'A caroline from Ballindine and leggings from Claremorris' . . .
> 'Up and down the market town and into Johnny Ward's' . . .
> 'My love went to England to earn a pound a day' . . .
> 'Your love went to England to sponge on the women' . . .)

Lines like these could be improvised, but some, it seems, were fixed. "They are as a rule very personal in character, but I suppose half their attraction lay in the fact that, under cover of the game, the singer could be insulting with impunity". (172)

A humorous song once popular all over Connacht is 'Túirne Mháire' ('Mary's Spinning-wheel'); it has been attributed to a poet named Owen MacGowan from Coolcarney, near Bunnyconnellan. It concerns a spinning-wheel belonging to an old half-blind lady named Mary Jordan; the wheel has been put out of action by some practical joker, but she blames the fairies and resorts to various means to have it repaired. (173)

Taréis a ndúirt me, níl sé i dtiúin
Go gcuirfidh mé a' siúl é amárach,
Síos go Cill Ala a' féachaint an easpaig
Go dtógfaidh sé suas ina láimh é.
Mar bhí sé mallaithe, ní féidir a bheannú
Go dté sé chun Ard Naoimh Pádraig,
Le neart a shoirne 's a mhéid a shloigfeadh,
Ní choinneodh ceathrar snáithe leis. (174)

(After all I've said, it isn't in tune,
Until I send it off tomorrow,
Down to Killala to see the bishop,
To let him take it up in his hand,
For it was cursed and cannot be blessed,
Till it comes to the Hill of Saint Patrick;
With the size of its snout and the amount it would swallow,
Four people couldn't keep it fed with thread.)

Another humorous Mayo song, 'An Chailleach', ('The Hag'), immortalises an old lady whose nimble fingers were put to less noble use than Mary Jordan's: her name was Molly Coakley, and she earned her place in folksong by stealing a golden guinea from a man called Micheál Ó Briain, of Druinnín, (Dringeen), who had given her lodging for a night. The following is an extract from his search warrant:

As Cill Íomair a d'éalaigh an chailleach
In aice le Baile an Róba,
As sin síos go Condae Shligigh
Agus thart le Coill an Tóchair . . .
'Séard a chuala mé ag Feichín Breathnach
Gur ionsaigh sí Dúiche Sheoigeach,
Is má castar leat i gConamara í,
Bain mo ghiní óir dhi. (175)

(Out of Killimor the hag escaped,
Hard by Ballinrobe,
From there down to County Sligo,
And over to Kiltogher (?) . . .
I heard from Festy Walsh
That she advanced on the Joyce Country,
And if you meet her in Connemara,
Get my golden guinea from her.)

It is good to know that the people of Mayo had humorous songs to sing in the dark days when they were given so many occasions to lament. Indeed, at times their merriment could reflect their relief at some relaxation of the misery which so often oppressed them. A case in point is that great satirical song 'Eoin Cóir' ('Honest Owen') by Riocárd Bairéad (Richard Barrett), the bard of Erris (1739-1819). The subject of this delightful mock-elegy was one Eoin Ó Conmacháin, (Owen Conway), a rapacious land-agent employed by the Binghams in Erris; he died in 1788

195

and is buried in the graveyard of Tearmon Ceathrach (Termoncarragh), about four miles north-west of Belmullet. (176) Barrett's song attributes exaggerated grief to the people who have most to gain from the tyrant's demise:

Nach é seo an scéal deacrach san tír seo,
In anacair chroí 'gus brón,
Ó fhágas tú Creagán an Líne
Go dté tú go dtí an Fál Mór?
A leithéid de screadadh 's de chaoineadh
Níor chuala tú ariamh go fóill,
Cé níl againne aon íonadh,
Ó cailleadh, faraor, Eoin Cóir!

(Isn't this the most pitiful story
That ever touched heart to the core?
Today we saw Owen to glory
From Creagan-a-line to Fallmore.
Such wailing and loud lamentation
Were ne'er heard in Erin before,
For we've lost our best friend in creation
The kind, tender-hearted Owen Cóir!)* (177)

Particularly happy is the alleged 'prayer' of one Seamus McGreevy:

'Sé dúirt Séamus Pheadair Mhic Riabhaigh,
is é ag agairt ar Rí na ndeor,
"Do réir mar bhí seisean do dhaoine,
Gurab amhlaidh a bheas Críosta dhó!"

('Twas thinking of all his good labours
Made Shamus so fervently pray,
"The same as he was to the neighbours
May Jesus be to him today!")* (178)

One of the song's editors offers this interesting tit-bit of information: 'It was a favourite song with the late patriotic Archbishop of Tuam, the Most Rev. Dr. MacHale, who sang it with great animation and spirit when he found himself in congenial company'. (179)

"LET US BE MERRY BEFORE WE GO"

One may be tempted to wonder if the Archbishop ever brought the same energy to a rendering of Barrett's other still-popular composition 'Preab san Ól', one of the best-known drinking-songs in the language:

Is iomaí slí sin a bhíonn ag daoine
A' cruinniú píosaí 's a' déanamh stóir,
'S a laghad a smaoiníonn ar ghiorra an tsaoil seo,
'S go mbeidh siad sínte faoi leac go fóill.
Más tiarna tíre, diúc nó rí thú,
Ní cuirfear pinghin leat a' dul faoin bhfód:
Mar sin's dá bhrí sin, níl beart níos críonna
Ná bheith go síoraí ' cur preab san ól.

(Why spend your leisure bereft of pleasure
Amassing treasure? Why scrape and save?
Why look so canny at every penny?
You'll take no money within the grave!
Landlords and gentry, for all their plenty,
Must still go empty — where'er they're bound:
So to my thinking we'd best be drinking,
Our bumpers clinking in round on round.)* (180)

196

It has been suggested — and it is quite plausible — that John Philpot Curran borrowed the metre of Barrett's song for his 'Deserter's Meditation' on the same theme, and that the English poet Lord Byron took it from there for use in one of his own lyrics.

"IT'S A LONESOME THING TO BE AWAY FROM IRELAND ALWAYS"

We have considered many songs of Mayo. We have rested on some of its mountains and by the banks of some of its rivers, wandered through the streets and markets of many of its towns; we have heard the clink of glasses and the sound of gunfire, the laughter of people at work and the sighs of people in exile. We have watched a procession of fine women and witnessed the heartbreak of their admirers. We have listened to stories of men enlisting in armies and fighting or deserting, and of men going down to the sea in ships, and often not coming back; we have seen men languishing in prison or hanging from the gallows, attended a wedding or two, and many a wake. It is appropriate that we should finish by looking at one song which offers, as it were, a microcosm of that varied Mayo experience: the joys of drinking in the company of fine women, the adventure of enlisting, the pain of exile, the threat of the law's long arm and the fear of the hangman's rope. It is fitting too that this song, like the one with which we began, should bear the title 'Contae Mhaigh Eo'. Various versions of this song exist, and it seems that it is in reality an amalgam of (at least) two separate songs. Some verses obviously concern a man who enlisted in the army and then deserted; others refer to a smuggler or pirate — named as Micheál Ó Bruadair, from Carrowkeel, in one account (181), and as Thomas Flavell (or Lavelle), from Inishbofin, in another (182) — who was arrested in Santa Cruz, and hanged. As is usual, the song provides little information which would allow a detailed reconstruction of the protagonist's circumstances, and no doubt the implications of certain verses commonly sung together are contradictory. Facts, however, seem to matter less to singers and listeners, than feelings, and much of the appeal of 'Contae Mhaigh Eo' is due to to its emphasis on its hero's sadness at not being able to revisit his native place or realise the desire of so many exiles: 'bás in Éirinn':

Agus dá mairfeadh mo shean-athair agam bheinn maith go leor,
Bheadh buidéal ins gach láimh liom is mé i gcomhluadar ban óg;
    Marach síor-ól na gcártaí
    Is an dlí a bheith ró-láidir,
Ní i Santa Cruz a fágfaí mo chnámha faoin bhfód.

Tá púnt is fiche amuigh agam i gContae Mhaigh Eo,
Is ní racha mé dá n-iarraidh choíche ná go deo,
    Ar fhaitíos go mbéarfaí thiar orm
    Is go ngabhfaí i ngeall le fiacha mé
Is go bhfáiscfí bóltaí iarainn ar bharr-iachalla mo bhróg.

Is go dtaga Cnoc na Cruaiche ar cuairt go hAbhainn Mhóir,
Acaill go Cúl Luachra ag buachailleacht na mbó,

197

Go ndéantar Iarla i gCliara
De Dhónal bheag Mac Riada,
Ní fheicfear mé go dtí sin i gContae Mhaigh Eo. (183)

(And if my grandfather were still alive, I'd be in fine form,
I'd have a bottle in each hand, and I in the company of young women;
If it weren't for my continual drinking
And the law being too strong,
It's not in Santa Cruz I'd be leaving my bones under the sod.

I am owed twenty pounds in County Mayo,
But I won't go looking for them now or ever,
For fear I would be caught there,
And seized on account of debts,
And that iron bolts would be clamped over the laces of my boots.

And until Croagh Patrick goes visiting the Owenmore,
And Achill comes to Cúl Luachra herding cows,
Until they make an Earl in Clare Island
Of young Donal MacGrady,
I won't be seen until then in County Mayo.)

FOCAL SCOIR

Great claims have been made for the quality of Gaelic folksongs, in respect of both music and words: Sir Arnold Bax, Donal O'Sullivan, Seán Ó Riada, Seán Ó Tuama and others have maintained that they are the most beautiful of their kind in the world. I do not feel competent to make such a claim, but I have no hesitation in saying that I find several of the songs, quite simply, perfect, and that I consider being able to enjoy them to be one of the main benefits of having some knowledge of the Irish language. — As to the seán-nós style of singing which is most often associated with them, it is, as the cliché has it, an acquired taste: I have found it a taste well worth acquiring. And incidentally, it may not be out of place here to pay tribute to those sean-nós singers — principally those of Connemara — whose talents have ensured the preservation as a living reality, into our own day, of so much of the material dealt with in this article: singers such as Seán 'ac Donncha, Máire Áine Nic Dhonncha, Darach Ó Catháin, Pádraig Ó Catháin, Seán Ó Conaire, Treasa Ní Mhiolláin, Micheál Seoighe, Tomás Ó Neachtain, Tess Bean Uí Chonfhaola, Sorcha Bean Uí Chonfhaola, Seosamh Ó Flatharta, Máirtín Mac Donncha, and, of course, the late Caitlín Maude, who died on 6 June 1982.

County Mayo can claim a not inconsiderable share in the heritage of Gaelic folksong. It is a heritage that any community could be proud to possess — or re-possess.

REFERENCES
Abbreviations used in the references

ACG: Micheál agus Tomás Ó Máille, *Amhráin Chlainne Gaedheal,* Connradh na Gaeilge, B.Á.C., 1905.

ACU: Muireadhach Méith, *Amhráin Chúige Uladh;* Atheagrán le Colm Ó Baoill, Gilbert Dalton, Dublin, 1977.

ADCC: Douglas Hyde, *Abhráin Diaga Chúige Connacht/Religious Songs of Connacht,* Irish University Press, Shannon, 1972.

AGCC: Douglas Hyde, *Abhráin Grádh Chúige Connacht/Love Songs of Connacht,* Irish University Press, Shannon, 1969.

ALR: Douglas Hyde, *Abhráin atá Leagtha ar an Reachtúire/Songs Ascribed to Raftery,* Irish University Press, Shannon, 1973.

AMS: Mrs. Costello: *Amhráin Mhuighe Seóla,* Talbot Press, Dublin, 1923.

BC 5:   Donal O'Sullivan (ed.), *The Bunting Collection of Irish Folk Music and Songs,* Vol. V.

CA 1:   Mícheál Ó hEidhin, *Cas Amhrán I,* Cló Chois Fharraige, 1979 (2nd ed.)

CCF: Mairghréad Nic Philibín, *Na Caisidigh agus a gcuid filidheachta,* Oifig an tSoláthair, B.Á.C., 1938.

CCU: Seán Ó Baoill, *Cnuasacht de Cheoltaí Uladh,* Comhaltas Uladh, 1944.

CG: Seán Óg agus Mánus Ó Baoill, *Ceolta Gael,* Mercier, 1975.

CM: Liam de Noraidh, *Ceol ón Mumhain,* An Clóchomhar Tta., B.Á.C., 1965.

CO: An t-Ath. Tomás Ó Ceallaigh, *Ceol na n-Oileán,* Oifig an tSoláthair, B.Á.C., 1931.

C1, 1:   Colm Ó Lochlainn, *An Claisceadal,* Iml. I, Faoi Coartha na dTrí gCoinneall, B.Á.C.

DCCU: Enrí Ó Muirgheasa, *Dhá Chéad de Cheoltaibh Uladh,* Oifig an tSoláthair, B.Á.C., 1934, 1974.

DG: Róis Ní Ógáin, *Duanaire Gaedhilge,* Comhlucht Oideachais na hÉireann, Tta., B.Á.C., 1921.

GAD: Seán Ó Tuama, *An Grá in Amhráin na nDaoine,* An Clóchomhar Tta., B.Á.C., 1978.

IM, 1:   James Hardiman, *Irish Minstrelsy,* Vol. I, Irish University Press, Shannon, 1971, (first published 1831).

IMS: P. W. Joyce, *Irish Music and Song,* Gill, Dublin, 1903.

IPS: Edward Walsh, *Irish Popular Songs,* 2nd ed., Gill, Dublin, 1883.

IST: Seán O'Boyle, *The Irish Song Tradition,* Gilbert Dalton, Dublin, 1976.

LC: M. Hannagan and S. Clandillon, *Londubh an Chairn,* Oxford, 1927.

MSFS: Tomás Ó Máille, *Micheál Mhac Suibhne agus Filidh an tSléibhe,* Oifig an tSoláthair, B.Á.C., 2nd ed., 1969.

ND 3:   Tomás Ó Concheanainn, *Nua-Dhuanaire, Cuid III,* Institiúd Ardléinn Bhaile Átha Cliath, 1978.

PPM: John O'Daly, *Poets and Poetry of Munster,* 1st Series, Dublin, 1849.

SI: Donal O'Sullivan, *Songs of the Irish,* Browne and Nolan, Ltd., Dublin, 1960.

REFERENCES

Note: The spelling of most quotations from older sources has been modernised in the interests of readability. Rhyming translations, marked with an asterisk, are approximate rather than literal.

(1) For example, Co. Mayo has furnished the longest and most complete versions of the religious song, 'Caoineadh na dTrí Muire', which was sung all over the country; cf. Angela Partridge, 'Caoineadh na dTrí Muire agus an Chaointeoireacht', in *Gnéithe den Chaointeoireacht* (eag. Breandán Ó Madagáin), An Clóchomhar Tta., 1978.Distinctive versions of widely-sung-songs — e.g. 'Bean an Fhir Rua' and 'Caisleán Uí Néill' — have also been collected in Mayo. (2) Some disjointed lines of the song, in imitation-English spelling, appear in an exercise-book Hyde used in 1873 when he was 13; (cf. ALR, p. vii). (3) ALR, pp 3, 5. (The text of the eight lines of the song quoted here is from ibid., pp. 96, 98). (4) ibid., p. 95. (5) ibid., p. 98. (6) ibid., pp. 223-230. (7) Cf. AGCC, pp. 123-129. (8) Donagh MacDonagh, *The Hungry Grass* (Faber & Faber). (9) CCF, p. 24. (10) ibid., p. 37. (11) Cf. ND 3, pp. 35-36. (12) Tomás Ó Canainn, *Traditional Music in Ireland,* Routledge and Kegan Paul, 1978, pp. 51-2. (13) ADCC, p 171. Hyde says the song is also known as 'An Bráithrín Buartha' ('The Troubled Friar'); in CCF, M. Nic Philibín reproduces a separate song with this title, though it

199

shares several verses with her version of 'An Caisideach Bán'. (14) CG, pp. 28-9. Seán Óg agus Mánus Ó Baoill *Ceolta Gael.* Mercier. (15) ADCC, p. 174. (All but the first two lines occur in a footnote to the main text). (16) ibid., pp. 176-7, footnotes. (The comments in parenthesis are Hyde's, as is the translation). (17) Máire Ní Scolaí, L.P. record CEF 029, Gael-Linn. (18) AMS, p. 90 and CCF p. 54. (19) ADCC p. 172. (20) ibid., pp. 172-3. (21) ibid., pp. 170-1. (22) Máire Ní Scolaí, op. cit. (23) CCF, pp. 55-7. (24) ADCC, pp. 174-5. (25) CCF, p. 54; AMS, p. 90. (26) CCF, p. 54, AMS p. 89. (27) CCF, pp. 54-5, AMS, p. 90. (27a) Donagh MacDonagh, op. cit. (28) MSFS, p. 116. (29) ACG, p. 97. (30) ibid. (31) ibid. (32) ibid., p. 156. (33) MSFS, p. 64. (34) ACG, p. 35. (35) Cf. MSFS, p. 3. (36) AGCC, pp. 10 & 11; I.P.S., p. 58. (For variants cf. AGCC, p. 12, and MSFS, p. 13.) (37) ND 3, p. 44. (38) AGCC, p. 9. (39) ibid., pp. 7, 9. (40) J.M. Synge, *The Playboy of the Western World,* Act 3. (41) Cf. CG, p. 38, and Máire Ní Scolaí, op. cit. (42) Text and translation are from the L.P. record, 'Grand Airs of Connemara', Topic, No. 12T177. (For a different version, cf. ACG, pp. 99-101). (43) Cf. GAD, p. 107. (44) Cf. DCCU, Réamhrádh. (45) L.P. Record, 'Amhráin as Árainn agus Conamara', CEF 038, Gael-Linn. Cf. also CO, p. 124. (46) ND 3, p. 42. (47) ibid. (48) Text and translation are from 'Grand Airs of Connemara'. (49) ibid. (50) Cf. GAD, pp. 30 et. seq. (51) CG, p. 85. (52) ibid., p. 84. (53) DCCU, pp. 277-8. (54) AMS, pp. 32-3; (translation altered at one point). (55) Cf. GAD, pp. 14 et seq. (56) SI, p. 67. (57) ibid., p. 66. (58) CM, p. 55. (An almost identical line occurs in a version recorded by Seán de hÓra, Gael-Linn CEF 063). (59) LC, p. 8. (60) BC 5, pp. 34-5. (61) Cf. IM, 1, p. 334. (62) ibid. (For an almost identical version, cf. PPM, pp. 128-130). (63) Cf. BC 5, pp. 41-4. (64) Cf. GAD, p. 229. (65) Cf. ibid., p. 232. (It has been suggested that the 'Chanson de la malmariée' may have derived from a type of May-day song which purported to celebrate marital infidelity; cf. ibid., p. 233). (66) DG, p. 16. (Cf. also L.P. record of Cantairí Óga Átha Cliath, Gael-Linn, CEF 023). (67) Cf. GAD, pp. 174-6. (68) Cf. ibid., pp. 190 et seq. (69) AMS, p. 126. (70) Cf. IPS, p. 86. (71) CO, p. 33. (Cf. also Darach Ó Catháin, Gael-Linn, CEF 040). (72) IST, pp. 88-9. (73) DCCU, p. 76. (74) ACG, p. 132. (75) ibid., p. 133. (76) DCCU, p. 76. (77) ibid., p. 77. (78) AMS, pp. 139-40. (The order of the verses has been changed, and 'uisge' in the last line altered to 'fuisgí' to accord with the practice of certain singers, e.g. Seán 'ac Donncha and Treasa Ní Mhiolláin). (79) MSFS, p. 6. (80) ibid. (81) ibid. (82) ibid., p. 7. (83) ACG, p. 84, with 'n-aol-chrobh', from IM, 1, p. 208, replacing 'maol-chruth'. (84) ACG, p. 83. (85) ibid., p. 85. (86) Cf. ibid., p. 222 and DCCU, p. 73. (87) DCCU, p. 72. (88) ACG, p. 50. (89) DCCU, p. 73. (90) ACG, p. 51. (91) CCU, p. 14. (92) AMS, p. 34. (93) ND 3, p. 41. (94) ibid. (95) ibid. p. 29. (96) ibid. (97) ibid. (98) ibid. (99) Cf. MSFS, p. 130. (100) Cf. DCCU, p. 70. (101) ibid., p. 69. (102) ibid., p. 68. (103) ibid. (104) ACG, p. 111. (105) Cf. SI, p. 95. (106) MSFS, p. 61. (107) ibid., p. 59. (108) DCCU, p. 110. (109) ibid., p. 111. (110) SI, p. 166. (I have used this version in print rather than that of DCCU, since the latter gives the less usual reading, "an iníon sin Uí Dhálaigh.") (111) DCCU, p. 111. (112) SI, p. 167. (113) Cf. ND 3, pp. 19-20. (114) ibid., p. 20. (115) Carson McCullers, *The Mortgaged Heart,* Penguin, 1975, p. 282. (116) ACG, p. 178. (117) Cf. ND 3, p. 72. (118) ibid., p. 5. (119) ibid. (120) MSFS, p. 69. (121) ND 3, p. 7. (122) ibid. (123) ibid. (124) ACG, p. 158. (125) George Moore, *Hail and Farewell,* Colin Smythe, 1975, p. 729, (note by editor, Richard Cave). (126) Joseph Hone, *The Life of George Moore,* Greenwood Press, 1973, p. 18. (127) ACG, p. 120. (128) ibid., p. 121. (Cf. also CA, 1, p. 79). (129) ibid. (130) Cf. MSFS, p. 121. (131) ibid., pp. 46-47. (132) ibid., p. 46. (133) ibid., p. 47. (134) ibid., p. 46. (135) ibid. (136) Cf. ND 3, p. 80. (137) ibid., p. 20. (138) ibid. (139) Cf. ibid., p. 77 and ACG, p. 187. (140) ND 3, p. 15. (141) ibid. (142) ibid. (143) ACG, p. 86. (144) Seán Lucy, *Unfinished Sequence and Other Poems,* Wolfhound Press, 1979, p. 45. (145) ND 3, p. 18. (146) Cf. ibid., p. 79, and ACG, p. 127. (147) ACG, p. 127. (148) ND 3, p. 18. (149) Cf. Niall Ó Dónaill, *Foclóir Gaeilge-Béarla,* Oifig an tSoláthair, B.A.C., 1977, p. 170. (150) ND3, p. 27. (151) Cf. ibid., p. 84. (152) ACG, p. 94. (153) DCCU, p. 26. (154) ibid. (155) ibid., p. 27. (156) ibid. (157) All the information given here on George Chambers is taken from Pádraig Ó Moghráin, 'Gearr-Chunntas ar an Athair Mánus Mac Suibhne', in *Béaloideas,* Iml. XVII — Uimh. 1-11, Meitheamh-Nodlaigh, 1947, (Educational Company of Ireland, 1949), pp. 3-57. (Cf. especially pp. 18-19, 46-47, and 51-56). (158) V. Gribayédoff, *The French Invasion of Ireland,* New York, 1890, pp. 94, 97; quoted in Ó Moghráin, op. cit., p. 46. (159) *State of the Country Papers,* 1st Series, Carton 408/653/16: State Papers Office, quoted in Ó Moghráin, op. cit., p. 55. (160) *Rebellion Papers;* 620/47/28, State Papers Office, quoted in Ó Moghráin, op. cit., p. 54. (161) *Kilmainham Papers,* 199, pp. 211-212 (Nat. Library); quoted in Ó Moghráin, op. cit., p. 52. (162) 'An Gaodhal', Meitheamh, 1885, p. 491; quoted in Ó Moghráin, op. cit., p. 46-47. (163) ibid. (164) ibid. (165) ibid. (166) Cl, 1, 2, pp. 5-6. (167) Cf. ACU, p. 51. (168) Cf. Cl, 1, p. 6. (169) AMS, p. 98. (170) Cl, 1, p. 11. (171) AMS, p. 94. (172) ibid., p. 97. (173) Cf. ibid., p. 83. (174) ibid., p. 82. (175) ACG, p. 125. (176) Cf. SI, p. 156. (177) ibid., p. 155. (178) ibid. (179) IMS, p. 4. (180) SI, p. 117. (181) Cf. ACG, pp. 165-6. (182) Cf. IM, 1, p. 337. (183) ACG, pp. 5-8.

THE GEOLOGY OF MAYO

by Barbara Buckley

The wide variety of geological structures and formations in County Mayo is responsible for the diversity of its topographical features. The overall topography is expressed in a landscape, which extends from relatively flat farmed fields in the east of the county, through large island-studded lakes renowned for their game fishing, to the naked quartzite peaks along the indented Atlantic coast, with their rugged cliffs interspersed with flat clean sandy beaches. The extensive tracts of blanket bog in the north of the county contrast sharply with the mountains of south Mayo, and illustrate the diversity of the scenic panoramas of the county.

The complexities of any landscape can be more fully appreciated if one understands the geological events which created the present topography. If one realises, when observing a particular mountain view, that possibly 500 million years have elapsed since the mountain mass was formed, the appreciation of the mountain's intricacies must surely grow. To assist in this understanding it is pertinent to outline briefly the geological calendar responsible for the earth's formation.

Geological history started about 600 million years ago with the end of the Pre-Cambrian era. That was followed by a series of epochs, each consisting of eras lasting several million years. Thus, the Cambrian (70 million years), the Ordovician (65 million years), the Silurian (40 million years), the Devonian (50 million years), the Carboniferous (65 million years), and the Permian (55 million years) eras combine to form the Palaeozoic epoch. The Triassic (32 million years), Jurassic (57 million years), and Cretaceous (71 million years) eras formed the shorter Mesozoic epoch. The most recent epoch, the Cainozoic, comprised the Palaeocene and Eocene (27 million years), the Oligocene (17 million years), the Miocene (19 million years), the Pliocene (5 million years), the Pleistocene (2 million years) and the Holocene eras. We are presently in the Holocene era, which commenced 10,000 years ago. When speaking in terms of millions of years the concept of time becomes difficult to grasp, but suffice it to say that the earth's crust, and hence our geological formations, took many millions of years to form, and have been undergoing weathering and erosion ever since. When considering the geology and scenery of Mayo it is helpful to divide the county into a number of areas with similar and distinctive features.

MWEELREA AND THE MURRISK PENINSULA

This area is bordered by Clew Bay on the north, Killary Harbour on the

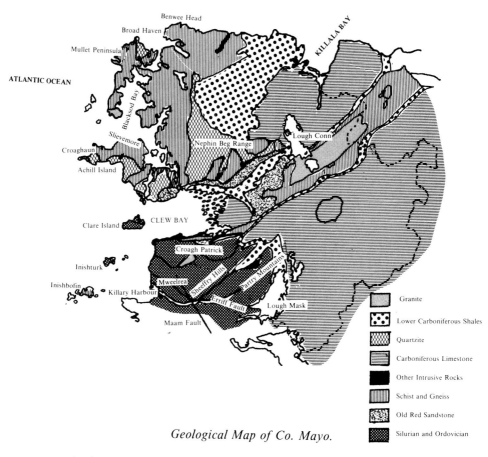

▨	Granite
⠿	Lower Carboniferous Shales
▩	Quartzite
☰	Carboniferous Limestone
■	Other Intrusive Rocks
▦	Schist and Gneiss
▨	Old Red Sandstone
▨	Silurian and Ordovician

Geological Map of Co. Mayo.

south, the Atlantic on the west, and Lough Mask and the Aille river on the east. Killary is the only fjord-like inlet in Ireland, and can be approached from many directions, but possibly the most breathtaking view can be seen from the small col at the north-western end of the Maam Valley (Co. Galway). From there can be seen the small village of Leenaun, snuggling into the mountainside at the bend in the dog's leg-type fjord. The Aasleagh Falls are at the northern end of Killary, where the Erriff river enters the fjord, seventeen kilometres from the mouth of the inlet. The harbour, or fjord, was formed by a fault, which was either a lateral, vertical or oblique movement of the earth's surface, resulting in displacement of the strata from their original alignment. Such faults were eroded by various agents to further increase the effects of the movement.

Mweelrea, (819m.), Connacht's highest mountain, is situated north of Killary harbour. A synclinal (downwards) fold of the substrata resulted in the formation of the mountain range starting with Mweelrea in the west, giving way to Ben Gorm, Ben Creggan, the Sheeffry Hills, Maumtrasna, and the Partry mountains on its eastern limit. This mountain range consists of substrata formed in the Ordovician era and are basically grits, sandstones, and conglomerates interbedded with slates and shales which underwent volcanic activity. This activity caused the volcanic dust and particles to form a rock known as tuff. Mweelrea rises out of the sea on its south and west side behind the sandy beach of Killadoon. On the eastern side of the peak are two corrie lakes or cums. Such lakes were formed by a build-up of ice, which later became a glacier. When it commenced its journey the glacier plucked out part of the mountain, resulting in a sheer cliff-back to the lake. Further east, the Mweelrea ridge is separated from Ben Gorm and Ben Creggan by Bundorragha valley, also formed by a fault, which was later deepened by denudational forces. The deepest part of the valley floor is occupied by Doolough, a deep lake surrounded by high foreboding hills. There is a lush stand of deciduous trees at Delphi Lodge, at the south end of the lake. The height of the surrounding hills gives an almost claustrophobic effect when travelling down the valley.

East and north east of Ben Gorm and Ben Creggan lie the Sheeffry Hills, which consist of grits formed during the Ordovician era. Between these hills and Ben Creggan lies Glenummera valley, which was formed by the erosion of a band of less resistant slate. The northern and eastern slopes of the Sheeffrys are pitted with corries, and the ridge shows evidence of nearby ice action in the presence of frost-shattered debris. Looking northwards from the Sheeffrys, one can see the characteristic cone of Croagh Patrick. This mountain mass differs from other quartzite mountains in Mayo, in that its rock substrata is Silurian in origin, rather than Ordovician, as in the Nephin Beg range. Croagh Patrick is visited annually by thousands of pilgrims, who have worn a path to the summit, exposing the sparkling quartzite. This path can be seen for kilometres around, particularly when the sun reflects off the wet broken fragments of the quartzite.

From Croagh Patrick several islands can be seen. The islands of Inishturk and Inishbofin rise out of the pounding Atlantic waves on the south west, while Clare island lies north west. This towering island is of particular geological interest as its substrata is divided by an extension of the Highland Border Fault, which runs along the south coast of Clew Bay. The western part of the island, with its Silurian sandstones, rises to 463m. at Croaghmore. The northern headland of Ordovician sandstone rises to cliffs 122m. high, while the eastern section of the island consists of Lower Carboniferous sandstones and shales. The most distinctive of the islands is the swarm of drumlins, whale-back type islands, which occupy the eastern section of Clew Bay. These drumlins were formed in the Pleistocene era, during a period of extensive glacial activity over most of Ireland. The most westerly (seaward) of these islands have been weathered by the action of waves, causing much of the limestone till of the islands to be deposited as spits, sand banks, and 'bridges' between the islands, giving rise to areas of backwater, leeward of the drumlins. The southern border of Clew Bay marks the western limit of the Highland Border Fault.

Murrisk peninsula is, therefore, bordered by a series of faults, namely, the Killary Fault to the south, the Highland Border Fault to the north, the Bundorragha Fault running north-south, and the Glenummera Fault east of the Bundorragha. The Erriff valley was formed by a fault which was later deepened by glacial action, as evident from the presence of hanging valleys and lateral moraines along the Erriff river banks.

To the east of the Erriff valley lies the high plateau of the Maumtrasna and Partry mountains. These Ordovician mountains do not provide such exciting scenery as the western axis of the Mweelrea syncline, although their southern borders are gouged by deep valleys and some corrie lakes. Two lakes can be seen beneath the summit of Buckaun, known locally as the Dirks, i.e. Lough Dirkmore and Lough Dirkbeg. These non-productive lakes are situated in the floor of a valley, otherwise covered with blanket bog. It is noticeable that where the turf banks have been cut large stumps of 'bog oak' have been exposed. These stumps are, in fact, remnants of pine (*Pinus sylvestris*) trees which grew in these areas, prior to the formation of the bog. From the southern side of the Maumtrasnas, one can look over the island-studded Lough Mask, whose north-east/south-west alignment is the result of glaciation in Iar-Chonnacht, which radiated from a point west of Leenaun. The lesser resistance of the Carboniferous limestone to a glacier's erosive forces has resulted in a deep lake with many islands near its shores. The Kilbride peninsula, with its Ordovician rocks, and volcanic fragments, separates two arms of Lough Mask, which penetrate deep into the surrounding mountains. To the west of the most northerly arm lies Lough Nafooey — a deep glacial lake, bordered by high majestic mountains. Its sandy beaches glitter like flashes of gold in this imposing valley.

CLEW BAY HINTERLAND

The hinterland to the east of Clew Bay lies along a syncline, with Carboniferous limestone near the surface, between Newport and Westport. This limestone is generally covered with glacial till, and numerous drumlins occur, giving a gently rolling landscape. The northern corner of the bay is bordered by Old Red Sandstone which, being less resistant than the adjacent limestone, gives rise to the Croaghmoyle Hills overlooking Beltra Lough. East of this area lie the uplands of granite which lead to the schists of the Ox mountains. The granite forms a backdrop to Lough Cullin, while the neighbouring Lough Conn has a limestone basin. The characteristic pitting of the limestone on the shores of Lough Conn and Lough Mask is attributed to the innate crystalline structure of limestone, coupled with constant wave erosion. Consequently, due to the interesting shapes formed, it is common to find specimens of this limestone placed on gate pillars, in rock gardens, and displayed as general garden ornaments. However, in their natural environment, these sharply-pitted rocks are a nuisance to moored lake boats.

NEPHIN BEG RANGE

The Nephin Beg range of mountains, formed from Dalradian quartzites, lies north west of the Clew Bay syncline. This impervious rock is weathered clear of vegetation on its peaks, creating knife-edge ridges and interesting terrain for the hillwalker. The peaks of this range are Nephin Beg (629m.), Slieve Car (722m.), Glenamong (630m.) and Nephin (806m.). Although the summits of this range do not appear to have been covered by ice glaciation, the lowlands have carved out valleys with glacial lake terraces. Nephin Beg and its neighbouring peaks rise out of the largest area of blanket bog in Ireland. It is possibly the most desolate region in the country, with fewer roads per hectare than any other part of Ireland. This treeless moorland covers schists and gneisses of Pre-Cambrian origin, which are among the oldest rocks in Britain and Ireland.

The blanket bog landscape is the doorway to some spectacular sea-cliffs, along the north Mayo coast, between Benwee Head and Downpatrick Head. Benwee Head has a natural sea arch with cliffs of almost 243m. To the west one can see the Stags of Broad Haven, which are the remnants of broken sea arches. To the east Dún Briste, at Downpatrick Head, is a superb example of a collapsed sea arch. The laminated substrata on the stack are a direct continuation of the adjacent cliff laminations. A prehistoric settlement on the stack points to a relatively recent collapse of the adjoining arch. Eastwards of the Nephin Beg range, and the northerly-facing schist and gneiss cliffs, is found a sloping area of Lower Carboniferous shales. These shales give way to the more fertile limestone area of north east Mayo, drained by the Cloonaghmore and Moy rivers, which enter the sea at Killala Bay. The Moy river is best known to angling tourists for its renowned salmon fishery.

THE MULLET PENINSULA

This peninsula assumes a peculiar shape, guarding Blacksod Bay to its east. It consists of schists with a triangle of quartzite at its southern tip. Glacial drift along the schists and gneisses of the rest of the peninsula contributes to the high calcium carbonate content of the beach sands of the area around Broad Haven Bay. The western coast of the Mullet is covered with sand dunes with peaty clays in the centre, and more acidic soils in the east. The bogs on the slopes of Termon Hill (105m.) once provided turf, but the supply is now depleted, exposing the shiny granite underneath.

ACHILL ISLAND

Achill island, the inverted L-shaped island, is the best known tourist resort in Mayo. Its scenery varies from sandy beaches to towering sea cliffs and large tracts of treeless bogs. The most westerly point, Achill Head, is approached from the cosy little beach of Keem. Along its sharp-edged ridge one can often find pockets of purple Achill 'amethyst'. Arising from Achill Head is the spectacular peak of Croaghaun (668m.), which plunges almost vertically to the wild Atlantic below. These magnificent cliffs are best seen from the sea, but offer a challenge to the intrepid mountaineer. Landward of Croaghaun is Lough Acorrymore — a perfect example of a corrie lake, with a backdrop of sheer mountainside. Not far to the east of this superb quartzite mountain is another equally impressive peak — Slièvemore. This schist mountain (672m.) looms over Dooagh village, Keel strand to the south, and Dooega to the north. It also shelters a corrie lake similar to that at Croaghaun. South of the long straw-coloured beach at Keel are the Menawn cliffs, and Cathedral rocks, which every Achill islander will tell you, with pride, are the most scenic cliffs in Ireland, and maybe even in the world. These quartzite cliffs must surely convince one of the potential beauty of any geological formation with quartzite as its main component.

EAST MAYO

With the exception of the granite mountain mass leading to the Ox mountains, Carboniferous limestone is found in east Mayo, from Killala Bay south to County Galway. This naturally more fertile substrata, corresponds with the most densely populated area of Mayo, with many small towns surrounded by agricultural land. Such landscape provides little of scenic interest when compared to the western part of the county.

A LANDSCAPE OF INTEREST

In Mayo one can find, within a day's journey, examples of volcanic activity, glacial formations, effects of weathering, whether destructive or constructive, expressed in a landscape varying from valley to valley. These forces have combined to produce a landscape of interest to the geologist, the botanist, the agriculturist, the adventurist, the rambler and tourist alike.

SOURCES
1. *Geology and Ireland* by W. E. Nevill.
2. *Geology and Scenery in Ireland* by John B. Whitlow.
3. *The Way that I Went* by R. L. Praeger.

THE MOUNTAINS OF MAYO

by Patrick McMahon

One of the most extensive areas of mountain and upland in Ireland is that which covers the western part of Co. Mayo, running almost unbroken from Lough Conn, in the north, to Killary Harbour, in the south.

These uplands are associated in many minds with the hardships and tragedies of the past. Generations of artists and writers have projected an atmosphere, which is almost tangible, and it is difficult in wandering through these hills not to succumb to images of the past. These images may be conjured up by a lonely mountain road, the scattered stones of a deserted cottage, or the faint outline of potato ridges high on a remote heather-clad hillside. However to-day, as more and more people turn to outdoor pursuits for leisure, these wild upland regions take on a different significance. For some, these summits and valleys offer a challenge and a sense of adventure. For others,immense satisfaction is achieved merely by being among the hills, and being able to absorb their special atmosphere of peace and tranquility. For whatever motive we are drawn to the hills, it is important that they be appreciated as a significant part of our heritage, and that as far as possible they be preserved as such.

NEPHIN MOUNTAINS

The following is a brief description of some of the more prominent mountain areas in Mayo, together with some indication on how to approach them. As one moves from north to south the first major range of mountains encountered is the Nephin Beg range. One is immediately confronted here with the problem of access. On the western side, the Mallaranny-Bangor road is up to 7 km. from the summit of the main ridge. Nephin Beg mountain itself is probably best approached from the south, following the road from Newport by Lough Feeagh to Shramore Lodge. From here the forest path should be followed, keeping left at junctions till the river is reached. This river must be forded, and while this is normally possible, a spell of rainy weather may create a different situation. However, assuming a successful negotiation of this obstacle, the journey will be continued along a gradually rising path. This path, which can be traced most of the way to Bangor, is the remains of a road, which in olden days was the route taken by many emigrants on their way to Westport, to board ships for America. The path can be followed for over three kilometres to the top of a broad pass. From here the route leaves the path and goes over, or around, a rounded hill about 407m. high (1336' on the map) and continues over rough-rising ground to Nephin Beg 629m.

(2065'), about 2.5km. further on. The view from the top is impressive, encompassing as it does, one of the most extensive areas of near wilderness in the country. Looking towards the west, the eye follows barren moorlands running down to Blacksod Bay, framed between the Mullet to the north and the imposing peaks of Achill to the south. Due to the length of the journey to the top of Nephin Beg, and to the remoteness of the area, the less experienced walker would be well advised to return by the same route. At the southern end of the Nephin Beg, both Glenthomas and Glendahork offer interesting horseshoe walks. The second of these two routes takes in a summit of 714m. (2343') which is, surprisingly, unnamed on the map. The Glenthomas route does not reach the same height, but does include a short section of the main ridge ,which is quite narrow, though not dangerously so. Before leaving these hills mention should be made of the complete traverse of the ridge, from Bangor to Mallaranny, taking in all the summits. This journey is regarded as an extremely tough one, and has been accomplished only by very experienced walkers

In contrast to the Nephin Beg range, Nephin Mór stands in isolated splendour to the east, overlooking Lough Conn. At 806m. (2646') it is the highest mountain in north Mayo, and the second highest in Connacht. Roads and laneways skirt the lower slopes giving good access. One route starts about 6km. north of Beltra on the road to Bellacorick. A fairly obvious route follows a broad ridge to the summit, and if one is lucky enough to arrive there on a clear day, the effort entailed will be amply rewarded. The views in every direction are magnificent and memorable.

ACHILL

We next turn our attention to Achill, whose beauty is widely recognised. The hill-walker will find much to interest him/her there, but, inevitably, his/her attention will be drawn to Croaghaun 668m. (2192'), and Slievemore 672m. (2204'). Croaghaun can best be climbed from Keem Bay by following the valley which leads upwards to the saddle between Benmore and Croaghaun. At a suitable point the slope on the right can be tackled, and the summit eventually reached. The cliffs which plunge from the summit to the Atlantic are truly awesome, and were once the home of the golden eagle. This strange landscape, with its precipices, and the austere rocky ridge of Achill Head contesting the great seas of the Atlantic, will linger long after in the mind. Slievemore, which is the highest point on Achill, can be approached from Doogort. The hill can be climbed by starting in the general direction of the summit, but keeping to the left of some rocky outcrops. A prominent ridge eventually leads to the summit, from which breath-taking views of Blacksod Bay and the Mullet can be enjoyed.

CROAGH PATRICK

South Mayo, which we now consider, is generally taken to be the area south of a line running east-west through Clew Bay. Much has been written about Croagh Patrick, 765m. (2510'), and over the years, thousands have annually taken the pilgrim path to the summit. The climb can be recommended at any time of the year, and if this can be achieved on a clear day, the reward will be one of the finest views in the country. The well-known pilgrim path is the obvious way to the summit. However, for the more adventurous, an interesting alternative is available. Starting from the highest point of a little-used road, which crosses a low gap about five kilometres east of the summit, the route goes westwards along a broad ridge, and eventually joins the upper part of the pilgrim path. Once the summit has been crossed the ridge can be followed, still running in the same direction, till at a suitable point the walker can head down to the Westport road.

SHEEFFRY MOUNTAINS

The view of the Sheeffry mountains from the summit of Croagh Patrick is most impressive. These mountains present a bare and stark profile. Long stretches of the main ridge lie at, or close to, 750m. high, and nowhere does it fall below 600m. but the approaches to it are either long, or steep, or both, depending on the route chosen. However, for the reasonably experienced hill-walker the first summit at the western end is a reasonable objective. Starting from the road at the southern end of Doo Lough, the route goes straight up to the crest of the ridge which runs almost parallel to the road. Turning right, (south-east), and following the steepening ridge, will bring the climber to the summit plateau, and a short distance further on to the summit cairn. The combination of steepness and short grass on this route may not be to everyone's liking. Across the deep valley of Doo Lough, steep rocky corries and buttresses rise to an intervening ridge, beyond which the seemingly ever-brooding Mweelrea lords it over all.

MWEELREA

Mweelrea, 819m. (2688'), is the highest mountain in Connacht. This height is accentuated by the fact that, on two sides, its slopes are seen to rise from sea level in one long sweep to its lofty summit. There are a number of routes to the summit, none of which can be considered easy. The most straight-forward starts on the western seaboard, where the road from Louisburgh, through Killadoon, runs out on the beach. From here, having crossed some fields and two rivers, the route goes directly towards the top. The slope gradually steepens, though not excessively, and does not relent till the summit is reached. The view from the top is in keeping with the splendour of the majestic mountain itself. Directly below lies the mouth of Killary Harbour, with its rocky shoals, while further out to sea the islands of Inishbofin and Inishturk fill the picturesque background. As the eye swings from the west through a wide arc to the south east, the sea and the Atlantic coastline are left, to be followed successively by views of the Twelve Pins and the Maumturk mountains; it is a magnificent panorama. If the weather is clear and dependable, an alternative route back can be recommended. This entails following the summit ridge southwards for some distance, and then leading straight down the long slope to Killary Harbour. Some rocky outcrops on this slope can easily be avoided. At the bottom, a rough path can be followed westwards, which leads back to the starting point.

BEN GORM MOUNTAINS

Directly south of the Sheeffry mountains lies the Ben Gorm range. This is a very compact group of hills, with many consistently steep slopes, which should be treated with great respect. The easiest gradients follow the long ridges which run eastwards from the two main summits, Ben Gorm 702m. (2303'), and Ben Creggan 695m. (2283'). A popular route to the summit of Ben Gorm follows the ridge which lies closest to Killary Harbour. The starting point for this is the car park near the famed Aasleagh Falls. On reaching the top of the ridge it should be followed to the left (westwards). From this ridge, steep slopes plunge down into the valley on the right. The route is fairly well defined, until, at about 600m. the ridge runs out into an extensive plateau. The summit, although only about 100m. higher, is a considerable distance away. Should conditions be unfavourable, the less experienced should consider retreating. However, those who continue to the summit will be well rewarded. In addition to fine views of Mweelrea and the Sheeffry mountains to the west and north, the southern view is again filled by the Maumturk mountains and the imposing Twelve Pins of Connemara. The return journey can be made by retracing steps, but again, an alternative, but longer route, is available. This entails descending the ridge north of, and parallel to, the one which was used for the ascent. There are some interesting rocky sections, but no danger is involved, though the drop into the valley on the left is impressively steep. At a suitable point lower down, the walker can swing into the valley on the right, and by following the river eventually reach the Aasleagh Falls.

MAUMTRASNA MOUNTAINS

Finally we come to the Maumtrasna mountains, an unusual range straddling the Mayo-Galway border. Individual summits are not a feature in this range, the significant characteristic being a long steep-sided valley, giving access to an extensive summit plateau. This plateau is 7km. wide at its greatest width, and even in clear conditions the highest point, 682m. (2239') high (and unnamed on the map), does not stand out with any prominence. For hill-walkers, most of the interest is provided by the valleys. A spectacular example is Skeltia, which runs north-eastwards from an area close to the north-eastern corner of Lough Mask. This valley, with brooding cliffs on both sides, gives a dramatic passage to the plateau. Some distance in from the edge of the plateau an O.S. marker indicates the summit of Maumtrasna mountain, 672m. (2207') high. A longer variation of this route involves following the rim of the valley and completing the horse-shoe at a high level. This is quite a serious undertaking, and should not be embarked upon by beginners. Numerous other valleys in the Maumtrasna mountains are well worth visiting. I would particularly recommend two: the Owenbrin, which divides the Partry mountains from the Maumtrasna mountains, and Glenacally, which runs southwards from Glenacally Bridge on the Leenaun-Westport road.

HILL WALKING

Within the limitations of a short article it has not been possible to be more detailed. I hope that this contribution will stimulate an active interest in hill-walking, but, a word of warning, hill-walking is for responsible people. Obviously one should not undertake a venture one is not capable of. Proper equipment, good footwear, suitable clothes and waterproofs, are essential. The weather at the top of a mountain may be very different from that at the bottom. Ask advice, or better still, for the first few journeys, travel with experienced companions. A map and compass should also be high on the list of priorities, even if the actual need for them is not foreseen. Their possession and use can add considerably to days of enjoyment on the hills "of sweet Mayo!"

SOURCES

1. *Irish Walk Guides/2 West* by Tony Whilde.
2. *Mountaineering in Ireland* by C. W. Wall.
3. *The Way that I Went* by R. L. Praeger.

MAYO WILDLIFE

by Michael Leonard

The term wildlife refers to all plants and animals which are not cultivated by man. *The traditional meaning* of the term is more restricted, and applies only to birds and wild animals which have some sporting, commercial or aesthetic value. Apart from Darwin's *"Origin of the Species",* the other literary classic which natural history has produced in Britain is Gilbert White's, *"The Natural History and Antiquities of Selborne",* first published at the end of the eighteenth century. The only comparable Irish text is Robert L. Praeger's *"The Way that I Went".* Although written almost half a century ago, it is still the finest guide to the beauties of the Irish countryside.

PRAEGER AND THE CLARE ISLAND SURVEY

Praeger, who was born in Co. Down in 1865, was fascinated by the rugged beauty of Achill, and described the north coast of Erris, with cliffs up to two hundred and forty metres high, as the finest cliff scenery in Ireland. The same cliff range was the haunt of the last Golden Eagle resident in Ireland in 1912, and the scene of the last reported sighting in 1931. Sadly, too, Praeger tells us that the last White-Tailed Eagle — a rare species, once plentiful in the West of Ireland — was shot on Clare Island in 1935. Robert Lloyd Praeger's name is of course irrevocably linked with beautiful Clare Island in Clew Bay. In 1903 Cecil Baring purchased Lambay Island in Dublin Bay, and sought Praeger's help in an attempt to discover all he could about the island. Praeger, then attached to the National Library in Dublin, suggested an intensive survey of the Flora and Fauna of the island. In 1905/'06 a score of specialists went on to the island in relays, and stayed with the owner. The results were exciting: — of the species collected, no fewer than seventeen were then new to the British Isles, and five were new to science. Praeger was so impressed that he decided to investigate a more remote western island. He selected Clare Island, off the Mayo coast, and during the years 1909—1911, a hundred specialists, including a number from the Continent, went to work on Clare Island. The result is now a milestone in the world of Biology. The findings were published in a series of sixty-seven separate reports, in three volumes; they are a credit to Praeger and to the Royal Irish Academy, which supported the research.

The Clare Island Survey is by any standards a monumental project. Of the total of 5,269 animals observed, no fewer than 1,253 species were found to be hitherto unknown in Ireland, 343 were unrecorded in Great Britain, and over one hundred were new to science. Of the 3,219 plants collected,

585 were new to Ireland, and eleven new to science. In a very special sense then, Clare Island was one of the first biological science field centres. In more recent times, Clare Island has entertained, and educated many, including investigator supreme, Hugh O'Donnell, and in the late seventies added nesting Gannets to its many charms.

CONSERVATION

The discovery of a new species of bird nesting in a country is always an exciting event, just as the extinction of an existing species is always sad. The Atlas project, carried out by the Irish Wildbird Conservancy jointly with the British Trust for Ornithology during 1968-'72, discovered the Goosander and its young in Donegal. The Goosander Duck, a near relative of the widespread resident, the Red-Breasted Merganser, is a welcome addition to a list of recent Irish gains. The list includes the Eider, Common Scoter Ducks, and the Fulmar Petrel, first discovered breeding in Ireland in 1911 at Portacloy, Co. Mayo. Mayo Fulmar counts, in the past decade, vary from one thousand pairs plus on Clare Island and Inishturk, to one thousand five hundred pairs on the north Mayo Cliffs, as well as smaller numbers on many other sites. That is part of the good tidings; on the other side of the coin, some species are endangered. The Peregrine Falcon, plumetting from three hundred metres above on an unsuspecting Pigeon or Dove, or the Salmon leaping majestically upstream to spawn, are but two of the wonders of nature on the verge of extinction in 1982. Such sights greeted the first people to reach our shores and have been a familiar part of life in Ireland since then. The Irish Hare, a distinct species, which is stockier than the brown hare, with much shorter ears and a white tail, has had its numbers dramatically reduced. The once indestructible Fox has now become a rarity in some counties, because of the organised killing of the animal for its skin. In reply to a Parliamentary question, on 9 December 1980, the Minister for Fisheries and Forestry told the Dáil that in the period from August 1979, when export licencing regulations were introduced, to April, 1980, 36,567 fox skins were exported. The beautiful Hen Harrier, which seldom breeds outside the Orkney Islands and northern Scotland, has a recorded population of approximately one hundred pairs in Britain and Ireland. A few have become established in North Wales, and on the West Coast of Ireland. A beautiful vagrant, the Belted Kingfisher, shot in Ballina in 1979 is now on display in our natural history museum in Dublin. The Heron-like Cattle Egret develops pink alluring legs during its breeding season, and in this century has achieved an astonishing expansion outside its native areas in Africa and south Asia. It is a very rare visitor to Ireland, and made its first reported crossing of the Atlantic in 1937.

Land drainage and all types of pollution effect our wildlife. While drainage is responsible, and indeed viable where good agricultural land is under-productive due to flooding, the drainage of marginal land is unnecessary and unwise. This land serves as a reservoir and regulator, absorbing water during periods of high rainfall, and releasing it slowly afterwards.

SEÓDAÍ MHAIGH EO

County Mayo provides ideal and diverse habitats for wildlife. Numerous mudflats, sandy estuaries, extensive sandbanks, and cliffs of varying heights, decorate the indented spectacular coastline, from Killala Bay in the north, to the Fjord at Killary harbour. Each of the offshore islands support a characteristic bird population. The most celebrated population is the colony of Barnacle Geese on the Inishkea Islands, off the Mullet, while Inishglora, between the two, has the largest colony of Storm Petrels off our coast. The colony, estimated to exceed ten thousand pairs, has been studied by the Extra Mural Department, Queen's University, Belfast. Inland Mayo, especially its larger lakes, provide an irreplacable habitat for our wildlife assets.

Lough Carra is of international ecological importance, because it has the largest Mallard population nesting in Ireland, with a population of approximately two thousand birds. It is also the best example we have in Ireland of a spring-fed limestone lake with extensive marl deposition. Other important wintering wild-fowl, on Lough Carra, include Shoveller and Gadwall Duck, which are of national importance. The waters of Lough Mask flow entirely underground to Lough Corrib, and that area has many small caves. The Mask, situated on the junction of Silurian slate and limestone, is of special ecological interest. The usual migrating birds, the Shrimp (Mysis Relicta), known locally as Ribe Robéise, are found in that region, and some interesting flora, including two St. John's Worts. Lough Conn is world famous for its Trout, Salmon, and its noteworthy race of Char. The nearby Pontoon woods have an excellent example of Atlantic Oakwood. The Common Scoter Duck breed is found on Lough Cullin, while nearby, the burnet *Sanguisorba officinalis* has its only site in the South of Ireland.

Lough Carrowmore situated in magnificent North-west Mayo, has some mediterranean heath (a species found only in Counties Mayo and Galway) on its shore. The most extensive community of mediterranean heath in Ireland grows on Mweelrea, just above Killary harbour.

Carrowmore lake, in its beautiful and lonely setting, is an important wintering haunt for Pochard, Tufted Duck, and small numbers of White-Fronted Geese.

The Mayo cliffs compare favourably with the Cliffs of Moher — Ireland's premier site for cliff-nesting species. The following facts and figures help to illustrate the point. Hump-backed Clare Island, already referred to, has important seabird colonies, especially: Fulmar, Kittiwake and Razorbill, (more than 1,300 pairs of each species). Guillemots, (800 birds), a Puffin-breeding colony, (more than 2,000 pairs), as well as large numbers of Storm Petrels in the breeding season. Inishglora has 10,000 pairs of Storm Petrels, the second largest colony in Ireland. All the Irish members of the Auk family are represented in Inishturk, including the rather scarce Black Guillemot, (28 pairs). The inaccessible Stags of Broad Haven, and Porturlin cliffs, have important seabird colonies. The latter has an unusual heather, resembling Mackay's Heath, growing on the cliff top. Mayo Bellavista can be seen on the Carboniferous cliffs of Downpatrick Head, with its seabird colonies of Kittiwake, Guillemot and Fulmar.

Drumleen Lough is the only known site for whorled Caraway between Donegal and Kerry. Croagh Patrick is one of the few Irish sites for the mountain ringlet butterfly, and has a rich Arctic alpine plant community. At beautiful Old Head, near Louisburgh, which is a favourite haunt of many birds, including breeding Nightjars, there is another example of Atlantic oakwood. Lough Meelick, adjacent to Killala esker, is the only known site for the introduced fish, *Liza ramode*. Blacksod Bay, with its large areas of inter-tidal mudflats, supports large populations of Waders, mainly, Oyster-Catchers, Ringed Plovers, Dunlins, Curlew, Redshank, and Bar-Tailed Godwit.

The Bar-Tailed Godwit feed on the widespread lugworm, with their long and noticeably adapted beaks digging the sand. Oyster-Catchers feed on cockles and other Molluscans. Dunlin and Redshank feed on smaller animal life, mainly ragworm and hydrobia shells. Brent Geese, from the Canadian Arctic, feed on eelgrass or the green seaweed *Enteromorpha*. Estuarine vegetation provides food for many species of duck, though the handsome Shellduck feed on invertebrata, leaving a semi-circular pattern on the surface. The Mullet is the nestling ground of the Red Necked Phalarope, which is the rarest breeding species we have in Ireland, and also a most interesting one. Unlike most Waders, the Phalaropes spend most of their time at sea and use the land only during the breeding season. They show an interesting adaptation to their aquatic life style; their toes have flattened scales to give added swimming power. The Red Necked Phalarope breeds throughout the Arctic region, and has its most southerly breeding post on the Mullet. It feeds on crustacea and larvae, by upending itself on the water. If its dietary organisms are too deep to be accessible by upending, the bird spins like a top creating turbulence, which brings the food nearer the water surface. It also shows a complete reversal of the usual courtship roles. The female Phalarope takes the initiative during courtship, and is more brightly coloured. The cock performs all the duties of nest-making, and rearing the young. Four eggs are laid in a grass cup, in late May or June, and are incubated by the cock for twenty days.

Most of the very few Snowy Owls seen in Ireland have also been reported from the Mullet.

Inishkea is the number one Irish site for Barnacle Geese, a winter visitor to Ireland. Almost three thousand Barnacle Geese come to Inishkea from the Greenland population of twenty-eight thousand. Six thousand Barnacle Geese spend winter on a handful of Irish sites and the remaining twenty-two thousand on the west coast of Scotland. About six thousand breed on the Arctic Island of Spitsbergen, and winter on the Solway Firth in Scotland. The third population of Barnacle Geese, all forty-five thousand of them, breed on the large island of Novaya Zemlya, between the Barent's Sea and the Kara sea, north of Russia. The very beautiful Barnacle Goose, with black, white and grey plumage, is the only Irish goose with a white face.

There are eighteen species of Seal, but only two breed in Ireland. There is a colony of Oceanic Grey Seals around Inishkea. The smaller Common Seal likes the shelter of inlets and harbours. The grey seal becomes sexually mature at five years of age, and one pup per mother is born on Inishkea, and other Western Islands, between early September and early November. Under the Wildlife Act 1977, it is illegal to kill seals without a licence.

BLANKET BOG

The very beautiful Blanket Bog of north Mayo is a must for inclusion in any list of elite Irish panoramic places, which stimulate and excite the imagination. It is at once lonely, awesome and rich in colour, especially in summer, when the heather is in bloom. Peatlands are unbalanced systems in which the rate of production of organic matter by living organisms exceeds the rate at which these compounds are broken down or respired. The result is an accumulation of an organic layer, which we call peat or bog. More than fifteen species of bog-moss, or Sphagnum, grow in Ireland, all found in boggy places, where they form thick soft masses and retain water like a sponge. Their older stems die annually, but due to the special conditions existing in our bogs, do not decay. This layer of dead bog moss is continually increasing in depth, and the lower compressed layers form peat or bog. As the peat grows, or thickens, the surface vegetation becomes isolated from underlying soil and rocks. The resulting environmental changes are accompanied by changes in the flora, which reflect the changing water and chemistry content of the bog surface. Bog is, therefore, constantly changing, growing and spreading. The dominant plant species growing on the Mayo blanket bog includes purple moor grass, black bog rush, heathers, bog cotton, sedges and mosses.

Irish bogs offer unrivalled opportunities for ecological investigations. For two decades now, An Foras Talúntais scientists, based at Glenamoy, have been engaged in valuable and interesting research. The Peatland Experimental station at Glenamoy was established by the Department of Agriculture in 1955, on lands occupied formerly by Min-Fheir Teoranta, (The Grassmeal Company).

GROUSE

Scientists classify all animals in a series of groups, starting with twenty-two phyla and go downwards through classes, order, families, (ending in-idae), to the actual species. In some cases, as with Mayo Grouse, there are sub-species, or races, based on geographical variation. The basic divisions within the animal kingdom are universally agreed. Birds belong to the Phylum Chordata (the animals with a spinal cord), within which they form the class Aves. This class is divided into twenty-eight orders, half of which have, or had, members in County Mayo.

The aforementioned Grouse was the subject of an interesting research project carried out at Glenamoy Experimental Station. The research programme covered population studies, habitat improvements, nutritional studies on heather (Culluna vulgaris), and studies on Captive Grouse. The Red Grouse was considered, in former times, to be the only endemic bird species in Britain and Ireland. Red Grouse (Lagopus lagopus), now include Willow Ptarmigan, Willow Grouse and Red Grouse. The British Red Grouse is reduced to the rank of subspecies as Lagopus lagopus Scoticus, while the Irish Red Grouse, formerly regarded as a subspecies of the British bird, has equal status with the name Lagopus lagopus hibernicus. The Red Grouse is an herbivore, feeding mainly on heather, and is characteristic of open moorland dominated by heather, with crowberry and bilberry providing alternative food.

RAIFTERÍ

No words of mine could do justice to the enormous variety, and depth of beauty, of Mayo's Natural history, so let us leave the parting words to Raifterí, An file:

"Tá an chuach 's an smólach ag freagairt a chéile ann,
Tá an Londubh 's an céirseach ag gur, os a gcómhair
An gúld-finse, 'n creabhar, 's an linnet i gcage ann
An maosgach ag léimnigh, a's an eala ó'n Róimh.
An t-iorlach as Acaill 's an fiach dubh ón gCéis ann,
An seabhac ar Loch Éirne 's an fhuiseóg ó'n mhóin.
's dá mbéitheá ann ar maidin roimh eirighe na gréinne,
Go gcloisfeá gach éan aca ag seinm san ngróbh".[1]

NOTE

[1] Translation by Douglas Hyde.

"There is the cuckoo and the thrush answering each other there,
The blackbird and the ceirseach hatching over against them,
The goldfinch, the wood-cock, and the linnet in a cage there,
The snipe leaping up, and the swan from Rome,
The eagle out of Achill and the raven out of Kesh Corran,
The falcon from Loch Erne and the lark from the bog,
And if you were to be there in the morning before rise of sun,
Sure you would hear every bird of them a-singing in the grove."

SOURCES

1. *Birds of Ireland* J. Darcy.

2. *Geology and Ireland* by W. E. Nevill.

3. *The Botanist in Ireland* R. L. Praeger.

4. *The Irish Landscape* by G. F. Mitchell.

5. *The Way that I Went* R. L. Praeger.

THE REEK

le tAthair Leon Ó Mórcháin

In his *Irish Sketch-book,* published in 1843, William Makepeace Thackeray describes a journey he made by horse-car from Clifden to Westport . He tells of one point on the Leenaun road where his young guide jumped excitedly from the car and, pointing to a mountain-peak on the horizon, shouted out: "The Reek! the Reek!" It must have been, in miniature, a moment of emotion, akin to that recounted by Xenephon when the Greek soldiers, journeying homewards, caught sight of the Euxine and shouted: "The sea! the sea!" The shapely cone of Croagh Patrick is not towering, 2,510 feet (765m.), but it does dominate the land — and sea-scape of the area between Clew Bay and the Killaries, which was known long ago as Aicill, and more recently as Iar-Umhal. It has a commanding and a unifying effect on the communities that live within sight. Geologically, the Reek is part of a very ancient rock fold known as the pre-Cambrian fold. Its rock-formation is of the metamorphic type, and the main constituent of the present mountain is quartzite, which explains why it has weathered so well, has resisted change such as any vegetation, and retains its distinctive shape.

PLACE OF PILGRIMAGE

Historically the mountain was originally known as *Cruach Aigli* (that is, the mount of the territory of Aicill), and it is mentioned as the site of a tribal battle, in the early second century of Christian times. Its real place in history relates to its connection with Saint Patrick, which later changed its name. In a scholarly analysis of the saint's writings, *Mise Pádraig* (1960), an Dochtúir Liam Mac Philibín suggests that the mountain was probably the place of Patrick's captivity in Ireland, and that this area was also the site of the Wood of Focluth, from which a vision of Irish youth called to him to *return.* The earliest actual reference to Patrick's prayer and fast on the mountain is in the writings of the seventh-century writer Tirechán, who states that, having approached from Aughagower, "Patrick went to Mount Egli to fast and pray on it forty days and forty nights, keeping the discipline of Moses and Elias and Christ". He also records the death and burial there of Patrick's charioteer, Totmael.

A tenth or eleventh-century work, the Tripartite Life, gives the date of that sojourn as Lent 441, linking it with the accession of Leo 1 as Pope, and adds that Patrick sent his nephew, Bishop Munis, to the new Pope, with filial greetings. This record, however, has not equal authority with that of Tirechán. Gradually, a pilgrimage of popular devotion grew, but how soon

218

The Reek. (Liam Lyons)

it became established we do not know. There are occasional references, like so many stepping-stones through the succeeding centuries, which allow us to conclude that the pilgrimage is at least nine hundred years old. The earliest of these is found in the *Chronicon Scotorum,* which states that in 1106 a pilgrim was struck by lightning on the mountain, and killed. The Four Masters, possibly referring to this same tragedy, record that a thunderbolt destroyed thirty pilgrims who were fasting and praying there, on Saint Patrick's Eve in the year 1113. Obviously there was a pilgrimage held then in association with the saint's feast-day in mid-March. An incidental reference in the *Annals of Boyle* recounts that Aedh O'Concubhair, King of Connacht, severely punished an outlaw for daring to molest a pilgrim to Croagh Patrick. The papal registers record that in 1216 the chapel on the summit was assigned permanently to the jurisdiction of the Archbishop of Tuam, for, like every Patrician foundation, it was hitherto directly subject to the Archbishop of Armagh. And in 1432, the registers record, Pope Eugenius IV granted certain indulgences to pilgrims, adding incidentally that 'a great multitude' resorts there on the last Sunday of July (which is still known as "Reek Sunday").

The known pattern of road communications, for those early centuries, clearly indicate the country-wide importance of Cruach Phádraic. A primitive trunk-road, called the *Tóchar Phádraic,* has been traced eastwards as far as Balla, and near this road in 1216 was founded the Abbey of Ballintober, which later became a traditional hostel for long-distance pilgrims to the Reek. In 1796-7 a French traveller to Mayo named De Latocnaye, describing the pilgrimage and the chapel which was at that time on the summit, refers to the presence there of a black bell of Saint Patrick, which, he says, was held in great veneration. Seemingly this bell was an heirloom of the Geraghty family, and was purchased for the National Museum by Sir William Wilde in 1871. The last of the history stepping-stones takes us into the present century: Archbishop Healy (1903-18) had been enthusiastically working for the revival of the pilgrimage to this site of national importance and had a modern chapel built on the site of the old Patrician one. He dedicated it on 30 July 1905.

TRADITION

So much for history. Tradition has, of course, added colour and embellishment. The more ancient traditions, which often nowadays masquerade as fact, concern the saint's style of prayer on the summit: his refusal to leave until God granted him his requests that the faith of the Irish would never fail; and that he would personally be their judge at the end of time. Tradition also associates with the Reek the banishing of serpents, and blends this somehow with a dismissal of devils or demons into a nearby mountain lake, which is still called "Loch na nDiabhal", or "Loch na nDeamhan". It was from this lake that the famous black bell was said to have been recovered during a drought. Tradition also links Croagh Patrick with two adjacent foundations; one on Caher Island, off the coast of West Mayo, (to which a *tóchar* now submerged, is said to lead), and the other the Church of Kilgeever, beside the blessed well called "Tobar Rí an Domhnaigh". An old local belief was that the stones from the top of the Reek, and indeed the clay from Caher Island, were preventives against rats!

NEW CHAPEL

The fidelity and veneration of the local people for Croagh Patrick as a sacred place is epitomised in the story of a man (variously named Robert Benn and "Bob o' the Reek") who, like a modern stylite, spent the greater part of his last fifteen years on the mountain-top, during the latter part of the nineteenth century. When he died his body was carried by the local people to the summit, and there buried beside the then ruined chapel. (Mr. Walter J. Heneghan of Louisburgh, who in 1905 worked as a youth with his father at the building of the new chapel, before his death told the present writer that, as they dug the foundations, they came upon parts of a human skeleton, which they re-interred somewhat to the south of the present building). The building of this new chapel was indeed a triumph of strength and endurance. All of the building appliances, including scaffolding, old-fashioned casing, and the cement, were carried by men and donkeys from the base of the summit. The necessary water was brought (at one shilling per can!) from Garraí Mór on the western slope. For those workmen, a mere station on the Reek would have been relative relaxation!

TRADITIONAL STATION

The traditional station, as distinct from the climb, which it includes, begins at the eastern base of that cone at Leacht Benain. (Benan was Patrick's successor in Armagh). The pilgrim walks seven rounds of the *leacht,* and then climbs to the top, by way of the steep passage known locally as "the ladder". One then walks fifteen times around Teampall Phádraic on top, seven times around each of the three mounds of Roilig Mhuire, and seven of the area of Garraí Mór. A corresponding number of Paters, Aves, and Glorias with one creed are said at each of these. In a Church re-juvenated by more imaginative and dramatic liturgies, such repetitious prayers and exercises are fast losing favour, but the same challenge, the call and the mystique of the Reek remain. The physical challenge is hardly more real than is the spiritual combat of which it is a parable. On any Reek Sunday morning, or indeed on any day of the now extended pilgrimage, along the slopes people are, consciously or otherwise, acting out a whole series of life-responses and situations, as well as continuing a tradition which disappears backwards into early Christian times.

A RECENT THEORY

A recent theory questions the accepted accounts of Saint Patrick's association with the mountain. It argues that such mass climbs were a common feature of pagan Ireland, and that there is no historical proof that there was an actual link with Saint Patrick, so that the tradition is spurious. The theory could perhaps be met with three points. The existence of an ancient custom of mountain-climbing in pagan Ireland could well mean that, as he did elsewhere, the saint gave a Christian dimension to a native practice. Since there is no written conclusive proof either way, the purchase of centuries of tradition must not be dismissed. This is quite apart from the vast weight of recorded opinions of historians, from Tirechán and the Tripartite Life down to Bieler and Bury. Indeed, Professor Bury states that Croagh Patrick is the one place where we can be sure that we stand in the saint's footsteps!

A PILGRIMS PROGRESS

The river of pilgrims flows on. The prayerful silence may nowadays be punctured by the decibels of transistors; a new arrangement — of *daylight* climbing only — may have ended the inspiring sight of a moving chain of lights upwards along the pilgrims' path, but, as with the mountain itself, the core remains. It reminds one of the *goodness* of salt; of the endurance of granite. Along that pilgrim path are, literally and figuratively, all ages of man; the carefreeness of youth, the difficulties of age, the hesitant, the adventurous, the persevering, the thoughtful, the loner, the group, and the couple. There is the eagerness of the base chastened into resignation at the summit, by the experiences and trials of the journey. It is life's mountain. It is a *pilgrim's progress.* For many an admiring Irish tourist — but for none more than a returning emigrant — there is in that familair cone, an atmosphere, a consciousness of awe and of 'nature', which echoes the cry: "The Reek! the Reek!"

SOURCES

1. *History of the Archdiocese of Tuam* Vols. 1 & 2 Rt. Rev. Monsignor D'Alton.

2. *The History of the County of Mayo to the close of the sixteenth century.* H. T. Knox.

KNOCK SHRINE

THE GOAL OF POPE JOHN PAUL II's HISTORIC
PILGRIMAGE TO IRELAND

by Thomas Neary

"Here I am at the goal of my journey to Ireland: the Shrine of Our Lady of Knock. Since I first learnt of the Centenary of this Shrine. . . . I have felt a strong desire to come here, the desire to make yet another pilgrimage to the Shrine of the Mother of Christ, the Mother of the Church, the Queen of Peace . . . . Do we not confess with all our brethren, even with those with whom we are not yet linked in full unity, that we are pilgrim people . . . . .

I am here then as a pilgrim, a sign of the pilgrim Church throughout the world, participating, through my presence as Peter's successor, in a very special way in the centenary celebration of this Shrine.

The Liturgy of the word of to-day's Mass gives me my pilgrim's salutation to Mary, as now I come before her in Ireland's Marian Shrine at Cnoc Mhuire, the Hill of Mary . . . ." (Homily of Pope John Paul II at Knock Shrine, on 30 September, 1979).

In December 1978 the Irish Episcopal Conference, at the request of His Grace, The Archbishop of Tuam, Most Rev. Dr. Joseph Cunnane, formally invited His Holiness Pope John Paul II to Ireland. The following is a brief extract from the invitation text: "So, by unanimous decision of our Episcopal Conference, we humbly and most respectfully invite Your Holiness to visit Ireland during the year 1979, and lead us in celebrating the Centenary of the Shrine of Our Lady, Queen of Ireland, at Knock, in the Archdiocese of Tuam". On 21 July 1979, at a Press Conference in Dublin, His Eminence, Cardinal Tomás Ó Fiaich announced that His Holiness had gratefully accepted the invitation and looked forward to this event with immense joy. In the course of the Cardinal-Primate's statement he said: "The Holy Father visits Ireland this year as a pilgrim to the Shrine of Our Lady at Knock". The news of the Holy Father's visit was received in Knock with the utmost feelings of profound gratitude and joy. Clergy, laity, and members of Knock Shrine Society were overwhelmed by the good news. All regarded the announcement as a great privilege, something unique in the history of the Papacy, and in the history of Ireland. For the benefit of those who may not be too familiar with the history of Knock Shrine, a short summary of the main events is given hereunder.

THE STORY OF KNOCK

It all started on Thursday 21 August 1879. The day began as an ordinary day in the lives of the people of Knock. They were doing their usual jobs of cutting the corn, saving the hay, and bringing home the turf. It started to rain heavily that evening. Mary McLoughlin and Mary Byrne were walking from the east, towards the south gable of the Church of St. John the Baptist. At some distance they saw a great globe of light enveloping the gable, and three figures standing there. At first they thought that they were statues, but when they came closer they found that there was movement and life. They immediately got very excited and ran home to gather the neighbours. On their return they recognised the central figure as that of Our Lady, dressed in white robes, with a crown on her head and a rose on her forehead. Her hands were raised in a posture of prayer like a priest at Mass. St. Joseph was on her right, with head and shoulders bowed towards her, as if out of respect. St. John was on her left, book in his left hand, and index and middle finger raised, as if preaching. To his left, and slightly behind, was an altar with a cross and lamb, around which Angels hovered. Although it was raining, and the rain was blown towards the gable by a south-east wind, the ground beneath the gable, and the gable itself, were dry. This was the miracle that accompanied the Apparition. The lights were seen also by Patrick Walsh, from a distance of nearly a kilometre, who thought that there was a great fire in the Churchyard. The reaction of the people who witnessed the Apparation was one of great joy and happiness. This feeling of joy and happiness was so great that many of them shed tears. All fell to their knees and recited the Rosary. Some of them went towards the gable to get closer to the figures. Mrs. Brigid Trench, an old woman of over seventy, tried to clasp Our Lady's feet, but felt nothing but the wall. Her exclamation summed up the attitude of all the witnesses: "A hundred thousand thanks to God and to the Glorious Virgin that has given us this manifestation".

COMMISSIONS OF ENQUIRY

The local Archbishop, Most Rev. Dr. John MacHale of Tuam, set up a Commission to examine the witnesses. The Commission examined fifteen witnesses, and reported that their evidence was "trustworthy and satisfactory". The Commission also investigated all possible natural explanations, including the magic lantern theory, and found them inadequate to explain what happened in Knock on that August evening. The Commission reported to Archbishop MacHale in the Spring of 1880. On 19 March 1880 Archbishop John MacHale met the first organised pilgrimage to Knock Shrine, which came from Limerick, at his residence in Tuam. In the presence of the Press, he received the pilgrims, and blessed them and their families. He said, "It is a great blessing for the poor people of the West, in their wretchedness, and misery and suffering, that the Blessed Virgin Mother of God has appeared among them". This completed the usual canonical procedure in the investigation of an Apparition. The usual procedure is that the local Bishop sets up a Commission to investigate the facts. If the Commission reports favourably, and the Bishop accepts the verdict, then the faithful may visit the scene of the Apparition. In the case of Knock, pilgrims began to flock to the Shrine, and brought their sick. Many extraordinary cures took place, and were reported in the public press. A second Commission was set up in

1936, by Most. Rev. Dr. Thomas Gilmartin, and the three surviving witnesses were examined. The three of them confirmed the evidence they had given in 1879. The verdict of this Commission was that the evidence of the witnessess was "upright and trustworthy". The Commissioners were very impressed by Mrs. Mary O'Connell (née Byrne), who gave evidence under oath on her deathbed. Having given her evidence she said: "I am perfectly clear about everything I have said, and I make this statement, knowing that in a very short time I am going before my God". She died six weeks later.

THE MESSAGE OF KNOCK

It may seem strange that there were no words spoken during this Apparition, no word was ever attributed to Our Lady by the witnesses. God can communicate with us in many ways and is not confined to words. The message of Knock is found in the very rich symbolism of the Apparition itself. After all, words are only symbols — sound symbols — and these can change from place to place, and from nation to nation. The language of the Knock Shrine Apparition is the language of the Crib, that has spoken to the hearts of Christians down the ages. It is a liturgical language, and transcends all language barriers, and all frontiers. Our Lady visited Knock Shrine at a time when the Irish people were hungry, miserable, oppressed and without hope. The potato crop had failed, and hunger and famine stalked the land. They had no security on their little farms, and evictions were the order of the day. They were suffering because of their religion. In these circumstances, Our Lady came to console them, to encourage them, and give them new hope. The Apparition was a heavenly vision, and she wanted them to know that she was praying for them before the throne of God. She wore a crown, and appeared as Queen of Heaven. The Knock Apparition, therefore, anticipated the decision of the Church in 1950 to define the dogma of the Assumption. This dogma declared that Our Lady was assumed body and soul into heaven, through a special privilege of Almighty God. St. John the Evangalist appeared as a bishop wearing an Eastern-type mitre. He seemed to be drawing attention to the altar, the Lamb and the Cross on the one hand, and to Our Lady on the other hand. He seemed to be saying, that in spite of all their difficulties, they should remain loyal to their faith and to the Sacrifice of the Mass. He also implied that they should listen to the teaching of the Church, and have confidence in their prayers, and the intercession of Our Lady. In this way they could solve their many problems in a peaceful manner, at a time when people were tempted to resort to violence and agitation. St. Joseph was there as a layman; he was appointed Guardian of the Church in 1882. His presence seemed to indicate the important role of the layman in the Church, and especially the layman's role in defending the Church. In the Apparition, the Church seemed to be represented by St. John - the Evangelist - and St. Joseph, and Our Lady was there as Mother of the Church, showing concern in her role as Mother. It is interesting to note

225

that Vatican II declared Our Lady to be Mother of the Church. It can be truly said that the Knock Apparition represents all the basic dogmas of the Catholic faith.

THE CHURCH'S ATTITUDE TO APPARITIONS AND SHRINES

It might be very useful to explain, at this stage, the Catholic Church's attitude towards Apparitions and Shrines. In 1877, two years before the Apparition took place at Knock, the Congregation of Rites was asked the following question:— "Does the Church approve of the Apparitions at Lourdes and La Salette"?. The answer given was as follows: "The Church neither approves, nor reproves, nor condemns apparitions as such. It simply authorises them as pious beliefs, based on purely human faith or evidence". It is quite clear, that no apparition gets any official recognition from the Church, be it Knock, Lourdes or Fatima. In other words an Apparition never becomes part of Church teaching. Every Catholic, be he Pope, Bishop, Priest or layman, is free to form his own judgment on the evidence presented. The Church does however recognise Marian Shrines, and assigns to them a very special role in the modern world. Knock Shrine has the full approval and recognition of the Church, and has received all the privileges granted to Lourdes, Fatima and La Salette. Not only is Knock Ireland's National Marian Shrine, it is also recognised as one of the world's major Marian Shrines; it has the same ecclesiastical status as Lourdes and Fatima. Knock Shrine has the full recognition and approval of the Catholic Church. It has received special honours and privileges from all the recent Popes.

FOUR POPES HONOUR KNOCK

On the 1 November, in the Marian Year, 1954, on the occasion of the proclamation of the new feast of the Queenship of Mary, His Holiness Pope Pius XII blessed the banner of Knock, in St. Peter's Basilica, and decorated it with a special medal. By kind permission of the Vatican Chapter, the statue of Our Lady of Knock was solemnly crowned on the feast of the Immaculate Conception 1954. The crowning ceremony followed the general lines of the ceremonial used in Rome when Pope Pius XII crowned the picture of Our Lady — Salus Populi Romani. The Knock Crown is also similar in design to that of the crown used in the Rome ceremony. In 1957 the Church of the Apparition of Knock became an affiliated Church of the Basilica of St. Mary Major in Rome, and special indulgences were granted to the stewards and handmaids of Knock, and to pilgrims, by the Sacred Apostolic Penitentiary. The indulgences were renewed in 1967 when His Holiness Pope Paul VI promulgated a revision of indulgences. A beautiful candle, blessed by His Holiness Pope John XXIII was presented to Knock Shrine on 2 February 1969, as one of the outstanding places of public devotion to Our Lady. His Holiness Pope Paul VI concluded the third session of the Second Vatican Council by celebrating Mass with twenty-four bishops, in St. Peter's Basilica, on the 21

November 1964. The bishops were chosen because they were the custodians of the most famous Marian Shrines in the world. Most Rev. Joseph Walsh, Archbishop of Tuam, was one of the concelebrating bishops, and he was selected because he was the custodian of Our Lady's Shrine at Knock. In April 1979 His Holiness Pope John Paul II sent a special videotaped message to the National Missionary Congress in Knock. Opening his address, the Holy Father said: "To all of you assembled at Knock to celebrate the National Missionary Congress; Grace to you, and peace from God Our Father, and the Lord Jesus Christ. I know that you have not only gathered for reflection on the great theme of the missions, but you have also come as pilgrims to pray at the National Shrine of Our Lady".

Monsignor James Horan, the man who brought the Pope to Ireland, welcomes Mayo's most distinguished visitor ever – Pope John Paul II – to Knock on 30 September 1979, watched by Archbishop Joseph Cunnane.

POPE JOHN PAUL II, A PILGRIM TO KNOCK

On the 30 September 1979 His Holiness Pope John Paul II came as a pilgrim to Knock Shrine. It was the greatest privilege that the Church could bestow upon any centre of Marian devotion. During his visit, the Holy Father met the sick and handicapped in the Church of Our Lady Queen of Ireland. He addressed 2,500 of them and gave his blessing. He also paid a special tribute to the handmaids and stewards of Knock, who he said were, "the servants of the Mother of Jesus, and servants of their brothers and sisters, also." His Holiness celebrated Mass and anointed the sick at a specially-constructed altar, in front of the new Church, for a congregation of close to half a million. During the Mass he entrusted and consecrated the Irish people to Mary, Mother of the Church. The Holy Father raised the Church of Our Lady, Queen of Ireland, to the status of a full Basilica, and gave an exquisite Golden Rose as his own special gift to the Shrine. This gift will be preserved at Knock as a lasting memento of his visit. After he had imparted his Apostolic Blessing to the pilgrims, Pope John Paul travelled by Popemobile to the new Shrine, at the south gable of the old church. There he knelt in silent prayer at the very spot where the Apparition took place in 1879. He blessed the Shrine, and lit a candle dedicated to Family Prayer.

THE BASILICA OF OUR LADY, QUEEN OF IRELAND

The Church of St. John the Baptist, where the Apparition took place, was dedicated in 1828, and bears the following inscription: "My house shall be called the house of prayer to all nations" (Mk. Ch. II. V.17); "This is the gate of the Lord; The just shall enter into it". (Ps. 117). These words were certainly prophetic, as Knock Shrine is now truly the house of prayer for people from all nations. On 6 November 1973 the feast of all the Saints of Ireland, His Grace the Archbishop of Tuam Dr. Joseph Cunnane, a native of Knock parish, turned the first sod for a new Church at Knock. The Church of Our Lady, Queen of Ireland, was blessed and dedicated by Archbishop Cunnane on Sunday 18 July 1976. The ceremony was attended by the late Cardinal William Conway, Primate of All Ireland, the other Archbishops, and Bishops of Ireland. The dedication ceremony was followed by the usual devotions and a concelebrated Mass. His Holiness Pope Paul VI had blessed the foundation stone of the Church on the 6 June 1974. The stone, which is a slab of Carrara marble bearing the inscription - "Pope Paul VI" - in blue lettering, was laid on the feast of Our Lady's Assumption, that same year. Circular in shape, and with a capacity to accommodate 20,000, the Church is divided into five chapels. The Church itself, without its ambulatory, covers a half hectare of ground, and is one hundred metres in diameter. The ambulatory, with thirty-two pillars, surrounds the basilica on the outside. Knock is a national shrine, and each of the thirty-two counties in Ireland has provided stone for a pillar. There is a plaque on each pillar with the name of the donor county. There is another national feature within the Church. There are four replicas of large medieval church windows, one from each of the four provinces, on the internal walls of the Church.

The Gable of the Church of the Apparition and the Basilica in Knock.

THE WORDS OF MONSIGNOR HORAN

The Parish Priest of Knock and Director of Knock Shrine is Rt. Rev. Monsignor James Horan. He was the architect and builder of modern Knock, and the man who brought the Pope to Ireland. With regard to Knock Shrine, Monsignor Horan has this to say: "I can assure each of you, that you will find a visit to Knock Shrine very satisfying. You will experience an atmosphere of prayer and devotion that uplifts the soul. The display of Christian faith by pilgrims, at the Shrine, has to be seen to be believed. Knock Shrine is a virtual oasis of peace and tranquility, in a world in which the stresses and strains of life are increasing day by day. It is a place where people visit out of sheer curiosity, and remain to pray. It is a holy place where many who have strayed from God, in a permissive and secularised society, experience God's love and friendship".

FROM THAT DAY OF GRACE

This article began with an extract from the homily of Pope John Paul II at Knock, and ends with another extract from the same homily:—

"It is fitting then, and it gives me great happiness to see, that the Irish people maintain this traditional devotion to the Mother of God, in their homes and their parishes, and in a special way at this Shrine of Cnoc Mhuire. For a whole century now, you have sanctified this place of pilgrimage, through your prayers, through your sacrifices, through your penance. All those who have come here have received blessings through the intercession of Mary. From that Day of Grace, the twenty first of August 1879 until this very day, the sick and suffering, people handicapped in body or mind, troubled in their faith, or their conscience, all have been healed, comforted, and confirmed in their faith, because they trusted that the Mother of God would lead them to her Son, Jesus. Every time a pilgrim comes up to what was once an obscure bogside village in County Mayo, every time a man, woman or child comes up to the old Church with the Apparition gable, or to the new Shrine of Mary, Queen of Ireland, it is to renew his or her faith in salvation that comes through Jesus, who made us all children of God and heirs to the Kingdom of Heaven. By entrusting yourselves to Mary, you receive Christ. In Mary, "The Word was made Flesh"; in her the Son of God became man, so that all of us might know how great our human dignity is. Standing on this hallowed ground, we look up to the Mother of God and say: Blessed are you among women, and blessed is the fruit of your womb".

SOURCES

1. *Knock 1879-1979* by C. Rynne.

2. *I Comforted Them in Sorrow: Knock 1879-1979* by T. Neary.

3. *The Apparition at Knock: A survey of Facts and Evidence* by Rev. M. Walsh.

4. *A Story of Knock* by D. O'Keefe.

MAYO INDUSTRIES

Table 1 records the list of manufacturing industries in County Mayo, the year of establishment in each case and the nature of the production.

Table 2 records the industrial employment of the county from 1973 to 1981. (2)

TABLE 1 MANUFACTURING INDUSTRIES

Year	Name	Location	Product
1829	Connaught Telegraph	Castlebar	Printing
1840	John Burke	Ballinrobe	Boats
1850	Matthew Gilligan	Claremorris	Coach Builder
1860	Issac Beckett Ltd.	Ballina	Sawmill & Joinery
1882	Western People	Ballina	Printing
1892	Providence Woollen Mills	Foxford	Blankets, Rugs etc.
1906	W. J. Duffy (Ballina) Ltd.	Ballina	Bread/Confectionery
1911	P. J. Henry & Co.	Charlestown	Mineral Water
1917	Austin Quinn	Castlebar	Gates, Railings
1917	Castlebar Bacon Co.	Castlebar	Meat Processing
1919	John Durkan & Sons Ltd.	Ballyhaunis	Wholesale Bottlers
1920	Cahill's (Ballina) Ltd.	Ballina	Bread/Confectionery
1920	B. Boyle	Ballyhaunis	Engineering
1926	T. Archer (Ballina) Ltd.	Castlebar	Joinery
1927	Gavin Bros. Ltd.	Castlebar	Bread/Confectionery
1930	Holsum Bakery Co.	Charlestown	Bread/Confectionery
1930	Claremorris Bacon Co. Ltd.	Claremorris	Bacon
1932	A. J. West & Son Ltd.	Ballina	Timber Mills
1932	V. Donnellan	Claremorris	Joinery
1932	St. Attracta's Knitting Industry	Swinford	Knitted Jumpers & Cardigans
1934	Irish Sewing Cotton Ltd.	Westport	Sewing Threads
1937	M. Gleeson	Shrule	Joinery, Coffins etc.
1938	Michael A. Keane & Sons Ltd.	Ballyhaunis	Kitchen Furniture
1940	Western Hats Ltd.	Castlebar	Headgear/Knitwear
1940	T. McNicholas (Macs Bakery)	Kiltimagh	Bakery
1940	Arthur Molloy, (Knappa Beg Stables)	Westport	Horse Shoes
1942	McIntyre & Sons	Charlestown	Mineral Waters
1947	M/s Hanley's	Claremorris	Bakery/Confectionery
1948	Lastra Foundations	Westport	Ladies Garments
1949	Mayo News	Westport	Printing
1949	Paddy Dunne	Kiltimagh	Bakery
1949	Ryarc Optical Services Ltd.	Castlebar	Opthalmic Lenses
1949	Morans Bakery	Castlebar	Bread/Confectionery
1949	James Connell	Ballyhaunis	Wood Furniture
1949	Tom Donnellan	Ballyhaunis	Furniture & Coffins
1950	P. J. Sweeney	Ballinrobe	Furniture
1950	T. Dunleavy	Ballinrobe	Furniture
1951	McAleer & Sons	Westport	Sheepskin Rugs
1953	Irish Spinners Ltd.	Kiltimagh	Yarn Spinners
1954	Westport Doubling Co. Ltd.	Westport	Doubled Yarns
1954	J. Payen (I) Ltd.	Ballindine	Gaskets
1954	North Connacht Farmers Co Ltd.	Killala	Milk Separating & Animal Feeds

Year	Name	Location	Product
1954	Austin Grogan & Sons Ltd.	Ballyhaunis	Concrete Products
1955	Western Pride Bakery	Ballinrobe	Bakery/Confectionery
1955	Ceimici Teoranta (Corroy)	Ballina	Liquid Glucose
1956	Lough Conn Milling Co.	Crossmolina	Animal Foods
1956	O'Hara's Bakery	Foxford	Bread/Confectionery
1956	Ronane Bros. Ltd.	Swinford	Furniture
1957	W. Carey	Ballindine	Joinery
1958	L. Molloy	Ballina	Concrete Products
1958	James J. Ronayne	Claremorris	Brush Stocks
1959	Achill Island Pottery	Achill	Pottery
1959	Patrick Mulloy	Kilmeena	Shellfish
1960	Ballina Printing Co.	Ballina	Printing
1960	Joe Butler	Kilmaine	Concrete Blocks
1960	D. K. Moran	Ballyhaunis	Furniture
1961	M. Conroy & Sons Ltd.	Claremorris	Tubular Steel Furniture
1961	Roadstone Ltd.	Castlebar	Concrete Blocks
1961	Ballina Concrete Co.	Ballina	Concrete Products
1962	Coughlan's Bakery	Westport	Bakery/Confectionery
1963	Western Chickens Ltd.	Ballyhaunis	Poultry Processing
1963	Westport Clothing Ltd.	Westport	Shirts Overalls etc.
1963	Cake Kitchen	Westport	Confectionery
1964	Carraig Donn Industries Ltd.	Westport	Handcrafts & Aran Goods
1964	Joe Berry	Westport	Printing
1964	Corcoran Bros.	Westport	Concrete Products
1964	John Halloran	Ballina	Car Trailers
1964	Ballina Mineral Water Co.	Ballina	Mineral Waters
1964	Min Fheir (1959) Teo.	Geesala	Grass Meal & Nuts
1965	R. Barrett & Co. Ltd	Ballina	Wool Processing
1965	North Connacht Farmers Co-Op	Ballinrobe	Milk Separating
1966	Popular Handkerchiefs Ltd.	Westport	Handkerchiefs & Towels
1966	Westport Engineering Works	Westport	General Engineering
1966	Newport Foundations	Newport	Soft Toys
1966	Michael Rowley	Swinford	Joinery
1966	John Corcoran	Ballina	Light Engineering
1967	Táirgí Kenman	Gaoth-Sáile	Childrens Garments
1967	Millstream Fireplaces	Ballina	Fireplaces
1967	Connacht Concrete Products Ltd.	Ballyhaunis	Concrete Systems
1967	Séamus Cashin	Castlebar	Printing
1967	Peter Flynn	Westport	Joinery
1967	Anne McBride	Westport	Marble Products
1968	CPAC Ltd.	Foxford	Instant Royal Icing
1968	P. J. Diamond	Ballina	Joinery
1969	Melody's Machinery Sales	Ballina	Tractors & Trailers
1969	Dalgan Wood Industry Ltd.	Shrule	Joinery
1969	John Luskin	Cong	Joinery & Furniture
1969	Corbin Manufacturing Co.	Claremorris	Leather Goods
1969	Clew Bay Seaweeds Ltd.	Newport	Seaweed Meal
1970	Tricia Models	Kiltimagh	Ladies & Childrens Outerwear
1970	Thomas Costello	Kilkelly	Wrought Iron
1970	J. Murphy & Sons	Ballinrobe	Trailer & Body Builder
1970	Terrybawn Pottery	Ballina	Handmade Pottery
1970	Coolcran Products	Ballina	Furniture
1970	Cronin Interiors Ltd.	Ballina	Joinery
1971	Injection Moulds & Dies	Ballina	Moulds, Jigs, etc.
1971	Barbat Clothing Ltd.	Bangor	Mens & Youth Clothing

Year	Name	Location	Product
1971	Swinford Manufacturing Co.	Swinford	Blouses
1972	A. O'Gorman & Co. Printing Works	Westport	Printing
1972	Clare Morris Ltd.	Claremorris	Sportswear
1972	Travenol Laboratories Ltd.	Castlebar	Medical Products
1972	Grumbacher (I) Ltd.	Castlebar	Artists & Eyeliner Brushes
1972	Redmonds Quality Printing	Castlebar	Printing
1972	North Connacht Farmers Co. Ltd.	Castlebar	Milk Separating
1972	Smith & McAndrew	Ballina	Quarry Works
1973	Shamrock Forge & Tool Co.	Ballina	Spanners
1973	John Joyce	Kilmaine	Trailers
1973	St. Mary's Hospital	Castlebar	Rug & Basket Making
1973	North Connacht Farmers Co-Op	Claremorris	Milk Collection
1973	Séamus Golden	Swinford	Engineering
1974	Gaelchloch Acla	Achill Island	Quartzite Quarrying
1974	C. Conradty (Claremorris) Ltd.	Claremorris	Carbon Brushes
1974	Halal Meat Packers Ltd.	Ballyhaunis	Meat Processing
1975	Thomas Duffy	Crossmolina	Engineering
1975	C. Collins	Ballina	Craft Products
1975	Devaney Bakery	Castlebar	Confectionery
1975	Home Improvements (Ballyglass) Ltd.	Claremorris	Aluminium Doors & Windows
1975	Michael Sloyan	Knock	Craft Furniture
1975	Cniotáil Ghaeltarra	Tuar Mhic Éadaigh + Muingí	Knitting
1975	Leictreon	Achill Island	Quartz Crystal semi Processing
1976	Ecotech Ltd.	Westport	Leather Goods
1976	Earraí Olann Corránbuí	Poll a Thomáis + Carrowteige	Knitted Garments
1976	Kennedy-Harlow Originals	Westport	Craft Products
1976	Caitríona Fashions	Inver	House Coats
1976	Richard Geraghty	Castlebar	Connemara Marble Products
1976	Peter McCarthy	Breaffy	Craft Leather Goods
1976	Pádraig Kelly	Ballyhaunis	Furniture
1976	Hollister Overseas Ltd.	Ballina	Plastic Medical Products
1976	North Western Laboratories	Ballina	Animal Test Centre
1977	Asahi	Killala	Acrylic Fibre & Yarn
1977	Murphy Bros.	Ballyhaunis	General Engineering
1977	Castlebar Farm Machinery Ltd.	Castlebar	Rebuilding Agricult-ural Machinery
1977	Tom Kilkelly	Balla	Engineering
1977	Travenol Laboratories S.A.	Swinford	Health Care
1977	Dubarry Shoe Makers Ltd.	Westport	Shoes
1977	Táirgí Stoighin Mhaigheó	Gaoth-Sáile	Concrete Products
1978	Allergan Pharmaceuticals Ltd.	Westport	Solution for Contact Lenses
1978	Jeoffrey Shackleton	Westport	Weaving
1978	Gerry Walsh	Balla	Furniture
1978	Séamus Malee	Knock	Printing
1978	Corcoran Engineering Ltd.	Castlebar	Engineering
1978	Martin Nyland	Kilkelly	Leather Goods
1978	Gentrad Ltd.	Ballinrobe	General Engineering
1978	J. J. Moran & Sons Ltd.	Ballinrobe	Sawmilling
1978	T. Murphy	Belcarra	Agricultural Machinery
1978	Patrick Boyle	Ballina	Furniture
1978	Ballina Fitted Furniture Ltd.	Ballina	Fitted Furniture

Year	Name	Location	Product
1978	Bácús Uí Dhoncha	Belmullet	Bakery/Confectionery
1979	Rowear Ltd.	Ballina	Pyjamas/Nightwear
1979	Paddy Butler	Ballina	Furniture
1979	Eurosil Ltd.	Ballinrobe	Silicone Rubber Hose
1979	Irish Gripper Ltd.	Ballinrobe	Carpet Grippers
1979	John Morley	Ballinrobe	Agricultural Engineering
1979	M. Gallagher	Ballyhaunis	Furniture
1979	Adela Precision & General Engineering Co. Ltd.	Castlebar	Toolmaking & Precision Engineering
1979	Mayo Plastics Ltd.	Castlebar	Recycling Plastic
1979	Murphy Stainless Steel Ltd.	Castlebar	Stainless Steel
1979	Michael Jennings	Castlebar	Wrought Iron Craft Work
1979	Oliver Kelleher	Castlebar	Sports Trophies
1979	Dual Mechanical & Precision Engineering Ltd.	Charlestown	Precision Engineering
1979	Kennedys Knitwear Ltd.	Charlestown	Knitwear
1979	T. C. Print Ltd.	Kiltimagh	Plastic Packaging
1979	West of Ireland Aluminium Ltd.	Kiltimagh	Aluminium Windows & Doors
1979	Patrick J. O'Connell	Westport	Brushes
1979	William Coffey	Westport	Monumental Sculptors
1979	Sara Perceval Designs Ltd.	Westport	Designed Beaded Garments
1979	Achill Industries Ltd.	Achill	Double Glazing
1979	Irish Crafts Ltd.	Westport	Woven Products
1980	T. P. Lynn	Westport	Marine Engineering
1980	Paul Taylor	Westport	Pottery
1980	Newport Fireplaces	Newport	Fireplaces
1980	Pádraic Walsh	Westport	Fireplaces
1980	Northern Feather Ltd.	Westport	Continental Quilt Material
1980	Seán Regan Engineering	Charlestown	Engineering
1980	James O'Connor	Castlebar	Picture Frames
1980	Terence Coleman	Castlebar	Disco Lighting
1980	Lawless Glass Ltd.	Castlebar	Sealed Double Glaze Units
1980	United Care Ltd.	Ballina	Electronic Bed Alert
1980	Seirbhísí Innealtóireachta Mhaigheo	Belmullet	Engineering Services & Products
1980	Ruibéar Chomhlacht Atlantach Teo	Belmullet	Rubber Soles
1981	Bellco Sports Ltd.	Killala	Footballs
1981	Farah Manufacturing Co. Ltd.	Ballyhaunis	Slacks
1981	Broc Teo	Achill Island	Grease Absorbent Mops

TABLE 2 INDUSTRIAL EMPLOYMENT IN MAYO 1973 — 1981

1973	3,087	1976	4,195	1979	6,400
1974	3,998	1977	4,423	1980	6,599
1975	3,986	1978	5,570	1981	5,879

SOURCES

1. I.D.A. Western Region Office. (Joan Aylward & Thomas Hyland). Údarás na Gaeltachta (Máire Ní Chonchúir).

2. E.S.R.I. (Michael Ross).

NOTE: The above list includes only those industries which were in operation on 01/01/1982.

A MAYO MISCELLANY

by Bernard O'Hara

Mayo is a county with numerous scenic, historical and archaeological treasures. The coastline of Mayo, from Killala Bay in the north east to the deep fiord of Killary harbour on the south west, has several resorts and delightful scenery. Its lakes and rivers add to the beauty of the county. The chief lakes of the county are: Ballin, Bekan, Ballymore, Beltra, Bunaveela, Caheer, Callow, Carra, Carrowmore, Castlebar, Cloonacurry, Carrowkeribly, Conn, Corrib, Cullin, Dahybaun, Doo, Eaton's, Fahy, Feeagh, Furnace, Island, Islandeady, Keel, Levally, Mannin, Manulla, Mask, Nacorra, Nafooey, Tawnyard and Urlaur.

The chief rivers of the county are the Moy (which flows into Killala Bay); Palmerstown (Killala Bay); Ballinglin (Bunatrahir Bay); Deel (Lough Conn); Glenamoy and Muingnabo (Sruwaddacon Bay); Owenmore with its tributaries Muinig, Oweniny and Munhin (Tullaghan Bay); Owenduff and its tributary Tarsaghaunmore (Tullaghan Bay); Newport and Bunowen (Clew Bay), and the Erriff and its tributaries Cross, Derrycraff, Owenmore and Owenduff (Killary Harbour).

CASTLEBAR

Castlebar, on the river Castlebar, is the county capital of Mayo. After the Normans conquered Connacht they built castles at strategic locations. A castle was built in the place we now call Castlebar, around 1240, by one of the Barry family from Buttevant, Co. Cork. The castle was called Barry's Castle, Caisleán a' Bharraigh. Castlebar town itself was founded at the beginning of the seventeenth century by John Bingham, ancestor of the Earls of Lucan. James I granted the town a borough-charter in 1611. The town returned two members to the Irish Parliament until the Act of Union (1800). Castlebar featured prominently in "The Year of the French" (1798), when the French/Irish force under General Humbert defeated the English under General Lake at "the Races of Castlebar". John Moore's grave can be seen beside the 1798 memorial in the Mall, and there is a memorial to some French soldiers at French Hill. The Mall, Castlebar, was once the cricket pitch of Lord Lucan and his family, but is now a town park. The Mayo Land League was founded by Michael Davitt in Daly's Hotel, Castlebar, now the Imperial, on 16 August 1879.

There is a tablet on the wall of the Imperial Hotel, which reads:

"In this house the National Land League was founded on August 16th, 1879, by Michael Davitt, without whose life and work we would not own our land to day. To his memory, and the memory of all those who helped in the Land War which our people, under his leadership, fought and won, the Land Project of 1949 is dedicated, on behalf of the Irish people, by the Government of Ireland, August 16th, 1949".

WESTPORT

Westport is situated at the S.E. extremity of Clew Bay on the Carrowbeg river. The town was designed by James Wyatt, an English architect (1746-1813). It was once an important sea port.

Rev. James Owen Hannay (1865-1950), the novelist who wrote under the pseudonym "George A. Birmingham", was the Church of Ireland Rector in Westport from 1892 to 1913. He was born in Belfast on 16 July 1865 and ordained in 1889. Some of his publications include: *"The Spirit and Origin of Christian Monasticism", "The Wisdom of the Desert", "A Wayfarer in Hungary", "A Padre in France", "An Irishman Looks at his World", "God's Iron: A Life of the Prophet Jeremiah", "Spanish Gold", "The Lost Tribes", "The Island of Mystery", "Up the Rebels", "A Public Scandal", "The Mayor's Candlesticks", "Fed Up", "Two Fools", "Appeasement"* and many more. He died in London on 2 February 1950.

Westport House is an elegant Georgian mansion situated on the site of an ancient castle of the O'Malley's. The original house was built by Colonel John Browne and his wife, ancestors of the present Marquess of Sligo. The east front was built in 1730 by the famous German architect, Robert Cassels. The house was completed around 1778 by James Wyatt, the architect who designed Westport town. There is a small zoo in the grounds of Westport House.

Westport House.
(Bord Fáilte Éireann)

MURRISK FRIARY

Murrisk Friary was founded in 1457 by Tadhg O'Malley. It was destroyed by Cromwellian soldiers. A man who apparently hailed from the Murrisk area and whose name long survived in folk memory was the Augustinian friar, Fr. Myles Prendergast. He was stationed in Murrisk in 1785, but was one of six friars in the ruined friary on Convent Hill, Ballyhaunis, in 1791. He soon returned to Murrisk, however, for he and another local man named John Gibbons joined the insurgents in the Westport area when the French landed at Killala in 1798. In the aftermath of the rising, he and Gibbons went on the run and evaded capture for a number of years. The exploits of 'an tAthair Maoilre' and his companion are celebrated in song and story; one of the songs in which he figures, called 'Na Buachaillí Bána', is ascribed to Raftery. Eventually, about the year 1802, Fr. Prendergast, John Gibbons and another man, Valentine Jordan, were surrounded in a hut in Gowlaun, in Connemara, by government soldiers. Apparently Fr. Myles and Jordan were shot dead, while John Gibbons (or 'Johnny Éamoinn' as he was known) was hanged in Westport by Denis Browne who is said, at least in one account, to have been his godfather.

CLARE ISLAND

Clew Bay is studded with picturesque islands. The best known is Clare Island, which occupies almost a third of the mouth of Clew Bay. (1,993 hectares). There is a daily boat service to the island from Roonagh Point, near Louisburgh (distance 6.5 kilometres). It is a mountainous island with Croaghmore peak rising to 463 metres. Clare Island is synonymous with Grace O'Malley, the formidable ruler of the area in the second half of the sixteenth century. Her castle on Clare Island was converted into a coastguard station in 1831. The ruins of a 16th century Carmelite Friary can be seen in the centre of the island. It was built in 1220 and was later linked with the Cistercian monastery in Abbeyknockmoy, Co. Galway. According to local tradition Grace O'Malley was interred in the friary following her death in 1600.

NEWPORT

Newport is situated on the north east corner of Clew Bay. Burrishoole Friary, nearby, was built by Richard Burke around 1469. It was a Dominican friary. The Shrine of Our Lady Queen of Martyrs at Burrishoole bridge commemorates two Dominican nuns, Hononia de Burgo and Honora Magaen, both of whom died as a result of brutal beatings by Cromwellian soldiers. Carraigahowley, or Rockfleet castle, near Newport, was once Grace O'Malley's principal residence.

ACHILL

Achill Island is the largest island off the coast of Ireland and one of the most popular holiday resorts in the country. It is joined to the mainland by the Michael Davitt bridge. Captain Charles Boycott once lived at Corrymore House, near Dooagh. Kildavnet castle, near the southern tip of the island, was a stronghold of Grace O'Malley. There is a ferry service from Bullsmouth to the islands of Inishbiggle and Annagh. John F. Deane, who was born in Achill in 1943, published a collection of poems *"Stalking After Time"* in 1977.

CLAREMORRIS

Claremorris derived its name from a Norman invader Maurice de Prendergast, who came to Ireland with Strongbow in 1170 and was later given a large portion of land in south Mayo.

Denis Browne (1763-1828) M.P. and High Sheriff for Mayo lived in Claremount House,Claremorris, now the Convent of Mercy. Browne was a big landlord in the area and also local magistrate.

The Claremorris Workhouse was opened in 1851 and closed in October 1918; in 1930 the building became the premises of the Claremorris Bacon Company. The famous Irishtown Land League meeting of 20 April 1879 was planned in Nally's Hotel, James St. Sir John Gray (1816-1875), who gave Dublin its Vartry water supply in 1863 and edited the *"Freemans Journal"* during the Great Famine, was born in Mount St. Claremorris. He was elected Lord Mayor of Dublin in 1868, but declined the honour. Monsignor Macken, who was appointed parish priest of Claremorris in 1922, wrote *"The Canonisation of Saints"*.

Castlemagarrett House was built in 1694 by Geoffrey Browne, after his marriage to a daughter of Daniel Prendergast, the previous owner of the estate. It is now a rest home for senior citizens.

Ballinasmalla friary, near Claremorris, was founded about 1288, by the Prendergasts, and occupied by Carmelite priests until the late nineteenth century.

IRISHTOWN

Irishtown is known as "the cradle of the Land League". It was there the historic meeting was held on 20 April 1879 which led to the start of the Land League. The locals who prepared the platform for that historic meeting on the land of Mrs. Higgins were: Jimmy Daly (Crimlin), Michael Cullinan (Drymills), Patrick Corr, John Corr, Jimmy Rattigan, Pat Ronayne, Andy Mullarkey, J. Leonard. The platform was guarded the night before by Pat Ruane, Thomas Daly and John Bourke.

CONG

Cong is situated on the isthmus between Lough Mask and Lough Corrib and was once the residence of the Kings of Connacht. St. Féichín of Fore founded a monastery at Cong in 627, and became its first Abbot. The monastery became an important centre of learning, and a bishopric in 1010. No trace of the monastery now remains. Cong Abbey was erected on the site of the monastery in 1120 by Turlough Mór O'Conor, who became

King of Connacht in 1106. The Abbey was built for the Canons Regular of St. Augustine. Rory O'Conor, the last High King of Ireland, spent the last twelve years of his life at Cong Abbey, where he died on 29 November 1198. He was buried in Cong, but nine years later his body was exhumed and buried beside his father, Turlough Mór, in Clonmacnoise, Co. Offaly. The abbey was plundered by William de Burgo in 1201 and 1202, but the family later became generous benefactors of the abbey. The abbey was reconstructed after a fire in 1203 by Cathal Crobderg O'Conor, who ascended to the throne of Connacht in 1205. Cong abbey was suppressed during the reign of Henry VIII, but the abbots continued to live locally. The last abbot died in 1829. The ruins of the abbey can still be seen; its chancel and part of the cloister arcade survive.

The film "The Quiet Man", directed by John Ford, and starring Maureen O'Hara, John Wayne and Barry Fiztzgerald, was made in Cong in 1951.

ASHFORD CASTLE

Ashford Castle, Cong, is one of the most elegant and luxurious hotels in the world. It is situated on the northern shore of Lough Corrib, the second largest lake in Ireland. The original Ashford Castle was built by the De Burgos in 1228. The Oranmore and Browne family built a shooting lodge on the grounds, in the second half of the 18th century. Sir Benjamin Lee Guinness purchased the estate in the Encumbered Estates Court, in 1825, and started to enlarge the castle. The property was inherited by Lord Ardilaun in 1865, son of Sir Benjamin. He rebuilt the castle over a period of thirty years, and incorporated the remains of the De Burgo castle in its castellated facade. He also landscaped the grounds. Ashford Castle was transformed from a stately castle to a luxury hotel by Noel Huggard. The work began in 1939, and was completed from 1972 to 1974 by John A. Mulcahy, who purchased the hotel in 1971.

Ashford Castle.

239

THE MASK/CORRIB CANAL

The Lough Mask-Corrib Canal is a 6.5 kilometres long canal built during the Great Famine to provide relief work and join Loughs Corrib and Mask. The work started in 1848 and was abandoned in 1858. The canal was never used because the water seeps through the porous limestone and flows in numerous underground rivers to Cong village.

There are over forty river caves in, and around, Cong. The best known is the Pigeon Hole, with sixty one steps down to the bottom, where the underground river can be seen rushing through.

MOYTURA HOUSE

Moytura House, three kilometres from Cong, was built in 1865 by Sir William Wilde (1815-1876), a surgeon and antiquary and father of the dramatist Oscar Wilde (1854-1900). Sir William published his best known book *"Lough Corrib and Lough Mask"* in 1867. (The house is now private property).

BALLINROBE

Ballinrobe is situated on the river Robe. The remains of the Augustinian Friary, founded about 1313, can still be seen.

Right Rev. Monsignor D'Alton was parish priest of Ballinrobe from 1911 to 1941. He was the author of *"History of the Archdiocese of Tuam"* volumes 1 and 2, *"The History of Ireland from the Earliest Times to the Present Day"*, and *"A Short History of Ballinrobe Parish"* in 1931. He died on 25 January 1941 and was buried in the Church ground in Ballinrobe.

Lough Mask Castle, which was built by De Burgo in 1480, is now a ruin 6.5 kilometres south west of Ballinrobe. Lough Mask House, nearby, was once the home of Capt. Charles Boycott (1832-97), who was ostracised by his staff and tenants in September 1880 during the Land War. (It is now private property). The ostracisation was led by the local priest Fr. John O'Malley (d. 1892). He was buried in the Catholic Church in the Neale. St. Cormac founded a monastery on Inishmaine on Lough Mask in the seventh century.

MOORE HALL

Moore Hall, in the parish of Carrownacon, was the Georgian home of a famous Mayo family, the Moore's of Moore Hall. John Moore (b. 1706), a descendant of a Yorkshire Protestant family married Jane Lynch Athy from Renville, Co. Galway, became a Catholic, and lived at Ashbrook House, Strade, Co. Mayo. One of their children, George (1729-1799), emigrated to Spain where he married Catherine de Kilikelly in 1765. George became a very successful businessman, and also inherited the family home at Ashbrook. George and Catherine returned to Ireland in 1792 and purchased 324 hectares around Lough Carra, and built Moore Hall there on Muckloon Hill. The inscription over the entrance reads "Fortis Cadere Cedere Non Potest", and is dated 1795.

A son of George and Catherine Moore, John (1767-1799), was elected President of the Republic of Connacht, after the French captured Castlebar in 1798. Another son, George (1770-1840), lived at Moore Hall and spent his time reading and writing. He married Louisa Browne and one of their three children was George Henry Moore (1811-1870), the politician and sportsman. He was an eloquent supporter of Gavan Duffy's tenant-right movement, and was elected M.P. for Mayo in 1847, 1852, 1857 (but unseated), and re-elected in 1868. George Henry Moore married Mary Blake from Ballinafad House, and they had four children. George Augustus (1852-1933), the eldest, became a famous novelist. Moore Hall and the surrounding area are vividly described in his novels *"The Lake"* and *"Hail and Farewell"*. Another son Maurice became a colonel in the Connacht Rangers, served in India, and later became an Irish Senator. He married Evelyn Handcock from Co. Galway. Their family did not live in Moore Hall. Some members of the Moore family, including George Henry Moore, were buried in Kiltoom, on the estate. Moore Hall was burned on 31 January 1923. Today, the ruin of Moore Hall stands lonely and deserted on the shore of Lough Carra.

Moore Hall in 1982.

BALLINTOBER ABBEY

Ballintober, Baile Tobair Phádraig, means the townland of the well of Patrick. It derived its name from a spring well, which descends from a natural arch in the rock where there is no stream, and in which St. Patrick was supposed to have baptised converts in 441. There was once a road from

241

Ballintober to Croagh Patrick, known as Tóchar Phádraig. Nowadays Ballintober is famous for its restored abbey.

Ballintober Abbey is one of the wonders of County Mayo. Mass has been said continuously in the abbey for 766 years, a unique record. It was 276 years old when Columbus discovered America. It is situated just off the main Castlebar-Galway road, and eleven kilometres from Castlebar. The monastery at Ballintober was founded in 1216 by Cathal Crobderg O'Conor (Cathal More of the wine red hand), King of Connacht, for Canons Regular of St. Augustine, and dedicated it to the Holy Trinity. The nave of the church was burned in 1265 and rebuilt in 1270. The abbey was deprived of its lands and possessions by Henry VIII. The church was wrecked and the roof burned by Cromwellian soldiers in 1653, but Mass continued to be said within its hallowed walls. Mass was also said there in the unroofed church during the Penal Laws, "in spite of dungeon, fire and sword". Archbishop John Mac Hale made an appeal for funds to restore it in 1846. Some work was done at the time, but it had to be abandoned because of the Great Famine. Some restoration work was done in 1889, on the initiative of the parish curate, Fr. Thomas Reidy. The chancel crossing and transepts were re-roofed under the direction of George C. Ashlin.

Ballintober Abbey. (Liam Lyons)

Ballintober Abbey will forever be associated with a great Mayo priest, Rev. Fr. Thomas A. Egan, who planned, organised, and restored the abbey in time for its 750th anniversary in 1966. An important excavation preceded the restoration, which located a large portion of the 15th century cloister arcade, a hospice for pilgrims, and some domestic buildings. The restoration work began in 1964 under the direction of its architect Percy Le Clerc. Fr. Thomas Egan in his booklet entitled *"The Story of Ballintubber*

Abbey" wrote: "Burned twice, suppressed, proscribed and still never utterly destroyed. Surely it deserves the proud title of 'the Abbey that refused to die' ". The story of Ballintober Abbey is an epitome of Irish history and symbolises the triumph of right over might.

Fr. Thomas Egan was born in Castlebar on 15 September 1909, and ordained on 23 June 1935. He was appointed to Ballintober in 1959. He died in Sir Patrick Dun's Hospital, Dublin, on 17 October 1979, and was buried in the grounds of Ballintober Abbey.

The ruins of Burriscarra Friary, which was founded by the McEvilly's for the Carmelites in 1298, can be seen five kilometres S.E. of Ballintober Abbey.

SEÁN NA SAGART

Seán na Sagart, the notorious priest hunter during the Penal Laws time, was a native of Ballintober parish. His correct name was John Mullowney. He was buried in the cemetery adjoining Ballintober Abbey.

MAYO ABBEY

St. Colmán founded an abbey in Mayo in the seventh century and it became known as "Mayo of the Saxons". The foundation developed into a medieval diocese, which gave the county its name. The ruins of the successor to St. Colmán's building can be seen in the village of Mayo.

BALLA

Balla owes its origin to St. Mochua (d. 637), who founded a church there in the seventh century. The monastery was destroyed by fire in 1179. William Henry Hamilton Maxwell (1792-1850), the novelist, was Church of Ireland Rector in Balla during part of the 19th century. It was there he wrote his popular work *"Wild Sports of the West of Ireland"* (1832). He also wrote novels and historical works. A native of Newry, Co. Down, he retired to Musselburgh, near Edinburgh, where he died in 1850.

KILTAMAGH AND FR. O'HARA

The development of Kiltamagh owes much to a great Sligo priest, Rev. Fr. Denis O'Hara (1850-1922), who was parish priest of Killedan from 1888 to 1923. During that time he organised the building of the houses which today constitute the town of Kiltamagh. He also organised water, sewerage, street lighting, and other facilities for the town. He was responsible for bringing the St. Louis nuns to the town.

Denis O'Hara was a native of Cloonacool, Co. Sligo. He was educated at Cloonacool, N.S., Ballaghaderreen, and Maynooth College, where he was ordained in 1873. He was curate in Killedan from 1873 to 1875, Curry 1875-77, and Ballaghaderreen 1877-1888. He was a strong nationalist, a member of the Land League, and a close friend of Michael Davitt and John Dillon. Fr. O'Hara spoke at the famous Gurteen Land League meeting of 2 November 1879. Michael Davitt, in his book *"The Fall of Feudalism in Ireland"* (ch. XV P. 192), wrote:

243

"Fr. Denis O'Hara spoke at the Gurteen meeting and began there a career of work for the good of the people, which has never been surpassed, if ever equalled by any priest who has laboured with the kindest of Irish hearts and the most level of Irish heads, for the protection and for the material welfare of the Connaught peasantry".

Fr. O'Hara initiated the purchase and distribution of the Costello estate around Ballaghaderreen. Many felt he should have succeeded Dr. McCormack as Bishop of Achonry in 1888. What was Achonry's loss was Kiltamagh's gain; he was appointed parish priest of Killedan (Kiltamagh). He built a church, two parochial houses, a cottage hospital, which was later used as the barracks, and brought the St. Louis nuns to Kiltamagh on 14 September 1897. They visited the people of the parish and gave advice on household management, and started a school to provide instruction in cookery, needlework, laundry and lace making. The Kiltamagh lace school won several prizes at the R.D.S. The nuns opened a secondary school in 1898, and it became the first boarding school for girls in the diocese of Achonry. The nuns took charge of the local girls national school in 1903. Fr. O'Hara was a member of the Congested Districts Board. He was bitterly disappointed when John Dillon was beaten in the 1918 General Election. Fr. O'Hara died on 26 April 1922, and was buried in Kilkinure cemetery, near Kiltamagh.

KILLEDAN

Killedan, on the road from Kiltamagh to Bohola, was the birthplace of the bard Antoine Ó Raifterí. A group of Franciscan monks settled in Killedan in the fourteenth century. Their church and buildings were destroyed in the seventeenth century, and the land was given to the Knox family. They restored the house and added an extension. The place was bought by the Taafe family around 1780. Frank Taafe was prominently associated with Raftery. Killedan House was purchased by the Mac Manus family, early in the nineteenth century, from the executors of Frank Taafe's estate. It was there Lottie Mac Manus formed the second branch of the Gaelic League in Ireland, and wrote her historic novels: *"The Silk of the Kine"*, *"The Professor in Erin"*, *"In Sarsfield's Days"*, and two on local folklore *"Within the Four Seas of Fola"* and *"The Middle Kingdom"*. Killedan House is now a ruin.

KNOCK

Knock is situated between Claremorris and Ballyhaunis. It's Marian Shrine, where the Apparition of the Blessed Virgin Mary, Saint Joseph and Saint John took place on Thursday 21 August 1879, is an international place of pilgrimage. The gable of the Apparition can still be seen. The Basilica of Our Lady Queen of Ireland was dedicated on 18 July 1976, and is the largest Church in Ireland. It cost £1.75m. and was financed by collections in Ireland and abroad. The graves of the visionaries can be seen in the "old" churchyard. Knock Shrine will always be associated with Monsignor James Horan. He built the Knock we know to-day.

James Horan was born on 5 May 1911 in the townland of Tooreen,

Partry, Co. Mayo, the son of Bartley and Catherine Horan, née Casey, and baptised two days later by the parish priest, Rev. James Corbett. He was educated at Partry N.S., St. Jarlath's College, Tuam, and graduated with a First Class Honours degree in Celtic Studies from Maynooth. After ordination in 1936, he worked for a number of years in the diocese of Glasgow. He then returned to the diocese of Tuam and worked in Ballyglunin, Co. Galway, Tiernee and Carraroe in Connemara, Tooreen, Co. Mayo, before his appointment as Curate to Knock in 1963. He was appointed Parish Priest of Knock in 1970, and Monsignor in 1979. Monsignor Horan was responsible for the erection of the new Basilica, hostels for the sick, St. Joseph's Rest House for residential invalids, a new Confessional Chapel, the processional Square, a folk museum, and the refurbishment of the Shrine of the Apparition Gable. The museum, the first in County Mayo, was opened on 1 August 1973 by Most Rev. Dr. Joseph Cunnane, Archbishop of Tuam. Thomas Neary has written an excellent guide to the Knock Folk Museum entitled "Ould Acquaintance". The area around the Shrine has been landscaped, and generous provision made for car parking. The shabby stalls, which once occupied the street of Knock, are gone. The street and approach roads were all resurfaced in 1979 by Mayo County Council. Monsignor James Horan, the man who decided to invite the Pope to Ireland, had the pleasure of welcoming Pope John Paul II to Knock Shrine and to Mayo on Sunday 30 September 1979.

Another man who has made an enormous contribution to the modernisation of Knock is His Grace, the Archbishop of Tuam, Most Rev. Dr. Joseph Cunnane. Archbishop Cunnane is a native of Coogue in the parish of Knock. He was ordained in 1939 and appointed Archbishop in 1969, in succession to Archbishop Joseph Walsh.

BALLYHAUNIS

The Augustinian friary of St. Mary the Virgin at Ballyhaunis was said by local tradition to have been founded in 1348 by the local Hiberno-Norman lord, Jordan Dubh Mac Costello, who was killed in battle in 1367. Later tradition, however, gives the founder as a descendant of Jordan Dubh, while the earliest documentary evidence seems to point to 1432, or thereabouts, as the actual foundation-date. The first name associated with the place in the written sources is that of a friar named Philip Nangle. (The Nangles — earlier de Angulos — were the parent-family of the Mac Costelloes, whose surname in time virtually supplanted that of Nangle in east Mayo). The friary became a religious centre, a school, a hospital, and a model farm for the people of the area. The friary was destroyed in 1608 and restored in 1641. In 1649, the prior, Fr. (now the Venerable) Fulgentius Jordan, and another friar were killed in the friary grounds by Cromwellian soldiers. Nevertheless, the friary continued in existence, albeit in a ruinous condition, throughout the period of the Penal Laws. D. B. Redmond, O.S.A., in his booklet *"The Augustinian Abbey of St. Mary of the Virgin, Ballyhaunis"* wrote: "For, despite the sword and flame, the famine and gibbet, the people of this Golden West clung as closely to Patrick's faith as did the ever-green ivy to the battered gables of the "Ould Abbey". " The work of restoring the building commenced early in the 1830s and continued, at intervals, for nearly a century. The building as it now stands, extended to cover the original site, was completed in the early 1930s. Ballyhaunis friary has been used as a place of worship from its foundation to date, and ranks after Ballintober as the second oldest such place in Mayo. The friary was the nucleus around which the town of Ballyhaunis developed.

The Braghlaghboy ogham stone is situated near Ballyhaunis in the townland of Island. The ruined Mannin Castle stands on the east shore of Mannin Lake, anciently called Loch na nAirneadh (the lake of the sloe-trees).

URLAUR FRIARY

Urlaur Friary, in the parish of Kilmovee, was founded in 1434 by Edmund Mac Costello and his wife Fionnuala, daughter of O'Conor Don, for the Friars of the Order of St. Dominick. It was destroyed by Cromwellian soldiers in 1654.

Kilkelly has a ruined medieval church built on the site of an earlier foundation of St. Ceallach, from which the village got its name.

CHARLESTOWN

Charlestown was built in the middle of the last century, on the initiative of Lord Dillon's agent, Charles Strickland, in opposition to Bellaghy, then owned by the Knox family. Strickland planned the new town and offered forty hectares of land, free of rent forever, to the first man who lit a fire in the first house to be built in the new town. The first house was completed in the summer of 1846. It was called Charlestown in honour of Charles Strickland. The story of its origin, growth, and decline has been recorded by John Healy in *"The Death of an Irish Town"*. John Murphy, the author of the play *"The Country Boy"*, is a native of Bellaghy.

KILLASSER

Killasser, Cill Lasrach — the Church of Lasair, got its name from Lasair, an eight century Irish saint, who blessed a church in Knockmullin townland and gave the parish its name from that day to this. The parish has a rich archaeological heritage, with Court Cairns in Cartronmacmanus, Coolagagh, Creggaun, a crannóg in Lower Lough Callow, and nearly 200 ringforts.

SWINFORD

Swinford town owes its origin to the Brabazon family, who were given land in the parish of Kilconduff during the Cromwellian settlement. The family originally came from Leicestershire in England and settled in Ballinasloe, Co. Galway. They were dispossessed of their land and castle by Cromwell on 12 August 1652. A member of the family, George, and his wife, Sarah, née Burke from Galway, went to Kilconduff. In all probability they called the place after the village of Swinford, near one of the former seats of the family in Leicestershire. Their son Anthony inherited the estate, and married Anne Molyneux in 1776. One of their four children was William, who became a Mayo M.P. He was responsible for the erection of a Protestant Church in 1801, a Post Office, a police station and a courthouse. He died a bachelor in 1840 and was buried in the Protestant graveyard. The estate was inherited by Hugh Higgins-Brabazon, William's nephew, who was a benevolent landlord during the Great Famine. After his death in 1864 the family emigrated to England, and the estate was later sold to the Congested Districts Board, who gave it to the Land Commission. Some of the land is now a public park under the control of local trustees. The Famine Grave can be seen at the back of Swinford hospital, where 564 victims were buried "without coffin, without sermon, without anything which denotes respect for the dead," as Michael Davitt recalled in his book *"Defence of the Land League"*.

Meelick is three kilometres S.W. of Swinford and has a fine Round Tower on the site of a monastery founded by St. Broccaidh. There is a stone in the cemetery with an inscribed cross: Or do Grieni ("a prayer for Griene"). Meelick was once the principal abbey in the barony of Gallen.

Meelick Round Tower.

247

THE O'DWYER CHESHIRE HOME

The O'Dwyer Cheshire Home in Lismirrane, Bohola, was officially opened by the President of Ireland, Cearbhall Ó Dálaigh, on 27 of August 1976, in the presence of Group Captain Leonard Cheshire, the English-man who pioneered such homes throughout the world, Thomas F. O'Higgins, the Chief Justice,and Paul O'Dwyer, the man responsible for its erection.

The home is built on the site of the O'Dwyer family home. The site was donated by the family, and funds were raised, on the initiative of Paul O'Dwyer, in New York, Chicago, Dublin, Mayo, and other places. The Department of Health also gave a grant. The home caters for physically handicapped people from the west of Ireland, and every effort is made by its staff to simulate the environment of a family home.

Paul O'Dwyer was born in 1907 in the townland of Lismirrane, Bohola. He arrived in New York on 21 April 1925 and studied law while holding a full time job. After a few years practising law on his own he became a partner with Oscar Bernstein, and soon won a national and international reputation as a champion of civil liberties. He was elected to the New York City Council in 1963, and ten years later became its President. He published his autobiography *"Counsel for the Defence", in 1979.*

William O'Dwyer, Paul's brother, was born in Lismirrane in 1890 and emigrated to New York in 1910. After working in various jobs he became a policeman, and later a lawyer, District Attorney for Kings County, Judge, and was elected Mayor of New York City in 1945. He was re-elected in 1949, and resigned after eight months to become President Truman's Ambassador to Mexico, a rare distinction for an Irish emigrant.

STRADE FRIARY

Strade Friary was founded by Jordan de Exeter around 1240 for the Franciscans, but was transferred to the Dominicans in 1252. The friary ruin contains a chancel with six small lancet windows. The rest of the building dates from the 15th century. The jewel of Strade friary is the magnificent sculptured tomb and canopy on the north wall. There are eight figure carvings on the front of the tomb, i.e. left to right, three crowned figures (The Magi), Christ showing the five wounds, a layman taking off his hat, a mitred bishop with a crozier, St. Peter, and St. Paul. There is also a fine high altar with elegant decorations. The founder's tomb was used by the Dillon family of Ballaghaderreen. Anne Deane, née Duff, Ballaghaderreen a cousin of John Dillon, was buried there. The inscription on her tomb reads:

"This monument is erected to her memory by her cousin John Dillon, Member of Parliament for East Mayo, who owes his life and all that he possesses to her loving kindness and generosity".

Michael Davitt was born in Strade (about a half kilometre from the friary; no trace of the house survives). He was buried in the cemetery beside the friary, in accordance with his wish.

The Founder's Tomb in Strade Friary.

FOXFORD

Foxford is built on the river Moy. The modernisation and development of
the town owes much to the Sisters of Charity, who established a convent
there in 1891. There was widespread poverty and misery in the area at that
time, and the Bishop of Achonry, Dr. Lyster, asked Mother Arsenius to go
to Foxford and "do something for the people". She was a person of ability,
vision, courage, and above all "a doer". She started a convent, a convent
school, helped the people of the area to improve their living conditions,
and started the Foxford Woollen Mills. When she decided to start the mills
she went to County Tyrone to talk with people involved in the woollen
industry there. She was told "to go home and say her prayers", advice she
ignored. She then met John Charles Smith, owner of the Caledon Mills,
Co. Tyrone, who gave every assistance possible. Mother Arsenius set

about the erection of the mills. J. C. Smith advised on the construction, layout, and selected the plant and equipment. He nominated the first manager of Foxford Woollen Mills, James Sherry, from his own staff. The Congested Districts Board provided a loan of £7,000 (which was later fully repaid), and a grant of £1,500 for staff training. The Providence Woollen Mills were opened on 2nd May 1892. Horace Plunkett and Charles Kennedy, members of the Congested Districts Board, set the first loom in motion. The Mills were an outstanding success. Today Foxford woollen products are world famous.

Agnes Morrough-Bernard (Mother Arsenius) was born on 24 February 1842, in County Kerry. She died on 21 April 1932, and was buried in the nuns plot beside the Catholic Church in Foxford. The inscription on her tombstone reads:

> "Sister M. Arsenius Morrough-Bernard
> First Superior Convent Divine Providence
> Foxford
> Died 21st April 1932
> Aged 91 years
> She hath opened her hand to the needy,
> and stretched out her hands to the poor"
>
> Proverb XXX 1.10.31.

Vergottini's bronze bust of Foxford born Admiral William Browne (1777-1857), "the Father of the Argentine Navy", can be seen near the church. The bust was moved to its present position in May 1982 by Mayo County Council. It was situated out the Swinford road in an obscure corner from 1957 to 1982.

The ruin of Ballylahan Castle is three kilometres south of Foxford, near Ballylahan bridge. It was built by Jordan de Exeter in the thirteenth century.

Foxford is the gateway to Pontoon, alongside Lough Conn and Lough Cullin, a district which is the anglers delight.

BALLINA

Ballina was founded in 1729 by Lord Tyrawley, and quickly developed into an important commercial centre and seaport. There is a monument in Ballina commemorating "The Year of the French", known as "the Humbert Monument". Part of the inscription on the monument reads:

> "In memory of General Humbert
> Sarrazin, Louis Octave Fontaine
> Bartholomew Teeling, Matthew Tone,
> Henry O'Keon, Father Conroy, Patrick Walsh
> And all the other gallant patriots
> who sacrificed their lives
> for the freedom of their country
> After the landing of the French at Killala 1798"

The ruins of an *Augustinian Friary,* founded by the O'Dowds in 1427, can be seen in Ardnaree. The Dolmen of the four Maols is a cromlech near

250

The Humbert Monument in Ballina.

Rosserk Friary.

251

the railway station. According to local tradition it marks the grave of four foster-brothers, who murdered Bishop Ceallach of Kilmoremoy in the sixth century, and were executed by the bishop's brother. The place has since been known as Ard na Riadh, Ardnaree, or the Hill of the Executions.

The ruins of two friaries can be seen on "the Moyne road" from Ballina to Killala. Rosserk friary was founded around 1441 by a man named Joyce for the Observantine Franciscans. The nave, chancel, domestic buildings, and several carvings are well preserved. Moyne Friary was founded in 1460 by Mac Uilliam Íochtarach for Franciscans of the Strict Obedience. It was one of the chief houses of study for young Irish Franciscans. It was burned by Sir Richard Bingham in 1590. The cloisters, nave, and chancel are still in good condition.

KILLALA

Killala became a monastic centre in the fifth century, and St. Patrick was supposed to have appointed Muredach first Bishop of Killala. Killala figured very prominently in "The Year of the French".

Killala's Round Tower was struck by lightning early in the last century, and repaired by Bishop Verschoyle in 1840. Rathfran Friary, N.E. of Killala, is the ruin of a friary founded in 1274 by Sir Richard de Exeter for the Dominicans. You can travel to Rathfran by going out the Ballycastle road from Killala and turning right after crossing the bridge over the Palmerstown, or Cloonaghmore, river. The friary was burned by Bingham in 1590, but the friars remained in the area until the eighteenth century.

The Breastagh Ogham Stone.

There are several neolithic sites in the area, and in the townland of Breastagh, north of Mullaghmore crossroads, there is an ogham stone, which was re-erected in 1853 by the Royal Irish Academy. The damaged inscription reads:

L(E)GG . . . SD . . .LENGESCAD MAQ
CORRBRI MAQ AMMLLONGITT.

It probably commemorates the grandson of the fifth century local king, Amolgaid. Kilcummin Strand, the site of the French landing in 1798, is in Lackan parish.

Errew friary was founded by the Barretts in 1413 for the Augustinian Canons, and is now a ruin 9.5 kilometres S.E. of Crossmolina, near the northern tip of a peninsula of Lough Conn. Nearby is a small oratory, which stands on the site of a monastery founded in the sixth century by St. Tiernan.

BELLACORICK

Bellacorick Generating Station is a milled peat station with a capacity of forty megawatts. The construction of the station commenced in May 1958; the first generating unit was commissioned in November 1964, and the second unit in January 1963. The capital cost of the station was £2.5 million. The plant comprises two 20,000 kilowatt turbo-alternators, driven by two boilers capable of producing 95,000 kilograms of steam per hour. The power is passed through transformers to the 110,000 volt transmission network. A supply is given to the local 10,000 volt and 38,000 volt distribution networks. All the milled peat is obtained by Bord na Móna in Bellacorick. During an average year the station burns about 305,000 tonnes of peat, and generates about 140 million units of electricity. (Employment 1982 — 120 people).

Bellacorick E.S.B. Generating Station (E.S.B.).

253

Bord na Móna began operations in Mayo in 1952, and in 1982 owned 10,000 hectares of bog in the county. On average they produce 310,000 tonnes of milled peat per annum with a 55% moisture content. (Permanent staff 1982 — 280).

The *Musical Bridge* at Bellacorick is a great local attraction. Musical sounds can be produced by running a stone along the northern parapet.

BALLYCASTLE

The ruins of St. Patrick's Church and Poll na Seantuinne — a puffing hole with subterrain and a channel to the sea — can be seen at Downpatrick Head, near Ballycastle. Thirty local people were drowned in Poll na Seantuinne in late September 1798, as they escaped British soldiers in the "mopping up operation" during "the Year of the French".

Dún Briste, off Downpartick Head, is a broken sea rock 63 metres by 23 metres, 45 metres high and 228 metres from the shore. It is a fragment of the cliff broken off by some natural cataclysm.

Belderg, sixteen kilometres N.W. of Ballycastle, is famous for the important archaeological excavations carried out there by its native son Dr. Séamus Caulfield and others. The Stags of Broad Haven are four rocks, 91 metres high, offshore from Glenamoy. The coast from Porturlin to Benwee Head is among the most beautiful in Ireland.

LAHARDAUN

Archbishop John Mac Hale was born in the townland of Tobernaveen, near Lahardaun. The home of the Doyle family now stands on the site of the Mac Hale home. A plaque, designed by Francis Hourigan, was erected on the Doyle home in November 1981 to commemorate the birthplace of the great Archbishop. There is a monument in the village in memory of Fr. James Conroy P.P. Addergoole, who was hanged in Castlebar for assisting the French in 1798. He was buried within the church ruins in Addergoole burial ground, near Lough Conn.

ISLANDS

There are numerous islands off the coast of Mayo. Eleven islands off the Mayo coast (excluding Achill) were inhabited in 1982. The population of these islands in 1956, 1966 and 1979 were as follows:

	1979			1966			1956		
	M	F	T	M	F	T	M	F	T
Clare Island	80	52	132	95	58	153	103	109	239
Inishbiggle	57	40	97	55	48	103	59	57	116
Inishlyre	6	6	12	6	11	17	7	12	19
Inishturk	55	30	85	52	39	91	54	56	110
Inishcottle	6	5	11	5	4	9	4	5	9
Inishgort	2	1	3	4	2	6	5	2	7
Clynish	2	2	4	2	2	4	4	2	6
Inishakillew	10	5	15	9	3	12	7	3	10
Illanataggart	—	1	1	—	1	1	1	2	3
Annagh	4	2	6	4	2	6	2	6	8
Knockycahillaun	1	—	1	2	2	4	2	4	6

Five islands became uninhabited between 1956 and 1966, i.e. Achill Beg, Islandmore, Inishraher, Crovinish, and Collan More. The remains of a monastery founded by St. Brendan, the Navigator, in the 6th century can be seen on Inishglora. According to an Irish legend, the children of Lir were said to have regained their human form on Inishglora, after living as swans for 900 years, and that they were buried there. The ruins of a monastery founded by Saint Colmcille can be seen on Inishkea North.

SOURCES

1. *A Dictionary of Irish Biography* by Henry Boylan.

2. *A Topographical Dictionary of Ireland* by Samuel Lewis.

3. Fr. Denis O'Hara: A Short Biography by Frank McCarrick.

4. *History of the Archdiocese of Tuam,* vols. 1 & 2. by Right Rev. Monsignor D'Alton.

5. Holiday Guide: County Mayo. Bord Fáilte.

6. *Mother Mary Arsenius of Foxford* by Rev. Denis Gildea.

7. *Shell Guide to Ireland* by Lord Killanin and Michael V. Duignan,(Michael V. Duignan, the distinguished Celtic scholar and archaeologist, was born in Castlebar, Co. Mayo in 1907).

8. *The Augustinian Abbey of St. Mary The Virgin, Ballyhaunis 1348-1948: A Historical Sketch* by D. B. Redmond O.S.A.

9. *The Death of an Irish Town* by John Healy.

10. *The Glory of Cong* by J. A. Fahy.

11. *The Moore's of Moore Hall* by J. Hone.

12. *The Story of Ballintubber Abbey* by Rev. Fr. Thomas A. Egan

13. Nollaig Ó Muraíle, Placenames Office, Ordnance Survey, Dublin.

SOME FAMOUS MAYO PEOPLE

by Bernard O'Hara

Several Mayo people achieved fame for one reason or another over the years. The following are short biographical notes on some of them, whose deeds, whether good or bad, are remembered today.

CANON ULICK J. BOURKE (1829-1887)

Canon Ulick Bourke was one of the most active promoters of the Irish language during his lifetime.

Ulick Bourke was born in Castlebar on 29 December 1829. He was educated in the Franciscan school in Errew, St. Jarlath's College, Tuam, and in Maynooth college, where he was ordained in 1858 by his cousin Archbishop John MacHale of Tuam. During his student days in Maynooth he wrote *"The College Irish Grammer"*. Fr. Bourke was appointed to the staff of St. Jarlaths in 1858, and became President in 1865. He was appointed parish priest of Kilcolman (Claremorris) in 1878, and was later raised to Canon.

He was one of the founders of the Society for the Preservation of the Irish language (1876), the Gaelic Union (1880), and Irisleabhar na Gaeilge in 1882. He wrote a series of articles for *"The Nation"* on "Easy Lessons on Self-Instruction in Irish". Fr. Bourke published *"The Aryan Origin of the Gaelic Race and Language"* in 1875, and *"Pre Christian Ireland"* (1887). He worked unceasingly for the revival of the Irish language.

Canon Bourke died in Claremorris on 22 November 1887, and was buried in Barnacarroll Church ground, Co. Mayo.

Claremorris born Proinsios Ó Maolmhuaidh published a biography of Canon Bourke, entitled *"Athair na hAthbheochana-Uilleog de Búrca"*, in 1982.

LOUIS BRENNAN (1852-1932)

Louis Philip Brennan, the inventor of the dirigible torpedo and the gyroscopic monorail, was born on 28 January 1852 at Main St., Catlebar, Co. Mayo, the son of a hardware merchant, Thomas Brennan, and his wife, Bridget, née McDonnell. Louis and his two older brothers, Patrick and Michael, did well at school. Patrick went to Australia in 1856, and accepted a teaching appointment in Melbourne. Michael (1839-1871) started work as a journalist with the *Connaught Telegraph,* and soon earned a reputation for himself as a caricaturist. He later attended art schools in Dublin and London, and became an artist of merit. Two of his paintings are in the National Gallery of Ireland: 'A Vine Pergola' and 'Church Interior at Capri'. He died in Algiers in 1871 and was buried there.

Thomas and Bridget Brennan sold their business in Castlebar in 1861, and emigrated with their youngest son, nine year old Louis, to Melbourne, Australia. Louis had a keen interest in difficult puzzles, and in mechanical toys. His inquisitive mind wanted to know how all his mechanical toys worked, and he experimented on extending their use and efficiency. After his primary education he went to Joel Eade's Technical College, in Collingwood, Melbourne, where he was an excellent student. Louis took up employment with an engineering firm and continued his inventive experiments.

INVENTIONS

Louis Brennan's first major invention was the dirigible torpedo, for which he was granted a patent by the Patent Office, London, on 1 February 1878, (patent No. 3359). The title of the patent was "Improvements in machinery for propelling and guiding vessels on land and through air and water". In 1880 he accepted an offer of £110,000 from the British Government for the "exclusive rights" to his invention and an invitation to go to England. Louis Brennan was manager of the Government Torpedo Manufacturing Plant, at Gillingham, Kent, which manufactured his own torpedo, from 1880 to 1896. On 10 September 1892 he married Anna Mary Quinn, also a native of Castlebar. They went to live in "Woodlands", in Gillingham, overlooking the river Medway. Louis and Anna had three children, Michael, Norah and Julie. Louis was a consultant to the Torpedo Manufacturing Plant from 1896 to 1907. He then invented his gyroscopic monorail at his home, and in 1910 it won the highest award at the Japan-British Exhibition in London. Despite the general reaction to the invention, it was not developed commercially. The Brennan family left "Woodlands" and lived at several addresses over the following twenty years. Louis Brennan took up employment with the Ministry of Munitions from 1912 until 1918, when he moved to the Royal Aircraft factory at Farnborough, where he invented a type of helicopter. However, the withdrawal of funds prevented the invention being made a commercial proposition. Louis Brennan had many other inventions to his credit, e.g. a two-wheeled "Gyrocar", a billiard marker, a window safety-catch, a pocket-sized recording machine, a mini lift for stairs, improvements in cylinders, pistons, high-speed wheels, mechanical starting devices for internal combustion engines, and many more. Norman Tomlinson in his book *"Louis Brennan: Inventor Extraordinaire"* listed thirty-eight patented inventions of Louis Brennan. (pp 87-89)

While on holiday in Montreux, Switzerland, Louis Brennan was knocked down by a car on 26 December 1931, and died as a result of the injuries received on 17 January 1932 in Montreux. He was buried in Plot No. 2454, St. Mary's Cemetery, Harrow Road, London NW 10, on 26 January 1932.

WILLIAM BROWN (1777-1857)

Admiral William Brown, "the Father of the Argentine Navy", is a national hero in Argentina. Streets, towns, and provinces have been named in his honour. His statue stands in front of Government House in "Paseo Colón", which is the continuation of one of the finest streets in Buenos Aires, named in his honour, "Avenida Alminante Brown". There are other plaques in his honour in Montevideo, Martin Garcia Island, and Carmen de Patagones. Units of the Argentinian Navy and the Navy Training College have been named in his honour. The Argentine Government had special coins with his effigy minted, and special postage stamps printed, to commemorate the bicentenary of his birth in 1977.

William Brown was born in Foxford on 22 June 1777. (Providence Road is generally accepted, locally, as the place of his birth). He emigrated to Philadelphia with his parents in 1786, at the age of nine. His father died shortly after arriving in Philadelphia. William started work as a cabin boy on an American merchant ship, and in 1796 joined the English Navy. He commanded an English merchant vessel in the war against Napoleon, but was captured by the French, and imprisoned in Verdun. He eventually escaped to London, where he obtained a job in the coastguard service, and married Elizabeth Chitty.

ARGENTINA

William Brown went to Buenos Aires in 1809 in command of his own ship, the "Eloise". His ship went aground during a Spanish blockade in 1811, and from part of the proceeds of the salvaged cargo, he purchased another ship, the "Industria", which was later sunk by the Spaniards. Brown then purchased two boats from the proceeds of an insurance policy, and with the help of a small group of Irish, Scotch and English sailors, captured a Spanish warship, which he brought in triumph to Buenos Aires. In 1814 the "Patriot Government" of the new Argentinian Republic asked William Brown to take charge of a squadron, to fight the Spanish Navy, then dominant on the seas off South America. William Brown accepted the invitation, and on St. Patrick's Day 1814 his flagship, Hercules, captured the strategic island of Martin Garcia. Argentina gained control of the River Plate and the estuary. He then captured Montevideo, the last stronghold of Spain on the south Atlantic seaboard. William Brown was then made Admiral. He organised and commanded the navy of the infant Republic of Argentina, and worked in close co-operation with General San

Martin, Liberator of Argentina, Chile and Peru. Admiral Brown defeated the Spaniards in the Pacific and in the south Atlantic, while San Martin defeated their forces on land. Brown took his ships round Cape Horn, captured several Spanish ships off Peru, and attacked the fortified seaport of Guayaquil. His ship ran aground, and he was forced to surrender.

DEATH

Admiral Brown retired in 1819, but the authorities called him back in 1826 to fight Brazil. He took command of the navy again, and won the decisive battle of Juncal against heavy odds. After the battle of Ios Pazos he broke the Brazilian blockade of Buenos Aires, and defeated Brazil in the harbours of Montevideo and Rio De Janerio. He visited his native Foxford in 1836. Admiral Brown commanded the Argentine navy in the war with Uruguay in 1842. He retired from the navy in 1845, and went to live in a small estate at Boca, near Buenos Aires. He died in Boca on 8 May 1857, and was buried in the Recoleta Cemetery, in Buenos Aires.

Admiral Brown is commemorated in Foxford to-day by a bronze bust, the work of the Argentinian sculptor Vergottini, (1957), and the parish hall is named in his honour.

CARDINAL D'ALTON (1882-1963)

Cardinal John Francis D'Alton was Archbishop of Armagh and Primate of all Ireland from 1946 to 1963.

He was born in Claremorris, Co. Mayo, on 11 October 1882. After attending the local national school he went to Blackrock College, Dublin, and later to Clonliffe College. He then proceeded to the Irish College in Rome, where he was ordained on 18 April 1908. After receiving his Doctorate in Theology he obtained an M.A. in Ancient Classics in 1910. Dr. D'Alton was then appointed a lecturer in Maynooth College, and later became a junior Professor (1912), Professor (1922), Vice President (1934) and President in 1936, a post he held until 1942. His published works include, *"Horace and his Age"* (1917), and *"Roman Literary Theory and Criticism – a Study in Tendencies"* (1931).

Dr. D'Alton was consecrated Coadjutor Bishop of Meath on 29 June 1942, and in June 1943 became Bishop of Meath. Bishop D'Alton was appointed Archbishop of Armagh and Primate of All Ireland on 25 April 1946, in succession to Cardinal McRory. On 12 January 1953, he was chosen as a Cardinal by His Holiness Pope Pius XII. Pope John XXIII appointed Cardinal D'Alton a member of the Central Preparatory Commission of the Second Vatican Council in 1960. He led the Irish hierarchy at the first session of the Vatican Council in 1962. Cardinal D'Alton died in Dublin on 1 February 1963, and was buried in the grounds of Armagh Cathedral.

JAMES DALY (1835-1910)

James Daly was editor of the *"Connaught Telegraph"* from 1876 to 1888, and during that time he won the respect of many for his forceful and courageous advocacy of land reform. He chaired the historic meeting in Irishtown on 20 April 1879, which started the Land League campaign.

James Daly was born in Boghadoon, near Lahardaun, in 1835. His father farmed 45 hectares on the Palmer estate there. John O'Connor Power (1846-1919) gave regular reports to constituents on his performance, following his election to Westminister in 1874. James Daly was a regular attender at such meetings, from which emerged the Mayo Tenants Defence Association in 1878, and later the Mayo Land League.

THE CONNAUGHT TELEGRAPH

James Daly and his friend, Alfred O'Hea, purchased *"The Mayo Telegraph"* newspaper in February 1876. They changed its title to *"The Connaught Telegraph"*, and made it the main organ in the West of Ireland for articulating the grievances of tenant farmers. Daly was an able and courageous writer, who wrote at length about the Great Famine in Mayo in addition to the land problems. *The Connaught Telegraph* under Daly became a very respected and influential newspaper. Following O'Hea's death in 1878, James Daly secured complete control of the newspaper in 1879. On the initiative of James Daly the Mayo Tenants Defence Association was established in October 1878 with the objectives of highlighting rack renting and ending evictions, but the Association was a failure. When Michael Davitt returned to Mayo in 1878, following his release from prison, he called on James Daly. Daly had publicised the conditions under which Davitt served his jail sentence, and John O'Connor Power M.P. had campaigned for his release.

THE LAND LEAGUE

The tenants of the Bourke estate in Irishtown met James Daly early in 1879 in Claremorris and asked him to publish their grievances. He rejected their request, in fear of libel actions, but advised them to hold a public demonstration and that he would publicise it. A meeting was held in Claremorris attended by James Daly, Michael Davitt, John Keane, J. W. Walsh, and P. W. Nally, at which arrangements were made for the demonstration. The meeting was held in Irishtown on 20 April 1879 and was chaired by James Daly. The speakers were: John O'Connor Power M.P., John Ferguson (Glasgow), Thomas Brennan (Dublin), J. J. Louden B.L. Westport, and Matthew Harris, Ballinasloe. *"The Connaught Telegraph"* gave the meeting good coverage. Charles Stewart Parnell spoke at a meeting in Westport on 18 June, which was once again chaired by James Daly. James Daly's advice to the people at the Westport meeting was: "feed your families, pay your suppliers and if you have money left pay the landlords". He also recommended social ostracisation of the landlords. The success of the land agitation led to the formation of the Mayo Land League in James Daly's Hotel in Castlebar in August 1879, and he was elected vice President. James Daly attended and spoke at over one hundred demonstrations during 1879. On 4 November 1879 he spoke with Michael Davitt, John Dillon and James Bryce Killen in Gurteen County Sligo. Some days later, Daly, Davitt, and Killen were arrested for alleged seditious speeches and sent to Sligo Jail. Their case commenced in Sligo on 24 November. Killen was defended by a Belfast solicitor, John Rea, who turned the court into a pantomine. The three accused were returned for trial in Carrick-on-Shannon, but on the morning of the trial the charges were withdrawn. After the introduction of the Coercion Act in 1881 James Daly was arrested and sent to Galway Jail, where he spent five weeks. A rift developed within a section of the Mayo Land League; Daly felt that it had deserted the social group for which it was founded, and left the organisation. He strongly opposed land nationalisation. He sold his newspaper in 1888 to Thomas Gillespie and became a full time farmer. James Daly died in 1910, and in the words of Joseph Lee, in *"The Modernisation of Irish Society 1848-1918"*, "is the most undeservedly forgotten man in Irish history". (p. 69)

MICHAEL DAVITT (1846-1906)

Michael Davitt, "the father of the Land League", was Mayo's most famous son and arguably Ireland's greatest patriot. He inspired from County Mayo the most successful movement in Irish history, and secured a radical change in land ownership in Ireland by constitutional means.

Michael Davitt's sympathy and concern ranged from the Irish tenant farmer to agricultural labourers in Ireland, the plight of the British working class, the Liverpool dockers, prison reform, the Boers in South Africa, and the Jews in Russia. He was a champion of the oppressed and the exploited world wide, and regarded the population of the world as one family. He believed strongly in inter denominational education, and that libraries, museums, and art galleries should be provided around the country. Michael Davitt was a master organiser, a tireless writer, with a passion for truth, honesty, and social justice for all mankind. He was a person of transparent integrity, with a mind too noble to harbour grudges, a man who attacked the social system of his time, but not the people in that system. T. W. Moody wrote:

"Michael Davitt served his fellow men under the impulsion not of any dogma but of a generous and compassionate spirit that surmounted all distinctions of class and circumstances no less than of religion and national origin".

Fellow Mayoman, John Healy, in a tribute to Michael Davitt in *The Western Journal,* in August 1979, wrote:

"he more than any other has shaped modern Ireland and left it for what it is to-day: a prospering island on the edge of Europe with the great gift of political stability without which there can not be any progress".

EVICTION

Michael Davitt was born on 25 March 1846 at Strade, Co. Mayo, the second of a family of five. His father, Martin, and mother, Catherine (Sabina) née Kealty, were tenants on the Knox estate at Strade. Martin was literate; Catherine could not read nor write, but nevertheless had a big influence on Michael. When Michael was four years old he saw his family evicted from their home during "the great clearances" because they were unable to pay the rent which had accummulated during the famine. Michael never forgot the eviction experience and the sight of his home being battered to the ground. The Davitt family emigrated to Haslingden in Lancashire, and Martin became a fruit hawker, and later a labourer. At the age of nine Michael started work in a local cotton mill as a mill-hand. Two years later his right arm was badly injured by a machine, and it had to be amputated just below the shoulder. He left the factory and attended a non denominational school, which had been recommended by his parish priest, Rev. Thomas Martin. The school had a big influence on Michael; he saw and accepted religious differences, and throughout his life never showed any trace of sectarian bigotry. He stayed there for four years, and then secured employment in Cockcroft's Post Office in Haslingden.

FENIAN

Michael Davitt joined the Irish Republican Brotherhood in 1865, left his job in the post office, and became an arms organiser in Britain for the I.R.B. He was arrested in London in May 1870 for his involvement in arms traffic to Ireland, and after conviction of treason-felony was sentenced to fifteen years hard labour, which was served in Millbank, Portsmouth and Dartmoor prisons. On 19 December 1877 he was released on a ticket of leave in response to an amnesty campaign, after seven years and seven months of degrading and inhuman treatment. His prison ordeal became well known in Ireland and he became a national hero. He was still a Fenian, but had become very critical of the methods and intolerance of Fenianism. Davitt returned to Ireland and to County Mayo, where he received a warm welcome. Michael then went to America to visit his family, who had emigrated from England in 1865 to Pennsylvania, where his father died in 1871. Michael Davitt had several discussions in America with leading Irish Americans, including John Devoy (1842-1929), Patrick Ford (1837-1913) editor of *"The Irish World"*, and John Boyle O'Reilly (1844-1890) editor of *"The Boston Pilot"*, and formulated the "New Departure", under which the Fenians and constitutional nationalists would pursue two objectives, "Home Rule" and Land Reform, a policy first suggested by James Fintan Lalor (1807-1849), in 1845. Michael Davitt was the first Irish leader to solicit American support for Irish problems.

IRISHTOWN

On his return from America Michael Davitt found social conditions in Ireland terrible, especially among the tenant farmers of Mayo, where there was considerable fear of famine and eviction. Michael Davitt and his friend J. W. Walshe from Balla toured the county. *"The Connaught Telegraph"*, with its motto "be just and fear not", carried stories of the tenants plight week after week. The land agitation really started at Irishtown, Co. Mayo, in April 1879. Walter Joseph Bourke, an absentee landlord in the Irishtown area, died in 1873. The estate passed to his son, Joseph, an army surgeon stationed at Hampshire. Some tenants on the estate were under threat of eviction in January 1879. Joseph Bourke, the absentee landlord, was a nephew of Canon Geoffrey Bourke, parish priest of Kilvine, whose name seems to have been incorrectly associated with the tenant grievances. T. W. Moody in his book *"Davitt and Irish Revolution 1846-'82"* wrote ... "responsibility for the harsh treatment of these tenants may well have been that of the absentee owner, Joseph Bourke, not that of his resident uncle, the canon". (p. 295). In February 1879 James Daly, editor of *The Connaught Telegraph,* Michael Davitt and others organised a protest meeting to be held in Irishtown on 20 April 1879 to ventilate tenant grievances in general. Michael Davitt invited the speakers, drafted the resolutions, but did not attend. The Irishtown meeting was attended by a crowd variously stated to be from 4,000 to 13,000, and was most successful; the eviction notices were withdrawn from the Bourke tenants and a general reduction in rents achieved. Many such meetings followed, most of which were attended by Davitt. Charles Stewart Parnell accepted an invitation from Michael Davitt and attended a meeting in Westport on 18 June 1879, at which Michael Davitt spoke, his first speech to an Irish audience on the land question.

Michael Davitt c. 1880 (John Devoy, The Land of Éire)

263

THE MAYO LAND LEAGUE

The Mayo Land League was founded, at a meeting convened by Michael Davitt, on Saturday 16 August 1879 in James Daly's Hotel, Castlebar, now the Imperial Hotel. The inaugural meeting was chaired by James J. Louden, Westport, who was elected President. The objectives of the Mayo Land League were: to abolish the existing land system, publicise rack renting, make all evictions scenes of public demonstrations, help evictees and to campaign for reform. The Mayo Land League was very successful and on the initiative of Davitt evolved into a National Land League within two months. Davitt persuaded Parnell to join the League. The National Land League of Ireland was inaugurated in the Imperial Hotel, in Sackville Street, Dublin on 21 October 1879, with Charles Stewart Parnell as President and Michael Davitt one of its secretaries.

On the 18 November 1879 Michael Davitt was arrested for an alleged seditious speech at Gurteen, Co. Sligo, on 2 November, and was imprisoned in Sligo Jail. The charge against him was later withdrawn and he was released. On the 1 February 1880, he addressed a big meeting at the place of his birth, during which he said: "I am standing upon a platform erected over the ruins of my levelled home and hope that one day I will have the satisfaction of trampling on the ruins of Irish landlordism". Michael Davitt helped Anna Parnell (1852-1911), a sister of Charles Stewart Parnell, start the Ladies Land League.

He then spent six months in America seeking support for the Land League.

THE LAND WAR 1879-'82

The Land War was a mass movement of passive resistance. It was initiated long before Mahatma Gandhi (1869-1948) preached the doctrine of non violent resistance to the people of India. Evictions were made scenes of great demonstrations, evictees were supported, and an embargo was placed on every farm from which people were evicted. Some intimidation and violence did take place, but, technically, the Land League was a lawful movement. The most effective weapon of the League was ostracisation; the most publicised incident took place at Lough Mask House, Co.Mayo. Captain Charles Boycott, a former British army officer and later an unsuccessful farmer in Achill, was appointed agent for the Lough Mask estate in 1873 by Lord Erne, an absentee landlord, who kept increasing the rents on the tenants. Soon they were unable to pay and eviction notices were served on eleven families. The parish priest of the Neale,Rev. Fr. John O'Malley, organised a campaign of ostracisation against Boycott in September 1880; no local did anything for him. Eventually men were brought from the Orange Lodges of Cavan and Monaghan to save the harvest for Captain Boycott at a considerable cost. Captain Boycott left Ireland and never returned. Fr. O'Malley and James Redpath, an American journalist who stayed with him during the campaign, gave a new word to the English language, boycott.

The British Government felt that the Land League was getting too strong and introduced the Coercion Act to suppress it. The leaders of the League were arrested; Michael Davitt had his ticket of leave revoked, and was sent to Portland Prison in February 1881. At the same time the Gladstone Land Act of 1880 conceded the three Fs i.e. fair rent, fixity of tenure and free sale, and established the Land Commission. It also introduced a system of dual ownership and established special courts, to which tenants could apply and have their rents fixed. The Land League members were not satisfied; they wanted ownership. The Land League issued its "No Rent Manifesto" ordering tenants to pay no rent at all. Violence erupted around the country as "The Invincibles" and other societies filled the vacuum left by the League following the imprisonment of its leaders. Charles Stewart Parnell concluded the Kilmainhan Treaty with Britain, which ended the Land War on favourable terms. The coercion policy was abandoned, the manifesto withdrawn, the Land League leaders released in May 1882, and plans were formulated to meet the objectives of the League.

TENANT PROPRIETORSHIP

Michael Davitt was well treated during his imprisonment in Portland in 1881. He had access to books and read widely. One book made a big impression on him " *Progress and Poverty*" by Henry George, which influenced him to think of land nationalisation as the solution to the Irish land problem. On his release he recommended land nationalisation but the tenant farmers would not accept it. Michael Davitt, always a realist and pragmatist, succumbed to their wishes and accepted tenant proprietorship as the solution. The British Civil Service blamed the Irish landlords for some of the consequences of the Great Famine. The landlords were not happy with the rents fixed by the special courts and realised that they would be better to sell the land to the tenants on favourable terms. A scheme of state aided land purchase was formulated. The tenants eventually became full owners of the land by a series of land purchase acts i.e. The Ashbourne Act 1885, Balfour Land Act of 1891, and especially the Wyndham Land Act of 1903. These Acts provided the finance which enabled the tenants to buy out their landlords and repay the loans with interest over a number of years. Joseph Lee, in *"The Modernisation of Irish Society 1848-1918,"* wrote: "In composition, tactics, ideology, the Land League ranked among the most effective and sophisticated movements in nineteenth century Europe". Whilst due tribute must be paid to its many members and the pioneering work of James Daly, Michael Davitt is rightly honoured as "the father of the Land League".

WHERE HAVE ALL THE LANDLORDS GONE?

Ireland was dominated by landlords in the eighteenth century. They had their own parliament, controlled the right to vote, and any laws enacted were not inimical to their interests. The landlord class nominated the magistrates to enforce the laws, and controlled the grand juries at county level. Some landlord privileges were eroded over the years but it was Michael Davitt and his friends in the Land League who pioneered the abolition of the system.

To appreciate the extent of Michael Davitt's contribution to changing the face of Mayo and Ireland one need do no more than read through this list of "the people who counted" in County Mayo in 1858 and ask how many of their descendants still retain the same address and occupy even a portion of their ancestors patrimony:

Colonel George Lord Bingham, Castlebar House, Carra; Lord John Browne, M.P., Westport House, Murrisk; R. W. H. Palmer, Esq. M.P., Kenure Park, Gallen; Colonel F. A. K. Gore, Belleek Manor, Tirawley; Sir Robert L. Blosse, Bart., Athavallie, Claremorris; Sir R. A. O'Donnell, Bart., Newport House, Burrishoole; Colonel C. Knox, Cranmore, Kilmaine; Denis Bingham, Esq., Bingham Castle, Erris; John Nolan Farrell, Esq., Logboy, Costello; Colonel the Hon. J. L. Browne, Neal Park; Hon. Theobald Dillon, Loughglynn House; Capt. the Hon. D. A. Bingham, Newbrook; Hon. Geoffrey Browne, Castlemacgarrett; Hon. W. S. Russell, Dalgan Park; Hon. Sexton H. Perry, Ballina; Sir Charles C. Domville, Bart., Prison; Sir Samuel O'Malley, Bart., Kilboyne House; George H. Moore, Esq., Moore Hall; Lieut. Colonel George G. O. Higgins Mountpleasant; Valentine O'C Blake, Esq., Tower Hill; Thomas S. Lindsay jun., Esq., Hollymount House; Captain St. George Cuffe, Deel Castle; Robert Ruttledge, Esq., Bloomfield; Annesley Knox, Esq., Rappa Castle; Mark Blake, Esq., Ballinafad; Mervyn Pratt, Esq., Enniscoe; James Howe Browne, Esq., Browne Hall; Captain Hugh Brabazon, Brabazon Park; Philip Taaffe, Esq., Woodfield; James Knox Gildea, Esq., Clooncormack; Major P. C. Lynch, Clogher House; Arthur Costello, Esq., Edmondstown; Oliver V. Jackson, Esq., Carramore; Captain Fitzgerald Higgins, Glen Corrib; William H. Carter, Esq., Sheane Lodge; Captain Ernest Knox, Castlerea; Charles L. Fitzgerald, Esq., Turlough; Anthony Ormsby, Esq., Ballinamore; Captain Henry W. Knox, Netley Park; Charles Lynch, Esq., Ballycurran Castle; John C. Walshe, Esq., Castle Hill; H. I. H. Browne, Esq., Rahins; Captain Maurice Blake, Cugalla; Captain Thomas Elwood, Kinlough; William C. Orme, Esq., Owenmore; Crosdale B. Miller, Esq., Millford; George J. O'Malley, Esq., Newcastle; Francis R. O'Grady, Esq., Tavrane; Joseph M. MacDonnell, Esq., Doo Castle; Godfrey Fetherston, Esq., Abbeyton; Charles Strickland, Esq., Loughglynn; Thomas Ormsby, Esq., Knockmore; Parsons Persse, Esq., Summerhill; William Symes, Esq., Ballina; George Clive, Esq., M.P., Claggan; Colonel J. F. Knox, Mount Falcon; James A. Browne, Esq., Brownhall; John Ormsby, Esq., Gortnerabbey; Thomas Paget, Esq., Knockglass; Anthony R. Bowen, Esq., Annefield; Thomas Ruttledge, Esq., Cornfield; Joseph Bourke, Esq., Curraleagh; Richard D'Arcy, Esq., Fisherhill; George C. O'Donnell, Esq., Melcomb House; Major John Knox, Greenwood House; John L.Bucknell, Esq., Turin Castle; D. W. Ruttledge, Esq., Barbersfort; Lieutenant-Colonel W. Knox, Springhill; Austin F. Crean, Esq., Ballinvilla; Captain H. Blake, The Heath; Robert Orme, Esq., Mountainville; Edmond Taaffe, Esq., Woodfield; John Bolingbroke, Esq., Oldcastle; William Malley, Esq., Ballyvary; Murray M. Blacker, Esq., Claremount; Patrick H. Lynch, Esq., Strandhill; Bernard M. Manus, Esq., Barleyhill; Thomas Palmer Esq., Summerhill; James D. Meldon, Esq., Belmont; Charles Coyne, Esq., Heath Lodge; Robert Tighe, Esq., Ballinrobe; William M. Fitzmaurice, Esq., Lagaturn; James Dillon, Esq., Coogue; Captain Roger Palmer, Carramore; John Cannon, Esq., Catlegrove; William Levingston, Esq., Westport; Geoffrey Martyn, Esq., Curramore; Edward Howley, Esq., Belleek Castle; Courtney Kenney,Esq., Ballinrobe; William Kearney, Esq., Ballinvilla; Frederick Lewin, Esq., Cloghens; Charles Joley, Esq., Dalgan Park; Charles B. Jordan, Esq., Thornhill; William J. Bourke, Esq., Ower; George R. Acton, Esq., Bridgemount; William Pike, Esq., Glendarary; Patrick J. Blake, Esq., Rockfort; Walter Bourke, Esq., Oldtown; Myles Jordan, Esq., Roslevin Castle; Edmund H. Perry, Esq., Ballina; Benjamin W. Jennings, Esq., Mount Jennings; George Ruttledge, Esq., Beechgrove; Matthew Atkinson, Esq., Glencastle; Joseph Kirkwood, Esq., Killala; Myles MacDonnell, Esq., Carranacon; Ormsby Elwood, Esq., Lacafina Castle; Edward P. MacDonnell, Esq., Caher House; Matthew Gallagher, Esq., Grallagh; James W. Garvey, Esq., Tully House; Lucas A. Treston, Esq., Brize; Dominick D'Arcy, Esq., Doo Castle; Joseph Blake, Esq., Lavally; Hugh Bourke, Esq., Hollywell; Patrick Tuohy, Esq., Oxford; James French, Esq.,

Frenchgrove; Emerson Dawson, Esq., Houndswood; William R. Kirkwood, Esq., Crosspatrick; Stephen Gibbons, Esq., Westport; James MacDonnell, Esq., Ahalard; Henry McCarrick, Esq., Aclare; Thomas Fair, Esq., Fortville; Daniel Madden, Esq., Glenulra; Hugh Wilbraham, Esq., Boathaven; Charles Crotty, Esq., Maumeen.

MARRIED

Michael Davitt left the I.R.B. in 1880 and thereafter became a constitutional supporter of Home Rule. He was appointed Patron of the G.A.A. after its formation in November 1884.

Michael Davitt went on a lecture tour of the United States in 1886, and met Mary Yore, whom he had met on a previous visit, in Oakland, California. Both of Mary's parents emigrated from Co. Meath during the famine. Mary Yore and Michael Davitt were married in Oakland on 30 December 1886. After a honeymoon in Monterey, Chicago and New York, Michael and Mary returned to Ireland in February 1887. A few friends, led by James Rourke, presented Mary with a pretty residence at Ballybrack, Dalkey, Co. Dublin, which was called the "Land League Cottage"; it was the only present Michael Davitt accepted during his career. (Michael and Mary had two girls, one of them died young, and three boys).

MEMBER OF PARLIAMENT

Michael Davitt was elected an M.P. in 1882, but was disqualified by a special vote of the House of Commons because he was a treason-felony prisoner on ticket of leave. He was defeated in the 1891 general election in Waterford by the New Parnellite leader John Redmond. Davitt won North Meath in 1892 but was unseated because of clerical interference. (A clerical campaign launched against Parnell by Dr. Nulty of Meath). Michael Davitt went bankrupt after the Meath election and lost all his possessions including his home. He was elected unopposed for N. E. Cork in 1893 but had to withdraw when he was declared bankrupt. While in Australia in 1895, he was elected an M.P. for South Mayo and East Kerry. He chose his native Mayo and sat in the House of Commons for four years. Michael Davitt was never happy as a parliamentarian and resigned his seat in protest against the Boer War. He then travelled at his own expense to the five continents, speaking and writing in the promotion of justice. His source of income was from his work as a free lance journalist.

WRITER

Michael Davitt was a prolific writer and earned his living with his pen. In addition to many minor pamphlets and numerous articles and letters in newspapers, he wrote six books: *"Leaves From a Prison Diary"*, *"The 'Times' - Parnell Commission speech delivered by Michael Davitt in Defence of The Land League"*, *"Life and Progress in Australasia"*, *"The Boer Fight for Freedom"*, *"Within the Pale: the true story of anti-Semitic persecution in Russia"* and *"The Fall of Feudalism in Ireland"*.

Michael Davitt never forgot his experience in industrial Lancashire, which influenced him to become a trade union activist and play a major part in the formation of the Irish Trade Union Congress in 1894. He campaigned enthusiastically for the British Labour Party in the 1906 general election at which it won twenty-nine seats compared with two in the preceding election.

Michael Davitt's Grave at Strade.

Michael Davitt's will epitomised his magnanimous nature. Its salient points were:

"Should I die in Ireland I would like to be buried at Strade, Co. Mayo, without any funeral demonstration. If I die in America I must be buried in my mother's grave at Manayunk, near Philadelphia, and on no account be brought back to Ireland, if in any other country (outside of Great Britain) to be buried in the nearest cemetery to where I may die, with the simplest possible ceremony. Should I die in Great Britain, I must be buried at Strade, Co. Mayo. My diaries are not to be published without my wife's permission. On no account must anything harsh or censorious, written in said diaries by me about any person dead or alive, who has ever worked for Ireland, be printed, published or used so as to give pain to any friend or relative. To all my friends I leave kind thoughts; to my enemies the fullest forgiveness; and to Ireland the undying prayer for the absolute freedom and independence which it was my life's ambition to try and obtain for her". (Dated 1st February, 1904).

Michael Davitt died in the Elphis hospital in Mount Street, Dublin, on 30 May 1906. The cause of death was acute septic poisoning of his jaw following the extraction of two teeth.

His remains were taken to the Church of the Carmelite Fathers, Clarendon Street, the following day, as he had requested before his death. It was the only Catholic Church in Dublin which did not refuse to accept the remains of his Fenian friend McCarthy in January 1878. His remains were then taken across Ireland by train to Foxford. A huge cortege joined the funeral to Strade, where Michael Davitt was laid to rest within a half kilometre of the place where he was born, just over sixty years before. Rev. Fr. P. Hunt, P.P. Strade, assisted by Rev. Fr. Denis O'Hara, officiated at the graveside.

The Celtic Cross over his grave bears an appropriate inscription to his memory in both English and Irish:—

"Blessed are they that hunger and thirst after Justice; for they shall have their fill" Matt. 5.
"In loving memory of Michael Davitt, who departed this life on the 30th day of May 1906, at the age of 60 years, R.I.P. This monument is erected by his wife, Mary Davitt".
"Blessed are they that suffer persecution for Justice sake for theirs is the Kingdom of Heaven". Matt. 5.

JOHN BLAKE DILLON (1816-1866)

John Blake Dillon was born in Ballaghaderreen in 1816, and educated privately before going to Maynooth with the intention of becoming a priest. He left Maynooth and went to Trinity College, Dublin. After graduating in Ethics and Mathematics, he studied law and was called to the Bar in 1841. John Blake Dillon, Thomas Davis (1814-1845) and Gavan Duffy (1816-1903) founded *"The Nation"* newspaper. He married Adalaide Hart from Dublin in 1847.

John Blake Dillon was involved in the unsuccessful rising of 1848, and escaped to France. He later went to America, and practised law in New York until 1855. The family returned to Ireland in 1855, and John Blake Dillon continued his legal career in Ireland. He was elected an M.P. for Tipperary in 1865, but died in Killarney on 15 September 1866, and was buried in Glasnevin cemetery.

JOHN DILLON (1851-1927)

Even though he was not born nor reared in Mayo, John Dillon, a son of John Blake Dillon, was very much associated with County Mayo. John Dillon was born in Blackrock, Co. Dublin, on 4 September 1851, while his mother was home from New York visiting her family. The first four years of his life were spent in New York, and then the family returned to Dublin. After taking a degree in Arts, John Dillon became a doctor in 1875. He was a regular visitor to his cousin, Anne Deane, née Duff, in Ballaghaderreen, who was really a second mother to him. John Dillon became an active member of the Land League. His first speech on the land question was in Claremorris on 13 July 1879, and he spoke at several meetings in the following months. He was imprisoned twice during the Land War, and again in 1888 for supporting the "plan of campaign" against high rents charged by absentee landlords. John Dillon was elected an M.P. for Tipperary in 1880, and for East Mayo in 1885, a seat he retained at each subsequent election until 1918. He was committed to Home Rule for Ireland by parliamentary means. After the O'Shea divorce case in 1890, the Anti Parnellittes formed the Irish Nationalist Federation and John Dillon was its chairman from 1896 to 1900.

He married Elizabeth Mathew on 21 November 1895. John Dillon joined the United Nationalist Party under John Redmond in 1900, and became leader of the Nationalist party following Redmond's death on 6 March 1918. Following the 1916 rising the Nationalist party lost support, and the attempt by the British Government to introduce conscription in Ireland further eroded their support.

In the December 1918 election in East Mayo, John Dillon, leader of the Nationalist party, was defeated by Éamon de Valéra, leader of Sinn Fein, by 8,843 votes to 4,451. The nationalist party only won six seats in the election and John Dillon retired from politics.

He died in London on 4 August, 1927.

FREDERICK R. HIGGINS (1896-1941)

Frederick Robert Higgins (F.R.H.), the poet and former Managing Director of the Abbey Theatre, was born in the R.I.C. Barracks, in Foxford, Co. Mayo, on 24 April 1896. His father, Joseph, an R.I.C. officer, and mother, Annie, née French, were both natives of Higginsbrook, Co. Meath. Frederick was baptised in the Church of Ireland in Foxford. The family moved to Meath when Frederick was quite young. He was sent to national school in Meath, and started working at the age of fourteen, with Brooks Thomas Co. Ltd., in Dublin, as a clerk. He left Brooks Thomas and started to write and edit magazines, which is chiefly what he did for the rest of his life. In August 1921 F. R. Higgins married May Moore, a harpist of note. He edited a trade journal, a woman's journal called 'Welfare', and 'The Shamrock and Irish, in which he started to publish some of his own poems.

270

Frederick and May moved to Mayo in 1929, and lived in Lake View Cottage, Brackwansha, Knockmore, overlooking Lough Conn, a house rented from the Brogan family. May entertained the neighbours on the harp and Frederick worked on his editing and writing. They returned to Dublin in 1932, and shortly afterwards moved into their own house, Dúrlas, Lower Dodder Road. F. R. Higgins met William Butler Yeats in 1933, and two years later both edited a series of broadsheets, which were published monthly by the Cuala Press. F. R. Higgins became a Director of the Abbey Theatre, and manager during its 1937 American tour. He was appointed Managing Director of the Abbey Theatre in 1938, and continued his editing work with the help of his wife. At that time he was editing the *'Irish Decorator'* and *'Builder's Review'*. F. R. Higgins published four books of poems: *"Island Blood"* (1925), *"The Dark Breed"* (1927), *"Arable Holdings"* (1933), *"The Gap of Brightness"* (1940), and wrote a one-act play: *"A Deuce O' Jacks"*, which was produced by the Abbey Theatre in 1935. He was a founding member of the Irish Academy of Letters.

F. R. Higgins contacted Bell's palsy in 1940, and died in Jervis Street Hospital in January 1941. He was buried in Laracor Church graveyard, near Trim, Co. Meath.

OLIVIA KNIGHT (1830-1908)

Olivia Knight, a popular contributor to *"The Nation"* newspaper between 1848 and 1860, was a native of Rathbawn Road, Castlebar, Co. Mayo. She became a teacher, and regularly contributed poems and articles to *"The Nation"*, under the pseudonym "Thomasine". All her writing had a strong nationalistic theme. She emigrated to Australia after her mother's death in 1860, where she married a journalist — Hope Connolly. Olivia died in Queensland in 1908, and was buried there.

HUBERT T. KNOX

Hubert Thomas Knox was the son of Colonel Knox of Cranmore, Co. Mayo, and of Lady Louisa, daughter of the 4th Marquess of Sligo. He entered the Madras Civil Service in 1868, but was forced by ill-health to retire young. He returned to Ireland, and became very interested in the study of archaeology.

Hubert Knox published *"The History of the County Mayo, to the Close of the Sixteenth Century"* in 1908, *"Notes on the Early History of the Dioceses of Tuam, Killala and Achonry"*, and contributed numerous articles on archaeology to the Journals of the Royal Society of Antiquaries of Ireland and the Galway Archaeological and Historical Society. Towards the end of his life, he had to employ others to examine and measure the monuments he described.

His article on the ancient "Burgus of Athenry", published in the Journal of the Galway Archaeological and Historical Society Vol. XI, No. 1 (1921), was his last publication. He left the Galway Society a large collection of photographs, taken by himself, before his death in 1921.

FR. PATRICK LAVELLE (1825-1886)

Fr. Patrick Lavelle became a national hero for his courageous stand against proselytism in Toormakeady, Co. Mayo, and for publicising the evictions which took place there as a result in November 1860.

He was born in Mullagh, Murrisk, under the shadow of 'Ireland's holy mountain', Croagh Patrick, in 1825. His father was a farmer but also had some off-farm employment. Patrick received his early education at a local hedge school, and went to St. Jarlath's College, Tuam, in 1840. In 1844 he went to St. Patrick's College, Maynooth, where he was a brilliant student, and was ordained a priest in 1851. After ordination he became a student of the Dunboyne establishment in Maynooth, doing research work, and in 1854 was appointed Assistant Librarian in the College. Later that year he resigned his post in Maynooth, and went to the Irish College in Paris as Professor of Philosophy. Fr. Lavelle's experience in Paris was far from happy. He became involved in a dispute with the Rector of the College, Dr. Miley, a Dublin priest, who had anointed Daniel O'Connell in Genoa in 1847. Fr. Lavelle was recalled to his native diocese, Tuam, in 1858, and appointed Curate in Mayo Abbey. Later that year Archbishop John MacHale appointed him Administrator in Partry, where a fanatical proselytising campaign was rife.

THE PARTRY EVICTIONS

Most of the land in the parish of Partry, in 1858, was owned by Bishop Thomas Plunkett, Church of Ireland Bishop of Tuam, Killala and Achonry since 1839. He spent most of his spare time in Toormakeady, part of the parish of Partry, rather than in Tuam. He decided that Toormakeady, on the shores of Lough Mask, was a fertile locality for his proselytising zeal, and built a number of schools, and a church, on his estate. The parents of the area were persuaded to send their children to the Protestant schools by Bishop Plunkett and his agents. As Archbishop John MacHale had refused to allow state national schools in his diocese, some parents in Toormakeady sent their children to the Protestant schools, to prevent eviction. Some people were evicted for refusing to co-operate. The local parish priest, Fr. Peter Ward, was unable to cope with the situation, and asked for a transfer. He was transferred to Williamstown in 1858, and replaced by Fr. Patrick Lavelle.

Fr. Lavelle tells us in his book, *"The Irish Landlord Since the*

Revolution", that 165 people were evicted in Partry for refusing to send their children to the Protestant schools prior to his arrival in the parish (P. 500). Fr. Lavelle tried on his arrival to deal amicably with Bishop Plunkett, but the intimidation and coercion continued. He then publicly appealed to the parents not to send their children to the Protestant schools. Bishop Plunkett retaliated. Tenants were summoned and fined for the most trivial of offences, and were abused by teachers and Bible readers. Bishop Plunkett secured sixty ejectment decrees against tenants at the Castlebar Assizes early in 1860. None of the tenants involved had arrears of rent.

A former priest in the parish, Fr. Conway, then parish priest of Headford, intervened and secured an agreement whereby Bishop Plunkett would not proceed with the evictions, and that Fr. Lavelle would drop his case against the Toormakeady parson, Rev. Mr. Goodison, for threatening to shoot him with a revolver. Bishop Plunkett did not keep his part of the agreement for long. With the help of soldiers from the Curragh, local police and the sheriff, Bishop Plunkett had seventeen families, sixty eight human beings, evicted and their homes demolished in the townland of Derryveeny on 21, 22 and 23 November 1860. The people involved ranged in age from a child in the cradle to a man of eighty. All had been warned to sent their children to the Protestant schools.

Fr. Lavelle published details of the Partry evictions, as they came to be called, in the press, and received wide publicity and reaction. Even *"The Times"* of London, in a scathing leader, described the behaviour of Bishop Plunkett as "a hideous scandal". Fr. Lavelle fought Bishop Plunkett's proselytism and landlord tyranny in the public press, and in the courts. Fr. Lavelle had two Catholic schools erected in his parish, one for boys and the other for girls, staffed by Franciscan Brothers. Fr. Lavelle's fearless courage and determination had won through. Bishop Plunkett left the parish in 1862, and died on 19 October 1866. He was buried in the Protestant churchyard in Toormakeady. His daughter, Catherine Plunkett, continued the fight for a short time, to no avail. She sold her property and left the parish. The Plunkett regime in Toormakeady was at an end.

CONTROVERSY

Archbishop Paul Cullen of Dublin (1803-1878) disliked any form of Fenian activity. Fr. Patrick Lavelle had strong Fenian sympathies, and in 1861 was elected Vice President of the Brotherhood of St. Patrick, a sister organisation of the I.R.B. When, the Co. Fermanagh revolutionary, Terence Bellew McManus (1823-1869) died in America in October 1860 his remains were brought to Dublin for burial in Glasnevin cemetery. Archbishop Cullen refused to allow the remains to lie in any church in his diocese, except for the funeral mass. Fr. Lavelle attended the funeral in Glasnevin, delivered a short eulogy, and recited the De Profundis. Archbishop Cullen complained about Fr. Lavelle to Rome. In May 1862 a meeting of the Irish hierarchy demanded that Fr. Lavelle resign from the Brotherhood of St. Patrick, and apologise publicly for his activities. Archbishop John MacHale opposed the decision, and Fr. Lavelle refused to comply. Fr. Lavelle wrote regular letters to the newspapers defending the Fenians and criticising Archbishop Cullen. Archbishop John MacHale saved him from disciplinary actions on several occasions. Fr. Lavelle was appointed Parish Priest of Partry in 1866. He was rarely out of controversy, and, in February 1867, attacked Bishop Moriarity of Kerry in a public letter in *'The Connacht Ranger"* for his statement that "hell was not hot enough nor eternity long enough" for the Fenians. He campaigned for nationalist candidates in several elections, and was a close friend of George Henry Moore, to whom he dedicated his book.

CONG

Fr. Lavelle was appointed Parish Priest of Cong in 1869, in succession to Dean Waldron, the priest who gave the Cross of Cong to the National Museum in 1839. The people of Cong did not approve of their famous Cross going to Dublin. Fr. Lavelle shared their sentiments. One day he went to the National Museum, broke the glass case surrounding the Cross of Cong, and walked off with the Cross, intending to bring it back to Cong. He was soon surrounded in the street by officials, and after protracted negotiations in his lodgings, which involved legal advisers, the Cross of Cong was handed back to the National Museum, where it has remained since. Fr. Lavelle figured prominently in the famous Galway Election of 1872, in which it was alleged that the Catholic clergy used undue influence and intimidation, and resulted in a Government Inquiry presided over by Judge Keogh. Fr. Lavelle was surprisingly quiet for the rest of his life, took no part in the Land League Campaign, and became very friendly with the Guinness family of Ashford Castle. He died on 17 November 1886 and was buried in Cong Abbey. The people of Cong erected a plaque in the church in memory of him. (It is at the back of the new church). The inscription on it reads: "Pray for the soul of Patrick Lavelle who in dark and evil days successfully fought the battle of faith and fatherland".

WILLIAM LARMINIE (1849-1900)

William Larminie, the poet and folklorist, was born in Castlebar, Co. Mayo, in August 1849, into a family descended from Huguenot emigrés. On graduating from Trinity College, Dublin, he became a civil servant and worked in the Indian Office in London. He retired without a pension in 1892, much to the annoyance of his mother, who did not approve of him leaving the security of the civil service. They both returned to Ireland and took up residence at the Prince of Wales Terrace, Bray, and William became a full time writer.

His published works include: *Fand and Other Poems* (1892); *West Irish Folk Tales and Romances* (1893); *The Development of English Metres* (1894);

Joannes Scotus Eriugena (1897); *Glanlua and Other Poems* (1899). He translated Joannes Scotus Eriugena's "De Divisione Naturae", but it was not published. He was the first to advocate the use of the assonance of Gaelic poetry in English.

William Larminie died in Bray on 19 January, 1900.

ANTONY MacDONNELL (1844-1925)

Antony Patrick MacDonnell was Lieutenant Governor of the United Provinces of Oudh and Agra in India, Under Secretary for Ireland at Dublin Castle, 1902-1907, and Baron MacDonnell of Swinford from 1908 to 1925. He was born at Shragh, near Charlestown, Co. Mayo, on 7 March 1844, and educated in Summerhill College and Queen's College, Galway. He joined the Indian Civil Service in 1864, and became an expert on the organisation of famine relief, about which he wrote *"Food-Grain Supply and Famine Relief in Bihar and Bengal"* in 1876. He was appointed Lieutenant-Governor of the United Provinces of Oudh and Agra in 1895, ruling over a population of forty million.

After his appointment in 1902 as permanent Under Secretary at Dublin Castle by George Wyndham (1863-1913), the Chief Secretary for Ireland, he made a major contribution to the drafting of the Wyndham Land Bill, which when passed became the most effective Land Act in transferring land from the landlords to the tenant farmers. Antony MacDonnell later served in Dublin Castle under Walter Long, James Bryce and Augustine Birrell, and helped draft the ill-fated Irish Council Bill, which proposed devolution. It was later withdrawn because of widespread opposition. Antony MacDonnell helped draft the University Act of 1908, which established The National University of Ireland and Queen's University, Belfast. He resigned in 1908, in disappointment with the failure of his devolution plan, and was created Baron MacDonnell of Swinford. He spoke frequently in the House of Lords on Irish and Indian problems, and chaired the Royal Commission on the Civil Service (1912-14). Antony MacDonnell died in London on 9 June 1925.

ARCHBISHOP JOHN MacHALE (1791-1881)

When Archbishop John MacHale died on 7 November 1881, he was ninety years of age, sixty-seven years a priest, fifty-six years a bishop, and the senior prelate of the Roman Catholic Church in the world. For over half a century he was the dominant figure in the West of Ireland, and a fearless champion of Ireland and its people. He campaigned enthusiastically for the abolition of the tithes, the repeal of the union with Britain, Catholic Emancipation, tenant rights, the amelioration of economic and social conditions, denominational education, and the promotion of the Irish language. The "Liberator", Daniel O'Connell (1775-1847), called him "The Lion of the Fold of Judah". Fellow county man, Michael Davitt, praised him for his "unwearied love for the Irish people, his unceasing efforts on their behalf, his high character and his personal worth". Rev. Fr. Jarlath Waldron P.P. Partry, in a lecture in Galway in December 1981, said: "Archbishop John MacHale was one of the greatest products of our race". There are some who are critical of many aspects of his career, especially the fact that he was instrumental in depriving a large section of a generation of an education. Whatever his failings may have been, he was certainly courageous, uncompromising, a lover of his country, and independent of power, honour, or purse.

BORN IN LAHARDAUN

John MacHale was born in the townland of Tobernaveen (in Gaelic Tobar Na Bhfiann, the well of the Fianna), near Lahardaun, in the parish of Addergoole, Co. Mayo, on 6 March 1791, the son of Pádraig Mór MacHale and Mary, née Mulkieran. Pádraig Mór was a farmer and inn keeper. John was baptised by Father James Conroy, P.P., Addergoole, for whom he later served Mass on numerous occasions. Gaelic was the main language in the MacHale home. John MacHale attended a local hedge school, and received lessons from a local scholar, Martin Callaghan. In 1798 he saw the French soldiers march through Lahardaun, and up the slopes of Barnageeha (the windy gap), on the side of Nephin, on their way from Ballina to Castlebar, where they defeated the British. The young MacHale later saw the remains of his beloved pastor, Fr. James Conroy, brought home to Lahardaun, after he had been hanged from a tree in Castlebar, on a charge of treason. John never forgot the deep emotion felt by him and the people of Lahardaun on Fr. Conroy's death.

MAYNOOTH

John MacHale later attended a classical school in Castlebar, run by Patrick Staunton, and in 1807 went to Maynooth as a clerical student. He was ordained on 26 July 1814 at the age of twenty-three. He was appointed a lecturer in theology in the college prior to his ordination, a post he held until 1820, when he was appointed Professor of Dogmatic Theology in Maynooth. In the 1820's he published a series of letters under the pseudonym "Hierophilus", in which he attacked proselytism, the tithe system, under which Catholics were obliged to contribute to the Church of Ireland, and appealed for Home Rule and Catholic Emancipation.

Pope Leo XII appointed Dr. MacHale Bishop of Maronia and Coadjutor Bishop of Killala in 1825, with the right of succession to the bishopric. He was consecrated bishop on 5 June 1825 in Maynooth College. Social and economic conditions in the diocese of Killala were terrible at the time, and there were few Catholic churches in the diocese. The new bishop visited every parish in the diocese within a short time, and in 1827 started the erection of St.Muredach's Cathedral in Ballina, which was opened in 1831. Bishop MacHale visited Rome in 1832, and was presented with a chalice for the new cathedral by Pope Gregory XVI, on whom he made a big impression. Dr. John MacHale became Bishop of Killala in May 1834 on the death of Bishop Waldron. He was well-known by then as an uncompromising nationalist.

TUAM

Bishop MacHale was one of three candidates nominated by the clergy of the Archdiocese of Tuam to fill the vacant see of Tuam, in June 1834, on the death of Archbishop Oliver Kelly. The British Government asked the Pope "not to appoint any agitating prelate Archbishop of Tuam". The Prime Minister, Lord Melbourne, sent an envoy to Rome to request the Pope not to appoint Dr. MacHale, "anybody but him". Pope Gregory XVI overruled the objections and appointed Bishop John MacHale Archbishop of Tuam. A huge crowd saw him off from Killala diocese on 14 October 1834. They followed him in procession to picturesque Pontoon, situated between Lough Conn and Lough Cullin, the boundary between the diocese of Killala and Tuam, where he was met by a congregation of priests and people from the diocese of Tuam. He then went to Castlebar, where he stayed overnight. The new Archbishop told a crowd in Castlebar that he would be: "the friend of the poor, the guardian of the orphan and the widow, the comforter of the afflicted, the scourge of the wrong doer, and the messenger of peace, uninfluenced by the smiles or the favours of the powerful". He reached Tuam on 16 October and received a tumultuous welcome.

ARCHBISHOP

Archbishop John MacHale carried out the duties of his office in a conscientious manner. He had a keen interest in the social conditions in each parish, and took a great delight in visiting parishes at Confirmation time, and on other occasions, on horseback. He was not content to confine himself to his own archdiocese, but exerted a big influence on all the important national issues of the day. On his appointment as Archbishop he continued to attack several aspects of British administration in Ireland in letters to Prime Ministers, ministers, members of Parliament, Rome, and in the public press. The national school system was introduced by Lord Stanley in 1831, but Archbishop MacHale opposed it, because of his fear of proselytism. He wanted a system of denominational education, and set up some schools in his diocese, staffed by christian brothers and nuns. The hedge school system survived longest in the diocese of Tuam. He opposed Sir Robert Peel's plan in 1845 for the establishment of three Queen's Colleges, to be sited at Galway, Cork, and Belfast, respectively, to provide non-denominational university education. He approved the establishment of a Catholic University in Dublin, but disagreed with the choice of Dr. John Henry Newman as its first Rector. The university was established in 1854. Archbishop MacHale opposed, with vigour, proselytism in his diocese, especially in Achill and Toormakeady. There was a period of bitter disagreement with Bishop Thomas Plunkett, the Anglican Archbishop of the United Diocese of Tuam, Killala and Achonry. Archbishop MacHale appointed Fr. Patrick Lavelle to Toormakeady in 1858, and he eventually defeated proselytism in that area.

Over the years Archbishop John MacHale and Archbishop Paul Cullen of Dublin disagreed on most issues, especially on the role of the priest in Irish society at that time.

The Great Famine of 1845-'49 was very severe in the Archdiocese of Tuam, and thousands died of starvation. Archbishop MacHale worked tirelessly during the famine period. He spent ten hours a day writing letters looking for help, acknowledging gifts, and helping his people in every way he could; it is said that he collected and distributed £80,000 during that period. He castigated the inertia of the British Government during the famine period in several public letters. The Archbishop was always a friend of the poor, and never turned a beggar away from his door.

The British Parliament passed the Ecclesiastical Titles Act in 1851, which made it penal for any ecclesiastic to use titles conferred by a foreign power. Shortly after the Bill was passed, Archbishop John MacHale attacked it in a public letter, and proudly signed the letter: "+John, Archbishop of Tuam". The Government decided not to prosecute, and the Act vanished into oblivion.

Archbishop John MacHale was a Gaelic scholar, an enthusiastic supporter of Irish culture, and regularly preached in Irish. He published a catechism and a prayer book in Irish, and translated the *Pentateuch, Homer's Iliad,* and many of *Thomas Moore's Melodies* into Irish. Dr. MacHale was one of four Irish prelates at the first Vatican Council, 1869-'70, and spoke at the Council against the promulgation of a decree on Papal Infallibility.

LAST YEARS

The last years of Archbishop MacHale were far from happy. He wanted his nephew, Dr. Thomas McHale, a professor at the Irish College in Paris, to succeed him, and bitterly opposed the appointment of Dr. John McEvilly, Bishop of Galway. Eventually, in 1877, Dr. McEvilly (1881-1902), a native of Louisburgh, Co. Mayo, was appointed as Coadjutor Bishop of Tuam by Pope Pius IX. In June 1879 a letter was published in *The Freeman's Journal,* signed by Archbishop MacHale, criticising the Land League meeting to be held in Westport. It is now generally believed that the letter was written by Dr. Thomas McHale, the Archbishop's nephew. Archbishop MacHale set up the first investigation into the Knock apparition, which took place on 21 August 1879. Dr. McEvilly moved to Tuam in August 1879, and took up residence in St. Jarlath's College.

Archbishop MacHale died on 7 November 1881. A banner was erected in Tuam which read: "Archbishop John MacHale, Ireland's greatest son, is dead". Two days later his mortal remains were laid to rest in the vault beneath the altar of St. Jarlath's Cathedral, Tuam. Monsignor D'Alton, in his History of the Archdiocese of Tuam, wrote: "It would have been better for his fame as well as for his peace of mind had he passed away a few years earlier. He had become almost a legendary figure, no longer in touch with living realities, and was made to appear out of sympathy with the movement led by Davitt and Parnell. And his peace of mind was sadly disturbed by the arrangements made for the government of his diocese in his closing years. He was a great man and a great ecclesiastic, without any doubt the greatest who had ever filled the throne of St. Jarlath".

Archbishop John MacHale celebrated the golden jubilee of his consecration as a bishop in June 1875. A white marble statue of the Archbishop, by the great Dublin sculptor John Henry Foley (1818-1874), subscribed for by the clergy of the Archdiocese, was erected outside Tuam Cathedral. The inscription on the statue reads: "Connacia Grata". (Connacht grateful). MacHale G.A.A. Park in Castlebar was named in his honour.

The Statue of Archbishop John MacHale outside St. Jarlath's Cathedral, Tuam.

JOHN MacBRIDE (1865-1916)

"I write it out in a verse —
Mac Donagh and Mac Bride
And Connolly and Pearse
Now and in time to be,
Wherever green is worn,
Are changed, changed utterly:
A terrible beauty is born".
W. B. Yeats.

The MacBride referred to by William Butler Yeats, in his poem, "Easter 1916", was a Mayoman, Major John Mac Bride, one of the sixteen leaders executed following the 1916 Easter Week Rising.

John MacBride was born in Westport, on 7 May 1865. His father Patrick, a native of Antrim, came to Westport in the late 1850's and became a merchant. Patrick MacBride died of typhus, at the age of thirty-five, just six months after the birth of his youngest son, John. (Another son, Joseph, was elected the first Sinn Féin deputy for West Mayo in 1918). John attended the Christian Brothers School in Westport. He worked for a while in a drapery shop, in Castlebar, and then went to Dublin to study medicine. He left college after a short time, and worked with Hugh Moore, a Dublin firm of chemists. In Dublin, MacBride joined the I.R.B.

EASTER 1916

John MacBride emigrated to London, and went from there to South Africa. When the Boer War started in 1899, he joined an Irish Brigade against the British, and became second in command, with the rank of major. Michael Davitt resigned his Mayo seat in the British House of Commons in 1900, in protest against the Boer War. Some friends in Westport and Arthur Griffith nominated John MacBride, then fighting in the Boer War, as a candidate in the by-election. The United Irish League nominated John O'Donnell, who easily won the seat. After the war, John MacBride went to Paris, where he married Maud Gonne on 21 February 1903. Maud Gonne (1866-1953) was the daughter of an English army officer of Irish descent, and an English mother. She became a prominent Irish revolutionary. John MacBride and Maud Gonne had one child, Seán, who was born in January 1904. John returned to Dublin, and secured a job with Dublin Corporation.

John MacBride offered his services to Thomas MacDonagh on Easter Monday 1916, and was second in command in Jacobs biscuit factory during the rising. He was captured after the rising, court-martialled, sentenced to death, and executed in Kilmainham Jail, on 5 May 1916.

He was buried in Arbour Hill, Dublin. On 4 August 1963, Éamon de Valéra unveiled a plaque on the house at the Quay in Westport in which John MacBride was born.

GEORGE MOORE (1852-1933)

George Augustus Moore, the famous novelist and art critic, was born at Moore Hall, Ballyglass, Co. Mayo, on 24 February 1852. His father was George Henry Moore (1810-1870), and his mother the former Mary Blake from Ballinafad. George Henry was a benevolent landlord, a racehorse owner, and an M.P. for Mayo. He was responsible for the erection of Carrownacon church, and according to local tradition none of his tenants died from want during the Great Famine 1845-1849.

George Augustus was sent to Oscott College, near Birmingham, in 1861. He did not like Oscott, and would have preferred to be at Moore Hall with his father's horses and to have become a jockey. George left Oscott when he was sixteen and returned to Moore Hall. Two years later, he consented to join the army. The family took a house in Kensington, London, to facilitate George Henry who was a Westminister M.P. at the time.

A tenant dispute took place in 1870, and George Henry returned to Moore Hall to deal with the problem, where he died suddenly. The death of his father changed the career plans of George Augustus. He decided to become a painter and went to Paris, while his mother remained in London. He met the avant-garde Impressionist group in Paris, and became very friendly with Édouard Manet. George soon discovered that he had not got the ability to become a painter, and returned to London with the intention of becoming a writer.

WRITER

George became a prolific writer. His first novel was *"A Modern Lover"* (1883), followed by *"A Drama in Muslin"*, *"A Mummer's Wife"*, and *"Esther Waters"*, which earned him considerable acclaim. He wrote many articles on the Impressionists, which made him a leading art-critic. He wrote: *"Confessions of A Young Man"* in 1888, *"Evelyn Innes"* in 1898, *"Sister Teresa"* in 1901, and *"Reminisences of the Impressionist Painters"* in 1906. Moore went to live in Dublin at 4 Ely Place in 1901, because of his opposition to the Boer War and his attraction to the emerging Irish Literary Renaissance. He soon became friendly with the leading Irish literary figures of that time, William Butler Yeats, George Russell, Lady Gregory, Oliver St. John Gogarty, John Millington Synge and Edward Martyn of Tulira Castle, in Galway, his first cousin. He helped to plan the Abbey Theatre. He published *"The Untilled Field"* in 1903, and *"The Lake"* in 1905. His masterpiece was *"Hail and Farewell"*, (Ave, 1911; Salve, 1912; Vale, 1914), in part an autobiographical trilogy with an account of the Irish Literary Revival and his assessment of its key characters, W. B. Yeats, George Russell and Lady Gregory. Moore disliked the Irish people, their politics, and their religion. He left Ireland in 1911 and afterwards lived at 121 Ebury Street, London, until his death. He never married. He wrote: *"The Brook Kerith"* (1916), *"A Story-Teller's Holiday"* (1918), *"Héloise and Abéland"* (1921), *"Conversations in Ebury Street"* (1924), *"The Pastoral Loves of Daphnis and Chloe"* (1924), and *"Ulick and Soracha"* in 1926.

George received a letter on 1 February 1923 from a friend, James O'Reilly, a steward on the Moore Hall Estate, informing him that Moore Hall had been burned. The burning took place during the Civil War. The estate was managed by Maurice Moore, a brother of George's, who had become a senator.

DEATH

George Moore died at 121 Ebury Street, London, on 21 January 1933. His cremated remains were brought to Mayo for interment on Castle Island, in Lough Carra, which was owned by the Moore Hall Estate. The urn was placed in a cavity cut in solid rock on Castle Island.

George Russell ("AE") wrote the oration, which was delivered by Richard Best. Part of it read:

> "He loved the land even if he did not love the nation. Yet his enmities even made his nation to be as much admired or loved as the praise of its patriots. If his ashes have any sentience they will feel at home here, for the colours of Lough Carra remained in his memory when many of his other affections had passed. It is possible that the artist's love of earth, rock, water and sky is an act of worship. It is possible that faithfulness to art is an acceptable service. That worship, that service were his. If any would condemn him for a creed of their's he had assailed, let them be certain first, that they laboured for their ideals as faithfully as he did for his".

A small granite cross was erected over a square granite plaque. The inscription on the cross reads "George Moore, Born 1852 Moore Hall, Died London 1933".

JOHN MOORE (1763-1799)

John Moore was appointed President of the Republic of Connacht on 31 August 1798, after General Humbert (1755-1833) captured Castlebar following the French landing in Killala Bay. It was an honour he held for one week.

John Moore was born in Alicante, in Spain, the son of George Moore, (1729-1799), and Catherine de Kilikelly, (originally Kelly), a Galway girl, who went to Spain with her father as a child. George, a native of Ashbrook, Strade, Co. Mayo, became very successful in the wine trade in Spain, returned to Mayo in 1792 and built Moore Hall overlooking Lough Carra. During their years in Spain, George and Catherine enjoyed life and considered themselves part of the Spanish aristocracy of the time. Their five children, two of whom died young, were born in Spain.

John, the eldest, was a problem child, and a very big disappointment to his parents. He was sent to school at Liege, but had little interest in education. After enrolling in the University of Paris to study Arts he went to London, with his younger brother George (1770-1840), to study law. He made little progress and drifted aimlessly for a few years. John did not like any kind of work. He eventually arrived in Dublin with the intention of studying for the Bar, but soon became involved with the Irish Republican

Movement, and abandoned his legal studies. On hearing that the French had landed in Killala, John Moore travelled to Mayo and joined General Humbert in Castlebar, much to the annoyance of his parents.

"PRESIDENT OF THE REPUBLIC OF CONNACHT"

After the French forces had routed the English in Castlebar, John Moore was appointed "President of the Republic of Connacht" on 31 August 1798. A week later he was captured by the English and imprisoned. George Moore did everything he could on behalf of his son, despite his acute embarrassment. A legal battle developed, between the military and civil authorities, about who should try the case. Denis Browne of Westport offered his services to the Government as Chief Prosecutor. John Moore was kept in prison for over a year and dragged from one court to another, and escaped execution, due partly to the intervention of the influential Whig historian Sir James Mackintosh, a close friend of George Moore, John's brother. A courtmartial sat to consider the case in November 1798, but it had to be adjourned because of the poor state of the his health. He was tried eventually and sentenced to transportation in November 1799. John Moore's health deteriorated considerably during his imprisonment. He was taken to Duncannon, on the Wexford side of Waterford harbour, to await a ship, and died in the Royal Oak Tavern there on 6 December 1799, while being kept under guard. He was buried two days later in Ballygunnon cemetery, outside Waterford city. On 13 August 1961 John Moore's remains were exhumed, and re-interred in a grave in the Mall, Castlebar, beside the 1798 Memorial.

DELIA MURPHY (1902-1971)

Delia Murphy was the ballad queen of Ireland during the nineteen thirties, forties, and fifties, and was responsible for the revival and popularisation of Irish folk songs. During her career she recorded nearly four hundred songs, the best known of which are: "If I Were a Blackbird", "Dan O'Hara", "The Moonshiner", "The Spinning Wheel", "Three Lovely Lassies from Bannion", "Coortin in the Kitchen", "Boston Burglar", and the "Connemara Cradle Song". Delia Murphy was part of the fabric of Irish life during her singing career, and encapsulated in her songs the values of the Mayo of her childhood. She sang about ordinary people, their problems, pleasures, and values, with love, affection and sincerity. On the stage, especially, she had a rivetting presence; Delia was a real trouper who had the inborn ability to put a song across. She told our contributor Fr. Waldron what the great John McCormack said to her:

"It takes a hundred things to make a singer, and a voice is only one of them. 'Deelyeen' you haven't the voice but, my God, you have the other ninety nine"!

ROUNDFORT

Delia Murphy was born on 16 February 1902, at Claremorris, Co. Mayo,

283

after her parents had returned from the U.S.A., where her father, John, had worked in the Klondike goldmines in Colorado. John Murphy was a native of Hollymount, and on his return to Ireland purchased Mount Jennings House, in the parish of Roundfort, and forty hectares of land. The family took up residence at Mount Jennings, a few weeks after Delia's birth. Delia had seven sisters and one brother. She attended Gortskehy national school for four years, and completed her primary schooling at Roundfort N.S. As a child, Delia came to know and love the folk culture around her, and was a frequent visitor to a local tailor, John Mooney, a blacksmith, Michael Cunningham, and to some travelling people, who were camped near her home. She had a keen interest in local lore and ballads, and showed an early capacity in music. After her secondary education at the Dominican Convent, Eccles Street, Dublin, she attended University College Galway, and graduated with a Bachelor of Commerce degree. She met Thomas Joseph Kiernan, then Inspector of Taxes in Galway and a part-time lecturer in U.C.G., who lectured to Delia's class in economics. They met socially one evening at a guesthouse in Salthill, where there was a birthday party. Delia was asked to sing, and he agreed to accompany her on the piano, which he played well. They started going out together, and were married in January 1924 in the University Chapel at St. Stephen's Green, Dublin. Thomas J. Kiernan was a first-class honours graduate from U.C.D., and later obtained a Ph.D. degree in economics from the London School of Economics.

SINGER

Thomas J. Kiernan was appointed First Secretary of the Irish High Commission in London in 1824. He and Delia lived in London from 1924 until 1935. Their four children were born in London, Blon (December 1924), Nuala (October 1928), Colm (November 1931), and Orla (July 1933). Delia sang at numerous parties and receptions, and became a close friend of John McCormack, the great tenor. Delia Murphy sang the Irish song "Una Bhán", at the request of John McCormack, in the London Studio of musician Herbert Hughes. A representative of H.M.V., who was present, was very impressed, and invited Delia to make recordings of some Irish ballads. She recorded nearly a hundred songs, and within a short time was top of the Top Twenty in Ireland. Her songs were broadcast regularly on the B.B.C., and many comperes there referred to her as "Our Delia".

The family moved back to Dublin in 1935, and Dr. Kiernan was appointed Director of Broadcasting in Radio Éireann. During the following fifteen years, Delia Murphy sang in concerts all over Ireland and became one of the most requested singers on Radio Éireann. She wrote, collected, and sang Irish ballads, with great feeling, love and kindness. Many of Delia's songs were women's songs, and she was an early champion of the rights of women. Dr. Kiernan was appointed Irish Ambassador to the Vatican in 1941. Delia and all the family went with him. They lived in Rome until 1946, when Dr. Kiernan was appointed the first

Irish Ambassador to Australia. He went as Irish Ambassador to Germany in 1955, to Canada in 1957, and to the United States of America in 1961. Delia went with him to each country, which she felt was her duty. Despite being the wife of an eminent ambassador, Delia Murphy retained her simplicity, humility, wit and charm, and her life-long love for the folk ballads of her country.

DEATH

Delia Murphy performed in Ireland, England, Italy, Australia, Canada and America.

She appeared once on Irish television, in January 1971 on Gay Byrne's 'Late Late Show'. She died suddenly in February 1971, and was buried in Deansgrange cemetery, Dublin. The inscription on her grave reads:

> "Dr. T. J. Kiernan 1897 — 1967
> Delia Murphy Kiernan 1902 — 1971
> May They Rest in Peace".

A memorial to Delia Murphy was unveiled at Annefield, Killeen's Cross, in what was once her fathers land, on Saturday 25 April 1982, by R.T.E. presenter Donnacha Ó Dúlaing, the compere of the popular radio programme "Highways and Byeways". The members of the committee responsible for the erection of the memorial, under the leadership of Rev. Fr. Éamon Concannon, were: Rev. W. Walsh P.P. Roundfort, Doreen Hennelly, Bridie Varley, Mary McGovern, Jody Brennan, Paddy Tierney, Sonny Hession, John Hession, Pádraig Nolan and Michael Mellett. The site for the memorial was donated by Paddy Tierney.

The Delia Murphy Memorial in Roundfort.

285

P. W. NALLY (1856-1891)

The Nally Stand in Croke Park is called after a Mayoman, Patrick W. Nally. In his youth, P. W. Nally was a brilliant athlete. He became involved in Fenian activities, was imprisoned, and died in mysterious circumstances in Mountjoy Jail.

Patrick W. Nally was born in Rockstown House, near Balla, on 13 March 1856, the eldest son of a prosperous farmer. As a youth he showed exceptional athletic ability, and won several prizes at athletic events around Mayo from 1875 to 1879. P. W. Nally met Michael Cusack (1847-1906) in Dublin in September 1879. Both discussed the state of Irish athletics and agreed to do something about it. Nally went home to Mayo and organised the National Athletic Sports of Mayo, with Charles Stewart Parnell as Patron. They were held on a field owned by Nally's father in Balla, and all competitions were open. They were most successful, and a similar event was held in 1880, at which Nally himself competed and won a number of competitions. He was extremely interested in forming a national athletics organisation. The success of the two athletic events organised by Nally helped set in motion the forces which led to the establishment of the Gaelic Athletic Association, in Hayes Hotel, Thurles, on 1 November 1884.

THE NALLY STAND

When the Mayo Land League was formed on 16 August 1879, in Castlebar, P. W. Nally was elected as joint secretary. He was not present at the meeting and subsequently declined to act. P. W. Nally had strong Fenian views from childhood. In the late 1870's he became the leading organiser of the Irish Republican Brotherhood in Connacht, and by 1880 was a member of its supreme council. His Fenian activities forced him to go "on the run" in 1880. He spent 1880 and 1881 in England, and returned to Ireland in 1882. He was arrested at the end of 1883, for participation in, what became known as, the Crossmolina conspiracy, and was sentenced to ten years penal servitude. During his imprisonment, P. W. Nally was offered bribes and pardon to give evidence to the "Times Commission" that Parnell was involved with the Fenians. His reply was: "not all the gold or honours that the Queen could bestow would induce Patrick Nally to become a traitor". Owing to his good conduct in prison, it was decided to release him on 27 November 1891. He died in Mountjoy Jail on 9 November 1891. The official cause of death was recorded as typhoid fever, but it was widely believed at the time that he died a victim of foul play. The funeral to the MacManus plot in Glasnevin cemetery on 15 November was huge, and his coffin was draped with the same flag which had draped the coffin of Charles Stewart Parnell, just a month before. The entire Central Council of the G.A.A. marched behind the coffin. A Celtic Cross was erected to his memory in Balla, and unveiled in January 1900 by Dr. Mark Ryan, London.

Patrick Mullaney, a native of Balla and the Mayo delegate on the Central Council of the G.A.A., was responsible for having the new stand in Croke Park called after Patrick W. Nally in 1953.

JOHN O'HART (1824-1902)

John O'Hart, the genealogist, was a native of Crossmolina, Co. Mayo. His ambition was to become a priest, but a series of family difficulties prevented him from persevering.

He joined the Royal Irish Constabulary, but left after two years to take up a position as a school teacher with the Commissioners of National Education.

He published *"Irish Pedigrees"* (2 Vols., 1876) and its supplement *"The Irish and Anglo-Irish Landed Gentry when Cromwell came to Ireland"* (1884).

ERNIE O'MALLEY (1898-1957)

Ernest Bernard O'Malley, the writer and revolutionary, was born in Castlebar in 1898. His family moved to Dublin when he was a child. He became a medical student, and had a minor part in the 1916 Easter Week Rising. He took an active part in the "War of Independence" and was wounded several times. By July 1921, he had risen from the rank of volunteer to officer commanding the second southern division of the I.R.A. He was director of organisation on the anti-treaty side in the Civil War, during which he was also wounded. After his capture, he was sentenced to death, but later reprieved. When in prison he was elected to Dáil Éireann. On his release from jail, he left Ireland, and eventually arrived in America. Ernie O'Malley broadcast several times on Radio Éireann and on B.B.C., and was the author of *"On Another Man's Wound"* and *"The Singing Flame"*, which describe his experiences. He was elected to the Irish Academy of Letters in 1947. Ernie O'Malley died at Howth, Co. Dublin, in March 1957.

GRACE O'MALLEY (c. 1530-1600)

Grace O'Malley was the legendary sea-queen of the west during the second half of the sixteenth century. She was born in West Mayo about the year 1530. Her father was Owen (Dubhdarra) O'Malley, chieftain of the barony of Murrisk, and her mother Margaret, daughter of Conchobhar Óg mac Conchobhair Mic Maoilseachloinn, a branch of the O'Malley clan.

Grace's interests were ships, trade, politics and power. On her father's death she made herself ruler of the district around Clew Bay.

At the age of sixteen Grace married Donal O'Flaherty, who ruled over a large part of Connemara. He owned Bunowen Castle, where they lived for some time. They had two sons, Owen and Murrough, and one daughter, Margaret. Grace became involved in both initiating and settling tribal disputes, and attacking merchant ships en route to Galway. She controlled the O'Malley clan's trading missions to Munster, Ulster, Scotland, Spain and Portugal. She engaged in pirating lucrative cargo, and levying tolls in return for safe passage through her domain.

Grace married Richard Burke, chief of the Mayo Burkes, in 1566, and they resided at Rockfleet Castle, situated on an inlet of Clew Bay. They had two sons Donal and Tibbot na Long. (Tibbot na Long was created first Viscount Mayo in 1627 by Charles I.)

Rockfleet Castle was attacked on instructions from Edward Fitton, first Governor of Connacht, on 8 March 1574, because of complaints from Galway merchants about Grace's activities in Clew Bay. Grace O'Malley and her followers defeated the invaders. She submitted to Sir Henry Sidney in 1576, but it did not effect her activities.

While plundering the lands of the Earl of Desmond in 1577, Grace was captured and imprisoned for eighteen months in Limerick gaol and Dublin Castle. Richard Burke died in 1583 and Grace claimed all his property.

She refused to submit to Sir Richard Bingham, Governor of Connacht, in 1583, and was arrested, but later released. She visited Queen Elizabeth I in London in 1593.

Grace O'Malley died in the year 1600 and, according to tradition, was buried in the O'Malley Tomb in the Carmelite friary on Clare Island. Anne Chambers, a native of Castlebar, published *"Granuaile – The Life and Times of Grace O'Malley"* in 1979.

FR. PATRICK PEYTON

Fr. Patrick Peyton, "the Rosary Priest", has brought his message about the importance of family prayer to the five continents. His message is simple: "A world at prayer is a world at peace". He has preached at enormous rallies all around the world, and organised hundreds of radio and television programmes. His faith in Mary, the Mother of God, his sincerity, dedication and humility, have influenced millions around the world.

Most Rev. Dr. Thomas Flynn, Bishop of Achonry, in a tribute to Fr. Peyton said: "Father Peyton is one of the best known missionaries of our day. At a time when the stability and sanctity of family life are under attack, he has focused attention on the need for prayer with his message that 'the family that prays together stays together'. With unfailing devotion to Mary he has travelled the world to make her known and has justly earned the title 'the Rosary Priest'. We are proud to claim him as a native son of the diocese of Achonry — one of our greatest".

Patrick Peyton was born on 9 January 1909, in the townland of Carracastle, in the parish of Attymass, County Mayo, the sixth child of John and Mary Peyton. John owned a small farm, and was in poor health. Most of the farm chores were done by his wife, Mary (formerly Gilliard, from Rathreedane, Bonniconlon), and family. John and Mary had four sons and five daughters. John Peyton was a devout Catholic, and observed an inflexible rule that the rosary was said by all the family together every evening. That nightly scene was Patrick Peyton's earliest memory and his most abiding. Patrick Peyton started in Bofield national school, Attymass, in May 1914, where his first teacher was Marie Loftus. He spent a short time in Bonniconlon national school and finished his schooling in Ireland with fifty-two days in Currower national school. Patrick desired to become a priest, but due to family circumstances was unable to continue his schooling.

EMIGRATION

Patrick and his brother Thomas decided to emigrate in 1927 to their three sisters, Beatrice, Nellie, and Mary, in America. They left Carracastle on 13 May 1928 and travelled by train from Ballina to Cobh. They arrived in Scranton, Pennsylvania, and stayed with their sister, Nellie. Tom obtained a job in a coal mine and Patrick became sexton of St. Peter's Church, Scranton. Patrick soon realised that he had a vocation and discussed his feelings with Monsignor Kelly of St. Peter's. He went back to school at St. Thomas's Christian Brothers, and Monsignor Kelly took care of the tuition fees. Tom left the coal mine and took over Patrick's job as sexton. Within a few weeks Tom decided to become a priest, and joined Patrick in the Christian Brothers. Monsignor Kelly also took care of his tuition fees. Tom and Patrick did the work in St. Peter's between them, so as not to be a burden on their sisters. In the Spring of 1929 a group of Holy Cross priests from Notre Dame, Indiana, gave a mission in St. Peter's, and the Peyton boys decided to join them. Monsignor Kelly (d. 1934) in a letter of recommendation for Patrick to the Holy Cross superiors wrote: "I envy the community or the Bishop that finally gets him". Tom and Patrick went to the Holy Cross minor seminary, under the shadow of Notre Dame University, in Indiana, in August 1929. After three years they were admitted into St. Josephs Novitiate, at Notre Dame, and both graduated in 1937. Patrick opted for the foreign missions, a decision which led to him going to the Foreign Seminary, in Washington D.C., and Tom went to another seminary in Washington D.C. for students who intended to remain in the United States.

TUBERCULOSIS

Patrick contacted tuberculosis in the winter of 1938 in Washington D.C., and spent most of the following year in hospital. He was making little progress and decided to place his trust in Mary, the Mother of God. He prayed and prayed, and asked that he be restored to health. His prayers were answered and he was released from hospital, in February 1940, a cured man.

Patrick had lost a years study, but in May 1941, a month before Tom's ordination, a cablegram arrived from Rome, which read: "Special dispensations are granted for the immediate ordination to the priesthood of seminarian Patrick Peyton". Patrick was thrilled. He emigrated from Ireland with Tom, studied with him, and in his heart wanted to be ordained with him. On 15 June 1941 Tom and Patrick Peyton were ordained priests, in the Church of the Sacred Heart at Notre Dame. It was a long journey from Carracastle to that day in Notre Dame, and Fr. Patrick Peyton tells us in his autobiography, *"All for Her "*, "at Notre Dame that day I gave my heart and soul in love to Mary. I promised her all the merit of my priesthood until death. The merit and the glory of every action I would ever perform would be hers and hers alone" (p. 85)

FAMILY ROSARY CRUSADE

Fr. Patrick, after spending a further year in the seminary to make up for the year he was sick, was assigned as chaplin to the Holy Cross Brothers at the Vincentian Institute, Albany, New York. It was decided that he should not go on the missions because of his illness. He decided, with the full approval of his superiors, to launch a national crusade to promote the family rosary, and started to give triduums all over the United States. The crusade was supported by bishops and Catholic organisations in the States. He started a radio programme in Albany to say the rosary over the air, which was most successful. Fr. Peyton and his helpers wrote thousands of letters enlisting support, and sought a national network for family prayer. Edgar Kobak, President of the Mutual Broadcasting Company, in New York, and the director of religious programmes, Elsie Dick, gave a half hour free time for such a programme. Fr. Peyton and his friends, including Bing Crosby, organised an excellent programme based on the rosary, and was broadcast nationwide on Mothers Day 1945. Fr. Peyton then secured the services of many film stars for a series of radio programmes, "Family Theatre of the Air", and help from advertising agencies, business executives, and Catholic organisations. Fr. Peyton paid a short visit to Ireland in 1946 and preached at Knock on 15 August. "The Family Theatre of the Air" was transmitted over the Mutual Network for the first time on 13 February 1947. The programme was a success, and ran weekly for almost ten years.

After launching his Family Rosary Crusade at the Marian Congress, in Ottawa in 1947, he spoke at rallies all around the United States, Canada, the Philippines, England, Ireland, Spain, Australia, New Zealand, Kenya, India and Latin America. Everywhere the crowds were huge. A crowd of approximately one and a half million heard Fr. Peyton speak in Rio De

Janeiro in 1962. The Family Rosary Crusade girdled the earth. Meanwhile, Fr. Peyton continued to give triduums around the United States, and organised the making and transmission of television programmes on each of the fifteen decades of the rosary, which were financed by various groups, chiefly converts. The programmes were very successful. Pope Pius XII described the fifteen rosary films as: "a massive undertaking that has been achieved with distinction".

Fr. Peyton received the Cross, "Pro Ecclesia et Pontifice", the highest award the Church can give a member of a religious congregation, in 1965.

ANTHONY RAFTERY (c. 1784-1835)

Anthony Raftery was the last of the Gaelic bards. (1) Dr. Douglas Hyde (1860-1949), the founder of the Gaelic League and first President of the Republic of Ireland, described Raftery as "the most remarkable man of whom he found traces in the West of Ireland". Most Irish people have some knowledge of Raftery from their school days, especially the poem about himself:

> "Mise Raifterí an file,
> Lán dóchais is grá,
> Le súile gan solas,
> Le ciúneas gan crá.
>
> Ag dul siar ar m'aistear,
> Le solas mo chroí,
> Fann agus tuirseach
> Go deireadh mo shlí.
>
> Féach anois mé,
> Is mo chúl le balla,
> Ag seinm ceoil,
> Do phócaí follamh". (2)

His poetry was not written down, but was memorised by his contemporaries in the region in which he wandered, chiefly the Gort/Loughrea/Athenry district of County Galway. His poems became part of the folk memory of that region. Most of Raftery's poetry has been preserved for us, and for prosperity, by two great Irish patriots, Lady Augusta Gregory (1852-1932) from Coole Park, Co. Galway, and Dr. Douglas Hyde. Dr. Douglas Hyde deserves the major share of the credit for immortalising the man he affectionately called "My Raftery". In 1903 he published thirty-five poems ascribed to Raftery in Gaelic, with English translations and background information, in *"Songs Ascribed to Raftery"*, being the fifth chapter of *"The Songs of Connacht"*. He published a second edition in 1933.

THE BARD FROM KILLEDAN

Anthony Raftery was born in the townland of Killedan, near Kiltamagh, Co. Mayo, in the year of 1784. (3) No trace of his home remains. The field where he was born is near Lisard, at the back of Killedan House. His father was a cottier, with less than one acre of land. His mother's maiden name was Brennan. Raftery immortalised his native townland in his most memorable poem, *"Conntae Mhaigh Eo"*:

"Cill Aodáin an baile a bhfásann gach ní ann.
Tá sméara súchraobh ann is meas ar gach sórt,
is dá mbeinnse im sheasamh i gceartlár mo dhaoine
D'imeodh an aois díom is bheinn arís óg".

There is a tradition in the parish of Bohola that Raftery attended the hedge school run by James McManus, in the townland of Toocanagh, for a short time. At the age of nine he had smallpox, which did not disfigure his face, but left him completely without sight. ("Le súile gan solas"). It was a traumatic experience for him. He began to learn to play the fiddle and violin, but never became a good musician. He was a regular visitor to Killedan House, then owned by the local landlord, Frank Taafe. One day Raftery was at a party in Killedan House and the drink got scarce. A servant was asked to take a horse and go to Kiltamagh for more drink. The servant asked Raftery to take another horse and go with him, which he did. According to local tradition, Raftery's horse fell at a sudden turning in the road, and broke it's neck. Raftery escaped uninjured. Frank Taafe was very angry when he heard the news, and banished Raftery from Killedan. Whether that story is true or not, Anthony Raftery left County Mayo and went to County Galway. Raftery was completely blind and penniless when he arrived in County Galway.

GALWAY

Anthony Raftery spent the rest of his life wandering the roads of south Galway, visiting house after house, bringing news of the happenings of the day, reciting his poems, playing the fiddle, drinking and talking about his experiences. He regularly played at dances at Kiltartan Cross on Sunday evenings. He had no formal education in Galway, but Lady Gregory records that he regularly had books read out to him, and that he did attend some classes in a hedge school in Ballylee, Co. Galway. He did marry, and had a son and daughter, but he and his wife became estranged. Raftery had no permanent home. Lady Gregory was told that Raftery spent three months in Galway Jail for composing a song against the Protestant Church. In his poetry, he scorned those who did not help him, and praised those who did. He was greedy for money, and never forgot to rattle the plate after a dance. People were afraid of him, because they believed that it was unlucky to be mentioned in his poems. An old woman in Gort Workhouse, who knew Raftery, told Lady Gregory that "Raftery would run people down, he was someway bitter, and if he had anything against a person he'd give him a great lacerating". He was small in stature, but very strong.

ORAL TRADITION

Raftery could not write, but fortunately his poems were preserved in the oral tradition by the people of South Galway for years. A few people in the area recorded his poetry in manuscripts, most of which were later collected by Lady Gregory and Douglas Hyde. Some of Raftery's poetry was undoubtedly lost. Lady Gregory collected what survived in the oral tradition of her locality. Douglas Hyde collected and collated the manuscripts. Their search for all manuscripts and folk memories of Raftery started around 1893. The most important manuscript, containing twenty-two poems, was located by Lady Gregory. It was written by Michael Kelly, a stone-cutter from Killeeneen, Co. Galway. (It is now in the Torna Collection in U.C.C.) Lady Gregory got the manuscript from another stone-cutter, Patrick Daly, Craughwell, (d. 1924), a relation of Michael Kelly. Other poems were collected from: Owen Ó Neachtáin, Galway (eight), Fr. Clement O'Looney, Loughrea, (five), Mr. Glynn, Tuam, Mr. Meehan, Thomas Hynes (oral), Thady Connlan, Killedan (Contae Mhaigh Eo), Francis O'Connor, James O'Mulloy and from a few others. There were also twenty poems in the Royal Irish Academy, Dublin, most of which were also in Michael Kelly's collection. Hyde started publishing Raftery's poems and translations as early as 1893, in *'Love Songs of Connacht'*, and the complete edition was published in 1903. Hyde acknowledged the big debt he owed to Lady Gregory, and dedicated his first collection of Raftery's poetry to her: 'I dedicate this book to Lady Gregory of Coole with great esteem and with gratitude', and in a verse wrote:

> "O noble lady, O patron of the poets
> Who lives far West in Coole of the dense high woods,
> Since you saved the fame of my Raftery from death
> I humbly offer you this reward from my hand!"

Douglas Hyde also wrote a play about Raftery — *'An Pósadh'*. (Thady Connlon gave "Killedan" or "Contae Mhaigh Eo" to the novelist Lottie McManus, Killedan, who gave it to Douglas Hyde. The McManus family had purchased Killedan House from the executors of Frank Taafe).

POEMS

Anthony Raftery composed poems about Irish history, contemporary events, pretty women, in praise of generous patrons, and about himself. Lady Gregory in her book, *"Poets and Dreamers"*, observed that Irish history at the time had been to a great extent learned from Raftery's poems by the people of Mayo and Galway. She also suggested that his stories and poems were so memorable that they displaced the folk tradition of the old stories of the Fianna. Douglas Hyde wrote:

"This blind man was a power in the country spurring the people against the payment of tithes and urging them against their enemies".

Raftery's chief historic poems were:

O'Connell's Victory

(Bua Uí Chonaill — about Daniel O'Connell's election victory in Clare).

293

The Galway Election	(Ar Election na Gaillimhe).
The Whiteboys	(Na Buachaillí Bána).
The Catholic Rent	(An Cíos Catliceach).

and, especially, The History of, (or Dispute with), the Bush, (An Seanchus (nó Caismirt) na Sceiche.

His chief love poems were:

Mary Hynes	(Máire Ní hEidhin).
Breedyeen Vesey	(Brídín Bhéasaidh).
Peggy Mitchell	(Peigí Mistéall).
Mary Staunton	(Máire Stanton).
Nancy Walsh	(Neansaí Breathnach).

The other poems published by Douglas Hyde were:

Lament for O'Kelly	(Caoineadh Uí Cheallaigh).
Patrick O'Donnellan	(Pádraig Ó Domhnalláin).
The Drunkard's Dispute with the Whiskey	(Caismirt leis an Uisce-Beatha).
The False Witness	(An Fhianaise Bhréagach).
The Wife of the Red-Haired Man	(Bean an Fhir Rua).
The Weaver	(An Fíodóir).
Barney Richard	(Bearnán Ristéard).
The Cholera Morbus	(An Cholera Morbus).
I am Raftery	(Mise Raifterí).
Anthony O'Daly	(Antoine Ó Dálaigh).
The Wedding at Shlahaun Mór	(Bainis an tSleáthain Mhóir).
The Drowning of Annaghdown	(Anach Dhúin — about the drowning tragedy in Lough Corrib in September 1828).
Lament for Thomas O'Daly	(Caoine ar Tomás Ó Dálaigh).
Ballinhevna	(Béal-Átha-na-hAibhne).
Father Leeam	(An tAthair Uilliam).
The God whose name was Jupiter	(An Dia dar b'ainm Jupitér).
John Conroy	(Seán Conroid).
William O'Kelly	(Uilliam Ó Ceallaigh).
Raftery's Repentance	(Aithrí Raifterí),

his confessions, in which he relates his wrong-doings, and asks God for forgiveness before taking him from the world.

His best known poem in Mayo is, of course, Contae Mhaigh Eo, which, according to folklore, was composed either to make peace with Frank Taafe, or to praise Mayo better than another poet could praise Galway.

DEATH

Anthony Raftery died on 24 December 1835, in the home of Diarmuid Cloonan, one kilometre from Craughwell village, Co. Galway. He received absolution, and was anointed by a local priest, Father Nagle. According to local folklore, Raftery had often stated that 'if God had a hand in it, it would be Christmas Day he'd die'. Timber was purchased by a few locals, and the coffin was made by a man from the village on St. Stephen's Day. The grave was dug on St. Stephen's Day in Killeeneen cemetery, but a big stone in the grave delayed the burial until that night. A local lady sent out two lighted mould candles. There was a sharp breeze blowing, but it never quenched the candles, and according to local folklore that showed that the Lord had a hand in it. The grave was completed that night, and Anthony Raftery was laid to rest near the gable end of the church in what is now known as Reilig na bFile, Killeeneen, just off the road from Craughwell to Kilcolgan, Co. Galway.

Anthony Raftery's tombstone in Killeeneen Cemetery.

TOMBSTONE

On the initiative of Lady Gregory a tombstone was erected over Raftery's grave in August 1900. Douglas Hyde tells us that it was Lady Gregory who thought of the idea "and it was upon her the cost, or most of it, fell". A ceremony was held at the grave on 26 August 1900 to mark the occasion, attended by many from the area and by Dr. Douglas Hyde, Lady Gregory, and Edward Martyn of Tulira Castle. The stone was made by Patrick Deely, Craughwell, who had years earlier collected the most valuable manuscript of Raftery's poems from Michael Kelly for Lady Gregory.

Anthony Raftery was treated very well by the hospitable people of south Galway during his lifetime; in death he has been idolised. Craughwell and surrounding areas regard him as one of their own. A statue of Raftery was erected in Craughwell in 1980 on the initiative of Galway historian, Rev. Fr. Martin Coen, Craughwell.

NOTES

1. In Gaelic Antoine Ó Reachtúra, Reaftaraí, Raifteirí nó Raifteri.

2. Translation:

"I am Raftery the Poet,
Full of hope and love,
With eyes that have no light,
With gentleness that has no misery.

Going west upon my pilgrimage
By the light of my heart,
Feeble and tired
To the end of my road.

Behind me now,
And my face to the wall,
A playing music
Unto empty pockets".

Douglas Hyde
Songs ascribed to Raftery p. 41.

3. 1784 is now generally accepted as the year of his birth.

4. Translation:

> "Killeadan (is) the village in which everything grows;
> There are blackberries and raspberries in it,
>   and fruit of every kind;
> And if I were only to be standing in the middle of
>   my people,
> The age would go from me and I should be young again". *Douglas Hyde.*

MARGARET BURKE SHERIDAN (1889-1958)

Margaret Burke Sheridan, the prima donna, is regarded as one of the greatest sopranos of all time. Her lovely voice charmed the crowds in the great opera houses of Europe, especially in La Scala, Milan, the Teatro Reale, Rome, the San Carlo, Naples, and Covent Garden, London. The memory of Margherita Sheridan is revered in Italy today. Seán T. Ó Ceallaigh, the second President of the Republic of Ireland (1882-1966), said in a tribute to her:

"In the history of music, the name of Margaret Burke-Sheridan is inseparably linked with the great names of Giacomo Puccini and Arturo Toscanini. In La Scala opera house in Milan, her triumphs are commemorated in bronze. The years she spent in Italy were, indeed, years of triumph succeeding triumph. She lived there in a glittering world of music and song and reigned in that world, a queen — the centre of admiration and applause".

CASTLEBAR

Margaret Burke Sheridan was born on the Mall, Castlebar, on 15 October 1889, the youngest in a family of seven. (There is a plaque on the actual house). Margaret Mary were the names given to her at Baptism, and some years later she used her father's second name, Burke, in his memory. She was only four when her mother and father died. She spent the following five years with a friend in Newtown, Castlebar. Canon Lyons P.P. Castlebar (1885-1911) arranged with Mother Peter McGrath, the prioress of the Dominican Convent, Eccles Street, Dublin, for Margaret to attend school there. Mother Clement, of Eccles Street Convent, gave Margaret her first music lessons. She showed exceptional musical talent and worked hard. After winning a gold medal at the Dublin Feis Ceoil in 1908, a sponsored concert was organised for her at the Theatre Royal in Dublin, and with the proceeds was sent to the Royal Academy of Music in London. Margaret met her godfather and family friend, T. P. O'Connor M.P., in London, who helped her in every way he could. Lady Randolph Churchill, mother of the future Prime Minister, Winston, also helped her. Margaret was a welcome artiste in the homes of many people in London. On one such occasion in 1911 she impressed the inventor of wireless-telegraphy, Guglielmo Marconi, who invited her to continue her career in Italy, and made the necessary arrangements.

ITALY

Margaret Burke Sheridan arrived in Rome to study under Martini and Emma Correlli. When Martini first heard her sing Madama Butterfly's entrance song, he said to her: "You have a wonderful voice, but you don't know the first thing about singing". Margaret worked hard at her singing, and within two years made her operatic debut in Rome, in La Constanzia. It was an immediate success, and she received a magnificent ovation. Arturo Toscanini, the great virtuoso conductor, heard her and invited her to sing Mimi in La Bohème. Margaret Burke Sheridan gave an outstanding performance, which led her to a long series of successful engagements in operas by Puccini. She made her debut in Covent Garden, London, in 1919, in the title role of Madama Butterfly. She returned to Italy and over the following sixteen years thrilled audiences with outstanding performances in operas by Puccini, Mascagni, Respighi and other composers. La Margherita Sheridan, as she was called in Italy, was a perfectionist and sought excellence in her art. She reached the zenith of her distinguished career with performances in the La Scala in Milan with Toscanini conducting. Pope Pius XI, when Archbishop of Milan, said: "heaven came very near when I heard her singing". When he became Pope he offered her the title Countess, but, with characteristic modesty and humility, she declined the honour. During her singing career in Italy, Margaret brought distinction not alone to herself but also to Ireland. She always stated that she was Irish and proud of it. When Terence Mac Swiney (1879-1920) died on hunger strike, at Brixton Prison on 24 October 1920, the San Carlo Opera House in Naples had to be closed, because it was announced:

"La Sheridan will not sing, her compatriot is dead". Margaret Sheridan never married. She was engaged to an Italian Count, but broke it off when she later heard that he was already married. Margaret had a severe illness in 1934 and lost confidence in her ability to attain her own high standards. She retired from singing in 1935 and returned to Dublin.

DIED

She went to America in 1950, on the invitation of the New York Foundation of Opera, to help in their search for talent. She made a few trips to America but never sang there. Margaret Burke Sheridan died in St. Vincent's Hospital, Dublin, on 16 April 1958. The Italian Ambassador to Ireland paid this tribute to Margaret Burke Sheridan on her death:

"She was a great friend of my country. Italy admired her and loved her. She was more than a prima donna, she was literally the first great lady of the opera houses in Rome, Milan and Naples. She made us the gift not only of her golden voice, but of her generous warm Irish heart. Toscanini and Puccini will ever be linked with her name."

She was buried in Glasnevin Cemetery.

MARTIN J. SHERIDAN (1881-1918)

Martin J. Sheridan, from Bohola, Co. Mayo, was arguably the most renowned athlete of our race. His achievements are not widely known in Ireland, because all his triumphs were won under the flag of his adopted country, the United States of America. During his illustrious career he excelled as a discus-thrower, in the high and long jumps, in the shot put and in the pole vault. He won nine Olympic medals, five gold, (four for the discus and one for the shot put), three silver and one bronze, a record for an Irish person. (That figure includes the medals he won at the 1906 Intercalated Olympiad, which was not an official Olympics.) King George of Greece erected Myron's famous statue of Discobolos (the discus-thrower of ancient Greece) in honour of Martin Sheridan in Athens Stadium, after the 1906 games. Martin won two gold medals in that 'Olympiad'. The King also presented him with a replica of the golden goblet used for coronation ceremonies in Greece. In addition to his Olympic triumphs, Martin Sheridan won twelve American Championships, thirty Canadian and Metropolitan titles, and three world all-round championships in 1906, 1907, and 1909. At an indoor meeting in Madison Square Garden, New York, in 1909, he achieved five firsts, two seconds, one third, and established two world records — a performance unequalled in the history of athletics.

Martin J. Sheridan was born in Bohola on 28 March 1881, the son of Martin Sheridan and Jane, nee Durkan from Swinford. Martin J. Sheridan attended Carrowgowan national school, and went to the Marist Brothers in Swinford for a short time. He was a very strong youth, and was able to easily win any local athletic event, or test of strength, with his own age group in Bohola. He also played Gaelic football and was a keen handballer. His brother, Richard, was also a good athlete, and won many events around Mayo, before emigrating to New York, where he joined the police force. Richard wrote regular letters to his parents, and gave glowing accounts of life in America. Martin was impressed and decided to emigrate. He bade farewell to his family and friends in Bohola, and left for America in March 1900. He went to his brother in New York, and soon secured a post in the New York police force.

OLYMPIC CHAMPION

Martin devoted all his spare time to athletics, and quickly won a reputation for himself as a discus-thrower. Within a year of his arrival in New York, Martin Sheridan established a world record with the discus. He won the discus event in the American championships in June 1904, with effortless ease, and was chosen as a member of the American team for the 1904 Olympic Games in St. Louis. Martin Sheridan won the discus event in the Olympics on 1 September 1904, with a new Olympic discus record, and became the first Mayoman to win an Olympic medal. Later that year he won the Canadian discus championship, came second in the shot and high jump, and turned in creditable performances in several other events. In 1905 he won the American All-Round Championship, a ten event athletic competition, and retained his Canadian discus title.

An Intercalated Olympiad was held in Athens in 1906, and Martin Sheridan was a member of the American team. The discus, the highlight of that Olympiad, was the traditional Grecian sport, going back to the days of the glory of ancient Greece. The Greeks regarded their national champion, Davidecas, as unbeatable. Martin Sheridan had other ideas. He astonished the huge crowd in the famous athletic stadium of historic Athens with his brilliance in winning the discus-throw, and established another world record. The crowd rose to acclaim the feat of the discus-thrower from Bohola. The following day, Martin Sheridan won his second gold medal, when he won the sixteen pound shot championship. He later won three silver medals in jumping events. The winning of two gold and three silver medals in the one Olympiad was an incredible performance. He arrived back in New York to a hero's welcome. The sports-writers of the day acclaimed him as the greatest track and field athlete of all time. In the 1906 games Martin Sheridan alone scored more points that all the athletes from the British Empire. Martin Sheridan won the American and Canadian discus championships in 1906, and retained them in 1907. He was a member of the American team for the 1908 Olympic games, which were held at Shepherd's Bush, London. Martin Sheridan won two more Olympic gold medals, in discus events, and a bronze medal in the long jump.

He went from London to Bohola, his first visit to his native parish since emigrating, where he was received like a king. He gave a series of exhibitions at Dundalk, Dungarvan, Dublin and Ballina. While in Bohola Martin left a vaulting pole to his parents, which he had received from the King of Greece after the Athens 'Olympics'. (That vaulting pole is now proudly displayed in Michael Clarke's licensed premises in Bohola alongside photographs and other records of the athlete). Martin Sheridan returned to America and regained his American and Canadian discus titles. A beautiful framed scroll of honour was presented to him in New York, which he sent home to his parents in Bohola, and is now a priceless treasure in the home of Michael and Margaret Sheridan, who live on the farm where the athlete was born.

MEMORIAL

Martin Sheridan was very successful in the New York police department, and was promoted to the rank of first grade detective. He never married. He contracted pneumonia in March 1918, and died, at the age of thirty-seven, in a New York hospital, and was buried in Calvary Cemetery, New York. A Celtic cross was erected over his grave. Part of the inscription on the cross reads: "Martin J. Sheridan, an intrepid American, an ardent lover of his motherland, a peerless athlete, devoted to the institutions of his country, and to the ideals and aspirations of his race". To perpetuate his memory the New York Police Department established the Martin J. Sheridan Award for Valour, and it is awarded each year to a member of the Police Department for bravery above and beyond the call of duty.

A memorial to Martin J. Sheridan was unveiled in Bohola, on 22 May 1966. The funds for it were raised in Bohola, Dublin and New York.

The people responsible for the erection of the memorial were as follows:

New York: Eugene R. McKenna, William J. Keary, Martin Killeen, Gene Tunney, (former heavyweight boxing champion of the world, whose parents came from Killedan), William O'Dwyer, John Feeney, James A. Fitzpatrick, Daniel Sheehy, Andrew J. Sheridan, (brother of the athlete);

Ireland: James V. Aitken, Éamon Mongey, Micheál Ó Cleirigh, Anthony Freney, John Forde, Francis Colgan, J. P. Roughneen, Liam O'Hora, Miko Clarke, John Walsh, A. O'Hora, J. Gavaghan, Joseph Colgan, Dr. A. Aitken, Mike Sheridan, Bernard Durkan, and Billy Durkan.

Some of Martin J. Sheridan's medals can be seen in the O'Dwyer Cheshire Home at Lismirrane, Bohola.

SOURCES

1. *A Dictionary of Irish Biography* by Henry Boylan
2. *All for Her: The Autobiography of Fr. Patrick Peyton C.S.C.*
3. *Davitt and Irish Revolution 1846-1882* by T. W. Moody.
4. Michael Davitt by T. W. Moody in *Leaders and Workers*. J. W. Boyle (Ed.)
5. *John Dillon: A Biography* by F. S. L. Lyons.
6. *John MacHale, Archbishop of Tuam* by Nuala Costello.
7. *History of the Archdiocese of Tuam.* Vol. 1 & 2. Rt. Rev. Monsignor D'Alton.
8. *Poets and Dreamers* by Lady Gregory.
9. *Songs Ascribed to Raftery* by Douglas Hyde.
10. *The Irish Landlord Since the Revolution* by Rev. Patrick Lavelle.
11. *The Moore's of Moore Hall* by J. Hone.
12. The Patriot Priest of Partry: Patrick Lavelle 1825-1886 by Cardinal Tomás Ó Fiaich.
13. The Story of Michael Davitt. by P. W. Leamy.

CHRONOLOGY OF HISTORICAL EVENTS

c. 5,000 million B.C. Earth formed.
c. 3,000 million to 11,000 B.C. Old Stone Age.
c. 11,000 — 3,500 B.C. Middle Stone Age (Mesolithic Age).
c. 8,000 — 6,000 B.C. The first people arrived in Ireland.
c. 3,500 — 2,000 B.C. New Stone Age (Neolithic Age). Man settled in Co. Mayo.
c. 2,000 B.C. — 350 B.C. The Bronze Age.
c. 350 B.C. — A.D. 500 The Iron Age.
c. A.D. 432 St. Patrick arrived in Ireland.
441 St. Patrick in Mayo.
627 St. Feichín founded a monastery at Cong.
    Mayo Abbey founded by St. Colmán.
c. 670 Bishop Tírechán wrote his account of the life of St. Patrick.
795 The Norsemen arrived in Ireland.
1014 Battle of Clontarf.
1111 Synod of Rath Breasail.
1120 Cong Abbey founded.
1123 The Cross of Cong was made in Roscommon for Turlough O'Conor.
1152 Synod of Kells. Mayo established as a diocese.
1169 The Normans arrived in Ireland.
1171 King Henry II in Ireland.
1199 Rory O'Conor died in Cong Abbey.
1216 Ballintober Abbey founded.
1220 Carmelite Friary founded on Clare Island.
1224 Death of Cathal Crobderg, last independent king of Connacht.
1235 Connacht conquered by the Normans.
1240 Strade Friary founded.
1274 Rathfran Friary founded.
1288 Ballinasmalla Friary founded.
1297 The first representative Irish parliament met in Dublin.
1298 Burriscarra Friary founded.
1313 Ballinrobe Friary founded.
1348 Ballyhaunis Friary founded (Traditional date).
1413 Errew Friary founded.
1434 Urlaur Friary founded.
1441 Rosserk Friary founded.
1457 Murrisk Friary founded.
1460 Moyne Friary founded.
1469 Burrishoole Friary founded.
1507 Accession of Henry VIII.
1517 The Reformation.
1540-43 Policy of "surrender and regrant".
1541 Henry VIII declared King of Ireland by the Irish Parliament.
1558-1603 Reign of Elizabeth I.
1569 Sir Edward Fitton appointed Governor of Connacht.
1570 Battle at Shrule. (Mayo Burkes v Fitton).
c. 1570 County Mayo established.
1585 Adam Magauran, last Bishop of Mayo, appointed.
    The "Composition of Connacht".
    Rebellion of the Mayo Burkes.
1588 The Defeat of the Spanish Armada.
1601 The Battle of Kinsale.
1609 Plantation of Ulster.
1611 Castlebar granted a borough charter.
1631 Mayo diocese absorbed into Tuam.
1635 The Strafford Inquisition.

1641 Rebellion in Ulster.
1649 Oliver Cromwell came to Ireland.
1652 Act of Settlement. (Plantations)
1653 Cromwell's soldiers plundered Mayo.
1690 Battle of the Boyne.
1695-1727 The Penal Laws enacted.
1795 Maynooth Seminary founded.
    The Battle of the Diamond (21 September).
    Ulster Migration to Mayo.
1798 United Irish Rising.
    "The Year of the French".
    The French arrived in Kilcummin Bay on 22 August.
1800 The Act of Union.
c. 1810 ST. Nathy's College, Ballaghaderreen, opened.
1828 *The Mayo Telegraph* launched on 17 March.
1829 Catholic Emancipation.
1831 National School System started.
1835 Death of Anthony Raftery.
1838 Poor Relief (Ireland) Act.
    Tithe Act.
1839 Oíche na Gaoithe Móire (The night of the big wind) 6 January.
1842 *The Nation* newspaper founded.
1845-49 The Great Famine.
1846 Birth of Michael Davitt.
1849 Queen's Colleges at Galway, Cork, Belfast opened to students.
1851 Ecclesiastical Titles Act.
1854 Catholic University of Ireland founded.
1858 Foundation of Fenian movement.
1860 The Partry Evictions.
1863 Claremorris Railway Station opened.
1865 Westport C.B.S. opened.
1867 Tithes abolished.
1869 Protestant Church disestablished in Ireland.
1878 Mayo Tenants Defence Association established.
1879 Irishtown meeting (20 April).
    Mayo Land League founded (16 August).
    Irish National Land League founded (21 October).
    The Apparition at Knock (21 August).
1879-82 The Land War.
1880 Boycotting of Capt. Boycott at Lough Mask House.
1882 Kilmainham Treaty.
    The Western People founded.
1883 Ballinrobe C.B.S. opened.
1884 The G.A.A. founded.
1885 Ashbourne Land Act.
1887 The bridge to Achill Island was opened by Michael Davitt.
1891 The Congested Districts Board established.
1892 Foxford Woollen Mills opened.
1893 The Cross of Cong presented to the Royal Irish Academy.
1898 Local Government (Ireland) Act.
    Mayo County Council established.
    St. Louis Convent Secondary School, Kiltamagh, opened.
1903 Wyndham Land Act.
1906 Death of Michael Davitt.
    St. Muredach's College, Ballina, opened.
1908 St. Mary's Convent Secondary School, Swinford, opened.
1910 St. Gerald's College, Castlebar, opened.
1912 Convent of Jesus and Mary Secondary School, Crossmolina, opened.
1912-14 Home Rule Crisis.
1913 Riots in Westport after the staging of "General John Regan".
1914-18 World War 1.
1916 Easter Rising.
1918 Conscription opposed.

Sinn Fein won majority of Irish seats in the General Election.
Representation of the People Act.
1919 St. Louis Convent Secondary School Balla, opened.
Santa Maria College, Louisburgh, opened. (Co educational).
The first Dáil met in Dublin.
First Republican Law Court
session in Ireland held in Ballinrobe on 17 May.
1919-21 The War of Independence.
1921 Anglo Irish Treaty, (6 December).
1911-23 The Civil War.
1925 Sacred Heart Secondary School, Westport, opened.
1926 2 RN — the Irish Radio Station opened. (New Year's Day).
1931 Coláiste Mhuire, Tuar Mhic Éadaigh, bunaithe.
1933 Ballina Vocational School opened.
Castlebar Vocational School opened.
1933-38 The Economic War.
1935 Westport Vocational School opened.
1936 Mayo won the All Ireland senior football title.
1937 Belmullet Vocational School opened.
Achill Vocational School opened.
1940 Convent of Mercy Secondary School, Claremorris, opened.
1942 Marist convent Secondary School, Charlestown, opened.
1943 Convent of Mercy Secondary School, Belmullet, opened.
1939-45 Second World War.
1945 St. Colmán's college, Claremorris, opened.
Coláiste Phádraig, Swinford, opened.
1948 First operation of the new bridge to Achill Island (29 September).
1949 The Irish Free State declared a Republic.
1950 and 1951 Mayo won the All Ireland senior football title.
1951 "The Quiet Man" filmed at Cong.
1954 Swinford Vocational School opened.
1957 Crossmolina Vocational School opened.
1961 Telefís Éireann began (New Year's Eve).
1962 Stella Maris Secondary School, Ballycastle, opened.
1963 "The Defence of the West" movement launched in Charlestown.
Ballinrobe Vocational School opened.
Claremorris Vocational School opened.
Kiltimagh Vocational School opened.
1965 The Anglo Irish Free Trade Agreement.
1966 Restoration work completed on Ballintober Abbey; 8 September — celebration of the
750th anniversary of its foundation.
1967 Charlestown Vocational School opened.
Lacken Cross Vocational School opened.
1972 Ros Dumhach Vocational School opened.
1973 Ireland joined the E.E.C. (1 January)
Knock Folk Museum opened (1 August)
The first sod turned for the new Basilica in Knock (6 November).
1976 Michael Davitt House, Castlebar, opened on 28 June
by An Taoiseach, Liam Cosgrave.
The Church of Our Lady, Knock, blessed and dedicated (18 July).
The O'Dwyer Cheshire Home opened in Lismurrane. (27 August)
1977 Ballyhaunis Community School opened.
1978 Balla Secondary School opened (community owned).
1979 Pope John Paul II in Knock (30 September).

NOTES ON CONTRIBUTORS

Barbara Buckley, a native of County Tipperary, is a lecturer in Biology in Galway Regional College. She has a special interest in natural history.

Gabriel Colleran, a native of Headford, County Galway, is a lecturer in Law in Galway Regional College.

Michael Leonard. Is Múinteoir Eolaíochta é i nGaillimh a bhfuil suim aige i ngach gné den dúlra. Gaeilgeoir é a bhíonn le clos ar R.T.E. go minic. Tá sé ina chomhúdar de na leabhair *Ó Ghaillimh go Ceann Boirne* agus *Gaillimh mae a Bhí agus mar Atá.*

Patrick McMahon, a native of Dublin, is a lecturer in the Mechanical Engineering Department in Galway Regional College. His chief leisure activity is mountain climbing.

Thomas Neary, a native of Knock, Co. Mayo, is vice principal of Balla Community School and the chief steward of Knock Shrine. He is the author of: *I Saw Our Lady, Ould Acquaintance, Knock: the Pilgrims Hope,* and *I Comforted Them in Sorrow: Knock 1879-1979.*

Máirtín Ó Direáin. Rugadh é ar Inis Mór, Árainn, sa bhliain 1910. I measc na saothar atá foilsithe aige tá: *Coinnle Geala; Dánta Aniar; Rogha Dánta; Ó Mórna agus Dánta Eile; Feamainn Bealtaine; Ár Ré Dhearóil agus Dánta Eile; Cloch Choirnéal agus Crainn is Cairde.* Chaith Máirtín Ó Direáin, ar éirí as a phost lán-aimseartha sa Státseirbhís dó, tamall mar aoi-léachtóir i gColáiste na hOllscoile i nGaillimh, agus ba é a nocht an leacht ar uaigh Phádraic Uí Chonaire ar ócáid chomórtha a bhreithlae, 100 bliain ó shin, i mí Feabhra 1982.

Peadar O'Dowd, a native of Galway, is a lecturer in Galway Regional College. He has a life long interest in archaeology and local history, and is the co-author of *Ó Ghaillimh Go Ceann Boirne* and *Gaillimh mar a Bhi agus mar Atá.*

Nollaig Ó Gadhra. Rugadh é i bhFíonach, Co. Luimnigh, agus tá sé ar fhoireann léachtóireachta Cheardcholáiste Réigiúnach na Gaillimhe. I measc an tsaothair scríbhneoireachta atá foilsithe aige tá ceithre leabhar beatháisnéise i nGaeilge ar: *Gandhi, John Boyle O'Reilly, Éamann Iognáid Rís,* agus *Richard J. Daley, Méara Chicago* — dhá dhuais-iarracht Oireachtais san áireamh. I measc na leabhar a ndearna sé eagarthóireacht orthu tá *Celtic Advance in the Atomic Age* agus *Cois Fharraige Le Mo Linnse,* bailiúchán aistí faoi Ghaeltacht na Gaillimhe a scríobh Seán Ó Conghaile (athair a chéile) agus a bhain go leor duaiseanna Oireachtais freisin.

Bernard O'Hara, a native of Killasser, Co. Mayo, is Head of the School of Business and Humanities in Galway Regional College. He is the author of *The Evolution of Irish Industrial Relations Law and Practice* and *Killasser: A History* (Ed).

An tAthair Leon Ó Morcháin, a native of Louisburgh, Co. Mayo, is parish priest of Rosmuc, Co. Galway. He is the editor of the Louisburgh Parish periodical — An Choinneal, which was first published in 1959, and a frequent broadcaster on radio and television.

Nollaig Ó Muraíle, a native of Knock, Co. Mayo, and a graduate in Celtic Studies of St. Patrick's College, Maynooth, is a Placenames Officer with the Ordnance Survey. He has written and lectured on various historical topics, both local and national and ranging in time from the early historical period to the present century, as well as on Gaelic literary activity in Connacht since the 17th century, on the placenames of several Irish counties, and on the Early Irish genealogies. He is at present engaged on a doctoral thesis involving the edition of Dubhaltach Mac Fhirbhisigh's Book of Genealogies and a study of the celebrated Tireragh scholar's life and work.

Desmond O'Neill, a native of Cloonlara, Swinford, in now living in Omeath, Co. Louth, where he runs an engineering business. He is researching the genealogies of the O'Neill families in County Mayo.

Dr. Brian O'Rourke, a native of County Laois, is a lecturer in the Department of Humanities in Galway Regional College. He is the author of the book *The Conscience of the Race – Sex and Religion in Irish and French Novels 1941-1973.*

Rev. Jarlath Waldron, a native of Ballyhaunis, Co. Mayo, taught history and Irish for twenty one years in St. Colmán's College, Claremorris, served for fourteen years in Cornamona, Co. Galway,and is now parish priest of Partry, Co. Mayo. He had done considerable research on various happenings in the archdiocese of Tuam during the last century.

ACKNOWLEDGEMENTS

The publishers wish to thank the following for permission to include copyright material in this book:

Publisher	Publication	Author/Editor
Browne & Nolan Ltd., Dublin	*Songs of the Irish*	Donal O'Sullivan
Chódhanna Teoranta, Corcaigh	*Amhráin Chlainne Gaedheal*	Micheál agus Tomás Ó Máille
The Educational Co. of Ireland/Talbot Press	*Amhráin Mhuighe Seóla*	Mrs. Costello
Faber and Faber Ltd. London	*The Hungry Grass*	Donagh McDonagh
Folklore Dept., U.C.D.	*Bealoideas Vol. XVII No. 1-11*	Pádraig Ó Moghráin
Gael Linn	*'An Caisideach Bán' CEF 029*	Máire Ní Scolaí
Gilbert Dalton, Dublin	*Amhráin Chúige Uladh*	Muireadhach Méith Atheagrán le Colm Ó Baoill
	The Irish Song Tradition	Seán O'Boyle
An Gúm	*Micheál Mhac Suibhne agus Filidh an tSleibhe.*	Tomás Ó Máille
	Dhá Chéad de Cheoltaibh Uladh.	Enrí Ó Muirgheasa
	Na Cáisidigh agus a gCuid Filidheachta.	Mairghréad Nic Philibín
Institiúid Ard-Léinn Bhaile Átha Cliath	*Nua-Dhuanaire III*	Tomás Ó Concheanainn
Irish University Press	*Abhráin Diaga Chúige Connacht*	Douglas Hyde
	Abhráin Grádh Chúige Connacht	Douglas Hyde
	Abhráin atá Leagtha ar an Reachtúire Editions 1 & 2.	Douglas Hyde
Mercier Press	*Ceolta Gael*	Seán Óg agus Mánus Ó Baoill
Routledge & Kegan Paul Ltd., London.	*Traditional Music in Ireland.*	Tomás Ó Canainn
Topic Records Ltd. London.	*L.P. "Grand Airs of Connemara".*	
Wolfhound Press	*Unfinished Sequence and Other Poems*	Seán Lucy

Our thanks are due to the following:
Central Statistics Office, Dept. of Education, National Gallery of Ireland, National Library, National Museum, National Portrait Gallery, London, Ordnance Survey Office, Placenames Office, Public Record Office of Ireland, and the State Paper Office, Dublin Castle.

Special thanks are due to: the staff of the library of Galway Regional College, Mary Kavanagh, Máire Finn, Bernie Kelly, and Ann Gray; Patrick McMahon and the staff of the Mayo County Library; the staff of the library of University College, Galway, and Galway County Library.

Thanks are also due to the following: Cyril Brady (G), Rev. E. Concannon (Roundfort), James Cuddy (G), Michael Clarke (Bohola), Seán Dunleavy (G), Donal Downes (G), Liam Egan (Castlebar), Rev. Dudley Filan (Killasser), Rev. Leslie Forrest (G), Rev. P. J. Gallagher (Ballina), Terry Gallagher (Castlebar), Colette Keaveney (G), Professor Colm Kiernan (U.C.D.), Patrick Lane and Martin Lane (Williamstown), Sister Mary Leavy (Swinford), Margaret Lundy (Bohola), T. J. McClatchie (Dublin), Mary McHugh (G), Seán Ó Dea (G), Colm Ó Hanlaí (G), Gearóid Ó Tuathaigh (U.C.G.), Liam Ó Maolmhichíl (Dublin), Éamon Regan (G), Sister Joseph Ronan (Foxford), Margaret Sheridan (Foxford), Michael and Margaret Sheridan (Bohola) and Seán Smyth (Castlebar).   G = Galway.

BIBLIOGRAPHY

Aalen, F.H.A., *Man and the Landscape in Ireland,* London, 1978.

Bagwell, Richard, *Ireland under the Tudors,* I-III, London, 1885-90/1963.

Bennett, R. J., *Seán na Sagart: The Priest Hunter,* Dublin, 1946.

Bew, Paul, *Land and the National Question in Ireland (1858-82),* Dublin, 1978.

Binchy, D. A., "Patrick and His Biographers: Ancient and Modern", Studia Hibernica 2, (1962) pp 7-173.

Bowen, D., *Souperism: Myth or Reality,* Cork, 1970.

Boylan, Henry, *A Dictionary of Irish Biography* Dublin, 1978.

Brett, Rev. T., *Mayo of the Saxons: Brief History of an Old See,* Dublin, n.d.

Browne, D., *Westport House and The Brownes,* Derbyshire, 1981.

Browne, Vincent, *Magill Book of Irish Politics,* Dublin, 1981.

Byrne, Francis John, *Irish Kings and High-Kings,* London, 1973.

Caulfield, Séamus, "Céide and Belderg Beg" (1980); "Neolithic Field: The Irish Evidence" in British Archaeological Reports, No. 48, Ed. H. C. Bowen and P. J. Fowler, 1978.

Census of Population, (Central Statistics Office).

Charlesworth, J. K., *The Geology of Ireland: An Introduction,* London, 1966.

Chambers, Anne, *Granuaile, the Life and Times of Grace O'Malley, c. 1530-1603,* Dublin, 1979.

Clarke, R. Dardis, "F. R. Higgins" in *The Irish Times* (12/01/1982).

Coen, Rev. Martin, "Gleanings", *The Connacht Tribune,* 1979-'80.

Coogan, B., *Miracles at Knock,* Dublin, 1979.

Corfe, Tom, *The Phoenix Park Murders, Conflict, Compromise and Tragedy in Ireland, 1879-1882,* London, 1968.

Costello, Nuala, *John MacHale, Archbishop of Tuam,* Dublin, 1939.

Curtis, Edmund, *A History of Ireland,* London, 1936/1961, *A History of Medieval Ireland,* London, 1938.

D'Alton, Right Rev. Monsignor E.A., *A Short History of Ballinrobe Parish* (1931), *History of the Archdiocese of Tuam* Vols. 1 & 2, Dublin, 1928.

Davitt, Michael, *In Defence of the Land League,* London, 1890. *The Fall of Feudalism in Ireland,* London, 1904.

de Búrca, Seán, *The Irish of Tourmakeady Co. Mayo: a phonemic study,* Dublin, 1958.

de h-Ide, Dubhglas, *Abhráin agus Dánta an Reachtabhraigh,* Báile Átha Cliath, 1933.

de Valéra, Ruaidhrí, and Ó Nualláin, Seán, *Survey of the Megalithic Tombs of Ireland,* Vol. II, Dublin, 1964.

Dolley, Michael, *Anglo-Norman Ireland,* Dublin, 1972.

Egan, Rev. Fr. Thomas, *The Story of Ballintubber Abbey,* (1967), *What to see at Ballintubber Abbey,* (1967).

Fahy, J. A., *The Glory of Cong,* 1960.

Finley, Rev. T. A., *The Story of an Irish Industry: Foxford and the Providence Woollen Mills.*

FitzGerald, John, J. (Ed.) *Mayo Men's Patriotic and Benevolent Association of the City of New York Centennial 1879-1979* booklet, New York, 1979.

Freeman, A. Martin, *The Compossicion Booke of Conought,* Dublin, 1936.

Freeman, T. W., *Pre-Famine Ireland, A Study in Historical Geography,* Manchester, 1957.

Gallagher, Edward, Thirty I.R.A. men defied 600 British troops at Tourmakeady, May 3, 1921, in *With the I.R.A. in The Fight For Freedom, 1919 to the Truce,* Tralee, n.d.

Gavin, Anthony, The Brabazons, Swinford G.A.A. Programme, 13/05/1979, Swinford, 1979.

Gildea, Rev. Denis, *Mother Mary Arsenius of Foxford,* Dublin, 1936.

Greer, Rev. James, *The Windings of the Moy with Skreen and Tireragh,* Dublin, 1924.

Gregory, Lady, *Poets and Dreamers,* London, 1903/1974.

Grose, F., *The Antiquities of Ireland,* London, 1791.

Gwynn, A., and Hadcock, R. N., *Medieval Religious Houses: Ireland,* London, 1970.

Hanly, Dáithi P., *The Church of Our Lady Queen of Ireland: a Guide,* Knock, 1979.

Harbison, Peter, *Guide to the National Monuments of Ireland,* Dublin, 1970.

Hayes, Richard, *The Last Invasion of Ireland,* Dublin, 1937/1979.

Hayes-McCoy, G. A., *Irish Battles,* (Chap. 4 'Knockdoe, 1504') London, 1969.

Hayward, R., *The Corrib Country,* Dundalk, 1943/1968, *This is Ireland: Mayo, Sligo, Leitrim and Roscommon,* London, 1955.

Healy, John, *The Death of an Irish Town,* Cork, 1968; *Nineteen Acres,* Galway, 1978.

Henry, Seán, *Tales from the West of Ireland,* Cork, 1980.

Herity, M. Eoghan, G., *Ireland in Prehistory,* London, 1977.

Herity, Michael, "A Bronze Age Farmstead at Glencree, Co. Mayo", in *Popular Archaeology,* Vol. 2, No. 9, March 1981, Hemel, Hempstead, Herts.

Hickey, D. J., and Doherty, J. E., *A Dictionary of Irish History Since 1800,* Dublin, 1980.

Hogan, Patrick, "The Migration of Ulster Catholics to Connaught 1795-96", Seanchas Ardmhacha Vol. 9, No. 2, 1979.

Hogan, Robert, (Ed.) *Dictionary of Irish Literature,* London, 1979.

Hone, Joseph, *The Life of George Moore,* London, 1936. *The Moore's of Moore Hall,* London, 1939.

Howley, Michael (Ed.), *The Rehabilitation of Michael Davitt,* Strade, 1966.

Hughes, Kathleen, and Hamlin, Ann, *The Modern Traveller to the Early Irish Church,* London, 1977.

Hughes, Owen, "Major John McBride, 1868-1916 — Patriot, Soldier and Martyr", Journal Westport Historical Society, Vol. 1, 1982.

James, Father, O.F.M., *The Story of Knock,* Knock, n.d.

Jennett, Seán, *Connacht – the counties Galway, Mayo, Sligo, Leitrim and Roscommon in Ireland,* London, 1980.

Jennings, Fr. Martin, "Swinford Workhouse and Union" in Swinford G.A.A. Programme 13/05/1979, Swinford, 1979.

Jennings, Paddy, *The Parish of Turlough – History and Tradition,* 1976.

Johnston, Edith Mary, *Ireland in the Eighteenth Century,* Dublin, 1974.

Kenney, James F., *The Sources for the Early History of Ireland: Ecclesiastical, an Introduction and Guide,* New York, 1929/Dublin, 1979.

Killanin, Lord, and Duignan, Michael V., *Shell Guide to Ireland,* London, 1962/'67.

Knight, P., *Erris: in the Irish Highlands and the Atlantic Railway,* 1836.

Knox, Hubert Thomas, *The History of the County of Mayo to the Close of the Sixteenth Century,* Dublin, 1908.

Knox, H. T., "Occupation of Connaught by the Anglo-Normans after A.D. 1237" in *Jnrl. of Royal Soc. of Antiquaries of Ireland,* xxxii (consecutive series), pp. 132-8, 393-406, and xxxiii, pp. 58-74, 179-89, 284-94, (1902 and 1903).

Knox, H. T., "The de Burgo clans, The Clann David Burke and the family of William, sheriff of Connaught" in *Jnrl. of Galway Archaeological and Historical Soc.,* iii, pp. 46-58 (1903-4).

Knox, H. T., "The de Burgo clans of Galway" in *Jnrl. of Galway Archaeological and Historical Soc.,* iv, 1905-6.

308

Larkin, Emmet, *The Roman Catholic Church and the Creation of the Modern Irish State 1878-1886*, Dublin, 1975. *The Making of the Roman Catholic Church in Ireland (1850-'60)*, North Carolina, 1980.

Lavelle, Rev. Patrick, *The Irish Landlord Since the Revolution*, Dublin, 1870.

Lavelle, Anthony, Series of articles on "Mayo in the Fight for Freedom" in *The Western People*, Ballina, January-February, 1965.

Lavelle, Rev. J. J., Addergoole.

Leask, H. G., *Irish Castles*, Dundalk, 1966.

Leamy, P. W., "The Story of Michael Davitt", *Mayo News*, 1946.

Lewis, Samuel, *A Topographical Dictionary of Ireland* . . . with statistical descriptions, London, 1837.

Lee, Joseph, *The Modernisation of Irish Society, 1848-1918*, Dublin, 1973.

Lyons, F.S.L., *Charles Stewart Parnell*, London, 1977/'78.

Lyons, F.S.L., *John Dillon: A Biography*, London, 1968.

Lyons, F.S.L., *Ireland Since the Famine*, London, 1971/'73.

Macardle, Dorothy, *The Irish Republic*, London, 1937/1968.

Mac Caomhánaigh, Pádraig, *Kao Er Wen, an tEaspag Éamann Ó Gealbháin*, Baile Átha Cliath, 1965.

MacLysaght, Edward, *Irish Families, Their Names, Arms, and Origins*, Dublin, 1957.

MacLysaght, Edward, *The Surnames of Ireland*, Shannon, 1969.

Mac Niocaill, Gearóid, *Ireland Before the Vikings*, Dublin, 1972.

Mac Suibhne, Peadar, *Paul Cullen and His Contemporaries, 1820-1902*, 5 Vols., Naas, 1961/'77

Maxwell, W., *Wild Sports of the West*, Dublin, 1936.

McCarrick, Frank, "Fr. Denis O'Hara, A Short Biography", (Hons. B.A., Thesis, St. Patrick's College, Maynooth, unpublished).

McGarry, Tony, *Historical Guide to Killala and District*, Killala, 1970.

McNally, Kenneth, *Achill*, Devon, 1973.

Mitchell, Frank, *The Irish Landscape*, London, 1976.

Moore, Colonel Maurice George, *An Irish Gentleman – George Henry Moore, His Travel, His Racing, His Politics*, London, 1913.

Moody, T. W., Martin, F. X., and Byrne, F. J., *A New History of Ireland*, Vol. III, *Early Modern Ireland, 1534-1691*, Oxford, 1976; (Chap. I, D. B. Quinn and Nicholls, K. W., 'Ireland in 1534'; Chap. IX, Clarke, Aidan, "The government of Wentworth, 1632-40"; Chap. XIII, Corish, Patrick J., "The Cromwellian Conquest, 1649-53"; Chap. XIV, Corish, Patrick J., "The Cromwellian regime, 1650-60").

Moody, T. W., *Davitt and Irish Revolution 1846-1882*, Oxford, 1981.
"Michael Davitt, 1846-1906, A Survey and Appreciation", Studies xxxv No. 138, June 1946.
"Michael Davitt", in *Leaders and Workers*, Ed., J. W. Boyle, Cork, 1966.

Moran, Gerald, James Daly, Paper read to Muintir Mhaigh Eo in Galway, March 1980.

Mullen, Michael, Series on Local History, *Connaught Telegraph, 1978-'80.*

Neary, Rev. J., *Notes on Cong and The Neale*, Dundalk, 1938.

Neary, Thomas, *Knock: the Pilgrims Hope*, Knock, *I Comforted Them in Sorrow: Knock, 1879/'79, I Saw Our Lady*, Knock, 1977, *Ould Acquaintance*, Knock, 1980.

Nesson, Eoin, *The Civil War in Ireland, 1922-1923*, Cork, 1966/'69.

Nevill, W. E., *Geology and Ireland, with physical geography and its geological background*, Dublin, 1963.

Ní Cheannain, Áine, *The Heritage of County Mayo*, Dublin, 1982, Stair Mhaigh Eo, uimhir 1 & 2, An Roinn Oideachais.

Nicholls, K. W., *Gaelic and Gaelicised Ireland in the Middle Ages*, Dublin, 1972.

Ó Cuív, Brian, *Irish Dialects and Irish Speaking Districts*, Dublin, 1971.

O'Boyle, Eamon, *Claremorris-Hub of the West,* Claremorris, 1980.

Ó Corráin, Donncha, *Ireland Before the Normans,* Dublin, 1972.

O'Donovan, John, et al, *Letters relating to the antiquities of the county of Mayo* (= 'Ordnance Survey Letters') vols. I and II (mimeographed edition, Bray, c. 1929 — originals in library of Royal Irish Academy, Dublin). Ordnance Survey Field Name Books of Mayo (1838).

O'Dwyer, Paul, *Counsel for the Defence:* The autobiography of Paul O'Dwyer, New York, 1979.

Ó Fiaich, Cardinal Tomás, "The Patriot Priest, Patrick Lavelle 1825-1886", JGAHS 1976, Vol. 35.

O'Hara, Bernard, (Ed.), *Killasser: A History,* Galway, 1981.

O'Hara, M. M., *Chief and Tribune, Parnell and Davitt,* Dublin, 1919.

O'Hegarty, P. S., *A History of Ireland under The Union 1800-1922,* London, 1952.

O'Keefe, D., *The Story of Knock,* 1949.

Ó Lochlainn, Colm, *Cruach Phádraic,* Ireland's Holy Mountain.

Ó Madagáin, Breandán, *An Gaeilge i Luimneach 1700-1900,* Baile Átha Cliath, 1974.

Ó Máille, Tomás, *Micheál Mhac Suibhne agus Filidh an tSléibhe,* Baile Átha Cliath, 1934.

O'Malley, Ernie, *On Another Man's Wound,* 1935; *The Singing Flame,* Dublin, 1978.

O'Malley, Edward, *Memories of a Mayoman,* Westport, 1981.

Ó Maolmhuaidh, Proinsias, *Athair na hAthbheochana:* Uilleog de Búrca, Baile Átha Cliath, 1982.

Mhac an Fhailigh, Éamon, *The Irish of Erris, Co. Mayo,* Baile Átha Cliath, 1968.

Ó Móráin, Pádraig, *Annála Beaga Pharáiste Bhuiréis Umhaill, A Short Account of the History of Burrishoole Parish,* 1957.

Ó Muraíle, Nollaig, "Filí Chúige Connacht sa naoú aois déag" i *Léachtaí Cholm Cille 1972, III Litríocht an 19ú hAois,* Má Nuad, 1973.

Ó Muraíle, Nollaig, "Toirialach Ó Cearúlláin" i *Léachtaí Cholm Cille IV Litríocht an 18ú hAois,* Má Nuad, 1975.

Ó Muraíle, Nollaig, "Swinford and its Name: Some Aspects of Swinford History", *Swinford Re-Echo,* Swinford, 1981.

O'Neill, Thomas P., *Sources of Irish Local History,* Dublin, 1958.

Ó Nualláin, Seán, "The Megalithic Tombs of Ireland" in *Expedition* (The University magazine of Archaeology/Anthropology, University of Pennsylvania), Vol. 21, No. 3, Spring, 1979.

O'Rahilly, Cecile, *Táin Bó Cúailnge From the Book of Leinster,* Dublin, 1967.

O'Rahilly, Cecile, *Táin Bó Cúailnge, Recension I,* Dublin, 1976.

O'Rahilly, Thomas F., *Early Irish History and Mythology,* Dublin, 1946, *Irish Dialects Past and Present,* Dublin, 1970.

O'Reilly, Right Rev. Bernard, *John MacHale, Archbishop of Tuam:* His Life, Times and Correspondence, 2 Vols., New York, 1890.

Ó Riordáin, Seán P., *Antiquities of the Irish Countryside,* London, 1965.

Orpen, Goddard Henry, *Ireland Under the Normans, 1169-1333,* Oxford, 1911-20.

O'Sullivan, William, (Ed.), *The Strafford Inquisition of County Mayo,* Dublin, 1958.

Ó Tuathaigh, Gearóid, *Ireland Before the Famine, 1798-1848,* Dublin, 1972.

Otway-Ruthven, A. J., *A History of Medieval Ireland,* London, 1968.

Pakenham, Thomas, *The Year of Liberty,* London, 1969/1972.

Peyton, Fr. Patrick, *All For Her:* the Autobiography of Father Patrick Peyton, CSC, 1967.

Pochin, Mould D.D.C., *The Mountains of Ireland,* Dublin, 1976.

Praeger, Robert L., *The Way That I Went,* Dublin, 1937-1980.

Redmond, D. B., O.S.A., *The Augustinian Abbey of St. Mary the Virgin, Ballyhaunis, 1348-1948, A Historical Sketch,* Dublin, 1948.

310

Rynne, Catherine, *Knock 1879-1979,* Dublin, 1979.

Seoighthe, Pádraig, *Diabhal Smid Bhréige,* Baile Átha Cliath, 1980.

Semple, Maurice, *By the Corribside,* Galway, 1981; *Reflections on Lough Corrib,* Galway, 1974.

Seward, William W., *Topographia Hibernica, or the Topography of Ireland, Ancient and Modern,* Dublin, 1795.

Simington, Robert C., *Books of Survey and Distribution, Vol. II, County of Mayo,* Dublin, 1956.

Simington, Robert C., *The Transplantaion of Connacht,* 1654-58, Shannon, 1970.

Simms, J. G., "Mayo Landowners in the Seventeenth Century" in *Journal of the Royal Society of Antiquaries of Ireland,* Vol. 95, Dublin, 1965.

Sheridan, Andrew J. (Ed.) *Mayomen's Patriotic and Benevolent Association of the City of New York Diamond Jubilee 1879-1954* Booklet, New York, 1954.

Skeffington, Francis Sheehy, *Michael Davitt, Revolutionary, Agitator and Labour Leader,* London 1908-1967.

Stock, Rev., Dr. J., *A Narrative of Killala 1798,* London, 1800, and Ballina, 1982.

Sullivan, A. M., *New Ireland,* London, 1877.

Tohall, Patrick, "The Diamond Fight of 1795, and the Resultant Expulsions", in Seanchas Ardmhacha, Vol. 3, No. 1, Armagh, 1958.

Tomlinson, N., *Louis Brennan, Inventor Extraordinaire,* London, 1980.

Viney, Michael, *Another Life,* Dublin, 1979.

Viney, Michael and Ethna, *Another Life Again,* Dublin, 1981.

Waldron, Tom, "Monuments and the men" in *Tooreen: hurling and community life* (25th anniversary commemorative magazine published by Tooreen Hurling Club, April 1982), pp. 39-40.

Walker, Brian M., (Ed.) *Parliamentary Election Results in Ireland, 1801-1922,* Dublin, 1978.

Wall, C. W., *Mountaineering in Ireland,* Dublin, 1976.

Walsh, Rev. M., *The Apparition at Knock: A Survey of Facts and Evidence,* Tuam, 1959.

Wilde, William, *Loch Corrib: Its Shores and Islands,* 1938.

Williams, Nicholas, *Riocard Bairéad Amhráin,* Baile Átha Cliath, 1978.

Whilde, Tony, *Irish Walk Guides/2 West,* Dublin, 1978.

White, Seán J., Articles on Ballintober, Strade, Moyne and Dún Briste in *The Irish Times,* 1979.

Whyte, J. H., *The Independent Irish Party, 1850-59,* Oxford, 1958.

Woodham-Smith, Cecil, *The Great Hunger,* London, 1962-1970.

Whitlow, J. B., *Geology and Scenery in Ireland,* London, 1974.

Younger, Calton, *Ireland's Civil War,* London, 1968-1970.

NOTE: A full list of sources used for the article entitled 'County Mayo in Gaelic Folksong' is given at the end of the article and not repeated here.

PERIODICALS

Annagh (Ballyhaunis),
An Choinneal (Louisburgh)
Bohola Post
Castlebar Parish Magazine
Mayo G.A.A. Annuals
Slabhra (Ballycastle)
Swinford Echo
Swinford Re-Echo
The Bridge (Ballinrobe)
The Word
Journal of the Royal Society of Antiquities of Ireland
Journal of the Galway Archaeological and Historical Society

NEWSPAPERS

The Connacht Tribune
The Connaught Telegraph
The Freeman's Journal
The Irish Independent
The Irish Press
The Irish Times
The Mayo Constitution
The Mayo News
The Mayo Telegraph
The Times (London)
The Western Journal
The Western People

INDEX

312